CW01216681

Migration, Diasporas and Citizenship Series

Series Editors: **Robin Cohen**, Former Director of the International Migration Institute and Professor of Development Studies, University of Oxford, UK, and **Zig Layton-Henry**, Professor of Politics, University of Warwick, UK.

Editorial Board: **Rainer Baubock**, European University Institute, Italy; **James F. Hollifield**, Southern Methodist University, USA; **Jan Rath**, University of Amsterdam, the Netherlands

The Migration, Diasporas and Citizenship series covers three important aspects of the migration progress. First, the determinants, dynamics and characteristics of international migration. Second, the continuing attachment of many contemporary migrants to their places of origin, signified by the word 'diaspora', and third the attempt, by contrast, to belong and gain acceptance in places of settlement, signified by the word 'citizenship'. The series publishes work that shows engagement with and a lively appreciation of the wider social and political issues that are influenced by international migration.

Also published in Migration Studies by Palgrave Macmillan

Bridget Anderson and Isabel Shutes (*editors*)
MIGRATION AND CARE LABOUR
Theory, Policy and Politics

Rutvica Andrijasevic
MIGRATION, AGENCY AND CITIZENSHIP IN SEX TRAFFICKING

Floya Anthias and Mojca Pajnik (*editors*)
CONTESTING INTEGRATION, ENGENDERING MIGRATION
Theory and Practice

Claudine Attias-Donfut, Joanne Cook, Jaco Hoffman and Louise Waite (*editors*)
CITIZENSHIP, BELONGING AND INTERGENERATIONAL RELATIONS IN AFRICAN MIGRATION

Michaela Benson and Nick Osbaldiston
UNDERSTANDING LIFESTYLE MIGRATION
Theoretical Approaches to Migration and the Quest for a Better Way of Life

Grete Brochmann, Anniken Hagelund (*authors*) with – Karin Borevi, Heidi Vad Jønsson, Klaus Petersen
IMMIGRATION POLICY AND THE SCANDINAVIAN WELFARE STATE 1945–2010

Gideon Calder, Phillip Cole and Jonathan Seglow
CITIZENSHIP ACQUISITION AND NATIONAL BELONGING
Migration, Membership and the Liberal Democratic State

Michael Collyer
EMIGRATION NATIONS
Policies and Ideologies of Emigrant Engagement

Enzo Colombo and Paola Rebughini (*editors*)
CHILDREN OF IMMIGRANTS IN A GLOBALIZED WORLD
A Generational Experience

Huub Dijstelbloem and Albert Meijer (*editors*)
MIGRATION AND THE NEW TECHNOLOGICAL BORDERS OF EUROPE

Thomas Faist and Andreas Ette (*editors*)
THE EUROPEANIZATION OF NATIONAL POLICIES AND POLITICS OF IMMIGRATION
Between Autonomy and the European Union

Thomas Faist and Peter Kivisto (*editors*)
DUAL CITIZENSHIP IN GLOBAL PERSPECTIVE
From Unitary to Multiple Citizenship

Katrine Fangen, Thomas Johansson and Nils Hammarén (*editors*)
YOUNG MIGRANTS
Exclusion and Belonging in Europe

Martin Geiger and Antoine Pécoud (*editors*)
THE POLITICS OF INTERNATIONAL MIGRATION MANAGEMENT

John R. Hinnells (*editor*)
RELIGIOUS RECONSTRUCTION IN THE SOUTH ASIAN DIASPORAS
From One Generation to Another

Ronit Lentin and Elena Moreo (*editors*)
MIGRANT ACTIVISM AND INTEGRATION FROM BELOW IN IRELAND

Catrin Lundström
WHITE MIGRATIONS
Gender, Whiteness and Privilege in Transnational Migration

Ayhan Kaya
ISLAM, MIGRATION AND INTEGRATION
The Age of Securitization

Majella Kilkey, Diane Perrons, Ania Plomien
GENDER, MIGRATION AND DOMESTIC WORK
Masculinities, Male Labour and Fathering in the UK and USA

Amanda Klekowski von Koppenfels
MIGRANTS OR EXPATRIATES?
Americans in Europe

Marie Macy and Alan H. Carling
ETHNIC, RACIAL AND RELIGIOUS INEQUALITIES
The Perils of Subjectivity

George Menz and Alexander Caviedes (*editors*)
LABOUR MIGRATION IN EUROPE

Laura Morales and Marco Giugni (*editors*)
SOCIAL CAPITAL, POLITICAL PARTICIPATION AND MIGRATION IN EUROPE
Making Multicultural Democracy Work?

Eric Morier-Genoud
IMPERIAL MIGRATIONS
Colonial Communities and Diaspora in the Portuguese World

Aspasia Papadopoulou-Kourkoula
TRANSIT MIGRATION
The Missing Link Between Emigration and Settlement

Prodromos Panayiotopoulos
ETHNICITY, MIGRATION AND ENTERPRISE

Dominic Pasura
African Transnational Diasporas
Fractured Communities and Plural Identities of Zimbabweans in Britain

Ludger Pries and Zeynep Sezgin (*editors*)
CROSS BORDER MIGRANT ORGANIZATIONS IN COMPARATIVE PERSPECTIVE

Shanthi Robertson
TRANSNATIONAL STUDENT-MIGRANTS AND THE STATE
The Education-Migration Nexus

Helen Schwenken, Sabine Ruß-Sattar
NEW BORDER AND CITIZENSHIP POLITICS

Olivia Sheringham
TRANSNATIONAL RELIGIOUS SPACES
Faith and the Brazilian Migration Experience

Evan Smith and Marinella Marmo
RACE, GENDER AND THE BODY IN BRITISH IMMIGRATION CONTROL
Subject to Examination

Vicky Squire
THE EXCLUSIONARY POLITICS OF ASYLUM

Anna Triandafyllidou and Thanos Maroukis (*editors*)
MIGRANT SMUGGLING
Irregular Migration from Asia and Africa to Europe

Vron Ware
MILITARY MIGRANTS
Fighting for YOUR Country

Lucy Williams
GLOBAL MARRIAGE
Cross-Border Marriage Migration in Global Context

Migration, Diasporas and Citizenship Series
**Series Standing Order ISBN 978–0–230–30078–1 (hardback) and
978–0–230–30079–8 (paperback)**
(*outside North America only*)

You can receive future titles in this series as they are published by placing a standing order. Please contact your bookseller or, in case of difficulty, write to us at the address below with your name and address, the title of the series and the ISBN quoted above.

Customer Services Department, Macmillan Distribution Ltd, Houndmills, Basingstoke, Hampshire RG21 6XS, England

New Border and Citizenship Politics

Edited by

Helen Schwenken
*Institute for Migration and Intercultural Research (IMIS),
University of Osnabrück, Germany*

Sabine Ruß-Sattar
University of Kassel, Germany

Selection and editorial matter © Helen Schwenken and
Sabine Ruß-Sattar 2014
Individual chapters © Respective authors 2014

All rights reserved. No reproduction, copy or transmission of this
publication may be made without written permission.

No portion of this publication may be reproduced, copied or transmitted
save with written permission or in accordance with the provisions of the
Copyright, Designs and Patents Act 1988, or under the terms of any licence
permitting limited copying issued by the Copyright Licensing Agency,
Saffron House, 6–10 Kirby Street, London EC1N 8TS.

Any person who does any unauthorized act in relation to this publication
may be liable to criminal prosecution and civil claims for damages.

The authors have asserted their rights to be identified as the authors of this
work in accordance with the Copyright, Designs and Patents Act 1988.

First published 2014 by
PALGRAVE MACMILLAN

Palgrave Macmillan in the UK is an imprint of Macmillan Publishers Limited,
registered in England, company number 785998, of Houndmills, Basingstoke,
Hampshire RG21 6XS.

Palgrave Macmillan in the US is a division of St Martin's Press LLC,
175 Fifth Avenue, New York, NY 10010.

Palgrave Macmillan is the global academic imprint of the above companies
and has companies and representatives throughout the world.

Palgrave® and Macmillan® are registered trademarks in the United States,
the United Kingdom, Europe and other countries.

ISBN 978–1–137–32662–1

This book is printed on paper suitable for recycling and made from fully
managed and sustained forest sources. Logging, pulping and manufacturing
processes are expected to conform to the environmental regulations of the
country of origin.

A catalogue record for this book is available from the British Library.

A catalog record for this book is available from the Library of Congress.

Contents

List of Tables   vii

Notes on Contributors   viii

New Border and Citizenship Politics: An Introduction   1
Helen Schwenken and Sabine Ruß-Sattar

Part I Introduction: The Politics of Redesigning Borders
Helen Schwenken and Sabine Ruß-Sattar

1 Constructing Voluntarism: Technologies of 'intent management' in Australian Border Controls   17
   Leanne Weber and Sharon Pickering

2 Malta and the Rescue of Unwanted Migrants at Sea: Negotiating the Humanitarian Law of the Sea and the Contested Redesigning of Borders   30
   Silja Klepp

3 Negotiating Mobility, Debating Borders: Migration Diplomacy in Turkey–EU Relations   44
   Ahmet İçduygu and Ayşen Üstübici

4 Building Borders on a Bias: The Culturalist Perception of Turkish Migrants in France and Germany and the Debate on Europe's Boundaries   60
   Sabine Ruß-Sattar

Part II Introduction: The Technologies of Bordering
Helen Schwenken and Sabine Ruß-Sattar

5 The Momentum of Contestation – Airports as Borderlands on the Inside   73
   Detlef Sack

6 The Interiorisation and Localisation of Border Control: A US Case   90
   Robyn Magalit Rodriguez

7 Outsiders/Insiders: How Local Immigrant Organisations Contest the Exclusion of Undocumented Immigrants in the US   103
   Mara Sidney

8	Conditions as Internal Borders: The Case of 'Security of Residence' for Third-Country Nationals in Austria *İlker Ataç*	123

Part III Introduction: Politics of Citizenship as Border Politics
Sabine Ruß-Sattar and Helen Schwenken

9	Border Control Politics as Technologies of Citizenship in Europe and North America *Kim Rygiel*	141
10	Troubling Borders: *Sans-papiers* in France *Catherine Raissiguier*	156
11	From Sangatte to 'The Jungle': Europe's Contested Borderlands *Helen Schwenken*	171
12	Labour Migration, Postcolonial Nationalism and Class Politics beyond Borders: The Case of the Turkish Party MHP in Germany *Jörg Nowak*	187
13	Emigration Policies and Citizenship Rhetoric: Morocco and Its Emigrants in Europe *Esther Mikuszies*	205
14	Coda *Sabine Ruß-Sattar and Helen Schwenken*	218

References	224
Index	253

Tables

5.1	Number of airport procedures in Germany, 1993–2011	82
5.2	Number of deportees, acts of resistance and failed deportations, 1998–2011	85

Contributors

İlker Ataç is a post-doctoral researcher in the Department of Political Science, University of Vienna. His areas of research include migration politics, international political economy and Turkish studies. Recent publications include *Politik der Inklusion und Exklusion* (2013, ed. with Sieglinde Rosenberger) and *Ökonomische und politische Krisen in der Türkei: Die Neuformierung des peripheren Neoliberalismus* (2013). Contact: ilker.atac@univie.ac.at.

Ahmet İçduygu is Professor of International Relations and Director of the Migration Research Program (MiReKoç) at Koç University. In 2010–2011 he was a Visiting Scholar at the Robert Schuman Centre for Advanced Studies at the European University Institute. He holds a PhD in demography from the Australian National University in Canberra. His current research is on international, migration, civil society, and citizenship, ethnicity and nationalism. Publications include *Citizenship in a Global World: European Questions and Turkish Experiences* (2005, edited with E. F. Keyman); *Land of Diverse Migrations: Challenges of Emigration and Immigration in Turkey*, (2008, edited with K. Kirişci); and 'The Politics of Irregular Migratory Flows in the Mediterranean Basin: Economy, Mobility and "Illegality"', *Mediterranean Politics* 12, 2, 2007, 141–161. Contact: aicduygu@ku.edu.tr.

Silja Klepp holds a PhD in legal anthropology from the University of Leipzig. She currently holds a post-doctoral position as Principal Investigator at the Research Centre for Sustainability Studies, University of Bremen, Germany. In her current research project on climate change and environmental migrants in the Pacific region, she integrates postcolonial perspectives and critical theories in the study of climate change adaptation. Her field research experience includes countries such as Kiribati, Vanuatu, New Zealand, Italy, Libya, Malta and Zambia. In 2012 she won the Christiane Rajewsky Award of the German Association for Peace and Conflict Studies for her PhD thesis on refugees and border control in the Mediterranean Sea. She is member of the German Young Academy of Scientists (*Die Junge Akademie*), and her fields of research include legal anthropology, political anthropology, migration and refugees, political ecology, and Science and Technology Studies. She recently published her monograph *Europe between Border Control and Refugee Law. An Ethnography of the Mediterranean Sea Border* (2011, transcript, in German). Contact: info@siljaklepp.de.

Esther Mikuszies is a PhD candidate in the Department for Political Science at the University of Kassel. She holds an MA in political science, contemporary history and public law from the University of Freiburg. She recently published 'Die Rechte von Migranten: Überlegungen zu aktuellen Paradoxen der Bürgerschaftspraxis' in *Kultur, Identität und Menschenrechte. Transkulturelle Perspektiven* (2012, edited by Sarhan Dhouib). Contact: esther.mikuszies@uni-kassel.de.

Jörg Nowak holds a PhD in social sciences from the University of Kassel. During 2013–2014 he was a Post-doctoral Visiting Scholar at the Tata Institute for Social Sciences in Mumbai, India. He also works as a freelancer in the field of social sciences, in particular on migration, racism and labour issues. His areas of interest are state theory, governance, labour struggles, migration and gender relations. Among his publications are *Public Governance und schwache Interessen* (2010, edited with Ute Clement, Christoph Scherrer and Sabine Ruß-Sattar) and *Geschlechterpolitik und Klassenherrschaft: Eine Integration marxistischer und feministischer Staatstheorie* (2009). Contact: joerg.nowak@gmx.de.

Sharon Pickering is Professor of Criminology and an Australian Research Council Future Fellow on Border Policing at Monash University in Melbourne. Publications include *Sex Work: Labour Mobility and Sexual Services* (2012, with JaneMaree Maher and Alison Gerard); *Borders and Crime* (2012, edited with Jude McCulloch); *Gender, Borders and Violence* (2010); *Sex Trafficking* (2009, with Marie Segrave and Sanja Miliovjevic); *Counter-Terrorism Policing* (2008, edited with Jude McCulloch and David Wright-Neville); *Borders, Mobilities and Technologies of Control* (2006, with Leanne Weber); *Refugees and State Crime* (2005). *Globalization and Borders: Deaths at the Global Frontier* (with Leanne Weber, 2011) documented and analysed over 40,000 border-related deaths in Europe, North America and Australia. Contact: sharon.pickering@monash.edu.

Catherine Raissiguier is Professor at the Women's and Gender Studies program at New Jersey City University. She is the author of *Reinventing the Republic: Gender, Migration, and Citizenship in France* (2010) and *Becoming Women/Becoming Workers: Identity Formation in a French High School* (1994). She has taught Women's Studies at SUNY/Buffalo, the University of Michigan, Middlebury College, University of Oregon, Oregon State University and the University of Cincinnati. Contact: craissiguier@njcu.edu.

Robyn Magalit Rodriguez is Associate Professor in the Department of Asian American Studies at the University of California, Davis. She received her PhD in sociology from the University of California, Berkeley. Her book M*igrants for Export: How the Philippine State Brokers Workers to the World* (2010) received an honourable mention by the Association for Asian American Studies. Currently, she is completing a book manuscript entitled *In Lady Liberty's Shadow: Race and Immigration in Post-9/11 Suburban New Jersey* (to be published in 2015). Contact: rrodriguez@ucdavis.edu.

Sabine Ruß-Sattar is Professor of Comparative Politics at the University of Kassel. She studied at the universities of Freiburg, Clermont-Ferrand and the Institut d'Études Politiques, Paris. Her research fields include studies on political representation and interest politics, transformation of Western democracies, political parties and the construction of social problems. Among her recent publications are *Zweite Kammern* (2010, edited with Gisela Riescher and Christoph Haas) and *Europa und der Arabische Frühling* (2013, edited with Peter Bender and Georg Walter). Contact: sruss@uni-kassel.de.

Kim Rygiel is Associate Professor in the Department of Political Science at Wilfrid Laurier University. Her research focuses on citizenship politics and the regulation of global mobility through border controls within North America and Europe. Her current research includes a project undertaken with Veronica Kitchen on the 'Securitization of Policing' and examines the convergence of internal and international dimensions of security and policing within the context of global governance and issues of terrorism, border security and the policing of migrants and citizens. She is the author of *Globalizing Citizenship* (2010), winner of the 2011 ENMISA Distinguished Book Award of the International Studies Association, and with Peter Nyers has co-authored *Citizenship, Migrant Activism and the Politics of Movement* (2011). Contact: krygiel@wlu.ca.

Detlef Sack is Professor of Comparative Politics at the University of Bielefeld. Among his research interests are securitisation and the monitoring of human rights standards, political transformation and theories of democracy. Recent publications include 'Europeanization through Law, Compliance, and Party Differences', in the *Journal of European Integration*, 34, 3, 2012, 241–260; 'Dealing with Dissatisfaction – Role, Skills and Meta-Competences of Participatory Citizenship Education' in *Education for Civic and Political Participation. A Critical Approach*, edited by Reinhold Hedtke and Tatjana Zimenkova, (2013); and *Regieren und Governance in der Bundesrepublik Deutschland* (2013). Contact: detlef.sack@uni-bielefeld.de.

Helen Schwenken is Professor of Migration and Society at the Institute for Migration and Intercultural Research (IMIS) at the University of Osnabrück, Germany. She is also a coordinator of the Global Research Network for Domestic Worker Rights. Her research interests lie in the field of migration governance, social movement studies and global gender issues. In her book

Without Rights, but not Without a Voice (2006) she analysed political mobilisations of undocumented migrants in the European Union, in particular in border regions. In 2014 she published *'We want to be the Protagonists of our own Stories' A Manual on how Domestic Workers and Researchers can jointly conduct Research.* Contact: hschwenken@uni-kassel.de.

Mara Sidney is Associate Professor of Political Science at Rutgers University, Newark. Her research and teaching interests address a broad scope of fields touching on public policy, race and ethnicity and urban politics. She studies US and Canadian policies at national and local levels and examines the political role played by non-profit and community-based advocacy organisations in the integration of newly arrived immigrants. Publications include *Multiethnic Moments: The Politics of Urban Education* (co-authored with Rodney E. Hero, Susan E. Clarke, Luis Fraga and Bari Anhalt Erlichson, 2006) and *Unfair Housing: How National Policy Shapes Community Action* (2003). Contact: msidney@rutgers.edu.

Ayşen Üstübici is a PhD candidate in political science at Koç University and at the University of Amsterdam, as well as an affiliated researcher at the Migration Research Center (MiReKoc) at Koç University. She holds a BA in sociology and Political Science from Boğaziçi University and an MSc in gender, development, globalisation from the London School of Economics. Her PhD dissertation is a comparative enquiry on irregular migration regimes from the perspective of state and non-state actors in Turkey and Morocco. She received fellowships and grants from the Bucerius PhD Scholarship Program 'Settling into Motion', the Center for Gender Studies at Koç University (KOÇ-KAM) and the Scientific and Technological Research Council of Turkey (TUBITAK). Her areas of interests are international migration, comparative politics, social policy and gender studies. Contact: austubici@ku.edu.tr.

Leanne Weber is Senior Research Fellow at Monash University in Melbourne, Australia. She researches border control and migration policing using critical criminological and human rights frameworks. Publications include *Policing Non Citizens* (2013); *Stop and Search: Police Power in Global Context*, (2012, with Ben Bowling); *Globalization and Borders: Death at the Global Frontier* (2011, with Sharon Pickering) and *Borders, Mobility and Technologies of Control* (2006, also with Sharon Pickering). Contact: Leanne.Weber@monash.edu.

New Border and Citizenship Politics: An Introduction

Helen Schwenken and Sabine Ruß-Sattar

In September 2012, participants in the Refugee Protest March to Berlin walk from Bavaria to Berlin to protest against the conditions under which asylum seekers are housed in Germany. At the moment of crossing the internal border between the states of Bavaria and Thuringia, they publicly tear apart the official documents they carry. Why did they do so? By entering another state they violate a regulation called *Residenzpflicht*, which forbids all asylum seekers to leave the state in which their asylum claim has been filed. The refugees consider this practice a violation of their human and refugee rights. 'We tear apart our documents that contain the labels "*Aufenthaltsgestattung*" [temporary residence title for specific purposes] or "*Duldung*" [exceptional leave to remain] and that come with all the restrictions.' (Refugee Protest March to Berlin, 2012). The refugees explain their intention to send the destroyed documents to the issuing administration, the Federal Office for Migration and Refugees (BAMF) combined with the demand to 'correct the mistakes', as one of the speakers for the protesters explains. They demand that the BAMF issues genuine residence permits, which do not contain any restrictions concerning their residency, keep them living in camps, bar them from taking up legal employment or keep them in dependence on food packages or food stamps. In this act of civil disobedience at an internal border, the refugees symbolically disrupt the restrictive German migration and asylum regime. The action also sheds light on the ambivalence of the concept of citizenship (Schwiertz, forthcoming): The refugees are disenfranchised by carrying the status of 'non-citizens'. At the same time, they claim rights and reject the disenfranchisement in an assertive 'act of citizenship'. An action qualifies as an act of citizenship 'when, regardless of status and substance, subjects constitute themselves as citizens – or, better still, as those to whom the right to have rights is due' (Isin, 2008: 18). This example from a wave of refugee protests in Europe in 2012 and 2013 illustrates at least three dimensions of the constitutive relationship between borders and citizenship: First, 'the external border is diffused throughout internal spaces of the state' as well as 'within the everyday lives of migrants', as Rygiel writes in her contribution.

Second, the restrictive as well as the radical democratic linkages of border and citizenship policies are apparent. It is a matter of societal forces and political climate as to which of the two dominates the political landscape. Third, borders and citizenship work as 'mechanisms of subject formation' (Raissiguier, this volume).

At the very core of politics, power and domination is generated through dialects of inclusion and exclusion, association and dissociation. Though, strikingly, empirical research in the social sciences has rarely linked the two key concepts closely intertwined with these processes: 'citizenship' and 'border'. However, the dynamics of change with regard to the respective political phenomena are apparent if one looks at the contemporary policies of states. These recent forms of border and citizenship politics are characterised by shifting boundaries both to the inside and outside. Many immigration states in the global North, as well as in Australia, attempt to move border zones beyond their own territories to intensify and externalise (the costs of) control. Emigration states though tend to react to the normalised phenomenon of migration by including their emigrants into the nation by creating novel forms of citizenship. However, a comprehensive coverage of the bordering dynamics under way cannot limit itself to a state-centric perspective. The genuine political agency and actions of migrants themselves can bring about change in border as well in citizenship politics (Però and Solomos, 2010: 7; Schwenken, 2006). Migrants are reaching out beyond the frontiers of their legal status for their immediate needs and interests as well as for social and political citizenship (Rygiel, 2011a; see part III of this volume).

Citizenship itself is an extremely complex concept and its meaning can only be approximated in relation to other key concepts of the modern world, such as state, nation or democracy. In a very abstract way it stands for the relation between a person and a political body, and can be defined as a membership conferring rights, but also inferring duties. The quality of this relation can vary in time and space, but also with regard to its supposed normative ideal form (see Kivisto and Faist, 2007). In the political thinking of the late twentieth century, a liberal tradition stresses citizenship as a bundle of rights, whereas a communitarian-republican tradition accentuates the obligation of the individual citizen towards the political community. Finally, in a more radical Rousseauean republican understanding of the concept, it is active political participation which makes a citizen. In the context of migration, the republican frame can be used by migrants to claim access to citizen rights on the basis of their contribution to the whole social body. It goes without saying that the concept bears an emancipatory potential since it implies not only equality before the law but also the right to 'make it' (see Nyers, 2003, 2008; Isin, 2008, 2009). On the other hand, citizenship brings political freedom only to members, or those who are perceived as such, and discriminates and excludes the non-belonging ones (for a recent critical analysis see Reiter, 2013). The same dialectic is at work in the modern twin-concept 'nation'. Both concepts have to be filled and socially constructed and are based on 'imagined communities' (Anderson, 1991). How these communities are imagined can very well be observed in the making of diasporas, as Mikuszies' contribution shows.

Actually, the same is true for our second key concept 'borders'. The authors of the volume consider borders neither a 'natural' feature of today's globalisation to govern migration, nor as a line drawn by governments to delineate their territory. Therefore, *New Border and Citizenship Politics* approaches the subject of borders as a genuine political and socially constructed phenomenon, focusing on its dynamic, conflictive and productive character. In our view a border is a 'larger socio-legal apparatus' (Griffin, 2011: 17), making the border a social institution and being socially embedded (Weber and Pickering, in this volume). Borders as institutions come with their respective border control technologies, material capabilities (such as visas and passports) and legal as well as normative underpinnings. Conventional narratives on migration, mobilities and borders privilege state actors as those being in power. The contributors to the volume, however, share the approach that those who cross borders, talk about them or who attempt to control them, are actively shaping them. They are shaping borders, but under asymmetrical power relations that also restrict them and impact on their experiences and identities (Guild and Mantu, 2011b: 1). Borders have been universalised only quite recently, especially since the 1880s (McKeown, 2008: 2–6). This often neglected fact leads us to the issue of contestations about borders. International borders are key sites of regulation and struggles about belonging and mobility. Therefore we stress the aspect of politics, or more precisely, of contested politics around borders and citizenship. Politicisation has to be conceived in a dual sense: first, migration is politicised and second, politics, including citizenship politics, are subject to migration-induced reconfigurations, because the diverse movements of people impact on the affected societies (Squire, 2011). Migrants become both subjects and objects of politics.

The volume consequently develops further the state of the art in critical border regime and migration studies (such as: Squire, 2011; De Genova and Peutz, 2010; Guild and Mantu, 2011a; Hess and Kasparek, 2010; Geiger and Pécoud, 2010, 2012, 2013). It brings together and confronts the findings of two social science strands of research – critical migration and citizenship studies – by linking them conceptually. The authors do so by borrowing from studies on scale and the transformation of statehood and sovereignty. In recent years the paradigmatic 'mobility turn' has been influential in various disciplines that deal with migration. We insist though on the analytical category of migration and an empirical and conceptual focus on external and internal borders. The concept of mobility contains 'both the large-scale movements of people, objects, capital and information across the world, as well as the more local processes of daily transportation, movement through public space and the travel of material things within everyday life.' (Hannam et al., 2006: 1). This includes migrations of all forms. However, we see a danger that considering all forms of spatial movements as 'mobility', shifts the attention away from 'differential mobility', that is, the fact that internal and external state borders are powerful means to channel movements and to create hierarchies of desired and undesired mobilities. Some proponents of the mobility turn are well aware that '[t]here are new places and technologies that enhance the mobility of some peoples and places even as they also heighten the immobility of others, especially as people try to cross borders' (ibid.: 2). The contributions in this volume, for example Klepp's study on the Mediterranean Sea border, analyse some of the oftentimes violent processes at internal and external borders, which do not necessarily result in immobility, but come with high costs for the migrants. Other contributions, such as the one from Ataç, point to one of the results of differentiated mobility, the stratification of rights, which are effects of national migration and citizenship regimes.

We link border and citizenship studies conceptually by understanding them both as forms of 'reaching out' to the inside and to the outside, though with contradictory outcomes. Further, we follow Rygiel in considering citizenship politics as a part of border politics, in particular concerning their securitising and biopolitical dimensions (Rygiel, 2010: 92, Rygiel in this volume). Ataç shows, for example in the case of Austria, how certain conditions to qualify for a secure residence status, or even citizenship, become a powerful tool for governing migrant populations, including terminating their legal presence in case they cannot fulfil the requirements, which are subject to often quite spontaneous change. Border and citizenship politics are thus intertwined.

Three dimensions of new border and citizenship politics

In order to make these contributions to current scholarship, we need to delve into three dimensions: First, who are the relevant actors shaping these processes and what is the relationship between agency and structure in this highly asymmetrical field? Second, we need to better understand the spatial dimensions of the 'reaching outwards and inwards'. Third, what are the decisive mechanisms and technologies of the outreach and when citizenship and border politics interact?

Agency in bordering and citizenship processes

As the opening example of refugee protests illustrates, the first objective of the volume is to discuss the agentive quality of migrants, which has often been underestimated (and sometimes overestimated) in migration studies. We critically build upon the scholarship of the 'autonomy of migration' – a research paradigm that has primarily been developed in Italy, France and Germany (e.g. Transit Migration, 2007; Mezzadra and Neilson, 2008; Hess and Kasparek, 2010). Political protest as well as migrants' regular and irregular border crossings do affect the very existence of borders; however, these take place under asymmetric power structures that apparently restrain migrants' agency (Benz and Schwenken, 2005). The authors argue from the common ground that borders and citizenship are elements of a juridical arsenal for classifying people in categories such as 'regular/irregular' or 'insider/outsider'. Some migrants experience that established classifications can be subject to – often sudden – change and assign lesser rights to them, as the contributions by Ataç and Rygiel show. Consequently, according to their legal status and public perception, migrants have or lack certain rights. In some cases, as the case study by Klepp on the search and rescue mission for migrant-refugees in the Mediterranean Sea concisely demonstrates, migrants are completely deprived of every right, even including their 'bare life' (Agamben, 1995). Contributions on citizenship and subjectivity in the third part of the volume relate to this question of who can be a rights-bearing and agentive subject. They conclude that 'impossible subjects' (Raissiguier, 2010: 2, 34 and in this volume) in fact do emerge, making the link between status, space and (loss of) subjectivity less rigid than an Agambenian reading (see also Rygiel, 2011a). Within a restrictive legal frame, migrants with an irregular legal status might be able to exercise economic and even political citizenship (see the debates that take place under the headings of 'acts of citizenship' and 'activist citizenship', i.e. Isin, 2009; Nyers, 2006a; Andrijasevic, 2010; chapter 5 in Squire, 2011). The two studies in the volume about undocumented migrants' resistance and movements by Schwenken and Raissiguier make clear that becoming a political agent is possible in spite of the official deprivation of rights which constitutes an integral part of any border regime. However, this agency is fragile, both from a perspective of temporality and the existence of windows of opportunity. Further, it is linked to hierarchical gender and racial orders and the embodiment of agency in certain spaces such as the French Republic and the border zone between France and the UK.

Two sides of the coin: Externalisation and internalisation of borders

A second scholarly debate addresses borders and border regimes and how to conceptually understand recent changes in border regimes. We consider borders not to be so much a means of closing off a territory, but rather a juridical device to stratify mobile populations. Following Michel Foucault's governmentality approach, one could argue that sovereignty is shifting from control over territory to control over people. The debates in interdisciplinary border studies mainly focus on the spatial aspects of borders. Here two moves are key: the internalisation – Rodriguez (in this volume) further distinguishes interiorisation and localisation of borders and their enforcement – and the externalisation of borders. Concerning the governance of external(ised) borders, the technologies between air borders, offshore and onshore borders differ (Sack, Klepp, Weber and Pickering, all in this volume). The authors make the troubling observation that at these types of borders, the rights of migrants and asylum seekers are at their most precarious and volatile. Border guards often apply dubious techniques of 'intent management' to filter out potentially undesirable or undocumented persons. Further internal borders became – through racial profiling and conditionalities for public services – ever-present for many (underdocumented) migrants or visible minorities. In many countries such 'backdoor border controls' (Varsanyi, 2008) have clearly increased over the past decade. Rodriguez (in this volume) argues that 'what is at stake in these border practices is... citizenship, particularly social citizenship'.

Besides these spatial changes, one also needs to take into account the cultural politics of redesigning borders. Every border – thus, including every attribution or deprivation of rights – has to be officially legitimised. The authors of this volume pay particular attention to the discursive and cognitive levels of politics. Accordingly, it imparts a special standing to analysis from a social constructivist perspective. İçduygu and Üstübici conduct an analysis of the construction of the meaning of migration in European Union (EU)–Turkey negotiations about the candidature of Turkey to the EU. In the past, borders have often been understood as a result of power relations and interests. In contrast to this rationalist view, a constructivist perspective enables us to reveal how identities and culturally preformed perceptions act on the formation of political interests and perceptions of power (Onuf, 1989; Hopf, 2002). For instance, Turkey's EU candidacy necessitates difficult changes for Turkey's policies in the field of asylum and immigration. However, up to now, immigration policies have been closely related to the Turkish understanding of Turkish national identity and conception of the state. Redesigning the European and Turkish border would consequently imply finding a new post-nationalist construction of the Turkish state as well as Turkish migration policies (Avci and Kirişci, 2006: 167). In addition to this, on the EU side, irregular migration is constructed as a threat and framed as a security problem (Huysmans, 2006). Consequently, the capacity to control migration by efficient border policies becomes a central power resource which at least equals military capacity in international relations and is also closely related to it as the militarisation of borders and of border control technology shows. Constructivist approaches also provide a venue for analysing how the construction of borders is legitimised in order to fulfil their multifold introverted and extroverted functions. Ruß-Sattar, for example, looks at the discursive patterns of the debate on Turkish EU membership in key EU member states. It is striking how domestic and foreign policy discourses on belonging and exclusion are intertwined in order to justify the borders of Europe.

Obviously, migration touches upon integral functions of sovereignty since the regulation of migration is directly linked to the question of control in terms of territory and population. However, exercising control does not mean securing a territorial borderline, but constructing and maintaining a complex border regime. Paradoxically, one of the main characteristics of these border regimes precisely consists in suspending the differentiation between 'in' and 'out', and thus contradicting a classical function of borders (McKeown, 2008: 8–10, 16).

Mechanisms in linking border and citizenship politics

The third main contribution this volume makes discusses the mechanisms and technologies through which borders are redesigned, shifted or 'embedded' (Weber and Pickering, in this volume). In this respect, the EU appears as a testing ground for new technologies of control in a multilevel polity. On the one hand, the EU externalises its border control to non-member countries through, for example, 'mobility partnerships' (Kunz et al., 2011), and on the other, the securing of borders takes place within the EU territory itself for instance by defining airports as borders on the inside (see Sack, in this volume). Comparable strategies of internal bordering processes can be observed, for example, in the US, where undocumented migrants are the object of a new range of repressive policies on the local level, as the contributions by Rodriguez and Sidney document. Drawing borderlines and immigration enforcement has been rescaled to the very local level. This trend can be considered as 'domopolitics', a reconfiguration of 'relations between people, state, territory. At its heart is a fateful conjunction of home, land and security. It rationalises a series of security measures in the name of a particular conception of home' (Walters, 2004). The border sneaks into the suburbs as well as the very private sphere. These changes are, as the case of the changing meaning of conditions for acquiring a secure residence status and citizenship in Austria (Ataç in this volume) shows, related to the stratification of rights and inequality (Rygiel, 2010: 12; Morris, 2002; Goldring et al., 2009), but – and here we see an important contribution of the volume – in conjunction with the scholarship in critical border regime studies. The linkage is crucial, because 'politics of citizenship are changing within the context of globalization and securitization' (Rygiel, 2010: 10).

These particular macro contexts also come into play when tracing the linkage of border and citizenship politics in emigration countries and from a transnational perspective of relations that span emigration and immigration societies. Two authors in this volume engage with strategically carried out activities of 'reaching out' by governments of emigration countries towards their (former) citizens. Also, every immigrant with mostly limited citizenship rights is at the same time an emigrant with sometimes limited citizenship rights in the emigration state (Brand, 2006; Fitzgerald, 2009; Coutin, 2007; Smith, 1997; Rodriguez, 2010). Mikuszies and Nowak analyse and discuss in their chapters the reconfiguration of citizenship and diaspora politics beyond borders for two major emigration societies in the

Mediterranean, Morocco and Turkey. In line with Rygiel, they show how these new forms of citizenship are characterised by simultaneous openings and closures, in particular with regards to exclusionary and potentially violent functions of nationalism. These contributions speak to recent studies attempting to systematise emigration states' relationships towards the parts of their populations residing abroad (e.g. see Ragazzi, 2009).

Hot spots and hidden spots

These three broader issues of the volume allow us to discern the broad picture of today's logics and techniques of new borders and citizenship politics. In this complex and interactive process, governments and their agencies, citizens as well as (undocumented) migrants, are changing notions and practices of borders and citizenship. If territorial borders seem to become more porous today, this only masks the political shift from a more territorial form of control to the control of subjects and subjectivities. Borders as a political phenomenon will not disappear; they undergo changes such as the one of externalisation and internationalisation. Analysing these changes from above, within and below allows us to attain a clear view on the transformation of statehood, sovereignty and citizenship in today's politics.

The volume focuses on selected regions and selected 'hot spots' of current border contestations (Rygiel, Schwenken, in this volume), but also less obvious and less visible locales, such as suburbs and cities (Rodriguez, Sidney, in this volume) or bureaucracies (Ataç, in this volume). Most contributions engage with the EU level and/or countries in the EU and its neighbourhood. A specific focus is paid to the Mediterranean and Turkey, given the dynamic developments of the borders in the region, including its sea borders, and the EU's declared strategic interest in that region. The contributions on the US and Australia have been chosen due to the empirically new development in the US where border controls have currently been shifting attention away from an exclusive perspective on the US–Mexican border to erecting internal borders. The Australian case also shows that the move towards the externalisation of border controls and their gradual social embeddedness is not a European specialty, but that Australia has also been a key laboratory for the development of extra-territorial control claims in the whole Asia-Pacific region (see also Wilson and Weber, 2008; Ryan and Mitsilegas, 2010).

The volume fills some of the gaps that exist in the current debates between migration, citizenship and border studies. We contribute to this scholarship by systematically taking into account that bordering processes and migration take place under conditions of asymmetric power relations and bend towards increasing inequality and the creation of exclusionary regimes; therefore we follow a perspective that does not lose sight of the structural conditions of mobility. These conditions create tensions; hence a perspective on politics rather than policies is crucial.

Overview of the chapters

The volume comprises three sections: 'The politics of redesigning borders' (part I), 'The technologies of bordering' (part II) and 'The politics of citizenship as border politics' (part III) with in-depth case studies by anthropologists, sociologists, political scientists and a demographer. Each of the three parts is introduced by the editors.

Part I: The politics of redesigning borders

In 'Constructing voluntarism: technologies of "intent management" in Australian border controls' Leanne Weber and Sharon Pickering take the reader to the 'world leader in border externalisation practices' aimed at preventing asylum seekers' arrival and deporting visa-violating non-citizens. The practices came under public attack and a major reform of Australia's immigration enforcement machinery was set in motion. The authors show that 'structurally embedding' the border has been a key border regime technology with the aim to better control access to work and essential public services. Although this 'surveillance fantasy' is, as yet, imperfectly realised, Weber and Pickering observe how it is geared towards 'voluntary' reporting by migrants. This would constitute a shift from the open deployment of coercive power against unwelcome non-citizens towards a neoliberal responsibilisation agenda in which coercive state practices are disguised beneath a veneer of individual choice. The chapter 'Malta and the rescue of unwanted migrants at sea: The humanitarian law of the sea and the contested redesigning of borders' by Silja Klepp addresses an issue that has recently been discussed quite critically – the securing of the sea borders and the related deaths of shipwrecked migrants. She poses the question why so many migrants have to die despite existing legal and normative provisions to save people in distress at sea. In her ethnography of the sea border she observes how responsibilities, for example for search and rescue operations, are particularly uncertain where a state is engaged in joint operations, operations in the territorial waters of another state or operations on the high seas. In the Mediterranean Sea, the policies of border control and the right of a sovereign state to control its territory clash with the claims of a functioning European refugee protection system and with some aspects of the humanitarian law of the sea. The chapter shows that it is not merely a case of enforcing legal norms created by international law. The process is much more complex: legal gaps are filled by regional actors, through informal or even illegal practices, asserting their own claims at their convenience.

The following two contributions take a different focus on the redesigning of borders, both with a focus on Turkey–EU relations. They illustrate what Vicki Squire (2011) has coined 'politicizing mobility'. Ahmet İçduygu and Ayşen Üstübici analyse in 'Negotiating mobility, debating borders: Migration diplomacy in Turkey–EU relations' from a social constructivist perspective the role and position of migration and asylum management issues in membership negotiations between the EU and Turkey. As this analysis reveals, the so-called 'Europeanisation' of the Turkish border and migration regime is often misunderstood as being a unidirectional projection of European power. On the contrary, it is a product of political interactions in which migration itself functioned as a resource in the hands of Turkey.

In 'Building borders on a bias: The culturalist perception of Turkish migrants in France and Germany and the debate on Europe's boundaries' Sabine Ruß-Sattar pays attention to the discursive processes of legitimising political orders. The case is instructive as borders are drawn in a post-national type of polity. The author focuses on debates in France and Germany, at the time being key EU players and the most outspoken opponents towards Turkey's accession to the EU. They also represent two historically opposed experiences of state and nation-building and its political logics of inclusion and exclusion. In contrast to Germany that traditionally emphasises cultural frames with regard to citizenship, nation and state-building, France's Republican model should make this highly improbable. However, in both national political arenas immigration and Islam have become highly politicised issues that now bias the perception of the pros and cons of Turkish membership.

Part II: The technologies of bordering

The second part of the volume is opened by Detlef Sack's 'The momentum of contestation – airports as borderlands on the inside'. He analyses the executive practices and the political struggles at one type of an internalised external border, European airports and in particular the case of Frankfurt-Main airport. A range of state and non-state actors are participating and applying varying discursive strategies in the deportation of migrants and resistance against it. Three political discourse coalitions were identified: the first interprets migration within the frame of repressive control and deterrence, the second focuses on the human rights standards for refugees and the norm of international law, and a third one understands the transit zone as a state of exception and perceives the border itself as the problem to be addressed. External borders in the inside of a nation-state are also analysed in the contribution 'Interiorisation and localisation of border control: A US case' by Robyn Magalit Rodriguez. She engages with the phenomenon that municipal governments across the US have increasingly introduced policies aimed at prohibiting the employment and settlement of undocumented migrants, in particular those from Latin America, despite the fact that the federal government is supposed to have sole authority over the admission and expulsion of immigrants. This chapter maps out the newly introduced border technology of 'back door' border policies in the state of New Jersey. Rodriguez argues that these are forms of 'domopolitics' (Walters, 2004). Their origins and motivations can be found not only in post-9/11 securitisation moves, but also in the meaning of suburbanism for American culture. Rodriguez draws an argumentative line between cultural politics, citizenship and new border and immigration control politics. While Rodriguez engages with anti-immigrant 'domopolitics', Mara Sidney shows that in the same state another set of actors follows a more welcoming approach. In 'Outsiders/insiders: How local immigrant organisations contest the exclusion of undocumented immigrants in the US' she examines how the reconfiguration of border and immigration control in the US affects local advocacy on behalf of immigrants. By applying different argumentative frames – the undocumented migrant as a rights-bearing subject, as a productive worker or as neighbourhood inhabitant – pro-immigrant advocates try to find the most resonating frame within a fragmented policy space. İlker Ataç is interested in the encounter of migrants with the state, precisely with bureaucratic procedures and requirements to remain in the country of their residence. In 'Conditionalities as internal borders: The case of "security of residence" for third-country nationals in Austria' he builds upon literature that considers integration policies as a tool of immigration policy that meanders between restricting and expanding the rights of third-country nationals. He shows that in addition to well-known 'cultural' requirements, such as integration or language tests, the fulfilment of income requirements is an additional powerful mechanism of this form of internal border control, which is part of current migration management.

Part III: Politics of citizenship as border politics

The first chapter in the third part by Kim Rygiel, 'Border control politics as technologies of citizenship in Europe and North America', elaborates the linkages between border and citizenship politics. Her understanding of citizenship radically diverts from classical liberalism. Citizenship is not considered just a modern legal institution, but as 'government' in a Foucauldian sense. It includes practices, discourses, technologies, forms of power and political subjectivities. Rygiel argues that, on the one hand, citizenship is increasingly being used to regulate mobility; on the other hand, 'transgressive forms' of citizenship are developed that go well beyond both the conventional use of the term citizenship as well as the control-oriented type. Also, the following chapter, 'Troubling borders: Sans-papiers in France' by Catherine Raissiguier, gives a powerful example of how migrants can also resist the strengthened border regime by finding and using the fissures in the hegemonic discourse. The chapter engages the surprisingly successful narrative of a 'French exception' in terms of immigration and citizenship and the ways in which the *sans-papiers*, undocumented immigrants, in France help us see contradictions within the narrative. By focusing on the *sans-papiers* movement and the critical arguments *sans-papiers* brought up in immigration discussions in France, the essay aims to challenge French understanding of citizenship, national belonging and equality. In the next chapter, 'From Sangatte to the "Jungle": Europe's contested borderland', Helen Schwenken also engages with the question in how far borders are challenged by actors that are in a structurally weak position. But here the spatial dimension comes into the game. Mobilisations of undocumented migrants at Eurotunnel in northern France are analysed, and despite the fact that the stay of the migrants in the borderland is only temporary, they managed to establish a decade-long series of protests and mobilisations, in particular due to their use of spatial conditions. However, at the end of the decade the migrants' informal settlements, called 'the jungle', were demolished. This lost battle can be explained by the fact that local and national state authorities themselves made use of territorial strategies. The chapter thus engages with the literature on the legal and spatial dimension of activist citizenship practices and border-related mobilisations.

Linking border and citizenship politics and considering them arenas of negotiation also calls for a perspective that includes countries of origin. This is taken into account by two chapters in the volume, first by Jörg Nowak and his case study on 'Labour migration, postcolonial nationalism and class politics beyond borders: The case of the Turkish MHP party in Germany'. Turkey offers an example of how political elites reach out across borders to emigrant communities, wishing to tap into their political resources. The article re-evaluates the available research on the MHP's German branch in the light of recent debates about state strategies and the transnational social spaces that involve immigrant associations. It is argued that the activities of the Turkish party MHP in Germany are embedded both in transnational capitalist strategies and the internationalisation of states. The wave of wildcat strikes in Germany in 1973 is presented as an example of how these transnational political linkages became effective in local workplace conflicts. In the last chapter of this section, 'Emigration policies and citizenship rhetoric: Morocco and its emigrants in Europe', Esther Mikuszies examines in what way Morocco's complex borderland situation shapes exclusive and inclusive tendencies in citizenship rhetoric. The country's colonial experience makes the border situation complex in terms of historical heritage, unresolved geographic border conflicts and internally constructed boundaries set by the monarchy. The author first examines how the Moroccan monarchy tried to expand sovereignty towards its large-scale community in Europe over the last 20 years. Second, she takes the interplay between 'controlling and courting' as a starting point to expand on official citizenship rhetoric. Here the contradictory nature of enabling and constraining citizens becomes obvious.

Acknowledgements

We thank the Fritz Thyssen Foundation (Germany) for generously funding two book-making workshops and the International Office of the German Federal Ministry for Education and Research (BMBF) for supporting the

German-Turkish mobility in this respect. In particular we would like to thank the hosts of these workshops: The Center for Global Affairs at Rutgers University, in particular Simon Reich, and the Center for European and Mediterranean Studies, in particular Michael Minkenberg, at New York University as well as Sinan Özbek from the Philosophy Department of Kocaeli University (Turkey) with whom we had the pleasure to conceptualise the workshops. Christine Göttlicher, Sunniva Greve, Jane Parsons-Sauer, Silvia Mann and Matt Rees supported us enormously in proofreading and organisational issues. Muriel's, Helen's daughter, patience in the months before and after her birth, when finishing the manuscript, is also highly appreciated.

Part I
Introduction: The Politics of Redesigning Borders

Helen Schwenken and Sabine Ruß-Sattar

In autumn 2013 the European public is mourning for almost 400 people – mainly from Eritrea and Somalia – who died on 3 October 2013 near the coast of the Italian island of Lampedusa when their ship caught fire and sank. Meanwhile, the European border agency Frontex posts a human-touch cover story on a rescue mission in the Mediterranean Sea on its website (Frontex, 2013). One could have the impression that the much criticised agency is in fact a life-rescuing agency. Below the cover story we find pictures of the new European Border Surveillance System (EUROSUR) that has been introduced in December 2013. We see men sitting in front of a row of large monitors with satellite images of Europe and in particular the Mediterranean Sea around the south of Italy. Ship icons on the monitors indicate the location of vessels potentially on mission by people smugglers and with unauthorised passengers on board. EUROSUR is supposed to monitor irregular migration flows and to impede the business of smugglers – and to save people's lives by spotting and rescuing them. The combination of surveillance and rescue is in line with statements issued by politicians such as European Commissioner for Home Affairs Cecilia Malmström, directly after the Lampedusa tragedy: 'We have to become better at identifying and rescuing vessels at risk. We also need to intensify our efforts to fight criminal networks exploiting human despair,' (quoted in Europarlamento 24, 2013). Empirically, one can raise doubts on how serious the link between rescue and securitised border control actually is. Only a few days after the 3 October tragedy, another ship sank close to Lampedusa and dozens of migrants died. Further, Frontex had to admit that it actively pushed back ships with refugees, although this practice had been declared unlawful by the European Court of Justice in 2012 (Monitor, 2013). From a discourse analytical perspective the linkage of security, blaming greedy people smugglers for the migrants' deaths and lifesaving missions by Frontex is characteristic of the current border regime. It allows increasing legitimacy for further Europeanising border controls and the introduction of new technologies. This discursive figure has to be situated in the broader shift from a security-driven approach to what is called migration management, which is often understood as a middle way between repressive control measures and a more liberal approach (Kalm, 2012; Geiger and Pécoud, 2010). What has to be taken into account, though, is the specific space the current debate refers to – the sea. European external borders and in particular their sea borders have been at the centre of redesigning the borders of the European Union (EU) (as well as Australia, as the contribution by Weber and Pickering in this volume shows). Why is the sea border so central in this regard? Border regime studies note a trend towards an externalisation and blurring of borders (e.g. Boswell, 2003; Transit Migration, 2007; Huysmans, 2000 and 2006). The national border, and in particular the sea border, is no longer a clear line with checkpoints guarded by easily recognisable border patrol staff. At the sea there is often a dispute over which state is responsible for saving shipwrecked migrants (see Klepp in this volume). In such an environment of divided responsibilities there is ample space for experimenting with new forms of border control. The Frontex logo visualises this approach: The logo contains the 12 European stars, a 'protective' blue circle around one of these stars and a green line from the top left to the bottom right. Both the blue circle and the green line are inside as well outside of the assumed territory of the European Union. The logo thus visualises the spatial understanding of the agency, controlling both in- and outside of the EU's territory.

This first part of the volume thus focuses on the contested territorial and political dimensions of attempts to redesign borders, in particular external borders. A variety of actors becomes visible that contribute to these processes – governments, border control units, international organisations, media, migrants and borderzone populations. The authors engage with the troubling finding that the meaning of how migration, security, control etc. are understood by different groups of actors often shifts throughout the political process. These strategic shifts are characteristic of the contested politics of redesigning borders and conditioning mobility. While the contributions by Weber and Pickering and Klepp focus on the control claims at to-be-redesigned borders, İçduygu and Üstübici and Ruß-Sattar engage with the cultural politics at play. Both contributions focus the developments in border politics with regard to the EU as the most striking case of the emerging postnational border constellation (Vobruba, 2010). As these case studies demonstrate, the often-used formula of a closed 'Fortress Europe' is indeed misleading and may be rethought, as Vobruba proposes, as a 'bazaar of mobility and migration' (ibid.). The results of negotiations on migration and border issues may in fact be related to package-deals in other policy fields. Further, the redesigning of borders can be observed not only at the frontlines – some of the scenes where these contested shifts take place are outside public visibility, such as in 'migration diplomacy' (İçduygu and Üstübici, in this volume) – but also at the sea, where from time to time the Pope or TV cameras are present and appeal to the humanistic conscience.

1
Constructing Voluntarism: Technologies of 'intent management' in Australian Border Controls

Leanne Weber and Sharon Pickering

Australia has attracted a dubious international reputation over the last decade for its harsh policies towards asylum seekers and has become a world leader in border externalisation practices aimed at preventing their arrival. At the same time, Australian governments have also historically shown a preparedness to use their internal enforcement powers to expel non-citizens who commit criminal offences or violate their strict visa conditions. These border control practices which operate, respectively, before and after arrival reflect the external and internal manifestations of the Australian border. Although openly coercive practices such as offshore interdiction, detention and deportation are the most visible and visceral aspects of Australian border control, new forms of border governance are emerging that seek to shape individual decision-making to promote 'voluntary' compliance with migration management goals at both onshore and offshore locations. This governmental project is pursued through what Rose (2000: 324) describes as 'technologies for the conduct of conduct'. A key onshore strategy is the construction of a 'structurally embedded' border (Weber, 2013), so that access to work and essential public services is so constrained that unlawful non-citizens are driven to report 'voluntarily' to authorities. With respect to the offshore border, the re-implementation in 2012 of the notorious 'Pacific solution' has been accompanied by propaganda campaigns aimed at discouraging asylum seekers from travelling to Australia by boat, and with strategies of persuasion intended to produce 'voluntary' returns amongst those who are not deterred. These developments in the biopolitics of border control – described in official documents as *'intent management'* – indicate a partial shift from the open deployment of coercive power towards a neoliberal responsibilisation agenda in which state authority operates through a veneer of individual choice. However, in contrast to the responsibilised citizenry proposed by Garland (1997) as reflecting a new technology of crime control, the aim is to create responsibilised *non*-citizens who will align their thoughts and behaviour with the border management goals of the Australian state and cooperate in their own exclusion.

Responsibilising non-citizens

In relation to the control of border crossing, intent management may be best understood as pre-emptive migration management. Rather than responding to an unauthorised border crossing with turn-around, prosecution or deportation, intent management seeks to impact the thoughts of those who have been profiled as 'undesirable' (see also Sack, in this volume). This represents a shift in focus away from individuals breaching border control or migration requirements, and instead towards pre-emptive strategies that aim to identify threats and make interventions *before* travel takes place. The desire to manage intent in relation to border crossings requires a range of elaborate processes to manage large populations of *potential* and *actual* travellers, only some of whom may seek 'migration outcomes' within Australia. Pre-emptive border control has much in common with pre-emptive policing endeavours (Weber, 2006; Wilson and Weber, 2008). In the context of criminal justice, Zedner refers to this development as a shift towards a pre-crime society, 'in which the possibility of forestalling risks competes with and even takes precedence over responding to wrongs done', and where the 'post-crime orientation of criminal justice is increasingly overshadowed by the pre-crime logic of security' (2007: 261–262).

Anticipating the risky traveller is now a focus for the Intent Management and Analytic section of the Department of Immigration and Citizenship (DIAC).[1] The aim is to pre-empt potential claims on Australia's refugee protection obligations and anticipate post-arrival compliance breaches, such as working when on a tourist visa. Australian immigration authorities describe their 'layered' approach to intent management as follows: 'The process starts *even before* the person books a ticket or lodges an application for a visa to enter Australia' (McCairns, 2011; emphasis added). This places intent management at the outermost edge in border policing – one that temporally occurs well before the usual preparatory actions associated with travel (e.g. buying a ticket or applying for a visa) and physically well before any border crossing. Those who are not intent-managed out of the system at this preparatory stage are then streamed into visa processing categories described as 'risk tiering':

> The client's details are assessed against a set of risk ratings. [The] key objective of risk tiering is to be able to predict high and low risk clients based on historical patterns, aligning processing effort to client risk levels. Depending on the risk rating, visa applications will be streamed to a particular processing queue: streamlined, standard, high rigour.
>
> (McCairns, 2011)

Those who are 'intent-managed' at either of these stages are effectively policed out of the licit market in the movement of people. Intent management links state actions to suspicion about potential travellers without assessing an individual's rightful need or desire to undertake an illegalized border crossing in relation to specific frameworks of human rights and without specific investigation or charges in relation to migration law.

Intent-management strategies display many of the features of classical deterrence. Both envisage a rational actor choosing a course of action by weighing up the costs and benefits associated with each of the available choices. But intent-management strategies also carry the hallmarks of distinctively neoliberal forms of governance described by Rose (2000: 321) as 'regimes for the continual, silent and largely invisible work of the assessment, management, communication and control of risk'. Rather than rely on the threat of punishment, these regimes mobilise a wider array of threats (such as the risk of drowning or shark attack); typically target threats to specific, 'high-risk' populations rather than the populace as a whole; often communicate risk statements through new social media and information technologies; and seek to manage intent by attempting to shape the field of choice through the application of risk-based technologies. And whereas deterrence may be understood as exerting either a general or specific impact on behaviour, intent management is expressed as a stage before action – acting on the thoughts (intentions) that may or may not fuel an 'undesirable' act. Although the technologies may not be as developed as the consciousness-penetrating techniques imagined by Orwell, intent management effectively expands the remit of border control/migration management in a way that hints at his vision of 'thought policing'.

After individuals have crossed the Australian border, intent management manifests most clearly in attempts to manufacture various forms of 'voluntary' self-policing. As a first step, DIAC annual reports assert that 'the department seeks to create an environment where people voluntarily comply with their visa obligations' while at the same time 'it actively identifies and locates those who are not complying with their obligations under Australia's migration laws, through robust enforcement strategies' (DIAC, 2012). Voluntary compliance is presented as preferable to the less palatable alternative of 'robust enforcement', and is to be promoted through the provision of information about visa conditions, overlaid with messages about harsh consequences for refusal to comply voluntarily. The promotion of voluntary compliance shares some of the characteristics of intent management, being directed towards influencing thought processes through the provision of information. It also has a pre-emptive quality, aiming to achieve border management goals while avoiding the necessity for coercive intervention.

Attempts to manufacture 'voluntariness' continue even when voluntary compliance with immigration controls has manifestly failed. 'Voluntary' reporting to DIAC offices consistently accounts for the vast majority of detections of individuals in breach of visa conditions. Significant increases in the detection rate have been attributed to 'a range of reforms' introduced in 2007–2008 'to encourage voluntary approaches to the department from non-complying visa holders' (DIAC, 2012). Individuals presenting themselves 'voluntarily' to immigration officials no doubt hope for a resolution of their visa breach through regularisation of their status. However in recent years, annual reports have also documented increasing numbers of expulsions of non-compliant individuals, which they attribute largely to departmental success in promoting 'voluntary' departures. The 2011–2012 annual report even claimed that the majority of removals *from detention* were voluntary (1689, compared with 86 'involuntary' removals), attributing a remarkable level of agency to a group experiencing mandatory and potentially indefinite incarceration. Since then, the reinstatement by the former Labor government of offshore detention in the Pacific has generated a new wave of 'voluntary' returns, primarily involving Sri Lankan asylum seekers facing long-term detention on Nauru (Pickering and Weber, 2014).

While voluntary compliance has much to recommend it when compared with the prospect of intense and potentially coercive enforcement, many questions arise about the quality of individual choice being exercised and the processes shaping the available options, not least of which is the underlying fairness of the legal provisions with which individuals are intended to comply. In relation to the intent-management practices described earlier, anticipating future breaches of border controls raises serious legal and ethical issues not least of which include the fairness and legality of discouraging those seeking refugee protection from carrying out their security-seeking plans. In the remainder of this chapter, we seek to shed some light on these questions by analysing in greater detail some of the techniques of intent management and voluntary compliance in operation at Australia's external and internal borders.

Managing travel intentions

Managing the travel intentions of undesirable travellers is an extension of the central pillar in border control in Australia, Europe and the US: pushing interventions and border control further out from the nation-state. In the case of Australia, managing travel intentions has been the focus of efforts to deter asylum seekers. The two most notable campaigns have been geared around two equally flawed premises: that undesirable travellers need to voluntarily make 'better choices', and that those 'voluntary' choices can be influenced by clearer messages sent by the receiving state.

In 2000, Australian immigration authorities commissioned an online advertisement trilogy: *The Trip*, *The Reception* and *Experiences and Expectations of Travellers*. Sharks, fires, crocodiles and snakes featured in the videos aimed at deterring asylum seekers from arriving without authorisation in Australia.

The message was clear: asylum seekers should seek asylum elsewhere as they face the risk of being eaten by sharks or crocodiles, incinerated in wildfires or attacked by poisonous snakes. The opening video, *The Trip*, includes the voiceover:

> They lied to them, promising state of the art boats with satellite navigation. What did they get? A run-down fishing boat at the end of its useful life. The boats often break down en route and are usually abandoned by their crew once they reach their destination. People are often left in remote areas thousands of kilometres from their destination. It is not worth the risk.
>
> (Carmody, 2000)

There is no available evidence that asylum seekers have fallen prey to the wildlife detailed, but the deterrent message was more general. The contentious issue is not the likely grounds for a protection application, but rather that asylum seekers should not bring those claims to Australia but voluntarily go elsewhere. The minister for immigration at the time remarked:

> Now when you see them [the videos,] you might think that they are a little sensational. You may think that they're horrific, and that maybe we're trying unnecessarily to scare people from coming to Australia. So I want to stress that the information in all of these videos is based on fact.
>
> (Carmody, 2000)

The minister toured the Middle East and Europe showing the videos to media in a kind of reverse promotion campaign. The information kit also included material that stated: 'paying people smugglers could leave prospective immigrants in debt to criminals who will demand you work for them selling drugs or force you and your family into prostitution to pay off your debt' and that asylum seekers 'face racial hatred and violence because citizens are angry at having to support them' (quoted in Uprooted People, 2001).

The most recent manifestation of the management of 'travel intentions' has been the 'No Advantage' campaign directed at asylum seekers travelling to Australia. By announcing that those interdicted at sea will be transported to offshore places (namely Nauru and Papua New Guinea) where they will remain in restricted conditions for an indefinite period, the Labor government sought to construct a rationality in which making the hazardous maritime crossing confers no advantage over a person who patiently waits in a neighbouring or transit country for processing by the United Nations High Commissioner for Refugees (UNHCR). The 'no advantage principle' was a key recommendation of the Expert Panel on Asylum that was charged with developing policy recommendations to prevent the loss of life of asylum seekers. Drawing on classical deterrence approaches, but also expanding the scope of interventions to include a range of positive and negative incentives, the set of policy recommendations includes a vast extension of the mandatory detention regime for unauthorised arrivals.

UNHCR wrote to the minister for immigration and citizenship commenting on the No Advantage principle in 2012:

> The practical implications of this are not fully clear to us. The time it takes for resettlement referrals by UNHCR in South-East Asia or elsewhere may not be a suitable comparator for the period that a Convention State whose protection obligations should use. Moreover it will be difficult to identify such a period with any accuracy, given that there is no 'average' time for resettlement... Finally, the 'no advantage' test appears to be based on the longer term aspiration that there are, in fact, effective 'regional processing arrangements' in place.
> (UNHCR, 2012: 2)

A compliant consumer of the 'no advantage' message would volunteer to stay in transit, go elsewhere, or return home despite this restricted range of 'choices' providing limited utility for those seeking durable protection. To reinforce this message, a renewed international online video campaign was targeted at asylum seekers in the region. An Australian government video promulgated via YouTube (Government of Australia, 2012) – presumably for consumption by potential asylum seekers – comes with the caption: 'We're working regionally to stop people smugglers. There's no advantage taking a boat when it's safer, cheaper and just as quick to use orderly migration options.'

Attempts to manage intentions in this way failed to produce the desired results, with numbers of arrivals increasing to unprecedented levels from the time the approach was introduced in August 2012 until the change of government in 2013 (Curr, 2012). A detailed list compiled by the NGO Safecom shows boat arrivals continuing unabated following the government announcement (Safecom, no date). As well-known refugee advocate Pamela Curr wrote:

> I asked an asylum seeker in Indonesia if the Government's attempts to spread word of Nauru by DVD to stop people would work: 'I saw that film. If Nauru like this people come more than before. [Because] the place for live in Nauru is more better than Indonesian detention and also Australia take responsibility for them.'
> (Asylum seeker in Indonesia who has tried two boats to get to Australia, quoted in Curr, 2012).

Having failed to manipulate the thought processes of asylum seekers in ways that deterred the boat arrivals, the former Australian government was forced to introduce new strategies of intent management. It soon became clear that the significant numbers of asylum seekers continuing to arrive by boat could not all be accommodated in the hastily erected tent accommodation on Nauru and Manus Island. The minister then issued a press release on 21 November 2012 that shocked refugee advocates with its severity and single-minded adherence to the 'no advantage' rule. Asylum seekers who arrived after the 13 August 2012 watershed of the introduction of the 'no advantage' rule would have the rule applied to them even if they were processed in Australia. In the minister's words: 'Consistent with "no advantage", people from this cohort going onto bridging visas will have no work rights and will receive only basic accommodation assistance and limited financial support' (Minister for Immigration and Citizenship, 2012). In the most extreme attempt to recreate an equivalent measure of uncertainty and misery as faced by those waiting in transit in the hope of being resettled in Australia, the minister announced that even those individuals recognised as being in need of refugee protection were to be issued only with temporary protection visas with extremely limited rights, 'until such time that they would have been resettled in Australia after being processed in our region' (Minister for Immigration and Citizenship, 2012).

For those who have refused to be intent-managed and began filling up the overflowing camps on Nauru and Manus Island, the government then constructed 'voluntary returns' through the manipulation of available options as a secondary strategy.

> Having failed to deter boat arrivals, the government now seeks to force a 'voluntary' return. It is this new strategy which strikes fear in the hearts of those Australians clinging to ideals of human rights. Asylum seekers arriving on Christmas Island are told that they will be sent to Nauru for an indefinite time, that their cases will not be assessed for a long time and that legislation has been passed which means that they may never see their families again. The darkest picture is painted of their lack of a future.
>
> (Curr, 2012)

So why have these threatening messages failed to alter thought processes? Roslyn Richardson has documented the unexpected ways messages regarding risks and punitive government policies were consumed and acted upon by asylum seekers. She found that asylum seekers are 'diverse, unpredictable and capable of producing a variety of interpretations of the messages they receive...the transmission and reception of Australia's deterrence "messages" are far from straightforward' (Richardson, 2010). Others have argued that these information campaigns are intended more for domestic consumption by electorates seeking tough border control policies from the major parties than future asylum seekers. However, as Curr notes, the manufacture of volunteerism in managing the travelling intentions of asylum seekers is *always* coupled with a punitive kick – even when labelled 'voluntary'.

In short, having made the poor choice of seeking asylum in Australia, a second and final opportunity is granted to an asylum seeker to determine an alternate course of action and avoid making another erroneous choice. So now the asylum seeker is encouraged, engaged, threatened and supported to volunteer for repatriation.

This process is equally subject to online infomercial blitz. The manufacture of removal as a voluntary opportunity is then advertised on 'infomercials' posted on the internet and in a Twitter feed from DIAC which creates a virtual scorecard of 'voluntary' returns by groups of irregular maritime arrivals identified by nationality. Like many others, British barrister Frances Webber (2011: 99) has questioned whether programmes of 'voluntary returns' of failed asylum seekers 'offer a genuine informed choice or are just an extension of deportation programmes'. She raises questions as to whether assisted returns are sustainable, safe or truly voluntary. In the instances described in the DIAC Twitter communications, those referred to are not 'failed asylum seekers' for they have not been through any refugee status determination process. Rather, they have either been 'screened out' (immediately deemed not to have raised a protection obligation) or, subject to communication with government officials, have decided not to make a claim for refugee status. The UNHCR has issued guidelines for voluntary repatriation of asylum seekers, which assert that choice must be 'informed' (which depends upon conditions in the country of origin) and 'free' (which is influenced by circumstances in the country of asylum) (Webber, 2011: 103). There are reports that some of those subject to voluntary return have been arrested upon arrival in Colombo (IRB, 2013). Since this action is likely to have been anticipated by the returnees, serious concerns are raised about the extent to which any choice made could be considered to have been a free and informed choice.

Australia is not the only liberal democracy to have employed strategies of intent management using novel and highly targeted modes of risk calculation (see Schwenken, in this volume). In response to high rates of deaths occurring during unauthorised border crossings across the US–Mexico border, the US government launched a 'harm minimisation' approach known as the 'Border Safety Initiative', which entailed sending patrols to find migrants in distress, and a greater emphasis on 'search and rescue' functions. Preventing dangerous (and unwanted) crossings across the desert was, however, the primary aim, corresponding to the focus on unauthorised boat arrivals by sea by the Australian authorities. In a way that is also analogous to the Australian context, the recording and classification of deaths by US agencies at this time was a means of validating their 'humanitarian' mission to reduce the harm of their own border enforcement practices which were explicitly designed to deter migrants by making it more dangerous to cross the border. As noted in a 2009 *Washington Post* article:

> In what may be among the lesser-known deterrents exercised by our nation's security forces, the Border Patrol is deploying up-tempo Mexican folk songs about tragic border crossings to dissuade would-be illegal immigrants.
>
> (Surdin, 2009)

This traditional form of communication is intended to influence the decision processes of potential border crossers through culturally appropriate messages. The lyrics of one of these songs (possibly losing some of its lyricism in the process of translation) included the lines: 'Before you cross the border, remember that you can be just as much a man by chickening out and staying. Because it's better to keep your life than ending up dead' (ibid.).

At the external border, these 'technologies for the conduct of conduct' stretch deterrence to its limits by intervening as early as possible and expanding the repertoire of threats beyond formal punishment, introducing distinctly neoliberal elements of pre-emption, responsibilisation and novel forms of risk communication. In the case of asylum seekers attempting to reach Australia by boat, assumptions that the potential suffering – namely loss of life during border crossing, or through indefinite detention, separation from family or ongoing precarious migration status – can be set against a safer alternative of remaining offshore – has proven to be a terrible miscalculation regarding the capacity for human suffering. As Curr (2012) explains, even the attempts to turn Nauru into a 'hellhole' of offshore detention have failed to influence the risk calculations of individuals who have experienced much worse:

> The fear of being killed or tortured is the root cause for people leaving homes, family, land and businesses. Having made the soul-destroying decision to leave all that is dear and head off into uncertainty, people feel that they have no choice but to keep moving and striving for safety and security. Australia offers this. Malaysia and Indonesia do not.
>
> (Curr 2012)

Constructing voluntary reporting

Once they are within Australian territory, non-citizens who become unlawfully present by overstaying their visa or breaching their visa conditions face a 'structurally embedded' border (Weber, 2013). This expanded border recruits law enforcement agencies, industry regulators, service providers, educational establishments, employers and private citizens into a migration policing role, along with DIAC compliance officers and state police who exercise enforcement powers under the Migration Act 1958.[2] Agencies that participate in these 'structural' migration policing projects are recruited through a variety of incentivisation schemes. These range from statutory requirements on service providers to check immigration status before providing benefits or services; to government funding arrangements that require proof of legal status in order to recover costs for the provision of medical services; to the threat of legal sanctions against private individuals who employ individuals who lack legal entitlements to work or remain in the country. Agencies can play an active role in identifying unlawful non-citizens by bringing them to the attention of DIAC in the course of checking their entitlement to receive services or benefits. In this case, migration policing agencies operate as 'switch point(s) to be passed in order to access the benefits of liberty' (Rose, 2000: 326).

In turn, fear of being detected by these agencies may narrow the options available to individuals for day-to-day survival to such an extent that they effectively decide to self-police. This comment by a senior official interviewed by one of the authors,[3] indicates that DIAC actively pursues this responsibilisation strategy.

> Already someone that's overstayed and disappeared and has no entitlements and Medicare benefits or... any form of social security benefit or anything like that, so they're very dependent on employment.... We're shifting where our resources apply and also... we're looking to these other ways of... making life difficult for people... so that they come in and see us.
>
> (DIAC official, cited in Weber, 2013: 142)

Faced with this web of information exchange and surveillance, it is not surprising that so-called 'voluntary' reports to DIAC officers are the fastest growing source of 'locations' of unlawful non-citizens, accounting for 82 per cent of unlawful non-citizens located by DIAC in the 2011–2012 financial year (DIAC, 2012). Embedding of the border through an ever-expanding network of immigration checks guarding access to essential services and opportunities, backed up in some cases with harsh sanctions for providing services to those without entitlement, creates a border that relies on exclusion rather than active efforts at detection. It is a border drawn around unlawful non-citizens themselves, intended to separate them from all that is necessary to sustain a reasonable life, so that 'voluntary' presentation to authorities becomes the only viable option.

DIAC annual reports note the success of unnamed departmental programmes designed to encourage voluntary reporting, claiming that the increase in 'locations' from 13,831 in 2010–2011 to 15,477 in 2011–2012 was due to a 'range of reforms to encourage voluntary approaches to the department from non-complying visa holders' that were instituted in 2007–2008 (DIAC, 2012). Determined overstayers and individuals with substantial community support may have the resources to resist the pressures to report. But if the removal of all options to sustain existence is achieved, the border will effectively have been internalised so that the governmental goal of managing intent is complete.

Once non-citizens who are unlawfully present in Australia are located by immigration authorities or report 'voluntarily' to DIAC offices, the next question that arises is whether the individual will make a 'voluntary' departure. Departmental publications indicate that, where necessary, status resolution officers work closely with affected individuals, seeking either to regularise their stay or smooth the pathway to removal.

> If an appropriate visa option is unavailable, clients are encouraged to voluntarily depart before the department pursues enforced removal. Effective status resolution is achieved through providing clear and accurate information and engaging early with non-citizens through targeted messages and communication products that deter non-compliant behaviour.
> (DIAC, 2012: 182)

In addition to deploying 'communication products', financial assistance is said to be provided 'to support immediate post return needs, when required', which may operate as a positive incentive in some cases. About 95 per cent of people who were removed from Australia in the annual reporting period 2011–2012 were said to have cooperated with removal arrangements (DIAC, 2012: 190). However, a small number of individuals resist their removal and considerable resources may be invested in securing their return.

Amongst this group – described in departmental documentation as 'entrenched clients' – considerable efforts are expended in constructing their 'voluntary' return. A consultants' report commissioned by DIAC on the 'management of forced removals' purports to present evidence from a 'client's perspective' that will inform strategies to encourage them to align their views with departmental goals (Hall and Partners, 2012). The report notes that, despite having exhausted all legal avenues to remain in Australia, these resistant clients resolutely describe themselves as Australian and harbour a distorted view of their entitlement to remain. The recommended strategies involve recruiting trusted third parties to encourage them to accept their fate. In order to pre-empt 'entrenchment' in the first place, it is suggested that community groups and migration agents should be encouraged to downplay the possibilities of achieving permanent residence to new arrivals; additionally, 'at-risk' clients should be made to understand that immigration decisions are based on 'evidence', rather than on whimsy or perceptions of moral desert – two perceptions that were said to be prevalent among this group.

The recommendations concerning 'entrenched clients' already appear to have made an impact on departmental thinking. The latest DIAC annual report asserts that: '[t]o progress each case to an outcome, status resolution officers engage openly and honestly with clients, and provide clear explanations about immigration decisions and their implications' (DIAC, 2012: 182). These 'explanations', it seems, are ideally provided as early as possible for those who are judged to be highly likely to refuse to leave. The consultants recommended that this 'at-risk' group should be identified from the instigation of compliance proceedings and required to submit a 'credible Plan B' with each application to stay, through wording on forms such as 'If, as is very likely, you are forced to leave, what will you do?' This introduces a marked pre-emptive mentality into the operation of after-entry border controls which is aimed at securing voluntary compliance as early as possible in the course of events.

At least some of these individuals will be rejected asylum applicants, some of whom are likely to have strong reasons to resist their return. Others may be motivated to resist their removal based on a range of grounds, including positive incentives to remain in Australia for financial and family reasons. One aspect of the many factors shaping the 'intent' of potential deportees that was absent from the consultants' report is the capacity of Australian immigration laws, and of those who apply them, to produce fair outcomes that will be accepted by those subjected to border controls. In relation to voluntary return programmes for asylum seekers in Europe, Webber (2011: 103) concludes: 'Virtually none of the schemes currently operating as "voluntary return programmes" from Europe meets the criteria for voluntariness. Voluntary return is instead offered as a less painful alternative to continued destitution followed by (inevitable) compulsory return.'

The consultants' report on entrenched clients notes the 'disproportionate' resources expended on their case management. It is relevant to ask what purpose is served by the efforts to construct the 'voluntary' return of even the most recalcitrant group. Efforts to manufacture voluntarism within the Australian immigration compliance system appear to stem from around 2007. This is the period following a series of scandals in which hundreds of Australian citizens were found to have been wrongly detained or even removed from Australia (Palmer, 2005). The sweeping reforms that followed were intended to restore legitimacy to the immigration enforcement process, while at the same time improving its efficiency through the application of advanced technologies and improved decision-making.

The systems in place to actively encourage compliance and intensively manage 'entrenched' departmental clients can therefore be understood as the management of political risk that might follow from the spectacle of forced deportation. This invisibility is a valuable political resource since, as Bauman (2002: 111) notes, forced expulsions 'make dramatic television and are likely to trigger a public outcry'. DIAC annual reports also characterise voluntary departures from the community as 'less expensive and less risky' than removals from detention (DIAC, 2012: 168). The production of 'voluntary' reporting and removal constitutes the subjects of internal border controls as freely choosing agents, as argued by Rose (2000: 337): 'Although the problems addressed by these new strategies of control are varied, at their heart lies the problem of control in a "free" society and hence the kinds of subjects that are imagined to inhabit and deserve such a society' (Rose, 2000: 337). An individual who transgresses internal border controls can therefore be viewed as having 'failed to accept his or her responsibilities as a subject of moral community' and is therefore responsible for his or her own exclusion.

Conclusion

Intent management provides a powerful additional tool to manufacture compliance, while the application of coercive power remains as an ever-present threat. Through technologies of intent management and the construction of voluntarism, those who are subject to Australian border controls at both the internal and external border are constituted as 'the responsible subject[s] of moral community guided – or misguided – by ethical self-steering mechanisms' (Rose, 2000: 321) – even as their actual or threatened expulsion from that moral community is always imminent. Their apparently free choice disguises the hand of government in pursuing its governmental project – recalling Rose's characterisation of contemporary governance as the 'largely invisible' control of risk. This locates responsibility for transgressing border policies with individuals, while concealing the operation of policies that constrain choice. These developments in Australian border control reflect the fundamentalist belief in rational choice inherent within neoliberalism and the establishment of the responsibilised individual as the subject of governance, while according considerable, and often hidden, power to government to shape the field of choice.

Notes

1. Since this chapter was drafted, a change of federal government has taken place in Australia and this department has been renamed the *Department of Immigration and Border Protection*.
2. Australian police are 'designated officers' under this legislation and engage primarily in the questioning (Section 188) and detention (Section 189) of those they believe to be 'unlawful non-citizens'.
3. Policing migration in Australia: An examination of onshore migration policing networks, Australian Research Council Discovery Project DP0774554.

2
Malta and the Rescue of Unwanted Migrants at Sea: Negotiating the Humanitarian Law of the Sea and the Contested Redesigning of Borders[1]

Silja Klepp

In recent decades, the margins of Europe's Mediterranean region have gone through enormous changes: national borders previously taken for granted have become contested external borders of the European Union (EU). Effects of the relocation of borders and of the European refugee protection system have been especially strong around the Mediterranean Sea: in particular, gaining access to the refugee protection systems of the EU has become increasingly difficult for these refugees. Responsibilities are particularly uncertain where a state is engaged in joint operations, in operations in the territorial waters of another state, or in operations on the high seas. Dilemmas also arise when migrants are rescued from shipwrecked boats. The legal responsibilities to rescue migrants at sea should be clear, but the actions taken vary according to which Search and Rescue Area (SAR Area) the shipwreck occurs in. In the Mediterranean Sea, the policies of border control and the right of sovereign states to control their territory clash with the claims of a functioning European refugee protection system and with some aspects of the humanitarian law of the sea.

The goal of this chapter is to understand why an increasing number of migrants has been dying at sea and what role various security forces of European nations have played in this context. First, background information concerning migration movements in the Mediterranean Sea between Libya, Italy and Malta in recent years is provided. Then, the chapter debates the different concepts regarding a 'place of safety' for the disembarkation of rescued boat migrants. Moving on to the empirical section of the text, the SAR operations at sea of the Armed Forces of Malta (AFM) are analysed. The findings show that SAR operations are not merely a case of enforcing legal norms created by international law. The process is much more complex: legal gaps are filled by regional actors, through informal or even illegal practices, asserting their own claims at their convenience. Thus, transnationalisation processes of law, such as the international SAR regime, create space for negotiation and manoeuvre.

By applying a legal anthropological perspective, processes of decision-making and practices of SAR in the Mediterranean will be analysed. The concept of a 'multi-sited arena of negotiation' (Benda-Beckmann et al., 2005: 9) has proved useful in analysing the migration policies of the EU, national Maltese policies and rescue operations across the Mediterranean Sea. This perspective allows a view of the interconnections and power relations between local, national and supranational actors, which acknowledges the complex character of the phenomenon of sea migration, SAR activities in the Mediterranean Sea and the development of law.

A broad, anthropological perspective on the interpretation and development of law covers all the relevant actors responsible for the creation and change of law. These include official institutions and legal experts such as judges, but also security forces in the border region. This inclusive approach illustrates the important interactions between the micro- and the macro-level, local and national interests, and conflicts that influence the implementation and interpretation of law (Benda-Beckmann and Benda-Beckmann, 2007: 54). The approach also captures actors and practices which seem to be marginal at first glance, but may have far-reaching influences and effects. This extended perspective on law shows how law develops in society and how diverse actors are creating law and practices that are relevant for refugees. Furthermore, it allows the detection of internal logics and constraints which determine the incidents and developments in the Mediterranean Sea. The logic of interaction and of operation in the maritime border region handling the phenomenon of boat migration will become more accessible in this way, making it easier to find ways of better protecting migrant and refugee rights – and lives – at sea.

To analyse these logics of interaction, methodological triangulation has been chosen, as it guarantees an insight into the complex and highly politically charged subject of boat migrants and SAR activities in Malta. Policy documents have been analysed as well as the legal framework on sea migration and EU border policies. Furthermore, diverse actors with different perceptions and viewpoints on sea migration in the Mediterranean Sea were interviewed. Field research in Malta was carried out in September and October 2007. Further field research was conducted in Libya in October and November 2006 and in Southern Italy from March to July 2007. Sixteen detailed semi-structured interviews were conducted in Malta, including interviews with commanders of the AFM, the director of the United Nations High Commissioner for Refugees (UNHCR) in Malta, and a Maltese journalist.

Sea migration between Libya, Italy and Malta

In recent years, border controls have been enhanced by European and national security forces; new policies have also been established, such as co-operation with North African transition states and countries of origin (Cuttitta, 2008: 46). Despite these measures, the numbers of arrivals in Italy and Malta increased. In 2008 in particular, an increase in arrivals of boat migrants was recorded, rising to 36,952 arrivals in Italy (Polchi, 2009) and 2704 in Malta. The arrival numbers dropped sharply after the enforcement of the so-called 'friendship treaty' (*trattato di amicizia*) between Italy and Libya in May 2009 and reached a new peak in 2011 after the fall of the Gaddafi regime: more than 60,000 migrants arrived by boat. In 2012 the arrivals seem to have dropped again. In Malta, most of the people arriving claim asylum and nearly 60 per cent acquire refugee status or a subsidiary protection status.[2] In 2011 more than 1822 missing and drowned migrants were registered (Fortress Europe, 2013) in the central Mediterranean. Undoubtedly, the number of unreported cases is much higher.

High levels of risk characterise the crossing of the Mediterranean Sea. There are passages that are quite short and proceed smoothly. And there are passages that finish tragically with the death of all travellers. If boats are in danger, the international system of SAR should be activated; their procedures are outlined below.

The international system of Search and Rescue

The humanitarian law of the sea dealing with SAR matters is formed by a network of formal maritime laws, as well as soft laws and traditions that are put into practice by various actors. The regime is monitored and formally developed by the International Maritime Organization (IMO) of the United Nations, but the organisation has few enforcement capacities. It is the coastal states that have a leading role in realising and implementing the regime: as members of the IMO and as signatories to crucial conventions on the law of the sea and of shipping, the coastal states are obliged to establish a functioning maritime SAR system. They are required to arrange for distress communication and coordination in their area of responsibility (SAR Area) and for the rescue of persons in distress at sea around their coasts (IMO, 1974, Chapter V).

The international SAR regime relies on the security forces of the naval forces or the coast guards of the coastal states. It also relies on the commitment to the longstanding maritime tradition of all seamen to rescue people in distress and their inclusion into the SAR system. All vessels at sea, including private commercial vessels, are part of the SAR system and have a duty to rescue (UN, 1982, Article 98).

The International Convention on Maritime Search and Rescue (IMO, 1979) requires the state parties to 'ensure that assistance be provided to any person in distress at sea... regardless of the nationality or status of such a person or the circumstances in which that person is found' (IMO, 1974, Chapter 2.1.10) and to 'provide for their initial medical or other needs, and deliver them to a "place of safety"' (Ibid., Chapter 1.3.2). It is clear that the international SAR system and the humanitarian law of the sea require granting assistance to any person in distress at sea. Nonetheless, political discussions over the responsibilities of the coastal states to save irregular migrants in distress and to disembark them in a 'place of safety' can hinder or delay immediate SAR actions. Furthermore, uncertainties linked to the concept of 'distress', which is not clearly defined in international law (Pugh, 2004: 59), leave room for interpretation on whether particular boat migrants should be rescued or not, as will be demonstrated in the following. As the political atmosphere on the island of Malta is crucial to the behaviour of all actors involved in issues regarding sea migration, including SAR actions, some background information on the Maltese situation concerning migrant landings will be given before discussing further SAR questions.

'We could be taken over' – a small island under pressure

The island of Malta, located in the central Mediterranean Sea between Tunisia, Libya and Italy, is a focal point regarding the arrival of refugees. The very densely populated country – Malta has approximately 410,000 inhabitants on 316 km^2 – has an enormous SAR Area. The relatively small Maritime Squadron of the AFM, consisting of 300 men and women, has to cover 250,000 km^2 of open waters, stretching from the Tunisian coastal waters almost to the Greek island of Crete (Grech and Sansone, 2009). The reasons for this enormous SAR Area are historical and are also connected to the lucrative income Malta derives from its Flight Information Region (FIR). An FIR is a specified region of airspace in which information services for aviation are provided. The size of the SAR region is linked to the Maltese FIR. Malta earns around €8.23 million yearly for air traffic passing over its SAR/ FIR region (Teixere, 2006: 174).

From 2002 to 2008, approximately 10,700 migrants landed on Malta or were rescued by the AFM in the Maltese SAR Area. Nearly all migrants landing on Malta intended to reach Italy, but bad weather conditions or other unforeseen circumstances prevented them from reaching their destination. In recent years, a heated political atmosphere regarding migrants coming by boat can be observed on the island. As Teixere states, one could talk of a 'climate of psychosis' (2006: 10) that has developed on the island regarding the phenomenon of irregular migration. Racism-inspired attacks like burning the cars of the Jesuit Refugee Service (JRS) or the burning of the house of a refugee advocate have occurred since the significant uptick in landings on Malta in 2002.[3]

The general perspective and the policy of the Maltese government in dealing with landing migrants were explained in an interview with Martin

Scicluna, official advisor to the Maltese government on irregular immigration. He illustrated the fears of the Maltese population regarding migration and emphasised the role of Malta being on the 'front line' of European border control.[4] In interviews with representatives of the Maltese government, it became clear that the government would do everything possible to avoid more migrants arriving.

On a European level, Malta feels disadvantaged by the Dublin II Regulation. This regulation was adopted by the member states of the EU in 2003. Its goal is to determine the member state accountable for an asylum claim and provides for the transfer of an asylum seeker to that member state. Usually, the responsible member state will be the state through which the asylum seeker first entered the EU. The island nation has made several appeals to other member states for more burden-sharing agreements in asylum issues, including their view that the country cannot handle the situation alone (Council of the European Union, 2009). The aim of the Maltese efforts is to negotiate special terms for the island due to its size and its dense population and to resettle most of the migrants in other EU countries.[5] Although a resolution of the European Parliament from April 2006 came to the conclusion that the Dublin II Regulation and its effects are not acceptable for Malta and other border countries (European Parliament, 2006), Dublin II has not been revised.

Who is responsible for migrants in distress?

In recent years, one of the most controversial issues in diplomatic relations between Malta and other countries has been the responsibility for the disembarkation of rescued migrants in the central Mediterranean Sea. In July 2006, the Spanish trawler *Francisco y Catalina* rescued 51 migrants from a disabled boat. Then the trawler headed for Malta to disembark the passengers on the island. The Maltese army stopped the vessel 60 miles off the coast, claiming that the migrants could not be disembarked on Malta. The Maltese government argued that the migrants had been rescued within the Libyan SAR Area and that they should be taken to Spain. The situation on board rapidly became unbearable as hygiene deteriorated and medical emergencies occurred. After one week of diplomatic quarrels, the trawler headed for Spain, where most of the migrants applied for asylum (Weinzierl and Lisson, 2007: 21). Similar incidents occurred in subsequent years.

The amendments to SOLAS and SAR

These cases all involve seamen of the civil shipping industry taking shipwrecked migrants on board; the crux of the problem concerns the difficulties in disembarking them afterwards. These circumstances mean a significant loss of time and money for ship owners and have created uncertainties regarding the consequences of rescue operations, meaning a weakening of the international SAR system. For this reason, the IMO decided to amend the SAR Conventions and the International Convention for the Safety of Life at Sea (SOLAS) which concern the international SAR system. These amendments were adopted by the Maritime Safety Committee (MSC) of the IMO on 29 May 2004 and came into force 1 July 2006 (MSC Resolution 153 (78), 2004a). In order to make the question of responsibility of coastal states more transparent, the new rules determine that the state responsible for a certain SAR Area is also responsible for finding a 'place of safety' to disembark shipwrecked people.

The question of where a person can be disembarked as well as the definition of a 'place of safety' point to another important aspect. These questions show how closely the humanitarian law of the sea and refugee law are interconnected when it comes to migration at sea. Usually, the closest port of call might be seen as a 'place of safety'. However, if boat migrants are potentially in need of asylum protection, choosing a 'place of safety' requires this to be taken into consideration. In the 'Guidelines on the Treatment of Persons Rescued at Sea' (MSC Resolution 167 (78), 2004b), it is stated, 'Disembarkation of asylum seekers and refugees recovered at sea, in territories where their lives and freedom would be threatened should be avoided' (Paragraph 6.17). This passage actually includes the principle of *non-refoulement*[6] of the 1951 Convention Relating to the Status of Refugees (The Geneva Convention). All boat migrants should have the opportunity to claim asylum and should not be brought to their home countries or a country where they risk human rights violations. According to information given to the ships' captains by the UNHCR and IMO on implementing the Convention, in cases where rescued boat migrants want to claim asylum, they should not only inform the next Rescue Coordination Centre responsible for SAR actions, but also contact the UNHCR, which can provide further assistance (UNHCR and IMO, 2006: 10; see Klepp, 2010).

In the heated debates concerning a 'place of safety' and rescued migrants in the Mediterranean Sea, the aforementioned aspects are of great importance when it comes to the Libyan state. Libya has no asylum system, and it also violates basic human and refugee rights (Klepp, 2011). Therefore it cannot be regarded as a 'place of safety' for migrants crossing the Mediterranean. Unfortunately, many migrants crossing the Mediterranean from Libya get into a distress situation while still in the Libyan SAR region.

The Maltese point of view

Although the Amendments to the International Convention for the Safety of Life at Sea (MSC Resolution 167 (78), 2004b) represent an attempt to facilitate and support the position of sailors who assist people in distress and to smooth the process of disembarkation, Malta has not signed these amendments. The government of the island has always insisted that rescued migrants should be taken to the nearest safe port from their place of rescue (Department of Information of Malta, 2010). The Maltese government also differs in its view of the protection of refugees' aspect in determining a 'place of safety', as various Commanders of the AFM, the authorities responsible for Maltese SAR operations, stated. Commander One accuses the UNHCR of interchanging matters of SAR and matters of refugee policy. He insists that migrants rescued in Libyan SAR waters or in Libyan coastal waters must be disembarked in Libya:

> UNHCR has said that Libya is not a safe place for disembarkation. So what does that mean? That anyone saved in Libyan SAR has to be disembarked in Malta as well? They are not separating the two issues! There is a safe place in terms of Search and Rescue and there is a 'place of safety' in terms of humanitarian law. These are two different things.[7]

The Maltese military command and government seem to deny the mutual relevance of the humanitarian law of the sea and refugee law, which plays a big role in defining a 'place of safety'. Malta insists on separating refugee law matters and SAR matters in dealing with migrants in distress. But the international SAR regime is also bound by refugee law. The commander mainly attacked UNHCR for its repeated statement that since there is no asylum system in Libya and detention conditions violate basic human rights standards, Libya cannot be considered a 'place of safety' for rescued boat migrants. On the contrary, the disembarkation of migrants in Libya would be a case of *refoulement* and would violate the Convention Relating to the Status of Refugees, which is also the legal basis of national (Maltese) and European refugee law (UNHCR, 2009b).

Uncertainties regarding the 'place of safety' and disembarkation of rescued migrants in the central Mediterranean Sea could impede rescue actions, especially by vessels of the civil shipping industry. Another point which is directly linked to possible fatalities at sea concerns negotiations between Malta and Italy about the responsibility of rescuing migrants in imminent danger and distress at sea. Italy regularly conducts SAR actions in the Maltese SAR Area to support the small island. In 2006, the Italian coast guard, the *Guardia Costiera*, carried out 289 SAR operations of migrants in distress in the Mediterranean Sea. It is remarkable that 135 of these operations – almost half – took place in the SAR Area of Maltese responsibility (Comando Generale del Corpo delle Capitanerie di Porto, 2007). Nonetheless, discussions about which country should take action can delay SAR measures in situations where delays can cost lives, especially since there are no fixed mechanisms to automatically delegate or regulate responsibilities. All actions taken by Italy in the Maltese SAR Area are based on *ad hoc* agreements of the SAR forces of the two countries.[8] In May 2007, an Italian vessel saved 27 migrants clinging to the tuna pens of a Maltese trawler which did not want to take the migrants on board. The migrants, who were found on the border of Libyan and Maltese SAR waters, were rescued after three days following a diplomatic controversy between Libya, Malta and Italy. One man died of dehydration (Viviano, 2007).

Some recent proposals on how to deal with the duties of refugee law in SAR actions focus on screening for potential refugees on board military vessels. Others reflect the argument that a distinction should be made between SAR interventions and border control actions in the Mediterranean Sea, working with a 'prevalence criterion' (Tondini, 2012: 74) that distinguishes the nature of the intervention. As Tondini (Ibid.: 73) argues, 'Human rights provisions such as the prohibition of collective deportation cannot be applied to a genuine SAR intervention.'

Carrying out these suggestions, however, would lead to a further weakening of the SAR system and to an even more restricted access to the EU. The clear distinction of SAR interventions and migration control is not possible in the Mediterranean Sea. 'There is a very thin line between "Search and Rescue" and border control. When the migrants are in distress, it's "Search and Rescue"; when they are not, its border control,'[9] as Commander One argued in an interview. That also the concept of 'distress' is a subject of international dispute and seems to be negotiable will be discussed below. Furthermore, the situation on board a military or coast guard vessel is too chaotic and too ambiguous for asylum claim screenings. Mentally and physically, these migrants are not in a situation where they should be interviewed. Furthermore, in the *Hirsi* case, where 24 migrants that were intercepted in international waters by Italian security forces and forced back to Libya in May 2009, the European Court of Human Rights (ECtHR) made it very clear: *refoulement* and push-back practices at sea, even those that occur extraterritorially, were unacceptable (Hertog, 2012: 3). With this decision, the ECtHR has followed the assessments of the UNHCR (2007a) and human rights representatives (Weinzierl and Lisson, 2007: 78). They assume that responsibilities with regard to potential asylum seekers crossing the Mediterranean Sea are clear at any time: anywhere a state exercises jurisdiction, that state is responsible for all potential refugees and their asylum claims.

Having discussed legal disputes and ambiguities concerning the disembarkation of boat migrants and the definition of a 'place of safety', it is important to discuss additional findings from Malta in 2007. These findings illustrate problems of the SAR system on the operational level in the Mediterranean Sea. These problems often remain invisible to the public.

'What does SOS mean to them?'

The Commanders of the AFM, who are responsible for SAR actions at sea, seem to be bound by a strong commitment to save migrants in distress.

As the three Commanders whom I interviewed stated, 'political aspects' should only play a role after the rescue, once the migrants were safely disembarked.[10] Nonetheless, political discussions around SAR responsibilities and the heated atmosphere on the island regarding irregular migration shape the behaviour of the AFM, as my study reveals. Legal loopholes and dodges are used to avoid SAR obligations. As a consequence, AFM practices that impede or slow down SAR actions, with serious consequences for migrants, will be described.

Malta has a small but highly professional Maritime Squadron. The Squadron's responsibility is maritime surveillance, maritime law enforcement and the execution of SAR operations at sea. As Commander Two stated during an interview, in contrast to other European states, the military in Malta is also involved in police roles. Due to the small size of the country, the AFM is the sole agency that has the resources to carry out complex rescue operations at sea: only the AFM has the necessary vessels, helicopters and aircrafts at its disposal.[11] Commander Two explained that the Maltese navy consists of nine ships and 300 men and women. It is no surprise that rescuing over 8000 migrants between 2002 and 2007[12] represented a great challenge to the Maltese SAR authorities.[13] However, Commander Two emphasised that as people of the sea, his troops feel committed to save every person in distress, including cases of irregular migrants.

As argued above, some negative aspects regarding SAR activities and the high number of fatalities at sea among boat migrants are caused by the large Maltese SAR Area and the limited resources of the AFM to handle its responsibilities. As the speaker of the Ministry of Interior stated, conservative Maltese estimates assume 600–700 fatalities per year in the area of Malta, Italy and Libya.[14] When asked about possible explanations for the fatalities at sea in recent years, Commander Two declared, suddenly in an angry tone: 'Who has told you that there are so many people dying at sea? So far we have rescued 58 boats! That's 1551 people. If the numbers carry on like that... We had the worst August on record.'[15] His outburst is very surprising, since the numbers of fatalities at sea are well-known to Maltese civilians, and even more familiar to the navy. Why is he reacting in such a harsh way to a question that is linked to a well-known and obvious fact? After interviewing Commander Two, more information was gathered about the situation at sea and the work of the AFM by speaking to representatives of other institutions. Neil Falzon, a representative of the UNHCR in Malta, illustrated how the UNHCR in Malta has actually become a 'maritime rescue organization' itself.[16] During the interview, he vividly described which moments he feared most during his daily work.

> Many times we receive calls in the office... Often directly from boats approaching. I mean, I pick up the phone and they say UNHCR, UNHCR we are sinking. Can you imagine my reaction? I hear people shouting in

the background and I panic. Or we receive calls from friends or relatives in Malta saying that they are arriving. So what do we do? We have a basic procedure: First we try to get all the information, number of people on board. Gender, age, nationalities, and we pass all the information to the AFM. What we have seen this year particularly is that the AFM is very reluctant to saying automatically 'OK, yes, we go and rescue them.' They ask, 'what kind of problem do they have?' I say the engine stopped, and they say, 'OK, we will look after it.' And then I call an hour later, because I call on an hourly basis. We call the AFM every hour. And they usually tell us, 'Yes, they [the AFM] have made contact with the boat, they [the migrants] didn't want to be rescued, we will not rescue them, they are moving steadily north.' And then they will leave them.[17]

The journalist Karl Schembri calls this practice of the AFM, described above by Neil Falzon, as 'passing the buck' to the Italian navy. The journalist, who has investigated several reports on SAR failures by the AFM, described the operation of the Maltese navy as a 'calculation': if there was any chance that the boat would have enough fuel to reach Italy, the AFM would take the risk of not immediately rescuing the migrants and 'pass the problem onto the Italians', expecting the Italian security forces to take care of the arriving boat.

One of the Maltese navy Commanders also described how the AFM often proceeds when it is informed about a boat entering its SAR Area: the AFM goes out with an offshore vessel. They approach the boat with a smaller boat and try to communicate with the people on board. Very often the migrants want to continue their journey north in order to reach Italy, as Commander One elucidated. In these cases they provide food, water and sometimes fuel for the boat and let them continue their journey to Italy. They inform the Italian SAR authorities and accompany the boat up to Italian SAR waters.[18]

As described above, the duty of rendering assistance is clear in cases of distress at sea. The SAR Convention defines the term distress as '[a] situation wherein there is a reasonable certainty that a vessel or a person is threatened by grave and imminent danger and requires immediate assistance' (IMO, 1979: Annex, Chapter 1, para. 1.3.11). However, this definition leaves room for interpretations in favour of non-intervention. Customarily, shipmasters are expected to be best placed to exercise their own judgment and reach an autonomous decision on rescues (Pugh, 2004: 59). Nonetheless, the AFM practice described above can have fatal consequences for the travelling migrants.

UNHCR representative Falzon identified the weak points of this method. He was aware of several incidents where migrants' boats were already identified or approached by the AFM, but afterwards obviously sank.[19] One of these boats was called the 'phantom ship' (*barca fantasma*) by the Italian media. The incident of the 'phantom ship' occurred in May 2007. A photo that was taken by the AFM and leaked to the press showed 53 men who were in distress on their small boat in Maltese SAR waters (Weinzierl and Lisson, 2007: 19). Regarding the incident, Falzon commented:

> The boat vanished. It was the famous boat; there was a photo in the newspapers... They were bailing out water, they were in evident danger. The Maltese insisted that there was no SOS. Come on!... I think that they literally want people to say: 'Yes, please save us!' Any other sign that the boat might not make it is a sign for them that they can help them but not rescue them. I mean the photo was taken by the AFM themselves. There was a man with a red T-shirt; there were buckets with which they were bailing out water. This boat vanished!... And like that boat, we are sure there are many, many more.[20]

When interviewed about the incident of the 'phantom boat', Commander One confirmed that the AFM had taken a photo of the boat from an AFM aircraft. But he refused to believe that this boat was in distress, explaining the AFM's definition of distress at sea thus: 'Distress is the imminent danger of loss of lives, so if they are sinking, it's distress. If the boat is not sinking it's not in distress. Even if it's six metres long and has 30 people on board.'[21] He confirmed that the Italian navy has a different perception; they would rescue every heavily overloaded boat. But how should the AFM react if the migrants on board do not want to be rescued by the Maltese navy, he asked rhetorically. The IMO emphasises that 'even if a ship's passengers show no sign of distress, the suspicion of trafficking and transport in unsafe conditions only entitles states to take action in accord with humanitarian principles' (IMO, quoted in Pugh, 2004: 59).

Regarding the communication with migrants at sea by the AFM, the Maltese journalist Karl Schembri documented a case in November 2005, which attracted great attention in the Italian media. The journalist photographed the official AFM logbook registering the orders given from the headquarters by radio to rescuers who were sent to track the boat on that day. The entries in the log book showed that the order – coming from Commander Two who was coordinating the SAR action from the AFM operations room at Luqa Headquarters – was to 'keep at a distance' from the boat carrying 200 migrants in force six winds on 17 November 2005 (Malta Today, 2006). The Italian SAR forces were informed late about a boat coming closer to their SAR region. The next day, the Maltese and Italian press published critical reports about the shipwreck of the migrants. Nine of them were found dead along the coast of Pozzallo, Sicily, between 20 and 30 of them were missing, and 177 were found on land, including five children and three women. In the following controversies, the Maltese Parliamentary Secretary stated that the migrants did not want to be rescued by Malta. Karl Schembri disagreed, noting, 'The day after in parliament Tony Abela, the parliamentary secretary who is responsible for the army, said that the immigrants had refused assistance. That was an outright lie. The migrants couldn't refuse assistance because they were never asked.'[22]

A volatile negotiation process

When is a boat in distress, and when must passengers be saved? In the controversies around these questions of rescuing people or not, it is becoming clear just how volatile the negotiation process is among actors in the Mediterranean Sea when it comes to irregular migration, border protection and humanitarian law of the sea. Looking back at the conversation with Commander Two, who got angry when asked about fatalities at sea, it seemed that he was caught between his moral and legal obligations as a sailor, and his obligations to the Maltese government as his employer. This dilemma of being both a sailor and a representative of the Maltese government (which is opposed to more landings) led him to deny the fact that many migrants at sea are drowning.

The complex links and disagreements of actors concerning SAR actions involving irregular migrants at sea become apparent in their differing notions of what it means to be 'in distress' and the conflicts regarding the amendments of the SAR and SOLAS conventions on the disembarkation of rescued migrants. All political levels and persons involved in the SAR of boat migrants are linked through a 'chain of interaction connecting transnational, national and local actors' (Benda-Beckmann et al., 2005: 9). This 'chain of interaction' is structured by power relations and restrictions that can reproduce or change it. The negotiable and political character of the drafting and implementation of law becomes evident in this 'multi-sited arena of negotiation' (Ibid.: 9) of the SAR system in the Mediterranean Sea. Internationally valid law is not simply enforced on the national and local level: the process is much more complex. On the ground, legal norms are modified and adapted by various actors pursuing their own agendas, sometimes through informal or even illegal practices (Merry, 2005: 224). In the Mediterranean Sea, the humanitarian law of the sea is ignored or modified according to political considerations and the manoeuvres of the governments of the coastal states that dominate the situation at sea. The perspective of the Maltese government that defines itself as a 'front-line-state'[23] in the battle of the EU against irregular migration has a significant influence on the practices of the AFM regarding SAR actions in the Mediterranean Sea. Even in cases where people are in immediate danger and distress at sea, political aspects can delay or even prevent SAR obligations.

In sum, the explosive political nature of sea migration begins to call into question the very legitimacy of legally binding SAR regulations. These regulations function as an 'open text' (Merry, 1997: 39) where global, European, national and local perceptions merge: 'both as resources and as constraints' (Ibid.: 45).

Under the pressure of a politically tense atmosphere as well as the grim realities at sea, AFM commanders have created their own mechanisms. On the one hand, these are inner psychological mechanisms, which conform to their own self-image as sailors who are ready to rescue every person in distress in line with the desires of their employers. On the other hand, external informal mechanisms have been developed to handle the demands of the oversized Maltese SAR Area and the paradoxical situation at sea – the duty to rescue unwanted migrants in distress (Lipsky, 1980: xiii). Any mechanisms created by security forces on site can be decisive for the future interpretation and development of this legal 'open text' (Merry, 1997: 39). Between the internal and external tensions of the local actors, new practices may be developed which shape the situation at sea and future (legal) cases. Currently, there are no political winners in the situation. In addition to many people dying at sea, the security forces themselves are also losing: they are at once caught in the dilemma of being pressured by one side to reduce their activities, and from the other side to more fully perform their tasks of saving the lives of migrants in distress.

In the Mediterranean area, questions of borders (as well as many other aspects of migration politics, such as the principle of *non-refoulement* (Klepp, 2010)) are not designed by the letter of the law, but are instead interpreted and redesigned according to a variety of political interests and power relations. Even regimes as strong as the SAR regime, based on a dense network of laws and traditions, must be studied in a wider perspective. Whether there will be a more effective SAR regime towards migrants in distress is difficult to predict. Criminally liable misconduct of security forces against boat migrants at sea is difficult to prove; incidents which result in fatalities are rarely punished. Moreover, Malta does not appear willing to sign the SAR and SOLAS amendments anytime in the near future. The failures of SAR at sea described in this chapter should not be read as a purely negative assessment of the AFM. Instead, insights into the inner logics of the border region create possibilities for responsible and rational actions by politicians, migrants, civil society and security forces alike. Furthermore, Malta alone cannot be blamed for all the legal and humanitarian transgressions at sea. The case of the so-called 'left-to-die' boat shows that even the involvement of NATO, Frontex, a French aircraft, the Italian MRCC and the Maltese MRCC led to the non-rescue of a boat with 63 passengers on their way from Libya to Italy. As the report of the Council of Europe's Parliamentary Assembly (PACE) revealed, only 11 passengers ended up surviving the 'catalogue of failures' and the lack of will on the part of all of these actors to rescue them (Hertog, 2012: 1).

Notes

1. A previous version of this article has been published in *International Journal of Refugee Law*, 23 (2011), 3, pp. 538–557. Permission for an updated reprint has been kindly provided by Oxford University Press.
2. Interview with Mario Friggieri, Director of the Maltese Refugee Commission (REFCOM), 3 October 2007, in his office in La Valetta.
3. Interview with Director of JRS Malta Father Paul Pace, 23 September 2007 in his office in Bikakara.
4. Interview with Martin Scicluna, Official Advisor to the Maltese Government on Irregular Immigration, 2 October 2007 in his office in La Valletta.
5. Interview with Martin Scicluna, Official Advisor to the Maltese Government on Irregular Immigration, 2 October 2007.
6. The principle of *non-refoulement* is set out in the 1951 Convention relating to the Status of Refugees: 'No Contracting State shall expel or return (*refouler*) a refugee in any manner whatsoever to the frontiers of territories where his life or freedom would be threatened on account of his race, religion, nationality, or membership of a particular social or political opinion,' (Article 33(1)).
7. Interview with Commander One, AFM, 5 October 2007 in the headquarters of AFM, Luqa Barracks.
8. Interview with Commander Calvinare, Comando Generale del Corpo delle Capitanerie di Porto, 26 June 2007 in his office in Rome.
9. Interview with Commander One (AFM), 05 October 2007.
10. Interview with Commander One, 05 October 2007. Interview with Commander Two, 21 September 2007 at the headquarters of the AFM, Luqa Barracks. Interview with Commander Three, 5 October 2007 at the headquarters of the Maritime Squadron of the AFM at the military harbour in La Valetta.
11. Interview with Commander Two (AFM), 21 September 2007.
12. Ibid.
13. Ibid.
14. Interview with Joe Azzopardi, spokesperson of the Ministry of Justice and Internal Affairs, 18 September 2007, in La Valletta.
15. Interview with Commander Two (AFM), 21 September 2007.
16. Interview with Neil Falzon, UNHCR Representative to Malta, 26 September 2007, in his office in La Valletta.
17. Ibid.
18. Interview with Commander One, 05 October 2007.
19. Interview with Neil Falzon (UNHCR), 26 September 2007.
20. Ibid.
21. Interview with Commander One, 05 October 2007.
22. Interview with Karl Schembri, 20 September 2007, in the office of the journal Malta Today.
23. Interview with Martin Scicluna, Official Advisor to the Maltese Government on Irregular Immigration, 2 October 2007, in La Valletta.

3
Negotiating Mobility, Debating Borders: Migration Diplomacy in Turkey–EU Relations

Ahmet İçduygu and Ayşen Üstübici

Borders and international mobility have become dominant themes in studies on contemporary global processes, yet relatively little has been said about the various dimensions of their interaction in international relations. This chapter intends to fill the gap by exploring twin issues: the crucial political dimensions attached to international migration and, often overlooked, the serious challenge border crossings pose to the states involved. In other words, the diplomatic and symbolic dimensions of international migration affect inter-state negotiations in the international arena in multiple ways. With the shift in migration issues, such as the securitisation of European Union (EU) borders, from low to high politics as a spillover effect of the EU integration process (Huysman, 2006), it is not surprising that migration and border diplomacy in this context has become a feature of membership negotiations on EU geography. In order to review the negotiation processes and salient debates in EU–Turkey accession talks, we adopt the concept of 'migration diplomacy' that refers to the analysis of changing border and asylum policies as an indirect form of foreign policy (Thiollet, 2011: 13) and the notion of EU-isation or Europeanisation defined as 'processes of construction, diffusion, and institutionalisation of formal and informal rules, procedures, policy paradigms, styles, "ways of doing things" and shared beliefs and norms to a European model of governance, caused by forms of cooperation and integration in Europe' (Bulmer and Radaelli, 2004: 4). Our analysis focuses on the ways in which Turkey–EU borders have been redesigned and their meanings reconceptualised by migration practices and policies in the EU–Turkey migration regime. It also elaborates on borders as reconstructed discursively by the EU but also by Turkey itself: EU–Turkey membership negotiations and Turkey's own 'migration transition'[1] both determine the nature of diplomatic manoeuvring when it comes to the question of borders and migration.

We acknowledge that discussions on migration and asylum issues in the context of EU–Turkey relations are not simply descriptions of a reality, but to a large extent part of the process of constructing this reality. In other words, borders and mobility are highly politicised themes in Turkey's affairs with the EU and used controversially in ideological debates. Increasing flows of irregular transit migration through Turkey into Europe during the 1990s and 2000s, for example, have contributed to the widely established perception of the EU–Turkey border as 'out of control' (İçduygu, 2011; İçduygu and Yükseker, 2012). Moreover, numerous politicians in Europe have publicly vocalised scenarios of 'invasion' by Turkish migrants as one outcome of Turkey's EU membership (Lagro, 2008). Yet another aspect is the growing frequency with which descriptions of the integration difficulties of Turkish immigrants already in Europe are laced with Islamophobic connotations (İçduygu and Karaçay, 2012: 20). Debates on the question of Turkey's accession to the EU have questioned the compatibility of their demographic and migratory regimes, and speculated on whether Turkey's EU membership would lead to the entry of young Turkish workers to the Union (Fotakis, 2004; Behar, 2006; İçduygu and Karaçay, 2012). As witnessed in discussions around several aspects of mobility across Turkey–EU borders, migration and border-related discourses are central to Turkey–EU relations due to their multiple implications for economic, social, political and demographic structures and processes in the EU. That is to say, what we call 'migration diplomacy' prevails in a variety of issues related to the causes and consequences of population mobility between Turkey and the EU.

We argue that a more informed view of the implications of mobility and border-related issues for EU–Turkey relations calls for the analysis of ongoing practices and discourses, focusing on the management of migration, which has become subject to a multifaceted negotiation process in the diplomatic arena. We concentrate on state actor perceptions of immigration, while acknowledging that some actors may in reality have a bigger say in the negotiation process. In this sense, Nowak's contribution to the current volume, which examines the role of a political party from the nationalist wing in the incorporation and exclusion of Turkish immigrants in Germany, complements our discussion on the role of the state in the making of migration policy. The analysis in our article, however, remains at the level of state and official discourses as embraced in international politics, partly because issues related to immigration are not yet part of Turkish electoral politics – through which public opinion is shaped – as is the case in the European or North American context. Also, the capacity and political influence of civil society has been curbed, although a number of civil society actors are highly critical of ongoing negotiations between Turkey and the EU, which they perceive as undermining migrant human rights.[2]

Against this background, the purpose of our paper is twofold: first, to map out migration and border-related discourses that have emerged from 'migration diplomacy' in the context of Turkey's accession to the EU, and to relate them to the reality of migration transition in Turkey; and second, to explore the dynamics involved in the EU-isation of migration policies in Turkey. We thus suggest that migratory flows between Turkey and European countries and the Turkey–EU accession negotiations have led to the redesigning of borders and of migration policies in Turkey.[3]

Turkey in the European international migration system: EU-isation of migration and asylum

As noted in the introduction, debates on international migration issues between the EU and Turkey focus on Turkey's role in the European international migration system, both as a country of emigration and as a country of immigration and transit. This triple role is repeatedly emphasised by the EU and officially referred to in a cornerstone document on EU–Turkey relations dated 6 October 2004 and entitled *Communication from the Commission to the Council and the European Parliament, Recommendation of the European Commission on Turkey's Progress Towards Accession*:

> (1) With over three million, Turks constitute by far the largest group of third-country nationals legally residing in today's EU. Available studies give varying estimates of expected additional migration following Turkey's accession. Long transition periods and a permanent safeguard clause can be considered to avoid serious disturbances on the EU labour market. However, the population dynamics of Turkey could make a contribution to offsetting the ageing of EU societies. In this context, the EU also has a strong interest in that reforms and investments should be made in education and training in Turkey over the next decade. (2) The management of the EU's long new external borders would constitute an important policy challenge and require significant investment. Managing migration and asylum as well as trafficking of human beings would be facilitated through closer cooperation both before and after accession.
>
> (European Commission, 2004)

This vision of Turkey as a potentially dangerous source of disturbance to the dynamics of migration and asylum in the EU corresponds to the pessimistic view of EU capacities to manage migratory flows (İçduygu, 2011). It likewise reflects the need for good governance of migration to the social and economic benefit of the EU (Kohler-Koch and Rittberger, 2006). For Turkey, new migration policies represent aspects of conditionality and socialisation in the EU accession process.[4] As a prerequisite for EU membership, it introduced reforms in the field of international migration. These reforms are at the same time indicators of Turkey's migration transition from emigration to immigration (İçduygu, 2011: 3). Convinced of this transition, policy-makers in

Turkey have begun to realise that new, complicated international migration management tools are an integral part of the process of integration into the global world in general and the EU in particular.

Turkey's role as a country of immigration and transit rather than one of emigration is highly visible in relations between the EU and Turkey today. Although the accession process has slowed down significantly and talks have not yet proceeded to the direct discussion of migration-related issues as presented in Chapter 24 on 'Justice, Freedom and Security', it would appear that migration and border-specific issues have gradually dominated EU–Turkey affairs. In fact, certain aspects of migration management have been among the most contested areas of EU–Turkey relations since accession talks began in 2005.

Documents such as the *EU Accession Partnership* (Council of the European Union, 2008) and the *National Action Plan for the Adoption of the 'EU acquis' in the Field of Asylum and Migration* adopted by the government in March 2005[5] reveal the intention of policy-makers in Turkey and in Europe to develop a migration and asylum management system in line with EU standards (Kirişci, 2007: 96). Developments in the area of migration and asylum management have clearly been part of Turkey's Europeanisation. The process in this area, however, has been slow as a result of uncertainty on the part of officials about Turkey's membership and the concern that Turkey as a non-member could become an EU 'buffer zone' (Kirişci, 2007: 96). Nevertheless, the Turkish government seems to be pursuing a policy of reforms to adopt and implement the EU *acquis*, partly because it still entertains the prospect of Turkish membership and partly because it has begun to register the need to regulate these areas in the country (Kirişci, 2012).

Although debates on migration and asylum that point to the role of Turkey as an immigration and transit country have prevailed in the accession talks, the issue of Turkish emigration to Europe has implicitly become part of the discussions, for example, on the management of visa regimes or on the assumed linkage between the readmission agreement and visa facilitation. Given the importance of Turkey's transition process from an emigration to an immigration country and the demographic aspects of Turkey's EU membership, Turkish emigration issues should not be fully divorced from the accession agenda.

Turkey–EU borders: A historical synopsis

Within the context of European migration systems, Turkey has traditionally been known as a country of emigration. Research since the late 1990s, however, shows that it has become a hub of transit migration into Europe and a focal point for asylum seekers originating from Middle Eastern and Asian countries such as Bangladesh, Iran and Afghanistan (İçduygu and Karaçay, 2012: 20). Turkey is now also host to workers from post-Soviet regions, who enter the country with valid documents but tend to overstay their visas (Yükseker, 2004), and to EU professionals (Kaiser, 2003) – further evidence that Turkey is turning into a 'migration transition country' (Kirişci, 2007). Coupled with Turkey's efforts to become a member of the EU, this transition process has brought pressure to bear on the 'overhaul of immigration and asylum policies and practices' (Kirişci, 2007: 91; İçduygu and Kirişci, 2009).

Emigration from Turkey

Migration dynamics in Euro-Turkish regions were shaped by the search for work in the expanding European economies of the 1960s in the context of Fordist guest worker programmes in the post-Second World War era (Akgündüz, 2008; Castles et al., 1984) and later by asylum flows throughout the 1980s and 1990s. Flows from Turkey to Europe have declined since the 2000s (İçduygu and Sert, 2009). Up to the mid-1970s, government agreements structured mobility patterns between Turkey and Europe (İçduygu, 2012: 13). Turkey saw emigration and the export of surplus labour as a strategy for the reduction of unemployment and the generation of revenue in foreign currencies (Abadan-Unat, 1976: 71). A bilateral labour recruitment agreement with the Federal Republic of Germany was signed in 1961. Similar agreements specifying the general conditions of recruitment, employment and wages were signed with other governments.[6] At the time, emigration was considered a policy for national and regional development rather than a foreign policy per se. Contrary to expectations and despite the economic downturn in Western Europe in the 1970s that brought labour recruitment in Turkey to an end, many 'guest workers' did not return to their home country (Gitmez, 1983; Wilpert, 1984; Lieberman and Gitmez, 1979). Turkish emigration to Europe continued in the form of family reunification and family formation, and most importantly after 1980, through asylum flows (Böcker, 1995).

The evolution of migration from Turkey to Europe was impressive. By the early 2000s, the number of people of Turkish origin living in Europe had reached over three million, with asylum flows from Turkey actively contributing to this trend (İçduygu and Kirişci, 2009; Abadan-Unat, 2002). According to statistics from the United Nations High Commissioner for Refugees (UNHCR), almost one million Turkish citizens applied for asylum in various European countries between 1980 and 2010, fleeing Turkey after military intervention in 1980, and later political and military violence in areas primarily populated by Turkey's large Kurdish minority. There is evidence that at the time irregular migration and the fraudulent use of the asylum channel was also common among economic migrants (Kirişci, 2007a: 92).

Turkey's income inequalities appear to have fed the push factors that fostered emigration in the 1960s and 1980s. Furthermore, the political instability of the 1980s and 1990s, the economic and political liberalisation of the 1990s, and the dynamics of contemporary globalisation all contributed to the emergence of various types of mobility in the last two decades and to new migration trends. These trends are characterised by a decline, on the one hand, in flows of labour migration, asylum seekers, irregular and family migrants, and an increase, albeit far less voluminous, in the movement of highly skilled professionals and students, on the other. Of the approximately 3.5 million people of Turkish origin living in Europe, about 800,000 have adopted the citizenship of their host countries. Turkish migrants and their European-born family members are the largest Muslim community in the EU, accounting for 0.6 per cent of the EU population (OECD, 2010). The perception that emigration from Turkey will increase if the country becomes a member of the EU is based on the persistent challenges posed by the need to integrate immigrants from Turkey into Europe rather than on this large numerical presence (Kirişci, 2007a: 92). Several actors, including ministries, governing political parties and those in opposition, have been engaged in the integration of emigrants, particularly in terms of maintaining transnational ties between immigration politics in the host country and politics in the home country (see Nowak's and Mikuszies' contributions, in this volume).

Immigration and transit migration through Turkey

Turkey's role as a 'migrant-sending country' has now been extended to include that of a 'migrant-receiving country' and a 'transit country'. International migratory movements to Turkey since the end of the 1970s have included transit migrants, irregular migrant workers, asylum seekers and refugees (İçduygu, 2003, 2006; Kirişci, 2002; Kaytaz, 2006). In addition, there is the legal immigration of professionals and retirees. Turkey's geographical proximity to migrants' countries of origin, the latter's cultural affinity with Turkey, and the political and economic turmoil and attendant security concerns in these countries have likewise impacted on this migrant flow to Turkey (İçduygu, 2006: 71). Another more visible group of migrants[7] in EU policy circles sees Turkey as a transit route to Europe rather than a final destination. Turkey's role as a transit country is a political construct driven by geographical factors, that is, its location at the crossroads between Asia, Europe and Africa with long, remote – and at times uncontrollable – borders, as well as by political factors, particularly the country's somewhat lax migration regime (İçduygu and Yükseker, 2012: 443). Thus, concerns in EU policy circles about Turkey's advance to a transit migration hub are based on the geographical reality that in the wake of EU expansion Turkey's borders could ultimately constitute the southeast land and sea borders of the EU. Even if Turkey merely remains a neighbouring country, irregular border crossings from Turkey will continue to be a burning issue and of vital concern to the EU.

It is true that Turkey's comparatively liberal border regime has given rise to transit migration. Transit migration alone, however, does not fully reflect the shift in Turkey's mobility patterns (İçduygu and Yükseker, 2012). The phenomenon of irregular migration (e.g. migrants with no legal status to reside or work in the country) in Turkey can be broken down into (a) transit migration, (b) shuttle or circular migration and (c) asylum-seeker and refugee movements (İçduygu, 2006: 71). Since there is a lack of reliable data on irregular migration in terms of volume and trends, we are often obliged to employ indirect measures.[8] Consideration of the countries of origin of irregular migrants suggests that those who enter Turkey from the south or the east are the most likely candidates for transit migration. While data on migrants detained by security forces indicates that between 51,000 and 57,000 would-be transit migrants entered Turkey each year in the early 2000s, today this figure has dropped below 20,000. Most transit migrants attempt to enter and leave Turkey illegally, enlisting the assistance of human smugglers (İçduygu and Toktaş, 2002). From 1996 to 2010, almost 800,000 irregular migrants were apprehended in Turkey; the above-mentioned assumptions suggest that almost 55 per cent were transit migrants. These figures pertain to the number of apprehensions and therefore include repeated apprehensions. The major source countries of transit migration to Turkey are Iraq, Pakistan, Afghanistan, Iran and Bangladesh (İçduygu and Yükseker, 2012: 443).

Another form of irregular migration to Turkey and one that affects Turkey's position in the European migration regime is 'shuttle' or 'circular' migration. 'Shuttle migration' defines those who make multiple trips to Turkey in search of economic gain. As a rule, shuttle migrants enter the country legally but occasionally overstay their visas. The Passport Law amendment introduced in February 2012 altered the rules of entry into the country and clearly impeded the multiple entries of circular migrants. In a sense, this pushed them into overstaying their visas and consequently, into further irregularity. Circular migrants usually make multiple trips in order to avoid overstaying their visas. Since the early 1990s, hundreds of thousands of shuttle migrants, mostly from the Commonwealth of Independent States (Yükseker, 2004), and more recently from Africa and Central Asia, have become 'suitcase traders'. Yet another form of circular migration consists of people from poor countries in Central Asia and the Balkans who work informally in Turkey on tourist visas, primarily in domestic service, the entertainment sector, sex work, construction, the tourism sector, agriculture and garment workshops (Kirişci, 2008a). According to data on apprehension by security forces, the top five source countries of irregular circular migrants are Moldova, Romania, Georgia, Ukraine and the Russian Federation (İçduygu and Yükseker, 2012: 448). It is difficult, however, to estimate the volume of circular migration. The flows between Turkey and former Soviet countries are partly the result of the general change in post-Cold War border regimes in Europe, and partly of liberal visa and border policies between Turkey and the source countries concerned. Given that Turkey is a growing economy on the cusp of its migration transition and that migrants now supply cheap labour force required in several sectors of the widespread informal economy, these relatively liberal entry policies can first of all be conceptualised as the 'economization of migration' (Parla, 2011: 75; İçduygu and Sert, 2012), and, second, as another form of migration diplomacy associated with the foreign policy activism of Turkey in the post-Cold War era (Öniş and Yilmaz, 2009).

Since the 1980s, Turkey has served as a transit route for both transit migrants and asylum seekers, primarily from unstable neighbouring countries. In the last 20 years, flows of refugees and asylum seekers have become a relatively minor component of the overall migrant flows to Turkey. Between 1997 and 2010, Turkey received around 50,000 applications from asylum seekers; more than 27,000 of whom were granted refugee status and resettled in other countries (İçduygu and Yükseker, 2012: 448–449).[9] Under the geographical limitation clause that accompanied Turkey's signature to the Geneva Convention, Turkey only accepts asylum applications from citizens of European countries.[10] The international community severely criticised Turkey for its geographical limitation principle, which it saw as seriously undermining the right to access asylum (Kirişci, 2007: 95). The majority of asylum seekers enter the country without documents and only those who have been resettled in third countries are permitted to leave the country as 'legalised transit' migrants. While most transit migration candidates seek asylum in the EU, others apply for asylum in Turkey, having crossed the border without the necessary documents, in despair at the long bureaucratic asylum and resettlement processes involved. In other words, Turkey's asylum system and border regime are constantly in the process of producing candidates for transit migration or resettlement through asylum. It is therefore understandable that the EU has a keen interest in increasing Turkey's capacity to receive irregular and asylum flows, and in controlling Turkey–EU borders to stop transit flows through Turkey.

Debating international migration in Turkey–EU relations: 60 years of migration diplomacy

With the signing of the Ankara Agreement in 1963, Turkey became an associate member of the then European Economic Community. In Article 12 of the Agreement, the 'gradual realisation of the free movement of workers among the parties' was envisaged and deemed extremely positive, in a sense complementary to bilateral labour agreements signed in 1961, when the demand for foreign labourers from Turkey on the European labour market was high (İçduygu, 2006: 40, 2010a: 59).[11] Forty-two years after the Ankara Agreement, negotiations between Turkey and the EU were finally launched on 3 October 2005. This step, seen as a 'historical milestone', at the same time signalled the beginning of a challenging process of negotiation for both Turkey and the EU. In striking contrast to the Ankara Agreement and the Additional Protocol, the Negotiating Framework approached the free movement of people in a negative light, rather as a remote possibility following long transitions and specific arrangements (İçduygu, 2010a: 59). Various reports by the European Commission on Turkey highlight this enlargement as different from previous cases, partly due to grave concerns about migration.[12]

In this context, discussions on international migration in the EU in relation to Turkey focus on two points of concern (Erzan and Kirişci, 2006; İçduygu, 2006, 2010a; İçduygu and Karaçay, 2012). First, will the free circulation of labour give rise to heavy migratory flows into Europe and subsequently to serious adjustment problems for both the labour market and the migrants concerned (this point is often made with special reference to adjustment problems encountered by Turkish migrants already settled in Europe (Kaya and Kentel, 2005))? Linked to this is the question of whether Turkey's demography can produce migration flows that will help to remedy the shrinking working-age population in the EU. Second, will Turkey, as a receiving and transit country, succeed in producing and implementing policies that comply with EU international migration and asylum regimes (İçduygu, 2010a: 62)? While the first point, the dominant topic in current discussions, is indeed related to future membership prospects, the second is a specific reference to Turkey's border control and management problems. Although this last point likewise refers to membership, it will remain a crucial item of negotiation in Turkey–EU relations even if the prospect of membership fades away (İçduygu, 2010a). Centred on these two lines of concern, state positions representing both sides have actively engaged, directly or indirectly, implicitly or explicitly, in migration issues during the negotiation process for membership. Here, the EU as the hegemonic actor is naturally a frequent agenda and tone setter, with Turkey attempting to tune the tone of the debates.

There was an obvious tendency to portray the key issue of 'free circulation of labour' in discussions on Turkish EU membership as an influx of Turkish migrants to EU countries. With unemployment in many EU states highly disturbing for native workers and even more alarming for migrants, the idea of placing restrictions on migration from a prospective member state was appealing (Erzan et al., 2006; Krieger and Maitre, 2006). Similarly, given the socio-cultural and ideological views and political interests prevalent in numerous EU states, it seemed advisable to prevent migration flows from Turkey at a time of growing concern about the integration of current immigrants from Turkey, about the definition of European identity, and the place of immigrants and especially Muslims in this definition (Lagro, 2008; see Ruß-Sattar, in this volume). Despite this fostering of pessimistic attitudes, some policy-makers and analysts prioritised demographic interests and enthused over the potentially positive contribution Turkish membership could make to the labour market needs of the EU economy, which was already suffering from a decline in the working-age population, on the one hand, and a growth in the elderly population, on the other (İçduygu and

Karaçay, 2012: 25–26).[13] Some argue that Turkey's reasonably young population could be part of the solution to EU requirements, particularly if the country makes efficient use of its 'demographic windows of opportunity' (Behar, 2006: 17–18; İçduygu, 2006) and invests in the education and training of its youth for contemporary labour market needs (Krieger and Maitre, 2006). Others in favour of Turkey's membership claim that its demographic transition in the next two or three decades may reach a stage where it can no longer export labour to other countries due to its own ageing population and the converse decline in the working population (Behar, 2006; Hancıoğlu et al., 2004).

The demography-related migration debate led to a series of critical arguments in Turkey with political implications for the climate of the country's EU membership adventure. First, strong objections to the idea of permanent restrictions on the right of workers from Turkey to free movement have been raised on numerous occasions. Such restrictions are seen as discriminatory by Turkish officials and against the fundamental values of the EU, which ensures free movement of persons, goods, services and capital.[14] Second, debates on the restriction of free circulation of labour reinforced the perception that the EU had lost its vision of full membership for Turkey (or had never had one) and instead begun to promote the notion of privileged partnership, particularly in anti-EU circles in Turkey. Prompted by these chains of reasoning, Turkish public policy-makers (and several analysts) gradually veered away from the idea of membership, arguing that 'Turkey should not be where it is not wanted'. In this sense, the question of free movement has triggered the use of 'migration diplomacy' on Turkey's part at almost every stage of the negotiations, including other migration issues between the EU and Turkey.

Apart from discussions on the 'free movement of labour', topics associated with Turkey's increasingly magnified role as a country of immigration and transit have gained considerable prominence in membership negotiations. With the battle against illegal immigration a priority in the EU's common immigration policy, Turkey's involvement in illegal migration flows since the 1990s, both as a source and a transit country, became one of the most contentious issues in the EU (Europol, 2009; Frontex, 2007, 2008, 2009). A number of broad EU policy areas, such as border security – physical control of the external borders of the EU – or combatting illegal border crossings, illegal employment, and the development of common asylum and return policies, have inevitably become intrinsic to preparations for accession talks with Turkey. Despite the close link between the many aspects of irregular migration and the common economic and political interests of the EU and Turkey, both parties appear to be tackling them with very different strategies and exclusively to their own benefit.

It could be expected that the EU and Turkey would have little difficulty in agreeing on the introduction of an integrated border management system and the development of a common asylum policy, once Turkey was convinced that the negotiations embraced a 'burden sharing' rather than 'burden shifting' perspective.[15] Again, Turkey's most important consideration stems from deep-seated doubts about the EU commitment to a fully fledged membership for Turkey.[16] Along these lines, it was argued that Turkish policy-makers had made vast efforts to adopt and implement the EU *acquis*: new legislation in 2002 criminalised the act of human trafficking, while 2003 saw the introduction of a new *Law on Work Permits for Foreigners* and new legislative arrangements in the *Citizenship Law* with implications for the battle against irregular migration and the protection of immigrant rights (Kirişci, 2007b: 24; İçduygu, 2010b). More recently, the Law on Foreigners and International Protection was enacted in April 2013. Rather than a question of burden sharing, these developments are perceived by the EU as the adoption and implementation of the *acquis* in the field of international migration. While there has been some impressive cooperative action with regard to designing a common asylum and immigration policy, and an enhancement of police and judicial cooperation, such as the preparations for the 'Law on Foreigners and International Protection', there are minefield areas where the negotiations have progressed at a snail's pace, as discussed below.

With regard to Turkey's position as a country of immigration and transit, four challenging issues are currently being tackled by the EU and Turkey. The first is related to the volume of irregular migrant flows from third countries to EU member countries, mainly to Greece, using Turkey as a bridge. As one aspect of irregular migration, transit migration constitutes a massive problem. Both the EU and Turkey are interested in finding a solution through individual and cooperative efforts. The debate around the construction of a fence by the River Evros to curb irregular crossings at the Turkish–Greek border, however, was a striking example of the highly questionable measures presented as part of the solution to irregular migration (see Rygiel, this volume).[17] In many instances both sides blame each other: the EU accuses Turkey of institutional inadequacy and unwillingness to fully combat irregular flows; Turkey, on the other hand, sees the resources and cooperation provided by the EU as insufficient (İçduygu, 2011: 14).

The other three issues are more specific: the establishment of a civilian 'border agency' to replace the current military-based institutional set-up to control, secure and manage Turkey's border; the 'lifting of the geographical limitation' to the *1951 Convention relating to the Status of Refugees*; the negotiation and conclusion of readmission and visa facilitation agreements with the Commission. Sharing borders with Iraq and Iran, and faced with the Kurdish separatist movement and conflict, Turkey has its own security concerns in relation to the defence and protection of its eastern and southern borders. The recent crisis in Syria has added a new dimension to this anxiety over the security of the eastern borders. This is the principal reason why it was reluctant to transfer border protection by the military to border management by a civilian authority, which is what the EU expects. After a long period of negotiation, Turkey finally began in 2010 to prepare for this transformation, although it has repeatedly stressed that this would be a step-by-step procedure and that a fully functioning system run by the civilian authorities would take time (see Kirişci, 2007b). Turkey is equally reluctant about the 'lifting of the geographical limitation' to the 1951 Convention, although it made a pledge to the EU to lift the geographical limitation on the origins of those seeking protection (in the Action Plan for 2005, Turkey had this legal change for the year 2012). Turkey feared, however, that removing this clause would open the country to vast numbers of asylum seekers and create a 'buffer zone' between Western Europe and countries in political turmoil (Kirişci, 2007: 96): 'Turkish authorities have tended to oppose the abrogation of this limitation clause until and unless concrete progress towards full EU membership takes place,' (İçduygu and Yükseker, 2012: 448). Similar anxiety is evident in Turkey's bargaining over the drafting and signing of readmission and visa facilitation agreements with the Commission. Signing a readmission agreement is inextricably bound up with facilitating a comparatively visa-free regime for Turkish citizens, at least in the eyes of the Turkish authorities. The EU, on the other hand, has encouraged Turkey to sign the readmission agreement as an incentive for negotiating visa facilitation. It has called for Turkey to de-link the two agreements, claiming that the supposed connection between the readmission and visa facilitation agreements is a figment of the Turkish authorities' imagination (İçduygu, 2011: 14–15).

Despite its complex and diverse nature, this area of bargaining for membership has the potential to reward each side. Both Turkey and the EU realise that any negotiations dealing with borders, migration or asylum either inside or outside the accession process will not only have an impact on the specific issue at hand, but also on the course of the process as a whole. In this sense migration- and asylum-related bargaining has witnessed frequent oscillation between the 'blame game' and an 'anchor for the accession period'. Mismanagement of the bargaining process carries the undeniable risk of reversing the process of accession (İçduygu, 2011: 15).

Conclusion

In the meantime, Turkey's accession talks have stalled and are unlikely to regain momentum in the near future. Within this grey environment, policy circles in the EU continue to be preoccupied with the question of emigration from Turkey to the EU and whether it would be a repeat performance of the post-Fordist guest worker regime experience, providing yet another challenge to the integration of communities from Turkey in Europe. In other words, debates on the terms and conditions of the free circulation of labour are still relevant to Turkey's future EU membership, given the European labour market's dire need for a younger labour force.

Apart from free circulation of labour, one of the dynamic areas of EU–Turkey cooperation – with or without membership prospects – is the border and migration management that stems from Turkey's new role in the European migration system as a transit and destination country. Both sides, the EU and Turkey, have somehow handled cooperation on border and migration management issues, albeit with ups and downs and at a slow pace, and have succeeded in adopting certain reforms to achieve the convergence of Turkish and EU policies and practices. The evolution of these policies and practices saw the emergence of a field of diplomacy for the benefit of good governance of borders and mobility-related issues. It seems that this diplomacy not only involves conformity, settlement and agreement but also conflict, dispute and disagreement. The EU side has criticised the slow pace with which Turkey is tackling migration management questions. Turkey, on the other hand, can hardly be expected to implement the difficult and costly changes that good governance of migration calls for while European leaders deliver outspoken statements opposing the country's full membership of the EU.

This chapter reflects the fact that membership negotiations between the EU and Turkey regularly engage in debates on the nature and characteristics of borders, border crossings and people on the move. Migration diplomacy clearly functions here as a tool within the framework of foreign policy and international relations. Theoretically and analytically speaking, the above-mentioned debates on the process of 'migration diplomacy' in the context of EU–Turkey relations challenge the Europeanisation arguments that have come to dominate discussions on policy-making in border and migration management in the EU space over time. The term Europeanisation often refers to the impact of the EU on individual member or non-member states. Its use, however, underestimates the power of the negotiating partners over the EU. Consequently, 'Europeanisation', particularly in a dynamic context such as Turkey's European integration, is likely to be subject to contestable interpretations in the mindsets of policy-makers and government officers. Europeanisation is not a smooth process. It involves ups and downs, and an occasional refusal to comply on the part of a negotiating partner (Weber, 2010). At certain stages, such as the preparation of the *National Action Plan in the Field of Asylum and Migration* referred to above, Turkey has been subject to conditionality as a *quid pro quo* principle, which links incentives to the required reforms in the management of migration and asylum resulting in the adoption of EU migration policies and institutions modelled after EU countries. Other debates, such as those on the free circulation of labour or the lifting of the geographical limitation on the origin of asylum seekers, have seen a process of differentiation, with the EU forced to recognise Turkey's individuality in terms of its specific political, judicial and economic situation, and its capacity and willingness to cooperate with the EU. At certain stages, it was the social constructivist or meta-theoretical perspective on the notion of socialisation with which the EU convinced Turkey and led it to accept the rules and regulations of migration and asylum promoted by the EU as normatively legitimate. Finally, there were phases where the principle of joint ownership governed the process and the EU supported Turkey in the development of voluntary legislative approximation to meet jointly chosen EU norms and standards in the field of migration and asylum. In the course of discussions on the *Law on Foreigners and International Protection*, for example, there was a growing consensus among Turkish officials that regardless of EU membership prospects Turkey needed a migration law (Kirişci, 2012). Indeed, the making of this new legislation on migration is a perfect example of how different processes of Europeanisation have come together, infused with historical legacies, and social and political values, and contributed to the redesigning of EU–Turkey border and migration regimes.

Notes

1. This term refers to a general shift in mobility trends, whereby developing societies typically go through migration transitions characterised by 'a sequence of initially increasing emigration, the coexistence of significant but diminishing emigration and increasing immigration to eventually become net immigration countries' (de Haas, 2011: 60).
2. The Association for Solidarity with Refugees (http://www.multeci.org.tr), Helsinki Citizens Assembly (http://www.hyd.org.tr) and the Migrant Solidarity Network (http://gocmendayanisma.org/blog/) are among the civil society actors whose perceptions of migration- and asylum-specific issues differ greatly from the official state perspective.
3. From an EU perspective, the EU has embraced the issue of migration as a tool in diplomatic relations with third countries, including Turkey (Boswell, 2003). Since the EU has been the most prominent actor in this 'migration diplomacy', the article focuses on EU–TR relations. We acknowledge, however, that Turkey utilises its border policies as indirect foreign policy, also vis-à-vis third countries.
4. See, for instance, Kirişci (2012) for the impact of socialisation and conditionality on the making of the Law on International Protection and Foreigners.
5. See the full document: www.imldb.iom.int/viewDocument.do?id=%7BB40DC463 -1DF2-4F43-ADC4-E928378E1CB7%7D, accessed 04 August 2013.
6. In 1964 with Austria, the Netherlands and Belgium, in 1965 with France, and in 1967 with Sweden and Australia. Less comprehensive agreements were signed with the UK in 1961, with Switzerland in 1971, with Denmark in 1973 and with Norway in 1981 (Franz, 1994).
7. Here we assume that migrants from countries in the Middle East, Asia and Africa (such as Iraq, Iran, Afghanistan, Pakistan, Sudan and Somalia) are transit migrants on their way to third countries, while migrants from Eastern Europe and the Commonwealth of Independent States (CIS) are circular migrants who frequently come to Turkey. Several empirical studies present evidence to support this assumption (İçduygu, 2003; Brewer and Yükseker, 2006; Parla, 2007; Kirişci, 2008).

8. Evaluation of the figures for those apprehended on charges of illegal border crossing or overstaying one's visa, for example, allows for comment on the extent of irregular migration to Turkey. Here data is compiled by the Bureau for Foreigners, Borders and Asylum within the Directorate of General Security at the Ministry of the Interior.
9. It should be noted here that Turkey's open border policy during the Syrian crisis following the extension of temporary protection to Syrian refugees as of October 2011 heavily increased the number of people in need of international protection in Turkey. At the moment, several hundred thousand Syrian refugees are subject to 'secondary protection' and not included in asylum-seeker and refugee statistics. Another trend in asylum applications is the growing number of Afghan citizens applying for asylum in Turkey. For a detailed elaboration of these figures, see the UNHCR Ankara Office webpage: http://www.unhcr.org.tr.
10. This is partly due to the nature of the refugee problem in post-Second World War Europe and partly a ramification of the anti-communist policies adopted by Turkey during the Cold War, which granted asylum to applicants from the Soviet Union and Eastern Europe. The flow of refugees to Turkey during this period, however, was insignificant (less than 8000 asylum applications from the Soviet Union and Eastern Europe) (İçduygu, 2003).
11. In reality, however, the conditions for a resolution on the free movement of workers as envisaged by the Additional Protocol of 1973 did not materialise between 1976 and 1986, as a result of which the free movement of workers never occurred (İçduygu, 2006: 40–41).
12. See, for example, the *Communication from the Commission to the Council and the European Parliament* referred to above.
13. Joschka Fischer, Former Vice-Chancellor and Foreign Minister of Germany, voiced his support for Turkey's EU membership on numerous occasions, for example, on the grounds of political, economic and demographic realism. See, for instance, Willis, Andrew (2010) 'Economic realism will ease anti-Turkish feeling, Joschka Fischer says', euobserver.com, 01 October, available at: http://euobserver.com/news/30932, accessed 02 August 2013.
14. Egemen Bağış, Turkey's Minister for EU Affairs and chief negotiator at the accession talks with the EU, is one of the leading politicians to voice his concern over discrimination against Turkish citizens in the case of visa policies: See, for instance, 'Visa restrictions are shutting Turkey out of the EU', Egemen Bağış, theguardian.com, 14 July 2012, available at: http://www.theguardian.com/commentisfree/2012/jul/14/visa-restrictions-turkey-eu, accessed 23 September 2013.
15. The impact assessment report prepared by the Ministry of the Interior states that

> While the capacity-building of the institutional and administrative structures regarding the return procedures of irregular migrants is underway and developing, it also surprisingly becomes clear that many bureaucrats at different levels carefully elaborate the pros and cons of the possible readmission agreement between the EU and Turkey often referring to the notion of 'burden-sharing versus burden-shifting' issues and voicing their concerns regarding whether Turkey's burden will be shared by the EU or vice versa. These concerns also often question whether the country's and its institutions' capacities are able to cope with the 'burden' of returning the irregular transit migrants sent in by the EU countries.
>
> (CFCU, 2012: 82)

16. Concerns that Turkey would never be considered eligible to join the EU prevailed from the outset (Zaman, 2007). This scepticism is even more valid today since no significant progress has been made in the negotiations, as stated by Ministry of Foreign Affairs Ahmet Davutoğlu (Zaman, 2013).
17. Plans for a wall on Greece's border with Turkey embarrass Brussels, *Guardian*, 11 January 2011, available at: http://www.theguardian.com/world/2011/jan/11/greece-turkey-wall-immigration-stroobants, accessed: 04 August 2013.

4
Building Borders on a Bias: The Culturalist Perception of Turkish Migrants in France and Germany and the Debate on Europe's Boundaries

Sabine Ruß-Sattar

In most German school manuals on politics and society, the history of European integration is illustrated with a picture of smiling people tearing down a barrier and opening up the border between France and Germany. Indeed, the dominant European narrative up to the 1990s was one of breaking through frontiers, opening and enlarging a free market space for people and goods, while constantly reshaping and deepening a very particular political union. In the aftermath of the Eastern enlargement of 2004, however, this process ground to a halt. The story now seems to be more about defining the boundaries of Europe, drawing new frontiers and establishing new and 'thicker' borders as a buttress against migrants from non-member states (Cardwell, 2009: 164). The history of European integration could be summarised as follows: 'an international cooperation project in the 1950s, to a policy-making project in the 1960s, an institutionally consolidated system in the 1970s and a system of trying to foster identity and citizenship in the 1980s and 1990s' (Bruter, 2005: XIV).

According to a widely accepted sociological assumption, collective identities emerge through interaction with the 'other'. In the case of the European Community, identity was created at the outset through old-style nationalism. During the Cold War this shifted to communism and, to a certain degree, to the US model of capitalism. Since 9/11, Islamic fundamentalism has surfaced as the 'other'. 'Contemporary boundaries are drawn between natives and immigrants from outside Europe to distinguish "us" from "them". Non-European foreigners are progressively ethnicised and made more foreign. But if the internal exclusion of particular social groups is not overcome, European society will have difficulty in evolving into a post-national entity,' (Öner, 2008: 164). Whether the European Union (EU) will develop into a genuine post-national entity based on the concept of 'collective identity' remains to be seen. Despite quite an advanced political and academic debate on European identity, empirical evidence referring to ongoing psychological processes is limited. Analysis based on Eurobarometer polls suggests, however, that the citizens of EU member states are still far from reaching agreement on the criteria to define the European in-group (Kaina, 2010). Will EU citizens ever become an 'imagined community' (Anderson, 1991)?

In this context, the enlargement debate with regard to Turkey is unique, since it is the only candidate country to date whose European qualities have been radically questioned. For some opponents, Turkey constitutes the European 'other'. Paradoxically, the debate peaked at the precise moment when Turkey – an EU candidate since 1999 – was approaching membership in legal terms in October 2005 and EU accession talks with Ankara had begun. Under normal circumstances Turkey was deemed to become a member by 2014, but the process has apparently lost momentum and members of the Turkish government have publicly cast doubt on this date as realistic.

Officially, of course, the conditions for EU membership are defined by the Copenhagen criteria. Recent European Commission progress reports on Turkey have confirmed its headway in coming closer to meeting the Copenhagen criteria, with particular reference to its new constitution. As the Gezi Park protests have made clear even to the most benevolent observer, however, problems persist in the area of freedom of speech and opinion, and human rights. The Cyprus question is also an obstacle to progress in the accession process. In terms of border politics, the case of Turkey's accession to the EU is exceptionally instructive. The EU is the forerunner of an emerging 'postnational border constellation' (Vobruba, 2010), where borders play a different role in international politics: unlike the old Westphalian world of states, here it is the quality of their functional control and selective permeability rather than their geographical location that is at stake. Indeed, Vobruba rejects the image of 'fortress Europe' and sees the EU on its way to essentially becoming a 'migration bazaar' (*Migrationsbasar*) (Vobruba, 2010). It should be understood that Turkey's accession to the EU also takes place in this bazaar, rendering membership negotiations largely a matter of migration diplomacy. The circumstances and tensions of EU–Turkey migration diplomacy are explored by Ahmet İçduygu and Ayşen Üstübici in this volume. Suffice it to say that Turkey's accession would mark a watershed in the European integration process, since it first and foremost implies a dramatic extension of European borders and borderlands – a 2949 km land border and 8330 km sea-coast border – and would open Europe to new migration dynamics.

Against this background, the following chapter approaches border politics from a more cultural perspective. Despite the acknowledgement of borderlines as drawn according to interests and power relations, it should be taken into account that if borders – not unlike other power phenomena – are to have a solid foundation, they must be legitimated by some form of rationale. In this view, the principal reason for analysing the EU membership debate lies in what it can teach us about the social construction of borders and of imaginary frontiers and their exclusive or inclusive political logic with regard to migrants.

To begin with I will briefly recall the argumentative dimensions of the debate on Turkey's accession to the EU. This serves to situate and analyse the pattern of the French and German debates. As the detailed comparative analysis of the debate on Turkey's membership has shown (Giannakopolous and Maras, 2005), the debate itself was particularly heated in these two countries. Their executive leaders, former French president Nicolas Sarkozy (2008–2012) and current German Chancellor Angela Merkel (2005–present), were the most high-profile European politicians opposed to Turkey's accession to the EU. Nicolas Sarkozy claimed that Turkey did not belong in Europe, advocating a Mediterranean Union instead, while the German Chancellor promoted a 'privileged partnership' that falls short of membership, a formula Ankara categorically rejects. In May 2009, Sarkozy and Merkel made a joint statement in Berlin declaring that they shared a common position on Turkey's accession, which was the offer of a privileged partnership but not full EU membership.

Without the support of these two key members of 'old Europe', Turkey has little hope of gaining membership of the EU. From a Turkish perspective, France is interesting for its particular role in the political imaginary of the country. Another justification for greater scrutiny of these two member states is their hosting of the highest share of immigrant populations of Turkish origin in Europe, with Germany as host to two-thirds of the overall EU presence. As a result, the debate could, first, be affected by the perception of mainstream society and the elites, and second, by the perception and voices of the immigrant population. In the following contribution I confine myself – due to lack of data – to examining the first aspect. This approach assumes that the controversies on Turkey at international or, more precisely, European level are connected to those on the domestic scene.

The patterns of argument on Turkey's EU accession and their shortcut: The Muslim migrant

Although several studies confirm that the debate on Turkey served to support the societies of EU member states in their search for a definition of 'Europe' and its boundaries (Walter, 2008), it would be misleading to call it a genuinely common and transnational European debate (Wimmel, 2006; Carnevale et al., 2005). Neither are there any typical national visions of Europe in these countries. The political landscape is complex, often with cross-cutting party lines between advocates for a more political or cultural understanding of 'Europe' and those in favour of a federalist, more supranational construction of the EU or one with a greater intergovernmental slant (von Oppeln, 2006: 62). According to some authors, the predilection for a certain structural form to the union can be traced back to the experience of nation-building (Wimmel, 2006).

Striking in this debate is that almost every fact cited can be applied to the pro or the contra category of arguments. It is not the purpose of this article to decide which is the more plausible interpretation, since the decision will ultimately be political. In addition to the binding constraints of the Copenhagen criteria for EU accession, the decision will depend on the method framework – risk-oriented or opportunity-oriented – used for interpretation. It seems that in member states where Turkey's accession to the EU is primarily framed as a set of domestic issues (migrant integration, secularism and religion, cultural and political rights), the risk-oriented interpretation prevails. Where it is regarded, on the other hand, as an issue of foreign policy (Turkey as a bridge or mediator to the Islamic world and strategic military ally), opportunity-oriented perception rules.

Furthermore, the positive view dominates the scene in countries where the political elite tends towards a less ambitious conception of Europe, and the public is less interested in the subject of Turkey's EU accession (the UK and Poland are for the most part in favour of a pro-atlanticist orientation of security policy, Spain and Italy for a rebalancing of the EU towards its south).[1] The geopolitical approach to Turkish accession prevails in this group. In contrast, a second group of countries, with France and Germany as frontrunners and including the Netherlands and Austria, is characterised by heated public debate and political and media discourses where cultural arguments arise more frequently. Turkey is constantly referred to as a Muslim country that would push the EU closer to the Middle East, create borders with Iran, Iraq and Syria, and bring Muslim immigrants into the EU. It could be argued that here the debate on Turkey not only serves to construct a European identity and European borders but also is linked to and fired by the national identity crisis within these societies and their prevailing national integration models.

Turkey's accession to the EU is perceived in these countries through the lens of domestic problems associated with integration. To use a phrase coined by Dutch social democrat René Cuperus, it is 'not the Copenhagen criteria, but the Berlin-Kreuzberg criteria' that in the eyes of the broader public measure Turkey's fitness for membership (Kreuzberg is a Berlin quarter with a high concentration of Turkish immigrants). In a speech in Brussels, Cuperus claimed that 'For the ordinary people it is not about the Copenhagen criteria, but the Berlin-Kreuzberg criteria, the Rotterdam criteria, the Marseilles criteria or the Vienna criteria! It's about the integration and successfully-living-together criteria' (Cuperus, 2005). Understandably, this shortcut is used by populist politicians when it comes to the complexities underlying the pros and cons of Turkey's membership. The so-called daily experience appears to give solid and immediate credence to one solution – in this case, exclusion.

The debate in Germany: A country of immigration in partial denial

Seeing the big picture calls for differentiation between the attitudes of political elites, the media debate and public opinion according to the polls. The debate on Turkey in Germany at the turn of this century focused on defining the borders of Europe. At the time, historians Hans-Ulrich Wehler and Heinrich August Winkler played a prominent role in setting the agenda of the media debate (Große-Hüttmann, 2005: 37). Once accession negotiations had got under way in 2005, however, the arguments in favour of defining the borders of Europe historically to the exclusion of Turkey largely disappeared. It comes as no surprise that one of the strongest voices in favour of Turkey's accession is that of German industry and its attendant organisation, BDI, which sees Turkey as a door-opener to markets in the Middle East and as a young society with vast economic potential. There are indeed close economic links between Turkey and Germany. Germany is the leading exporter to Turkey (with €14.5 billion) and boasts 2700 German companies in Turkey, among them BASF, Mercedes and MAN. At the same time, Germany is the largest importer of Turkish products, which amounted to €9.1 billion in 2006. The country has approximately 6000 Turkish companies with 360,000 employees, a third of whom are German (Zentrum für Türkeistudien, 2006).

In terms of party politics in general, parties leaning towards the left tend to be in favour of EU enlargement to embrace Turkey. The Social Democratic Party is nevertheless home to strong supporters such as former chancellor Gerhard Schroeder as well as to opponents such as former chancellor Helmut Schmidt. Since 9/11, a key argument of supporters in Germany has been the need to refute the 'clash of civilizations' hypothesis – an argument used prominently, for instance, by former German minister of foreign affairs Joschka Fischer. In contrast, the argument referring to Turkey's cultural distinctiveness as too diverse is used frequently in the Christian Democratic and Christian Social Union parties and coincides to a certain degree with the wider German public view. Indeed, the public debate is primarily dominated by discussions on the integration of migrants in Germany and women's rights.

In the 1980s, 1,500,000 citizens of Turkish origin were resident in Germany. By 2005, when Turkey was officially awarded the status of EU candidate, these figures had risen to 2,600,000. One in every three immigrants from Turkey has been naturalised, an evolution that peaked with the reform of 2000, only to decline subsequently as a result of legal attempts to prevent dual citizenship.

Turkish associations and immigrant lobbies in Germany support Turkey's accession to the EU, but – as Prime Minister Recep Tayyip Erdogan stated in February 2008 in his speech in the Cologne Arena to thousands of Turkish Germans – the Turkish expatriate lobby could be more effective in defending its interests. German Turkish associations see Turkey's potential EU membership as a means of finally putting paid to second-class citizen status for Turkish immigrants in Europe (Leggewie, 2000: 214). However, there is still some road ahead. According to the polls, Chancellor Merkel's objection to full membership has its stronghold in German public opinion. In August 2008, only 19 per cent of German interviewees of an French Institute of Public Opinion (IFOP) study declared their support for accession, 61 per cent stated the contrary, while the remaining 20 per cent were undecided (Fourquet and Simon, 2008: 7).

Official German politics since the turn of the century have finally recognised Germany as an immigration country. Recent times have seen a broad debate in politics and civil society on integration, Islam and European values. 'The media discusses questions such as How can we make a multi-ethnic and multi-religious society work? What are universal human rights and where does German law conflict with arguments for cultural peculiarities? What can a host society demand of immigrants and are Turkish immigrants willing to respond?' (European Stability Institute, 2006).

As one observer notes,

> The topic of Turkey's entry is inextricably linked to the debate over how integration of the millions of Turkish immigrants that already live in Germany has fared and how unemployment figures would be affected [...] The fear that 'parallel societies' have emerged and diverged in German cities and are already beyond any real legislative or cultural reach has dominated the debate on integration and injected a new level of suspicion into German life.
>
> (Schäfer et al., 2005: 2–3)

There are, of course, other issues that contribute or have contributed to Turkey's negative image in Germany. Germany hosts a relatively strong Kurdish community, which draws particular attention to the problems of political and cultural minorities in Turkey – an issue likewise addressed by EU annual progress reports. An impact of the Kurdish conflict on Turkey's image in Germany appears to exist in the 1970s and 1980s, the factor was dimmed down 'since the Balkan wars and post-September 11 radicalisation of the Muslim world [generated] a new appreciation of the achievements of the secular Republic of Atatürk among Germans' (Stelzenmüller, 2007: 116). It has always carried less weight than the perceived problem of integrating immigrants.

In the autumn of 2010, a book entitled *Deutschland schafft sich ab* (Germany is abolishing itself) became Germany's best-selling non-fiction book ever. The author, Thilo Sarrazin, a former Bundesbank governor and member of the centre-left Social Democratic Party (SPD), presented a scary scenario, predicting the intellectual and general decline of Germany, taken over by Muslim immigrants hostile to knowledge and disinterested in culture. Despite unanimous criticism of the book by the media, the public response was enormous.

There is an unfortunate lack of empirical evidence on evaluative citizen processes. It can, however, be deduced from the analysis of public discourse on Turkey that much of the opposition to Turkey's membership is linked to the perceived failed integration of the existing Turkish population in Germany. In his Ph.D. thesis, Bülent Kücük detects in the EU–Turkey debate migrant fantasies of creating an 'Orient within', since their religion, Islam, makes integration impossible. To exemplify this he quotes from an article by German historian Hans-Ulrich Wehler in the liberal German newspaper *Die Zeit* (2002/38): 'Muslim minorities all over Europe have proved to be incapable of integration, choosing to live exclusively among themselves. Germany has of course no problem with foreigners, simply one with Turks' (Wehler cited in Kücük, 2008: 187, own translation).

Culturalist lines of argument come as no surprise in Germany, considering its trajectory of nation- and state-building. But is Constanze Stelzenmüller right when she claims that 'only the German debate on Turkish EU membership is inextricably intertwined with a debate on the very nature of German identity in the twenty-first century' (Stelzenmüller, 2007: 110)? Let us take a look at France, which is commonly in confrontation mode with Germany as a result of its conception of nation and citizenship (Brubaker, 1992).

France: A 'post-republican fortress'?

A priori, historical experience and traditional political patterns make France an unlikely candidate to oppose Turkey's accession on the basis of cultural arguments. Its traditional Republican model is based on citizen equality regardless of religion, ethnicity or race (see Raissiguier in this volume). Its political principles were a source of inspiration during the process of founding the modern Turkish republic, notably those referring to secularism. And yet, it was probably French officials at the diplomatic level who initially put forward cultural arguments. French public opinion and the political elites see Turkey's accession to Europe with heavy scepticism. As IFOP polls demonstrate, the percentage of accession supporters dropped from 32 per cent in 2004 to 20 per cent in 2008 (Fourquet and Simon, 2008). In the French political system, which is characterised by weak intermediary structures, public opinion carries considerable weight. In the course of a constitutional reform, former president Chirac went so far as to introduce an obligatory referendum on EU enlargements in 2005. The article was abolished in June

2008, however, when France took over the EU presidency and was wary of damaging French–Turkish relations.

Turkey's accession to Europe would mean the end of Europe – this dramatic statement was made in 2002 by Valérie Giscard d'Estaing, former French president and current President of the European Convention. He pointed to geographical, cultural and historical reasons. Interestingly, geographical aspects are more frequently cited in France than in Germany, a fact that Sabine von Oppeln explains with the strong territorial character of the French nation-building process.

With regard to the debate on Turkey, we should bear in mind the general scepticism of the French about the EU and its enlargement. This culminated in the French 'No' in the referendum on the European constitutional treaty in 2005. Scepticism about Turkey goes hand in hand with Euroscepticism. However, opposition to Turkey's accession can also be found among the supporters of European integration.

French Armenians, on the other hand, have succeeded in becoming an unexpectedly influential group in French politics. Their local concentration in major cities such as Lyon, Marseilles and Paris gives them electoral leverage. The success of Franco-Armenian lobbying is documented by the law that defends the denial of the Armenian genocide – one that has harmed French–Armenian relations for many years. The current rapprochement of Turkey and Armenia could have a positive impact on the official French position on Turkey's EU membership.

Is it possible against this background to genuinely compare Germany and France in the context of my assumption that the culturalist argument against Turkey's membership is based in both countries on a perceived domestic problem with the integration of immigrant populations? Despite its compelling economic advantages, two prominent issues in the French debate hamper support for Turkey's admission: immigration and Islam. Both are highly politicised issues in France today. An in-depth analysis of the French discourse on Turkey convincingly demonstrates the impact of this conjectural context. Beyza C. Tekin summarises his findings as follows:

> Fear of the collapse of the French social model, the sentiment of *déclinisme*, the perceived loss of control of the European integration process and rising scepticism toward Europe, the high concern with immigration and the inability of the French model to deal with diverse cultural identities in society, and the rise of the extreme right *lepénisation des esprits* were all found to cast a shadow on the opposing discourse.
>
> (Tekin, 2010: 211)

In 2002, it came as a shock to republican forces in France when right-wing Jean-Marie Le Pen, who owed his success to populist anti-migrant and anti-establishment rhetoric, reached the second round in the presidential elections. In the subsequent elections of 2007, it was Nicolas Sarkozy who succeeded in gaining a number of votes from *Front National* supporters, with a mixture of tough measures on irregular migration and insecurity, the promise to be inclusive towards French citizens, and the promotion of diversity.

Some of his policies showed strong evidence of populism, clearly suggesting the political crisis that prevailed in France. President Sarkozy launched a three-month debate on national identity, which had unintended side effects. It provided a platform for xenophobic resentment, revealing yet again the emergence in France of a closed idea of nation. This is also manifest in the French malaise over Islam, which is highly politicised in France. In the public perception, Turkey is Islam, and Turkish immigrants in France ultimately end up in the same stereotype mould as 'Muslim Arabs' (Moïsi, 2006). This unfortunately links the debate on Turkey to the French debate on Muslim headscarves, which is seen as a symbolic test case for the values of the laic French Republic. Since France rejects data collection on the basis of ethnic, racial or religious categories, there are no polls referring specifically to French citizens of Turkish descent. The US-based Pew Research Center, however, polled European Muslims and came up with a somewhat surprising fact: over a third of French Muslims admit to having had a bad experience as a result of their religion or ethnicity. This places them at the top of European discrimination rates. Nonetheless,

> French Muslims are the most integrated and are less likely than others to primarily identify as Muslims and more often see themselves as French first. They are more likely to say they want to adopt European customs than are Muslims in other European countries. German Muslims are the most likely to consider Europeans hostile, although fewer report a bad personal experience.
>
> (Pew Research Center, 2006: 16)[2]

When Sarkozy announced a debate on *laïcité*, the French Republican mode of regulating the relationship between religion and the state, it was broadly seen as an attempt to surf on anti-Muslim resentment during the then up-coming electoral campaign. From the French perspective, Turkey's own version of republican *laïcité* could have been considered a strong asset for EU membership and helped to promote a republican mode for the inclusion of Islam. This is not the case, however. As Kemal Kirişci states in his article 'Religion as an argument', Turkish Muslimness has become more and more accentuated in the debate (Kirişci, 2008b: 31). The AKP, a party with a perceived Islamic background, has come under suspicion in France in the context of the secular character of Turkish politics. Ironically, it was the then acting French president, Nicolas Sarkozy, who broke with secular tradition in French politics when he spoke on 14 January 2007 of the French as 'the heirs of 2000 years of Christianity', thus emphasising a discordant Turkey that 'has no place in Europe'.

French people who question the secular character of the Turkish state, however, are not necessarily would-be members of a Christian club: if Sarkozy could be dubbed a post- or 'neo-republican' (should there be a desire to desist calling him a French-style neo-conservative), the opposition stemmed from republicans who abhorred religion and state control in the public sphere.

The burden of a historical path in French politics, which helps to explain current perception patterns, is certainly not a reference to the traditional concepts of *nation* and *republic*. As a recent study reveals, the construction of an 'immigration problem' is linked to the colonial past, an issue recently raised in the public debate by new social groups such as the *Indigènes de la République*.

To sum up, the French debate on Turkey's EU bid is far more influenced by culturalist arguments than would be expected, considering the French traditional concept of citizenship and nation. Analysis of the French press confirms that reporting 'focuses mainly on Turkey as being culturally, geographically and religiously different from the EU member states'. (Hamid-Turksov, 2012: 142).

Turkey's EU accession = inclusion of migrants in Europe?

In the opinion of prominent Turkish representatives in Brussels, the objection of French and German leaders explains the dwindling Turkish enthusiasm for membership of the EU.[3] The impact of this objection is confirmed by several surveys, which revealed a significant loss of confidence in the two countries among the general public. According to one survey conducted by the Ankara-based International Strategic Research Organization (USAK) in August 2009, France was ranked third by the general public on the list of countries seen as a threat and Turkish public opinion of Germany as a friendly country was in rapid decline (USAK, 2009). In October 2004, 8.2 per cent of Turkish people saw Germany as a friendly country. By December 2005, this had dropped to 4.8 per cent, while in August 2009, only 0.64 per cent of Turks were of this opinion.

Of the 1100 Turkish interviewees, 56 per cent saw 'religious and cultural differences and historical prejudices against Turkey' as the principal obstacle to Turkey's entry into the EU. Since the EU is primarily perceived in Turkey as an economic and political union, cultural reasons for the exclusion of Turkey must be regarded as unacceptable and even offensive. The view that Europeans are hostile to Muslims has, however, gained currency since 2006 in Turkey (+13 percentage points in 2011) (Pew Research Center, 2011). Political leaders also suspect that Europe's reluctance to admit Turkey as a member is based on cultural prejudice within the confines of the EU as a 'Christian Club'. This culturalism could impact negatively on the climate of the accession talks and on *migration diplomacy* (see İçduygu and Üstübici in this volume).

Interestingly, despite a considerable lack of confidence in the two leading members of the EU, the USAK survey of 2009 indicated that Turks envisaged their future in the EU (USAK, 2009). When asked where Turkey's future lies, 56.36 per cent saw it with the EU. In October 2004, however, this figure had exceeded 61.04 per cent. Other opinion polls also point to a decline in support for EU membership among the Turkish population.

Why should European politicians attempt to rekindle this support? Based on the reflections set out above, there are at least two good reasons: the process of democratisation in Turkey and the integration of immigrants, notably Muslim migrants from Turkey and elsewhere. Despite our lack of solid empirical evidence, election polls in Germany have shown that conservative electors of Turkish descent balk at voting for the Christian Democrats (CDU), a result of resentment towards their migration policy and their stance on Turkey's EU accession. As former British foreign minister, Jack Straw, stated at Bosporus University in November 2007: 'By welcoming Turkey into Europe, we will prove how two cultures can not only exist together, but thrive together in a modern world. Accession means a more pluralist, tolerant and inclusive Turkey – and a more pluralist, tolerant and inclusive Europe,' (Straw, 2007, cited in Arvanitopolous, 2009: 163).

Notes

1. According to an IFOP poll in August 2008, 41 per cent of Spanish interviewees were undecided, 29 per cent were for and 30 per cent against Turkey's accession. A similar picture emerges for the UK, where as many as 54 per cent were undecided, 20 per cent were pro and 36 per cent against (Fourquet and Simon, 2008, ES 9, UK 13).
2. This is reminiscent of Etienne Balibar's warning: resentment tends to surface as soon as migrants are integrated and thus become serious rivals to the established members of mainstream society.
3. Observers at government level are curious about Turkey's heavy engagement in its Eastern and Middle Eastern neighbourhood and whether this might be an indication of its search for alternatives to EU membership and paving the way for an independent role as a regional power. They also wonder whether Turkey is genuinely moving towards Europe. On the other hand, it seems likely that the Turkish government will still want to become part of Europe and at the same time avail of the economic advantages of markets in the Middle East. After all, a Turkey that is a major player in the Middle East can use this as an asset in negotiations for EU accession (Fuller, 2008: 145).

Part II
Introduction: The Technologies of Bordering

Helen Schwenken and Sabine Ruß-Sattar

While the first part of the volume has predominantly focused on processes of extending and redesigning external borders and of demarcating a political and 'cultural' space, the second part turns towards internal borders and, in particular, zooms into the concrete technologies of these borderisation processes. The term 'technology' has to be understood in its dual meanings: First, technologies in their literal meaning and second, in a Foucauldian sense as technologies of government. What does 'internal borders' mean and how are they related to external borders? McKeown shows in his detailed historical study on the globalisation of border controls how the development of institutions and technologies of border control has been an ongoing process for more than '150 years of globalization'. Given the 'multiple diplomatic, administrative, and legal pressures... it took finesse to develop the practical institutions of migration control in the ways that simultaneously justified extraterritoriality and exclusion' (McKeown, 2008: 9). The practice of enforcing external borders has become a standard technique of modern sovereign nation-states to allow free mobility and equal access to services and law in the inside of a nation-state. The current trend to increasingly introduce different forms of internal border controls – such as the examination of documents in trains, asking for proof of legal residence for the delivery of public services etc. – has to be seen in the light of the widely acknowledged failure of immigration control (Castles, 2004). One of the forces that contributes to the failure is for example an interest group's activities, such as employers 'needing' low-wage workers that undermine control claims.

The authors in this section point to two technologies in particular: the technology of rescaling migration and border control and the technology of classifying migrants. The chapters by Detlef Sack, Robyn Rodriguez and Mara Sidney focus on the rescaling dimension of internal bordering practices. Sack's chapter on the 'air border' also complements the one by Klepp in the Part I on the 'sea border'. The control practices at airports, as analysed by Sack, are certainly most illustrative for the internalisation trend and the presence of external borders on the inside. Rodriguez' and Sidney's chapters have to be read as complementary. While in the US Rodriguez diagnoses the rise of anti-immigrant sentiments and consequentially an orientation towards 'domopolitics' (Walters, 2004), Sidney looks at politics of inclusion and the de-emphasising of border and immigration control. She identifies three modes how pro-immigrant groups refer discursively to undocumented migrants in order to lobby for the extension of their rights and access to public services. Her chapter draws our attention not only to the technology of rescaling, but also of classification. While the (federal) state classifies migrants and even US-born children as 'undocumented', pro-migrant groups attempt to re-label these migrants. While 'domopolitics' are oriented towards an exclusive, nativist 'we', Sidney stresses the attempts in neighbourhoods to include undocumented migrants as 'locals'. Border regimes indeed have their local equivalent, or become even 'structurally embedded' as Weber and Pickering as well as Rodriguez illustrate in this volume. The contribution by Sidney, as well as the chapters by Rygiel, Raissiguier and Schwenken in Part III of the volume, shows that border regimes are not homogenously repressive and control-driven, but contested.

As briefly mentioned, there are numerous examples of an internalisation of external borders, but there are noticeable differences between them. The chapter by İlker Ataç attempts to make sense of the fine-grained internal controls creating a number of foreigner 'sub-classes' which he observes in the Austrian case. Ataç hypothesises that the technology of classification and stratification is a response to post-national trends of increasing the rights of third-country nationals by international – in Europe through Europeanisation – dynamics. The chapters point to a general question that is dealt with more explicitly in Part III: how inclusive or exclusive do societies attempt to be? By the practices that Sidney documents, one could also critically conclude that the insider–outsider dichotomy still prevails, even when the 'insider' status is also granted to undocumented 'locals'. These cases show that bordering technologies are quite similar to and interact with citizenship technologies.

5
The Momentum of Contestation – Airports as Borderlands on the Inside

Detlef Sack

> States have a legitimate right to control their borders and manage the entry of foreigners, but methods employed to prevent unauthorised entry of migrants must allow for those seeking protection to be identified so they can claim asylum. Safeguards must be employed to ensure that asylum seekers are not returned to any country without having their claim examined within a fair process first.
>
> (Hungarian Helsinki Committee, 2008: 7)

The quote spotlights the particular tension that constitutes one of the most dynamic elements of bordering processes. It suggests that state authority should be fair. In order to prevent unwanted acts, however, state authority rationale may see a breach of the rule asserted in the quote as advantageous. 'Not being fair' can be a deliberate strategy to 'manage' migration risk assessment as Weber and Pickering show in the case of Australia and Klepp with regards to Search and Rescue missions in the Mediterranean Sea (both in this volume). European migration policy draws on such a strategy and implements a policy of deterrence at its borders via military force, the police and the administration. Its dynamic element derives from its concurrent pursuit of a strategy of being fair. European regulations state their commitment to international law and human rights standards for refugees in order to restore, sustain and enhance European Union (EU) legitimacy as an imagined 'civilian community'. Migration policy gains its momentum from this inherent discursive ambiguity, which gives room for contestation and the

---

I am grateful to Sabine Ruß-Sattar, Helen Schwenken, Mara Sidney, Nursemin Sönmez, Andreas Vasilache, Julia Wirsbinna and the participants of the workshop 'Migration and Borderlands: Dynamics of Exclusion and Inclusion', 14–16 April 2011, Büyükada Island, for their helpful comments.

struggle between different discourse coalitions. These coalitions focus on either deterrence or human rights issues and are equipped with asymmetric resources and capacities. This chapter elaborates on the construction of border space and the struggle it entails, and focuses on airports as a specific type of border. These are understood as borderlands on the inside. The inherent ambiguity of migration policy at airports stems from the interplay between establishing a transit zone as a 'state of exception' and honouring *non-refoulement*, a principle of international law that ensures refugees will not be deported to countries where they are likely to face serious human rights violations. Airports and other semi-offshore camps under the administrative authority of any state that accepts the rule of law and international conventions to protect refugees are the spaces where border politics acquires a specific dynamic. It is the organisational capacity of the established legal system (that is, the multi-level court system and a wealth of law firms), the access to migrants by NGOs and like-minded lawyers, and the visibility of the place that distinguishes inside borderlands from those on the outside. In the wider transitional space beyond, international law is unlikely to be enforced where, for various reasons, jurisdictions cannot be held accountable. This should not veil the conflicts and daunting conditions migrants experience at airports or internal camps. Taking Frankfurt-Main airport, the hub of German aviation, as a case in point, the chapter sheds light on the dynamic element that shapes border politics in a particular context. It also focuses on a specific group: unauthorised migrants and asylum seekers.

To contextualise border practices, the chapter first sketches the principal features of European migration policy, with particular reference to the regulation of air borders. Following conceptualisation of the airport as a space of contestation, it discusses executive practices at European airports and their implementation. The case of Frankfurt-Main airport begins with an overview of the 'airport procedure' for asylum seekers and its implementation, as well as a discussion on the changing architecture of the space itself. Airport deportation practices are observed and the transit zone is shown to be a dynamic border space, one that has been shaped by deterrent administrative practices, marked-up humanisation initiated by NGOs and lawyers enforcing the rule of law, and individual acts by resistant migrants. Three political discourse coalitions with varying functions were identified in border contestation: the first interprets migration within the frame of repressive control and deterrence, while the second discourse coalition focuses on the human rights standards for refugees and the norm of the international law. A third coalition takes the transit zone as a state of exception and perceives the border itself as the problem to be addressed.

The patterns and dynamics identified in this microstudy of Frankfurt-Main airport resemble those constituent to EU migration policy as a whole. The chapter closes with a look at the distinguishing feature of the airport as an inside borderland in contrast to external frontiers. It is argued that the territorialised state of the *organised* rule of law makes a difference and, based on the established field of multi-level national and European court systems and numerous law firms, that the human rights discourse coalition has, to a certain degree, been effective.

European Union migration policies

Migrants' access to European airports and their regulation is part of the overall migration policy of the EU and its member states (Boswell and Geddes, 2011: 51–75, see the contribution by Klepp, in this volume). European migration policy is divided into four regulation areas: mobility of European citizens, legal immigration for socio-economic reasons, admission for asylum seekers and unauthorised migration.

In the interests of a common migration policy, the EU strives for 'partnership and cooperation with third countries for the purpose of managing inflows of people applying for asylum or subsidiary or temporary protection' (European Union, 2009: art. 78, para. 2). The EU expresses the commitment of European migration policy to international law.

For the purposes of this chapter, the general context of European migration is confined to the regulation of two migration types: asylum and unauthorised migration. Both are permeable and overlap. Some political refugees are reluctant to apply for asylum due to poor prospects of success. Others consider the asylum procedure an opportunity to become legalised. Once an asylum application has been turned down, however, only a fine line exists between asylum and unauthorised migration.

Under legislation on political asylum in the EU (Boswell and Geddes, 2011: 151), the Dublin II regulation guarantees that asylum seekers submit only one application within the EU. (European Council, 2003: art. 3, para. 1). This regulation led, in practice, to what critics of EU migration policies call the 'marshalling yard' (Pro Asyl, 2008: 1): refugees and asylum seekers are sent back to where they had their first contact with a member state of the EU. The Dublin II regulation is combined with the EURODAC regulation, which provides for a fingerprint database to identify asylum seekers (European Commission, 2007: 1). In 2011, the European Court of Justice ruled that member states should not transfer asylum seekers to Greece despite its registration in the EURODAC because the Greek authorities had failed to execute migration policies in line with European norms and guarantee fundamental human rights (European Court of Justice, 2011: para. 44). The judgement is based on four elements: human rights standards of European and international law, knowledge acquired through monitoring by NGOs (such as Amnesty International) and international organisations, the commitment of the lawyers who filed the complaint, and a court of justice interested in holding the administration of a member state to account.

Asylum seekers are likewise contingent on the entry regulations to the territory of the member state concerned: Council Directive 2005/85/EC confirms the principle of *non-refoulement* (Council of the European Union, 2005: art. 2). Applications made at the border or in a transit zone are explicitly covered by this directive (Council of the European Union, 2005: art. 35, para. 1). The respective procedures ensure the stay of the refugee at the border and transit zone or within its proximity, immediate information on rights and obligations, access to interpreter services, a personal interview before the application decision, a legal adviser or counsellor and, in the case of unaccompanied minors, a representative. Should a decision not be made within four weeks, the applicant will be granted entry to the territory (Council of the European Union, 2005: art. 35, para. 3). The EU return directive (European Parliament and Council of the European Union, 2008) addresses irregular migrants subject to expulsion. It establishes common standards for departure periods and entry bans, as well as the commitment to international law. It also stipulates requirements for the detention of irregular migrants:

> Unless other sufficient but less coercive measures can be applied effectively in a specific case, Member States may only keep in detention a third-country national who is the subject of return procedures in order to prepare the return and/or carry out the removal process, in particular when: (a) there is a risk of absconding or (b) the third-country national concerned avoids or hampers the preparation of return or the removal process. Any detention shall be for as short a period as possible and only maintained as long as removal arrangements are in progress and executed with due diligence.
> (European Parliament and Council of the European Union, 2008: art. 15).[1]

In general, EU member states are obliged to implement EU legislative acts and the administration of borders (Boswell and Geddes, 2011: 145). In accordance with the overall process of European agency-building (Rittberger and Wonka, 2011), it comes as no surprise that the EU launched Frontex. The task of this independent agency is to control external borders, set up technologies, and produce knowledge on irregular migration (Boswell and Geddes, 2011: 145–146; see Klepp, in this volume). With regard to the air border, Frontex states: 'The aim of Frontex Air Border Sector is to help Member States grapple with the challenge of detecting illegal entries to the EU at airports and yet maintain the smooth, efficient flow of enormous numbers of legitimate passengers,' (Frontex, 2010: 45). The agency identified more than 150 European airports as entry points of irregular migration and set up a number of actions to interfere with this unauthorised mobility flow (Frontex, 2010: 45–51), 12 of which were conducted between 2008 and 2010 (Frontex, 2010: 91).

In sum, much of EU migration policy on asylum and irregular migration can be defined as securitisation (Buzan et al., 1998) and the prevention of unauthorised migration. Securitisation is likewise a reference point for the most dominant discourse coalition (Boswell and Geddes, 2011: 41–43), with direct control and deterrence as its chief narrative mechanisms (Carling and Hernández, 2011: 52–53). At the same time, the policy proclaims its formal commitment to international human rights standards. Addressing the fundamental norms of a transnational humanitarian order in the interests of an imagined European civilian community allows the EU to gain legitimacy. Hence, the discursive ambiguity between deterrence on the one hand and respect for human rights on the other hand is constitutive in the policy arena.

Airports as spaces of entry and control

The spatial pattern of migration in Europe has changed notably during the last 20 years as national borders became European borders. Germany, among others, benefits from this new pattern as a result of externalising its control costs. Airports, however, remain points of entry and borderlands on the inside.

Identifying airports as inside borderlands calls for an understanding of the space itself. From a critical geography position (Soja, 1995; Swyngedow, 1997), it is a product of built environment, technologies, social contestation, politics and routines. The airport is a nodal point between transnational mobility and the access to localities. On the one hand, airports as borderlands are sites of waiting zones, aisles, counters and other facilities, and, on the other hand, of personal control. Five control technologies (CCTV surveillance, security checks, passport control, databases and boarding) are a matter of routine. Political regulation is built into the architecture, with vast halls dedicated to security checks, where counters and routes are designed differently for (non-)citizens. Security checks and passport controls are not merely the result of legislative acts. They are also social practices that include informal cultural and racial profiling as one of the 'rules in use'. Studying airports as contested borderlands goes beyond the built environment and its technologies, administration, social practices and local 'rules in use', and turns to the struggle between different 'political discourse coalitions' (Leifeld and Haunss, 2012: 382), all of which are equipped with power resources to a varying degree. In a Foucauldian adapted variant (Miller and Rose, 2008), these coalitions consist of narratives, core policies, practical expertise, strategies and resources with which affiliated collective or individual actors make meaning of mobility, migration, the airport, the need for its regulation and favourable execution.

Regarding the situation of unauthorised migrants in particular, transit zones at inside borderlands are instructive places. Although on the territory of the state and the respective airport, they are located outside their territorial jurisdiction, that is, beyond official state borders. This is where the unauthorised who wish to cross the border are detained – a no-entry zone. The executive practice of allocating unauthorised persons testifies to the character of migration policies. Political disputes on status and care focus on 'the migrant' in his or her weakest position: migrants in transit zones can be seen as the reduction of human beings to 'bare life', suspended from the law in a permanent 'state of exception' (Vasilache, 2008: 130–132; Agamben, 2005). In terms of international law, Hathaway asserts that a certain control policy became more common in the borderlands 'with states apparently prepared even to deem parts of their own territory to be outside their own territory, with the hope of thereby avoiding protection responsibilities to persons present therein' (Hathaway, 2005: 298).

Despite deterrent no-entry policies, the 1951 Geneva Convention on the Status of Refugees establishes a fundamental norm of access to states, which is binding for the signatories. Article 33 declares the principle of *non-refoulement*: 'No Contracting State shall expel or return (*refouler*) a refugee in any manner whatsoever to the frontiers of territories where his life or freedom would be threatened on account of his race, religion, nationality, membership of a particular social group or political opinion.' This principle does not apply to refugees convicted of serious crimes who would constitute a danger to the community (Hathaway, 2005: 300; Boswell and Geddes, 2011: 35). The legal obligation not to send refugees back to countries where life and liberty would be at risk constrains the state's prerogative to stipulate procedures for entry to its territory as the norm of *non-refoulement* (Hathaway, 2005: 301). Thus, from a legal position airport transit zones are by no means areas where migrants are reduced to 'bare life' in a constant 'state of exception'. They remain legal subjects protected by international law.

It is not surprising that some states tried to circumvent their international obligations by defining airport transit zones as extraterritorial. This was common practice at Charles de Gaulle Airport in Paris, France, in the late 1980s and early 1990s. The procedure was governed by decrees and orders from the French Ministry of the Interior, not by law. The short proceedings for asylum seekers and the designation of the transit zone as extraterritorial to French state territory came under pressure from the French Constitutional Court and the European Court of Human Rights. Complaints were filed with strong support from anti-racism NGOs. In 1991, the French government introduced a law on special airport procedures, which was passed by the National Assembly in mid-July 1992, allowing asylum seekers to be held for up to 20 days in the transit zone. Interestingly, the European Court of Human Rights stated in 1996 that airport transit zones belong to the territory of the state concerned. An area that legally suspends guarantees of the European Convention on Human Rights is therefore non-existent. These norms are in force at all borderlands (Leisering, 2008: 3–6). Again, this did not derive from party politics or social mobilisation alone. The struggle between the discourse coalitions took the form of 'legal politics'.

Executive administration and monitoring at European airports

Legal politics, however, is based on the knowledge and expertise of dealing with practices at airports. Research on human rights up to now has confirmed the gap between talk and action (Landman and Carvalho, 2010). Ratification of an international convention does not necessarily involve implementation. Information on the 'rules in use' at the inside borderland relies primarily on monitoring by NGOs and international organisations. From a methodological perspective, this kind of knowledge production is ambivalent: monitoring produces information on implementation and the state of refugees in transit zones to generate expertise for political contestation and at the same time to strengthen the organisation itself. Lack of sound scientific research, however, and the unavailability of border authority and United Nations High Commissioner for Refugees (UNHCR) internal reports (which do exist) make the NGO perspective the sole illustration of the situation at European airports.

Summing up monitoring reports on the removal centres and detention facilities at seven European airports (Hungarian Helsinki Committee, 2008; UK Border Agency, 2009; Council of Europe, 1991), the concerns of the human rights discourse coalition encompass administrative practices as well as the built environment. The following executive practices were the subject of repeated criticism: arbitrary and *ad hoc* implementation by border guards, intransparency or lack of information on legal proceedings, no access to appropriate translation, no interviews with refugees, and no trained staff to deal with traumatised migrants (Hungarian Helsinki Committee, 2008: 51–53). It should also be noted that

> despite the availability of court review against refusal of entry, it is in practice almost impossible to appeal the decision on non-admission to the territory. This is mainly due to the lack of understanding about procedures and legal remedies, the unreasonably short period of time for taking legal action against the return decision and the difficulties relating to access to legal advice.
>
> (Hungarian Helsinki Committee, 2008: 53)

Monitoring also revealed shortcomings in the delivery of basic needs such as water, food and blankets (UK Border Agency, 2009: 12–13). The legal norms of international conventions and European directives are breached by systematic non-information, intimidating control, long and opaque procedures, and administrative behaviour inappropriate to the specific situation of refugees. When it comes to transit zone sites, that is, removal and detention centres, the picture is again demeaning. Concerns have been raised about sleeping facilities, unisex washrooms, poor ventilation and extreme temperatures in buildings, harsh lighting, and lack of worship space and access to telephones (UK Border Agency, 2009: 12–13; Hungarian Helsinki Committee, 2008: 53). NGO monitoring indicates that the inside borderland space is shaped by local facilities and executive 'rules in use' that in reality leave refugees and unauthorised migrants in a 'state of exception'. On the other hand, 'the migrant' is not reduced to 'bare life'. Instead he or she is deliberately subject to unaccomplished legal norms in the transit zone. The practices detected by NGOs bear little resemblance to techniques of persuasion. On the contrary, they influence migrant risk assessment by means of repression, which is similar to what Weber and Pickering depict in this volume in the case of Australia. However, the gap between the formal commitment to human rights standards and the executive 'rules in use' is likely to trigger the gradual transformation of the border. Administrative practices and the discursive ambiguity entrenched in the space have paved the way for contestation, as unmet expectations and legal norms provide political discourse coalitions with room for manoeuvre in challenging European migration policy on the basis of civil norms upheld by European institutions.

The 'airport procedure' at Frankfurt-Main airport

The discursive ambiguity of border politics and its inherent dynamic also characterises the particular situation at one of the largest intercontinental aviation hubs in Europe: Frankfurt- Main airport. With 56.3 million passengers in 2011, it is the third largest airport on the continent (ranked after London-Heathrow [69.4 million in 2011] and Paris-Charles de Gaulle [60.7 million in 2011]), and by far the most important in Germany (ranked before Munich [37.6 million in 2011] and Düsseldorf [20.3 million in 2011], Eurostat, 2013). Due to the new spatial pattern of European migration policy (see above), Germany has displaced its land border activities to the EU member states that control the external borders of the European 'area of justice, freedom and security' but remains a migration destination area.

A review of the role of Frankfurt-Main airport as a borderland is of advantage here: in the course of a contentious debate on migration policy in 1992–1993, the German parliament not only amended the article on political asylum in German Basic Law, albeit this right was markedly restricted. It also passed a law on asylum procedures (*Asylverfahrensgesetz*), which came into effect in July 1993. The law encompasses a 'third-country regulation' whereby asylum-seeker applications are to be rejected if those concerned arrived via a safe third country. As a result of its geographical location, Germany's entry points for asylum seekers have been reduced considerably. Airports were deemed crucial logistical hubs for unauthorised migration by the incumbent Christian Democratic-Liberal government, which led to the establishment of an airport procedure to regulate access (Huber, 2004). The initiative came from the conservative Christian Democratic Party. The vast majority of Social Democrats, the second catch-all party in Germany and somewhat left-of-centre, supported the new migration policy and aligned with this discourse coalition (Welge, 2009: 4). The regulation set up by a Christian Democratic-Liberal legislative majority has been retained since 1993: by a Social Democratic-Green coalition cabinet (1998–2005), by a Grand Coalition (2005–2009), and, again, by a Christian Democratic-Liberal cabinet (since 2009).

The airport procedure entails a decision on the entry of unauthorised migrants and asylum seekers. If migrants do not apply for asylum they are subject to immediate removal. If they come from a 'safe third country' or seek asylum at border control, the procedure is set in motion. Migrants are required to advocate for their asylum application in a hearing organised by the Federal Office for Migration and Refugees (Bundesamt für Migration und Flüchtlinge, BAMF). If the application is 'obviously without cause', entry is denied. Applicants must appeal to the courts for temporary legal protection within three days. The administrative court responsible (*Verwaltungsgericht* Frankfurt-Main) then decides on the admission within a fortnight (Huber, 2004). BAMF must allow entry if the decision cannot be made in the short-term, that is, within two days, if the court cannot decide within a fortnight, or if adequate medical assistance for the migrant cannot be organised at the airport. This procedure was subject to adjudication by the German Constitutional Court, which authorised it in 1996 provided certain standards were observed. The latter are those listed by European Directive 2005/85/EC (*Bundesverfassungsgericht*, 1996: para. 166; Council of the European Union, 2005). Interestingly, three judges cast a dissenting vote. They saw the airport procedure as incompatible with human rights standards of the Basic Law.

Statistics can be instructive when it comes to the general development of airport procedures. A notable decline in procedures was observed between 1995 and 2005. Since then, however, there is evidence of a slight increase. The figures are difficult to interpret as they show the effects of EU and German border politics in flux as well as of transnational push factors for migration, such as regional civil wars, tightened autocratic practices, increased human rights violations and economic downturns. However, they do point to shifting trends in borderland traffic. The ratio of documented proceedings (applications filed by migrants) to permitted entries indicates the relevance of the airport transit zone: The higher the share of permitted entries, the lower its importance. Beginning with 1995, the share of permitted entries was 91.8 per cent in that year but dropped to 62.9 per cent in 2000 and 42.6 per cent in 2005. It rose to 76.8 per cent in 2010 and 94.5 per cent in 2011 (see Table 5.1). This increase in the ratio of proceedings to permitted entries is matched by the large number of proceedings in 2010 and 2011 and the significant decline in absolute numbers of decisions taken at the airport

Table 5.1 Number of airport procedures in Germany, 1993–2011

Year	All proceedings	Entry	Decision within two days	Accepted	'Obviously without cause'	Appeals to court	Appeals permitted	Appeals dismissed
1993	979	772	235	5	229	221	104	104
1994	2581	2378	206	0	204	166	23	139
1995	4590	4213	357	0	355	284	59	223
2000	1092	687	416	8	407	348	24	347
2005	427	182	236	0	235	181	19	148
2010	735	565	57	0	55	36	0	35
2011	819	774	60	0	60	50	1	49

Own compilation, sources: Bundesamt für Migration und Flüchtlinge quoted from Welge, 2009; Bundesamt für Migration und Flüchtlinge, 2012: 53, annual inconsistencies due to decisions on appeals from the previous year.

since 2009. In other words, airport transit zones as inside borderlands were highly relevant during the early and mid-2000s.

In almost all cases, detainment at the airport means rejection of applications as 'obviously without cause'. Two ratios shed light on executive practices in transit zones. First, the share of appeals to court indicates that migrants were at least informed of this option, be it by border guards, administrators of the proceedings, private lawyers or migrant peers. In addition, it shows the calculus assessment of migrants to appeal with good prospects. The share of appeals was 80 per cent in 1995, 85.5 per cent in 2000, 77 per cent in 2005, and 65.5 per cent in 2010 (see Table 5.1). The 2000s are defined by a relative decline in appeals and challenges to executive practice. Further research will be required to establish whether this is due to lack of information or a different appraisal of migrants. Furthermore, the number of permitted appeals testifies to executive decisions considered inappropriate to the standards of formal and informal rules. The figure should, however, be interpreted with caution. An overlapping if not congruent mindset of the executive administration and lower administrative courts suggests frequent contact, social networks and professional socialisation. Granting an appeal is therefore evidence of a wrong decision and deviance from the standards in place. The share of permitted appeals was 20.8 per cent in 1995, 6.9 per cent in 2000, 10.5 per cent in 2005 and 0 per cent in 2010. Taking into account the two ratios, appeals and permitted appeals, airport procedures and executive practices in transit zones stabilised during the 2000s. This suggests that the rules established were increasingly considered as appropriate by the practitioners and judges involved.

In summary, official statistics reveal that the establishment of specific rules in use as an element of border space coincided with a significant reduction in the number of migrants in the transit zone since the mid-2000s.

This borderland, in other words, has lost some of its factual importance and become dislocated following the transfer of migrants to internal accommodation.

Turning to the sites in question yields further information on the rules in use and the spatial character of the borderland. Due to its hub function for transcontinental aviation, Frankfurt-Main airport became the focal point for most airport procedures in Germany (Flughafen-Sozialdienst, 1998: 38; Welge, 2009: 25). The airport is located in the state of Hesse, whose government is partly in charge of airport administration. During the period in question, three cabinets were in power: a Social Democratic-Green coalition (1991–1999), a Christian Democratic-Liberal cabinet (1999–2003, 2009–2013) and a Christian Democratic cabinet (2003–2009). There is no evidence that party differences impacted executive practices in the transit zone.

Again, monitoring by NGOs within the human rights discourse coalition remains the sole source of information on this borderland. From the outset of the new procedure, an old building with 13 rooms located in the transit zone of Frankfurt-Main airport was used as accommodation for 70 detainees. Washing facilities were unisex and limited in number. Due to permanently closed windows the room climate was stuffy. Detainees were allowed to walk around a fenced field for one hour twice a day. Border control had to be called picking them up from the building. The 'typical' situation of the unauthorised migrant in transit zones, including uncertainty of applications, lack of information on legal procedures, fear of removal, language barriers, psychosomatic illnesses and traumatisation were aggravated by confined space, overcrowding and the length of detainment (Flughafen-Sozialdienst, 1998: 9–10). According to the Protestant charity Diakonisches Werk, 305 persons were held longer than 19 days in the facility in 1997. 58 persons were forced to stay more than 30 days; in two cases detention exceeded 100 days. The situation was exacerbated in 1999: 159 persons were detained at the removal centre for more than 30 days, 33 for more than 100 days and 12 for more than 200 days. In a letter to Amnesty International, Germany, 31 refugees criticised the 'inhuman and degrading conditions' at the facility. Between 1997 and early 2000, 18 suicide attempts were recorded. In May 2000, a 40-year-old Algerian woman committed suicide after seven months at the removal centre. Implementation of the airport procedure was put on the Human Rights Commission agenda of the German parliament (Sack, 2000). The facility was operated by personnel from the social services of the Protestant and Catholic churches, who were criticised by the Agency for Migration and Refugees and the conservative-liberal government of the state of Hessen, in office since 1999, for their public exposure of conditions at the removal centre. May 2002 saw a new purpose-built facility in the airport transit zone to house the removal centre, Border Control and an administrative unit of BAMF. In comparison with the old building, the space for a scheduled 100 detainees almost doubled. Sports facilities, a playing field and two places of worship were added. The Protestant and Catholic churches lost their contract to operate the facility but can still access migrants at the removal centre in an advisory capacity. Custody of detainees has been contracted to a private security corporation, which must schedule at least one woman per shift to address gender-specific needs. The facility is guarded by standard technical surveillance, such as CCTV and card readers. The overall administrative operation of the removal centre and social assistance for the detainees was taken over by the state of Hesse. The facility became 'socialized' when BAMF and the government sought to control the removal centre and its outgoing information, on the one hand, and staff became redundant due to a general decline in the number of asylum seekers, on the other (Land Hessen, 2005; compare Menz, 2009). As a result the situation of airport detainees was depoliticised and disappeared from the public eye (Welge, 2009: 1). Apart from a shift in the public mood to other border topics such as the situation on the coast of southern Spain, in the Mediterranean (see Klepp, in this volume) or at the Turkey–Greece border (see Rygiel, in this volume), three developments are worth noting. First, the removal centre and the circumstances under which migrants were detained at the airport improved and were 'humanized'. Second, information on the facility came under state control from the mid-2000s. It can be assumed that information has a different bias to that of the church welfare services that originally ran the facility. Third, statistics in Table 5.1 show that capacity utilisation altered significantly in 2008. The number of airport procedures since then has remained at less than capacity.

In addition to information gathered from official statistics (see Table 5.1), qualitative data is available on a number of Frankfurt-Main airport proceedings. Commissioned by the NGO *Pro Asyl*, 32 cases were scrutinised. Although a small and non-representative sample (Welge, 2009: VI), it gives some insight into administrative practices. To begin with, hearings were conducted in an atmosphere described as 'grilling' rather than questioning. Migrants encountered a general sense of mistrust on the part of BAMF personnel, who questioned their credibility and need for asylum. Traumatised migrants and victims of gender-specific persecution were at times confronted with relentless interrogation by BAMF staff. In some instances, asylum seekers did not have the mental and physical abilities to follow the proceedings. Lack of or contradictory information on the side of the asylum seekers was not clarified but taken as evidence of non-credibility. BAMF information on human rights situations in some countries of origin was biased and incomplete, namely, in Eritrea and Myanmar. BAMF tends to refer in its decisions to Border Control minutes taken after the immediate arrival of the migrants. Finally, adequate translation was identified as problematic (Welge, 2009: 220–230).

Since monitoring by NGOs may be biased to producing knowledge in the interests of the organisation, this non-representative study should be interpreted with caution. Bearing this in mind, the study suggests first that the hard-won humanisation of the built environment coexists with administrative practices of mistrust, hostility and deterrence. Second, it gives statistic-based information on the qualitative character of the rules in use and on the decline in appeals. Again, 'intent management' (see Weber and Pickering in this volume) draws on repression rather than persuasion techniques to alter the migrants' individual risk assessment.

Deportations from Frankfurt-Main airport

Airport procedures cover the arrival flow of unauthorised migrants by aviation and, to a minor degree, its departures. Borderlands on the inside and their transit zones are likewise locations for expulsion. According to the German government, the number of deportees from German airports decreased from 34,756 in 1988 to 7188 in 2011 (Deutscher Bundestag, 2000; Deutscher Bundestag, 2012). These figures derive from the annual parliamentary enquiry by The Left Party (Table 5.2). Government data also show the importance of Frankfurt-Main airport and the statistical refinement due to on-going monitoring. The former is reflected by the number of deportees. In 2000, 30 per cent of 32,443 persons expelled were deported from Frankfurt-Main airport. In 2011, the share was 42.5 per cent (Deutscher Bundestag, 2001: 3; Deutscher Bundestag, 2012: 1). The statistics became more refined as additional data on state or private escorts, target countries, and acts of resistance were submitted and include successful acts of resistance by deportees since 2005. Forthwith, 'the migrant' was rendered visible as an additional political actor for contestation of the spatial character of the airport and was signified and 'resurrected' as an active subject of resistance and a reference point. The same holds true for deportation refusals by pilots

Table 5.2 Number of deportees, acts of resistance and failed deportations, 1998–2011

Year	Number of deportees from German airports	Number of deportees from Frankfurt-Main airport	Successful acts of resistance by deportee	Failed deportation due to refusal of pilot/air carrier
1998	34,756	n/a	n/a	n/a
1999 (until 11.1999)	27,025	n/a	n/a	n/a
2000	32,443	9794	n/a	n/a
2005	16,865	n/a	298	95
2010	6907	3098	99	52
2011	7188	3056	122	39

Own compilation, source: *Deutscher Bundestag, 1999–2012*.

and air carriers. In quantitative terms, these acts of defiance are negligible: 1.7 per cent of all deportations for successful acts of resistance by the deportee and 0.5 per cent for refusal by air carriers. Nevertheless, their numerical presence in the airport border space extends the group of actors with subject status in contesting the space.

This is one of several outcomes of the struggle over the departure flow from the border space. Frankfurt-Main airport as an inside borderland reached the public agenda after the death of a deportee from Sudan in 1999. In 2000, the anti-racism network 'No one is illegal' launched the campaign 'deportation class – no deal with expulsions'. To raise awareness of deportations, the campaign used the corporate design of previously state-owned Lufthansa, the biggest German air carrier, and made a public scandal of the practice of transferring irregular migrants abroad. The network organised camps, art events, airport rallies and online demonstrations. Against the advocacy of the anti-racism movement, both the air carrier and the airport operator filed complaints against the use of the corporate design and imposed an airport ban on participants in the demonstration (Spiegel online, 15 June 2000, 20 June 2001; Deportation Class, 2002). Hence politicisation of the border region shifted from an arrival migration flow and the detention of unauthorised persons at the airport to practices of deportation and the violation of human rights standards.

Similar to practices at the Frankfurt-Main airport removal centre, a platform to monitor deportations at odds with human rights standards was initiated in 2006 by the regional Catholic and Protestant churches and entitled *Forum Abschiebungsbeobachtung am Flughafen Frankfurt am Main* (FAFF) (Forum for the Observation of Deportations at Frankfurt-Main Airport). The forum consists of representatives from the police, UNHCR, the two churches, Amnesty International, Pro Asyl and the Refugees Council in Hesse. It meets every three months to discuss the humanitarian aspects of deportation from the airport. The churches each sponsor one observer. Between July 2009 and June 2010 the two observers witnessed approximately 300 deportations. They reported on the lack of food and poverty of the expellees, their medical state and airworthiness, family separations, the behaviour of the police, transport staff and private security, the situation of children and deportation under the Dublin II regulation to other EU member countries in charge of processing asylum applications (FAFF, 2010). With observation FAFF pursues a specific goal: 'The aim of observing deportation is to render a space not open to the public transparent... The members of FAFF are convinced that observing deportation de-escalates and has led to transparency and to improvement of the expelling process,' (FAFF, 2010: 15–16). Thus, by monitoring the border region, it contributes in particular to humanising administrative practices intended to deter (Kalinock and Göller, 2007; Kalinock and Schicke, 2008; FAFF, 2009 and 2010). The spatial character of the inside borderland is essentially shaped by a political compromise. Here, policies of securitisation and deterrence are tamed and humanised with catch-up political struggles that lead to a certain degree of humanisation and of visibility of 'the migrant' as a subject.

These policies, however, produced an unintended side effect, transforming the airport from a contested border space into a general space of contestation. In 2003, a demonstrator of the anti-deportation rallies was banned from the entire airport area. The airport operator, which acts as a private borderland authority, attempted to forestall demonstrations by imposing bans and enforcing restrictive house rules. The demonstrator in question filed a complaint, claiming that her right of assembly had been severely restricted. Three courts ruled against her. As the ultimate level of decision, the German Constitutional Court (Bundesverfassungsgericht), on the other hand, took a different perspective and in 2011 ruled that her right to freedom of assembly and freedom of speech had been breached. Two arguments were crucial to the court's decision. The first saw the pending case as a matter of ownership and as an obligation to civil rights. The airport operator, Fraport AG, argued that it was a private company, and that although the state of Hessen (31.5 per cent) and the city of Frankfurt (20.12 per cent) held the majority of Fraport AG shares, the entire corporation was on the stock market and must therefore be seen as a private subject not directly committed to guaranteeing civil rights. The three previous court proceedings had pursued a similar line of argument. The Constitutional Court did not. It ruled that as long as public jurisdictions held the majority of shares, they had a strong influence on the company. A mixed-economy enterprise of this kind must be understood as a state entity and guarantee fundamental civil rights such as freedom of assembly and freedom of speech (Bundesverfassungsgericht, 2011: para. 45–60). The second argument highlighted the functional character of the space: freedom of assembly in the form of access to public space and communicative forums must be guaranteed (Bundesverfassungsgericht, 2011: para. 68). The airport is characterised as a space 'designed with places to stroll and talk, and areas for shopping and gastronomy. It is therefore open for general public traffic and communication' (Bundesverfassungsgericht, 2011: para. 72). Beyond security areas and transport facilities, the airport (the entity for travellers, migrants, customers and employees) has a general public audience to which collective opinions can be addressed (Bundesverfassungsgericht, 2011: para. 78). Security matters and air traffic operations may restrict freedom of assembly (Bundesverfassungsgericht, 2011: para. 87). Imposing a blanket ban on airports for political reasons, however, and prohibiting demonstrations in general was refuted as disproportionate. Even minor nuisances are to be accepted (Bundesverfassungsgericht, 2011: para. 106). This adjudication was the culmination of contesting the border space and led to the redefinition of private shopping malls as public communicative forums. It does not apply, however, to airport sites where in- and outflows of unauthorised migration are administered within the frame of securitisation and deterrence.

Conclusion

As the case study shows, EU migration policy patterns are being shaped in a specific way. To begin with, border politics at Frankfurt-Main airport are characterised by an ambiguity similar to that inherent in European policy: the tension, if not contradiction, between deterrence and human rights. Frankfurt-Main airport in particular and airport procedure in general constitute a place and a course of action that is deliberately insurmountable. The regulatory framework, however, includes a commitment to the standards of international law. This ambiguity triggered contestation of the specific character of the space, whose bordering practices have an innate structural tension.

The pattern of contestation cannot adequately be explained by party differences in the German context. The airport procedure and its regulation was set up, accepted and retained over the last 20 years by various coalition cabinets. This also holds for executive practices at Frankfurt-Main airport, which have been organised and supervised by both left- and right-of-centre cabinets. Puzzling in terms of the assumption that parties matter is the proportionate decrease in airport proceedings that took place under a Christian Democratic cabinet. Hence parties and their programmatic cleavages do not sufficiently explain the conflict at hand. Close scrutiny of political discourse coalitions, on the other hand, contributes to an understanding of the struggle and its dynamics. Their pattern at Frankfurt-Main airport also resembles that of European migration policy. One discourse coalition interprets unauthorised mobility as a dangerous and uncontrolled flow, against which the state and its citizens should be protected. It pursues a policy of securitisation and deterrence with strict regulation, surveillance technologies, exclusive and isolated areas, harsh executive practices and systematic ill-treatment of migrants, thereby highlighting the repressive side of 'intent management' at borders (see Weber and Pickering, in this volume). With regard to the case study, a grand coalition of the two German catch-all parties (the conservative Christian Democrats and the Social Democrats), the Agency for Migration and Refugees, Border Guards, local administrative practitioners and the lower administrative courts are affiliated to this coalition. A second discourse coalition focuses on human rights standards for refugees and pursues a policy of humanisation and fair treatment in line with European and international law. NGOs, church welfare organisations, lawyers associations and higher courts are among those that refer to this problem definition and act in the interests of migrants. The third discourse coalition identified here understands the airport as a deliberately organised state of exception for unauthorised migrants, and pinpoints the border itself as the problem.

Some NGOs, anti-racism movement activists and individual migrants act within this frame. The three political discourse coalitions adopted separate functions in engaging with borders. As a result of the asymmetrical distribution of resources, the first of these set up the agenda for strict regulation, enforced their policy, designed and built the place, and established its rules in use, since it has political majorities, finance and personnel at its disposal, and commands the administration and state-run violence. The second coalition undertook humanisation and organised expertise through monitoring and legal politics, its chief method of holding the government accountable to human rights standards of international law. The third, insurrectionary coalition increased the cost of the rules in use with acts of resistance, which ultimately led to a borderland change.

This change sees a humanisation of the place and of administrative rules, on the one hand, and a form of dislocation, on the other. The decrease in airport procedures is matched by the dwindling relevance of the transit zone in relation to refugee camps and facilities across Germany. In essence, the general principle of dislocation and relocation of borders seems little different from the shifting spatial patterns of European migration policy. It derives, however, from the specific local spatial compromise in flux.

When it comes to the feature that distinguishes the inside borderland from external frontiers, it is useful to recap the former's essential discursive ambiguity and structural dynamic. Again, the touchstone is not the conflict between a deterrent policy of securitisation and human rights standards but rather the jurisdiction of the rule of law and organised legal logic. The key distinction is the probability that unauthorised migrants will be displaced from the inside borderland at low cost to territories where the rule of law is not in place because it is not organised. In other words, the moveable border element (tension between deterrence and human rights) gains momentum at the inside borderland, as lawyers, legal associations and higher courts have an interest in enforcing the rule of law, thereby increasing the likelihood of legal politics. Unauthorised migrants are formally subject to international law in all areas. At the borderland on the inside, however, the organised rule of law can hold the executive administration to account and change the rules of use by implementing international law. This systematically predisposes the borderland on the inside to invest 'the migrant' with the status of a legal cosmopolitan subject.

Note

1. This directive was the first legislative act under the co-decision procedure within the area of migration policy and includes a strong role of the European Parliament (Boswell and Geddes, 2011: 139–143).

6
The Interiorisation and Localisation of Border Control: A US Case

Robyn Magalit Rodriguez

In 2010, Jan Brewer, the Governor of the State of Arizona, signed SB 1070, a highly controversial law that has come to symbolise new attempts in the US by sub-national governmental units (in this case, state governments) to introduce legislation to prohibit the settlement and facilitate the expulsion of immigrants, especially undocumented Latinos. Despite much opposition, in June 2012 the US Supreme Court actually upheld the law's most hotly contested provision. It deemed that the law's requirement that law enforcement officers ask whether individuals they apprehend during the course of their regular duties are indeed legal residents of the US was constitutional (Liptak, 2012). By September 2012, a federal judge ruled that Arizona police could begin enforcing SB 1070. According to critics, like the American Civil Liberties Union (ACLU), the law allows state and local police to racially profile Latinos. In the State of Arizona, being Latino and 'immigrant-looking', often synonymous with 'undocumented-looking', is practically a criminal offence that renders one possibly subject to deportation. Since the passage of SB 1070, many other states have followed suit. There has been a great deal of discussion and debate about the ways states bordering Mexico and other states in the American South such as Alabama and Florida have been attempting to introduce similar anti-immigrant legislation (e.g. see Robertson, 2012). However, state attempts to regulate the settlement of immigrants are a national trend. Even before SB 1070 was signed into law, the National Conference of State Legislatures reported that in 2009, state governments considered over 1500 laws related to immigration. 353 became law in 48 states in 2012 (NCSL, 2012).

Just as importantly, though overlooked in national news headlines and only recently garnering attention among scholars, anti-immigration legislation has also started to be introduced at the level of the *municipal* government. One study suggests that between May 2006 and September 2007, anti-immigrant ordinances were considered by over 100 cities and counties in 30 different states. In addition to enhancing cooperation between local police and federal immigration enforcement officers, these local ordinances prohibit immigrants' employment (through employer sanctions and day labourer prohibitions), as well as prohibit their settlement (through rental restrictions or restrictions to immigrant children's access to education) and promote 'English only' legislation (Esbenshade and Obzurt, 2007–2008; Gilbert, 2009). These ordinances are 'back door' attempts to regulate immigration (Varsanyi, 2008); that is, while these policies may not explicitly address the issue of undocumented immigration, they nevertheless are ultimately intended to target those presumed to be undocumented – generally Latino immigrants.

This chapter maps the various local initiatives that restrict immigrants' settlement in and facilitate their expulsion from different towns and cities across the state of New Jersey. I suggest that border enforcement and the notion of 'homeland security' is increasingly taking place in new sites and on a different scale. There has been a new interiorisation and localisation of 'border enforcement'. Border enforcement has been 'interiorised' in that it no longer only takes place at the site of national borders (in the case of the US, the border that has incited the most concern with respect to immigration has been the US–Mexico border), but instead is taking place within the interior of the US. Border enforcement has become 'localised' in the sense that sub-national police units are becoming engaged in the work of border enforcement. However, it is not always the local police doing that enforcement. Local government representatives, from housing inspectors to school officials, are also taking up the task of 'border security' which has not only taken the form of detention and expulsion, but also the prohibition of immigrant settlement (see Weber and Pickering, in this volume, for similar developments in Australia). The range of policy instruments that has been advocated for, and in some cases successfully implemented in, different towns and cities in New Jersey, moreover, normalises immigration enforcement. Hence, 'citizen' organisations and ordinary people have articulated discourses of and taken on the practices of border enforcement as well. This perspective shows the reverse side of Mara Sidney's analysis of NGOs at the local level who are working to tear down internal barriers by actively promoting solidarity and inclusion of undocumented migrants (see Sidney, this volume). What is at stake in these border practices is American citizenship, particularly social citizenship and the restriction of its benefits and entitlements, only to those who are deemed to be genuine citizens. These border practices are ultimately about securing the boundaries of belonging in communities. Local authorities and citizens take up the task of border security and enforcement in the most intimate of sites: the site of the 'home'.

The securitisation of migration and the rise of the 'Homeland Security State'

The interiorisation and localisation of border security politics has continued to intensify since 9/11. City, county and state government officials introducing laws to regulate the settlement of immigrants as well as to ultimately expel them often justify their actions as necessary in the absence of what they perceive to be adequate federal immigration restrictions. Yet, it was national security policies passed in the wake of the 9/11 terrorist attacks of New York's World Trade Center that have enabled local authorities to introduce measures to restrict immigrants and immigration. In other words, if city, county and state governments are responding to what they claim is a failure of federal policy on immigration, their very ability to respond is in large part possible because of federal policy. This federal policy, while spurred by national security concerns, is ultimately designed to fix on heightening the surveillance, apprehension, detention and deportation of immigrants, both documented and undocumented. However, the genealogy of contemporary immigration policy reaches back to 1996, with the Illegal Immigration Reform and Immigrant Responsibility Act (IIRIRA).

Despite its foundations in pre-9/11 immigration policy, the present immigration enforcement regime is marked by important distinctions. Since 9/11, the regulation of migration has come to be increasingly a national security concern. What we are witnessing is a 'securitization of migration' (Huysman, 2000) and the rise of the 'Homeland Security' state (De Genova, 2007). In the US, this means that national security and immigration enforcement is aimed not only at securing the nation's borders against external threats, but the interior of the 'homeland' from perceived threats. What the current regime does carry over from IIRIRA, and indeed more effectively implements, is the localisation of immigration enforcement. Under the IIRIRA, a programme known as 287(g) was introduced. This programme enables local police to be trained and certified as federal immigration enforcement agents (Wong, 2012).

To secure the 'homeland' since the rise of the Homeland Security State is to police the borders of the nation-state against immigrants and terrorists, who have become conjoined in the minds of lawmakers on all levels and among ordinary people. Indeed, terrorism and criminality has also become connected in the sense that both terrorism and criminal activity can lead to feelings of anxiety and insecurity. Hence, undocumented, so-called 'illegal' immigrants are seen as the primary suspects for disturbing a sense of domestic peace. 'Illegals' are ultimately 'criminals' and therefore only a small step away from being 'terrorists'. Today, the undocumented immigrant is often construed not only as having a propensity to criminality, but even a predisposition to commit acts of terrorism. A person willing to violate immigration codes, so the logic goes, is highly likely to commit a number of crimes and perhaps even terrorist acts; this is a logic that has shaped municipal immigration struggles in New Jersey.

While today's homeland security state apparatus is aimed at protecting the 'homeland' (i.e. the nation-state), it is also about protecting the 'home' (i.e. the neighbourhood or local community). The ordinances that have been introduced, particularly by municipal governments, address issues and concerns that are at the centre of what many Americans believe to be their birthright and that constitutes the key elements of the 'American Dream': safety, housing and education. It was African Americans' exclusion from these aspects of the 'American Dream,' for example, that defined their 'second-class citizenship'. Not surprisingly then, these issues are all at the centre of contestations over American citizenship in towns across the country, if not simply across the state of New Jersey. The 'border' is both a literal and a figurative one. The 'border' that is perhaps most meaningful to many Americans is the 'border' that demarcates the place where they live – the boundaries that enclose their neighborhoods and homes. This border is also ultimately a border or boundary not just defining a geographic space, but defining the difference between citizen and non-citizen, a boundary that is also a racialised one, defining whites as citizens and non-whites as non-citizens. For example, in a study similar to mine, Adler (2006) discusses the impacts of immigration enforcement on the Latino community in Chambersburg, NJ. She describes how specific neighbourhood spaces were literally 'defended' by earlier generations of whites against previously defined 'outsiders':

> Several informants mentioned how Puerto Ricans, the earliest Latinos in Trenton, were not allowed in Italian Chambersburg. Columbus Park rests on the edge of the neighborhood and it was there that the ethnic boundaries of the district were defended by its youth.
>
> (Adler, 2006: 54)

This chapter conceives of the interiorisation and localisation of border enforcement as an enforcement of the boundaries of social citizenship as it is most intimately experienced and understood on an everyday basis as much as about the enforcement of actual geographic boundaries (on the relationship between bordering and citizenship practices, see also Rygiel, in this volume). Indeed, these processes are related, as social citizenship is generally tied to residence (or employment) within a specific geographic space. More and more, Americans are feeling economically 'insecure'. While this feeling of economic insecurity has been especially acute since the financial crisis, the fact is that American social citizenship has been under attack since the 1980s with the rise of 'Reaganomics', which marked the beginning of aggressive attacks on public goods and services, including but not limited to welfare. Even under the Clinton administration, the attacks on entitlements did not wane, as that administration introduced major reforms to the welfare system. According to Barlow, Americans' 'new focus on local autonomy and local control has become an increasingly important way for racially and nationally privileged people to fend off the downward pressure of globalization' (Barlow, 2003: 84).

Moreover, I argue that the rescaling of border politics is linked to what William Walters calls 'domopolitics'. He argues,

> [D]omopolitics implies a reconfiguring of the relations between citizenship, state and territory. At its heart is a fateful conjunction of home, land and security.... [I]t has powerful affinities with family, intimacy, place: the home as heart, a refuge or sanctuary in a heartless world; the home as *our* place, where we belong naturally, and where, by definition, others do not.
>
> (Walters, 2004: 241)

For Walters, domopolitics describes the logics of homeland security politics in the contemporary post-9/11 world, but I would suggest that domopolitics actually plays itself out on a much smaller scale. Moreover, domopolitics arguably has a longer genealogy and is linked to the 'American Dream' as defined by suburban living. Suburban living refers to owning a house located outside of urban centres. What is notable about the interiorisation and localisation of border enforcement in New Jersey is that it is taking place generally in the suburbs.

This chapter is a case study of New Jersey, where the interiorisation and localisation of border enforcement is especially stark, as many municipalities across the state have garnered national media attention for their initiative and zealousness in introducing and implementing anti-undocumented-immigrant municipal policies. Border enforcement ranges from outright expulsion (either through detention or through deportation as a result of local governments' cooperation with federal authorities), or prohibitions against settlement (through restrictions of migrants working and living in specific localities), to intimidation and violence against migrants on an everyday basis.

The localisation and interiorisation of border enforcement: The case of New Jersey

The case study, as mentioned earlier, focuses on the state of New Jersey. New Jersey is an especially important locale for examining the interiorisation and localisation of border enforcement. First, New Jersey is far from the US–Mexico border, yet it has been an active site of immigration enforcement. It therefore exemplifies 'interiorisation'. Second, several of its municipalities have earned national attention for being among the first to introduce local ordinances regulating or prohibiting migration. It is thus a good example of 'localisation'.

Local-federal cooperation in immigration enforcement

Post-9/11 homeland security measures encouraged increased linkages and cooperation between local police units and federal immigrant enforcement officers. The Department of Homeland Security did not mandate local-federal cooperation; however, local (both municipal and state-level) governmental units took the initiative to cooperate with Immigration and Customs Enforcement on both a formal and informal basis.

Mayor Donald Cresitello of Morristown, New Jersey made national news in 2007 (three years before Arizona Governor Jan Brewer signed SB 1070), appearing on National Public Radio (NPR) and the Cable News Network (CNN), announcing that he was applying to the so-called the 287(g) programme, a federal programme which deputises local police as immigration enforcement officers (ICE, 2012). Cresitello, a Democrat, was among the first mayors in the country to apply for the programme and the first to do so in New Jersey (Rockland, 2008; NJ.com, 2009).

In an interview on NPR, when Mayor Cresitello was asked why he applied to the 287(g) programme, he replied:

> [F]irst of all, it's...a homeland security issue. Morristown manages an airport, for police protection. It's a major hospital, major office buildings and certainly, we need to be working closer with Homeland Security. As was indicated with Fort Dix a week ago, these problems can be uncovered at a local level. It'd be easier if there's cooperation. Also, with the increased problems with day labourers, with stacking, federal, criminal violations of federal immigration law we felt and I personally felt that it was better if we would be directly in contact with and participate with ICE [Immigration and Customs Enforcement] in any investigations going to take place in Morristown.
>
> (NPR, 2007)

Here, Cresitello sees his efforts at applying to the 287(g) programme as continuous with and an enhancement of national security imperatives. In the mayor's view, Morristown has what might be considered strategic targets for terrorists (a hospital, an airport, or corporate offices). In this statement, he not only represents the securing of Morristown as linked with the securing of the nation, he represents terrorism as linked with undocumented migration. The threat of Islamist terrorists such as those who were charged with conspiring to attack Fort Dix is linked to 'problems with day labourers' (Russakoff and Eggen, 2007).

Cresitello's application to the 287(g) programme was the target of both support and opposition by various local, state and national groups (Fahim, 2007b; Hassan, 2007a; Hassan, 2007b; Duffy, 2009). Notably, the Morris County government, with whom Cresitello would have to cooperate in order to be accepted into the 287(g) programme, rejected the mayor's request to open an unused wing of the Morris County jail to hold immigrant detainees apprehended upon the Morristown police's deputisation under 287(g). Among the concerns raised by officials was the cost to the county that reopening the wing would have (Llorente, 2008). However, in 2007, the same year Cresitello applied to the 287(g) programme, the state's Attorney General, Anne Milgram, issued a directive that clarified and ultimately sanctioned cooperation between local police and federal immigration authorities. The directive states, 'While immigration enforcement is primarily a federal responsibility, State, county and local law enforcement agencies necessarily and appropriately should inquire about a person's immigration status under certain circumstances,' (Corzine and Milgram, 2007). By the end of 2007, the number of undocumented immigrants who were arrested for immigration violations was double the number in 2006. ICE officials attribute this increase to closer work with local police (Donohue, 2007). They Morris County government's rejection of Major Cresitello's request and hampered his 287(g) application, yet after the Attorney General's directive, Morristown was among New Jersey's top cities referring undocumented immigrants to ICE (Hassan, 2008). Indeed, immigrant rights advocates report that immigrants 'had been questioned about their status during routine traffic stops – especially in rural areas – or witness interviews' by local police which advocates described as 'overzealous enforcement' (Fahim, 2008). This is a clear example of the interiorisation of 'border enforcement' and the normalisation of this kind of practice among local police.

Attorney General Milgram's directive clarifying local-federal cooperation with respect to immigration status was issued directly after the execution-style killing of who were described in many local news accounts as 'college students' in Newark in 2007. Much was made in the press as well as by officials, not only of the undocumented status of the suspected killers, but of their nationalities: Peruvian and Nicaraguan. The racial or ethnic backgrounds, as well as the gender of the victims are left unmentioned, but their status as 'college students' is highlighted. Significantly, Cresitello, in other interviews, explains that his interest in deputising local police as immigration agents was also prompted by a murder committed by an undocumented Honduran immigrant. The focus on the undocumented status and the nationality (specifically their origins in Latin America) of these perpetrators is linked to older discourse of Mexican immigrant criminality that has circulated since the debates to end the Bracero Programme (1942–1964) (Jacobson, 2008). Both Mayor Cresitello and Attorney General Milgram draw connections between undocumented migration and criminality. Street crime, similar to terrorism yet also qualitatively different, contributes to feeling 'unsafe', yet safety is the defining characteristic of suburban life.

Despite Milgrim's directive essentially sanctioned local-federal cooperation on immigration matters yet, county officials in other parts of New Jersey applied to the 287(g) programme to formalise that cooperation. In 2008 Hudson County and then in 2009 Monmouth County each secured a Memorandum of Understanding with the Department of Homeland Security to begin the process of having their county police trained and certified as ICE agents (ICE, 2012).

From the municipal (Morristown), to the county (Hudson and Monmouth) to the state (New Jersey) level, government representatives have attempted to, and in some cases have been successful, in formalising cooperation between local police units and ICE. Indeed, among these initiatives are those (i.e. applications to the 287(g) programme) which attempt to extend federal immigration enforcement authority to law enforcement officers locally. These are all examples of the localisation of immigration enforcement as linked to Huysman's (2000, 2006) concept of the securitisation of migration. Moreover, the arguments advanced by officials draw connections between undocumented immigration, terrorism and criminality. Border security becomes interiorised in the process.

Because immigration enforcement has increased dramatically (despite many state and local government officials' claims that enforcement mechanisms under the Department of Homeland Security are not sufficient), federal authorities have had to outsource the detention of immigrants to county facilities. Federal facilities cannot accommodate the growing numbers of immigrants that are being swept up in the housing, workplace and street raids that have become so commonplace. At the same time, contracting to house immigrant detainees from ICE raids can be a lucrative source of revenue for local governmental authorities (Kirkham, 2011). In other words, if local authorities are taking the initiative to extend and expand the scope of their policing in order to perform the functions of immigration enforcement, federal authorities have sought cooperation with local authorities in detaining undocumented immigrants they are already apprehending and rewarding local authorities for that cooperation. In the state of New Jersey, there are presently five counties with ICE contracts (ICE, 2013).

While county jailers are receiving federal funding for partnering with ICE, many have failed to comply with or, as immigrant rights and detainees claim, have wilfully neglected federal standards governing the treatment of immigrant detainees. Activists report that several detainees have died in jail and that there is widespread neglect in county facilities. Indeed, a federal audit of New Jersey's county jails confirmed that several county jails in New Jersey were in fact problematic (Department of Homeland Security, 2006; Fisher, 2007) and even after the audit, reports of abuse continued to surface (Bernstein, 2009). Among the most egregious cases were at the Passaic County jail, where attack dogs were used against immigrant detainees in ways that detainees as well as advocates likened to torture techniques deployed against post-9/11 detainees in Guantanamo Bay; indeed, Muslims and Arabs were targeted in particular (Bernstein, 2006). Here we see the implicit connections jailers make between the undocumented and terrorists in their treatment of immigrant detainees.

Prohibiting immigrant settlement

Other municipalities have attempted to regulate the presence of immigrants within their jurisdictions, not through policies of policing, detention and ultimately expulsion, but through housing and employment exclusions.

A number of municipalities have tried to introduce ordinances that require local officers to more stringently enforce housing codes against 'stacking', or to fine landlords who rent properties to undocumented immigrants. 'Stacking' refers to the situation where the maximum number of residents allowed to occupy a single residential property is exceeded. While it may be argued that college and university students, for example, are often 'stacked' in residential units, and that indeed, 'stacking' may be a strategy more and more families engage in as they make new kinds of housing arrangements to cope with today's financial crisis (see for example, Armour, 2009; Mykyta, 2012), it is immigrants, especially Latino immigrants, who have been and are likely to continue to be the target of housing code enforcement. This was the case, for example, in Englewood, NJ (Glazer, 2004). Indeed, housing code enforcement ultimately mobilises non-police officials as well as private citizens to play a role in the regulation of immigration.

In 2006, the mayor and township committee of Riverside, NJ, unanimously approved a measure that made it the very first municipality in New Jersey to enact legislation that would penalise landlords or home sellers who rented or sold residential property to undocumented immigrants. Moreover, attempts to introduce and pass similar codes have occurred in other municipalities. The borough of Bound Brook had already been cited by the US Department of Justice in 2004 for waging a campaign to drive out Latinos through its housing code enforcement practices, which the town settled; however, four years after this citation, the borough council president attempted to (re)introduce a housing code that would require landlords to verify prospective tenants' immigration status. Alongside this code, the council president attempted to introduce a policy that would require local police to check the immigration status of those they arrest, as well as a policy to deny borough contracts to businesses that hire undocumented immigrants (Brunstein, 2008). A housing ordinance was also introduced in Middletown (ibid.).

Mexican immigrants have not been the only group that has suffered from the enforcement of 'stacking' laws. In Woodbridge Township, NJ, there is a high concentration of Indian immigrants. In 2006, the mayor had made the announcement to step up the enforcement of housing codes, and Indians were disproportionately targeted (Fahim, 2007a). Alarm about the increasing Indian immigrant population in neighbouring communities has continued to be sounded. According to one council member in Edison, NJ, some community members have complained that 'immigrants have been buying up homes, rather than people who worked hard to establish the community' (Berger, 2008).

Often passed alongside housing ordinances are ordinances that prohibit immigrant day labourers from seeking employment on the street. Indeed, when Riverside's township council unanimously voted to ban the selling or renting of property to undocumented immigrants, it also voted to ban the hiring of them. In 2003, Freehold Borough closed a 'muster zone' where employers went to seek day labourers. Though the ordinance was challenged by immigrant advocates and the borough ultimately settled the lawsuit in 2006, the mayor vowed to continue to enforce housing codes (Spoto, 2006). In addition to Freehold, Lakewood began deliberations on introducing a measure to get rid of day labourers as well (Santos, 2006).

Local officials have even tried to prevent the children of immigrants from attending school. In Fairview, NJ, the superintendent, David Verducci, ordered five children to be expelled from a local elementary school when he learned that their parents were undocumented. The superintendent was later instructed to readmit the children by the state's Department of Education (Newman, 2002). Nevertheless, a 2008 report by the American Civil Liberties Union (ACLU) found that the phenomenon was much more widespread across the state of New Jersey (Education Week, 2008).

Furthermore, local officials have attempted to prohibit immigrant entrepreneurs as well as other businesses catering to bilingual and multilingual customers to stop using languages other than English in their signage. This was the case in Bogota, NJ, when Mayor Steve Lonegan, a leader in New Jersey's conservative movement, launched a campaign to eliminate a Spanish-language McDonald's billboard. His crusade, like that of Cresitello's, made national headlines, once again putting New Jersey on the national immigration politics map (Alaya, 2006; Bernstein, 2007).

All of these examples of attempting to regulate housing, employment, schooling and even marketing to immigrants, mainly Latinos, are further examples of both localised and interiorised border enforcement. Here, the localisation of border enforcement does not merely refer to local policing efforts, but indeed to the role of other local authorities from housing code enforcers to school officials in restricting immigrant settlement in local communities. The interiorisation of border enforcement is reflected in the ways that immigrant settlement is being regulated at the level of the town or city. The aim by local authorities is to prevent immigrants from enjoying the already limited rights of social and cultural citizenship. It is about reifying the 'border' around, or boundary between, citizen and non-citizen to ensure that the enjoyment of security of employment, housing and the social reproduction of children is denied to those who are considered 'outsiders'.

Normalisation of immigration 'enforcement'

While local, county and state officials have all played a role in border enforcement, it must be noted that they often do so together with organised anti-immigrant groups. For instance, chapters of the New Jersey Citizens for Immigration Control have been forming up and down the state. The group is aimed not only at supporting anti-immigration federal legislators and legislation but also at fighting to limit state and local benefits for immigrants. Their website declares, 'The Migration Policy Institute reports that it costs New Jersey taxpayers about $400 million annually to support illegals with public benefits! Help us fight free hospital care, disability, and other benefits for illegals. We also oppose legislative proposals to give them favourable in-state college tuition and driving "privileges"' (NJCFIC, 2012). Following Mayor Cresitello's lead, a group has also taken on what it calls 'Project 287(g)' to encourage other municipalities to apply, as Mayor Cresitello did, for the training and deputisation of local police. In July 2007 they went on foot in Bergenfield to collect signatures in support of 287(g) and had planned to go before the Bogota Borough Council on 19 July 2007 to encourage the Council to apply for the programme. Later that month, Bogota's mayor confirmed that he would, like Cresitello, put forth an application under 287(g). Mayor Lonegan already had links with the United Patriots of America, a local New Jersey anti-immigration group. Lonegan declared, 'any immigration whatsoever that violates the laws of this country should not be tolerated. We've now allowed America to become a free-for-all' (Perez, 2005).

In addition to the Project 287(g) campaign, and often part of it, the group has mobilised public forums and demonstrations against undocumented immigration in different municipalities across the state in the last two years. In June 2008, it held a forum on 'the Effects of Illegal Immigration on the New Jersey Taxpayer' in Sayreville, NJ; the month before that (in May) the group organised an Anti-Illegal Immigration Rally in Lakewood. Additionally, in 2007, the group organised a Rally for Immigration Control/287(g) in Fairview.

Perhaps to avoid accusations of racism, the group does have links with anti-immigration Latinos, most notably the group, 'You Don't Speak for Me'. Moreover, the group makes distinctions among 'legal' and 'illegal' Latinos, but these distinctions are classed. While anti-immigrant, presumably white groups attempt to define membership by virtue of legal status, they also attempt to define membership by virtue of class. Mayor Cresitello, who has participated in activities organised by groups like the New Jersey Citizens for Immigration Control, makes distinctions between Latino groups, as suggested in a radio interview: 'Certainly we have a wonderful Columbian community that came into the country legally, they're established businesses, they purchased homes and fixed their homes just like other groups before them and there's no tension... [T]he resentment is that illegal groups simply congregate on the streets'. Of course, it may well be, too, that middle-class Latinos have joined together with anti-immigrant groups to make their own claims to membership within particular communities. What is interesting also about the New Jersey Citizens for Immigration Control is the way it links undocumented immigration with terrorism; one of the main organisations it has featured in its activities is the 9/11 Families for a Secure America.

Immigration politics, moreover, have come to be normalised in daily life. An article on bullying programmes in elementary schools describes how an 11-year-old girl suffers from bullying at her school. She says, 'It's hard to ignore them. They call me "immigrant," and girls tell me, "You're so ugly, your clothes don't match"'. Meanwhile, Sikhs, often misrecognised as Arab Muslims, have increasingly suffered from racially motivated violence since 9/11. In Hightstown in May 2008, a high school student's turban was burned, while in Hoboken earlier in 2008, a woman tried to remove a man's turban while he was dining in a restaurant (Coyne, 2008).

Conclusion

The enforcement of borders has not always been about flows of immigrants from other countries, but actually the drawing up and enforcement of borders on a much more intimate level – that is, at the level of municipalities, towns and cities, neighbourhoods where people live out their everyday lives; in places people call 'home'.

Though not the focus of this chapter, immigrants, their advocates and government supporters have responded in numerous ways to these attempts at preventing immigrant settlement in different communities. Many local authorities, often in response to the actions of their counterparts in other municipalities, are actively welcoming immigrants, regardless of immigration status, as Mara Sidney also shows in her chapter. In New Jersey, the city of Trenton ordered local police not to call immigration officials when they apprehend a person who they suspect or may actually be undocumented. The mayor of Hightstown took a similar stance (Llorente and Perez, 2005).

Immigrant rights activists have engaged in more conventional political action and have turned local officials out of office during elections. This was true in the Riverside case, as voters ousted the Republican mayor, Charles Hilton, under whose leadership and initiative anti-immigration local ordinances were introduced. Due to the drastic economic effects it had on Riverside and the mayor's own admission that the policy may have been ill thought out, citizens of Riverside decided to end his tenure (Pearsall, 2006). In Freehold the Borough's ordinance against day laborers the matter was decided in court, as local immigrant rights activists sued the Borough Council and ultimately forced the municipality to settle with the day labourers named in the suit (Spoto, 2006). At the same time, immigrant rights activists and advocates have also attempted less conventional means to safeguard undocumented migrants' lives. For instance, though largely failed, immigrant rights groups attempted to form 'Rapid Response Teams' in different neighbourhoods. The idea is that immigrants who suspect that immigration enforcement agents might apprehend them call on these teams to prevent agents from doing their jobs, even if it means physically getting in between immigrants and agents. In a highly unusual case, a member of the clergy negotiated with ICE directly, advocating for the release of immigrants in their custody (Semple, 2011).

The point I hope to underscore in this chapter is that we need to consider 'border' politics at different sites and on a different scale, on a more local scale within today's Homeland Security State regime. Indeed, border politics under the Homeland Security State regime is ultimately about the politics of 'home,' that is, who belongs in a town or municipality, who it is that should count as a neighbour, and who it is that should count as a friend. 'Home' for most Americans is the suburbs. The suburbs are where American citizenship, as a white, middle-class franchise, is exercised and achieved. New Jersey in particular was among the first states where the suburb as a social experiment was born. What occurs in New Jersey, therefore, offers insights into processes taking place nationally. The Homeland Security State is one that functions around a domopolitics; hence it has become interiorised and localised. The borders that are at stake are not national ones, but the fences that encircle the suburbs.

7
Outsiders/Insiders: How Local Immigrant Organisations Contest the Exclusion of Undocumented Immigrants in the US

Mara Sidney

Non-governmental organisations (NGOs) serving immigrants in US cities face a complex policy domain that poses significant obstacles to their goals of helping immigrants to settle, to forge new lives and to become part of the community fabric. One major hurdle is the negative image of unauthorised immigrants that dominates US policy and politics, casting them as threats to Americans' safety, security and quality of life. NGOs respond that unauthorised immigrants are embedded in local community life through work and family, and frequently through longstanding residence. They are very much interconnected with other community members, although they frequently encounter punitive and exclusionary laws and policies, which treat them as outsiders. A second feature of the immigration policy domain is its fragmentation across government levels. While the national level of government dominates policy-making and implementation, state and local policies importantly shape immigrants' day-to-day experiences. NGOs therefore target different levels of government for resources or policy changes, depending on their particular mission. This chapter examines how local immigrant-serving NGOs navigate this challenging landscape, creating discursive frames that counter the negative image of unauthorised immigrants as they pursue, at various levels of government, their goals of enabling immigrants to build lives in US cities.

Both outside and inside borders

The experiences of unauthorised immigrants in the US illustrate how borders come inside the nation-state, and become part of social interactions in communities. National policies operating inside communities exclude unauthorised immigrants from many parts of the workplace, from many social benefit programmes, from access to financial aid for higher education and from other realms of activity and social participation. The threat of discovery, detention and deportation is ever-present. State and local policies sometimes echo this exclusion, fortifying these internal borders through the denial of driving licences, of reduced-cost university tuition and the like. Borders thereby work to hinder immigrants' security and socio-economic mobility. Yet as they are excluded in so many ways by these internal borders, unauthorised immigrants and their advocates also challenge and even overcome them. Their US-citizen children and relatives, their work lives, and their lives as neighbours all attest to the ways in which these immigrants 'cross' borders and exist as citizens of sorts, inside the nation-state. Moreover, some state and local policies officially include them through, for example, enforcement of workers' rights, provision of services in their native languages and other measures.

In its presentation of NGOs that challenge the exclusion of unauthorised immigrants, this chapter complements Rodriguez's chapter (this volume). She illustrates how borders come inside local communities when national policy leverages the manpower of local law enforcement. She presents cases of local officials defending their communities against immigrants, especially unauthorised immigrants. My analysis shows alternative scenarios in which local organisations respond to various oppressive policies by asserting a perspective on immigrants that places them very much inside and even legitimately inside communities. NGOs work on a variety of fronts to help immigrants settle and prosper. This sort of work is what Rygiel theorises (this volume) as 'practices of citizenship', here implemented on behalf of, and by, those for whom legal citizenship is not possible. Her theoretical and empirical depictions of resistance to, and solidarity against, oppression complement my analysis.

My analysis is informed by literature in the fields of public policy and migration studies. A growing body of work documents the role that NGOs play in serving and advocating for immigrants (e.g. Bloemraad, 2006; de Graauw, 2008), consistent with the growing role of NGOs across policy domains generally (Salamon, 1995; Smith and Lipsky, 1993). In addition, studies have documented the multilevel governance of immigration in localities (Tolley and Young, 2011), whether *de facto* (the case primarily in the US) or through formal partnerships across government levels (e.g. in Canada). The study of policy discourse is by now well-established, and work in many areas of public policy shows how organised interests deploy ideas strategically in service of their policy goals (Fischer and Forester, 1993; Stone, 2002). Public policies advance sets of ideas about policy problems as much as they set in motion a series of specific instruments to address those problems (Schneider and Ingram, 1997; Yanow, 1996). My work sits at the nexus of these bodies of literature, by demonstrating that NGOs serve immigrants as much by promulgating alternative ideas about them as by offering concrete services to help them make their way in US cities.

The chapter begins by setting the context in which pro-immigrant NGOs work in the US, including discussion of the population of unauthorised immigrants and the policy history that gave rise to this group of people. I sketch the distinctive roles of national and subnational governments in immigration policy-making, which result in a fragmented policy sphere. The chapter then profiles three local immigrant-serving organisations in Newark in the state of New Jersey, which represent distinct types of NGOs. Each interacts with different levels and sectors of government, and develops narratives about undocumented immigrants that reflect its mission and its government targets. Each works in its own way to break down the national borders inside communities through dissemination of alternative ideas about immigrants and through service provision to them. That is, NGOs differently situated in the city and pursuing different goals develop different perspectives on the groups they serve, including undocumented immigrants. When NGO staff members employ narratives about undocumented immigrants, they do so partly strategically to advance their goals, but the narratives also reflect actual knowledge about these people that they have gained as they carry out their missions on a daily basis.

Unauthorised immigrants in the US

In 2011, the US was home to 40 million immigrants, representing about 13 per cent of the total population. The Census Bureau estimates that about 54 per cent of immigrants come from Latin America (including Mexico), about 27 per cent from Asia, 13 per cent from Europe, 4 per cent from other areas including Africa and Oceania, and 2 per cent from Canada (US Census Bureau, 2010). The top five sending countries include Mexico (29 per cent), India (4.6), the Philippines (4.5), China (4.1) and Vietnam (3.1) (Pew Hispanic Center, 2013). These migration flows fuel a growing diversity in the US, where Latino and Asian populations represent the fastest growing in the country; it is estimated that by 2043 there will no longer be a majority racial/ethnic group (Cooper, 2012). Of the immigrant population, 72 per cent have legal status and 28 per cent do not (Passel and Cohn, 2011). In 2011, it was estimated that about 11 million immigrants were unauthorised (Passel and Cohn, 2012).

Trends and national origins

The population of unauthorised immigrants in the US was estimated to have grown significantly from 1990 to 2007, at which point it began to decline (Passel and Cohn, 2011). Today's estimated population of about 11 million people represents a tripling of the 1990 population and growth by one-third since 2000, when it stood at 8.4 million (ibid.). The peak in recent years was an estimated 12 million people in 2007. The majority (58 per cent) of unauthorised immigrants are Mexican, with 23 per cent from other Latin American countries, 11 per cent from Asian countries, 4 per cent from Europe and Canada, and 3 per cent from African and other countries (Passel and Cohn, 2011: 11). An estimated one million were under the age of 18 (Pew Hispanic Center, 2013).

Passel and Cohn attribute the decline in unauthorised immigrants to declining numbers of Mexican immigrants generally, and among the undocumented (2012). That is, in 2000 the majority of immigrants arriving from Mexico came illegally, whereas by 2010, the majority came as legal immigrants and the numbers had fallen significantly (from 770,000 to 140,000 people) (ibid.). Estimated numbers of unauthorised immigrants from other countries remain unchanged since 2007. These authors suggest that several factors have driven declining numbers of Mexican immigrants including the 2007–2009 recession and the subsequent slow recovery, increases in deportation and other enforcement activities, and changes in conditions within Mexico.

Unauthorised immigrants inhabit an uncomfortable position in the US, being 'at once welcome and unwelcome' (Ngai, 2004: 2), at once outside the nation in the sense of formal membership and legitimacy and inside the nation in the sense of being part of ethno-racial communities, mixed-status families and the labour force (ibid.). Indeed, the Pew Hispanic Center reports that '[i]n 2010, nearly two-thirds of unauthorised immigrants had lived in the US for at least a decade, and nearly half (46%) were parents of minor children' (Pew Hispanic Center, 2013: 3). We can think of policies regarding unauthorised immigrants as emphasising either their insider or outsider status – that is, policies that would enable immigrants to regularise and to stay with their families would acknowledge them as insiders, whereas policies that aim to identify and deport them acknowledge their status as outsiders.

Public opinion, discourse and policy images

Public opinion about immigration in the US is marked by concerns about unauthorised immigrants, and indeed, public discourse on the subject of immigration, both in the media and among government officials, is dominated by discussions of unauthorised immigrants as outsiders. When polled, majorities of US residents state that immigration should be restricted, and levels should decrease. A slight majority thinks that immigration is more of a problem than an opportunity, and most believe undocumented immigrants drain public resources (Bloemraad and de Graauw, 2011). They also believe that most US immigrants are illegal, which (as noted above) is not true (ibid.).

Dominant discourse and policy about unauthorised immigrants emphasises their outsider status. But debates about immigration in the US also have long been marked by narratives about the 'right and wrong kinds of immigrants' (Newton, 2005: 139). Unauthorised immigrants in particular have been characterised as the 'wrong' kind – that is, as freeloaders who use resources otherwise destined for taxpaying citizens, as inherently criminal given their unauthorised border crossing, as engaging in criminal activity in the US (ibid.). Such images appear in Congressional debates on immigration policy and are used to justify the adoption of increasingly punitive border enforcement policies (ibid.), such as those described below. Because of the dual outsider/insider status of unauthorised immigrants, other competing images certainly are available, and indeed are used by immigrant rights' advocates to argue for legalisation and for less punitive enforcement. Unauthorised immigrants are in many cases longstanding members of communities and many have American-born (therefore US-citizen) children; they participate in the work force and pay taxes; and many young people without documentation aspire to attend college. Thus advocates seek to persuade policy-makers that they are insiders and, contrary to conventional wisdom, the 'right' kind of immigrants after all.

Immigration policy history: The emergence of undocumented immigrants

What often becomes lost in today's policy debates about unauthorised immigrants is the fact that the US creates this group of people through its policies regulating migration and restricting categories of migrants. Imposing caps on immigration flows or strictly conditioning or making impossible the regularisation of immigration status, coupled with the longstanding labour demand in the US (in particular for Mexican workers, but others as well), give rise to unauthorised migration. Studies document that enforcement may lead to changes in the routes, methods and costs that unauthorised migrants bear to cross the border, but tend not to stop migrants from coming (e.g., Andreas, 2009; Massey, 2007). Despite an ebb and flow to the numbers, as noted above, one could argue that unless US policy changes fundamentally, some degree of unauthorised migration will always occur. Indeed, as McKeown argues, exclusion has long been at the heart of migration control, even as regulations also enabled cross-border movement in keeping with liberal ideals about individual freedoms (2008).

The 'problem' of unauthorised immigration was born after 1924, with the passage of that year's Immigration Act, which imposed national quotas on immigration. Prior to that time, and notably when migration from Europe was at its peak, immigration was largely unrestricted, with the exception of the Chinese Exclusion adopted in 1882. For most migrants, then, there were no rules to break, they entered freely and began their new lives. But administrative mechanisms of exclusion developed for Chinese people were employed more broadly a few decades later (McKeown, 2011).

Although the 1924 Act excluded the Western Hemisphere from the quotas it imposed on the rest of the world, new requirements for passports and visas affected Mexican immigrants. State Department workers, unhappy with Washington's decision to leave Mexican immigration unrestricted, started to deny visas to Mexicans at high rates, enforcing literacy tests, bans on contract labour and using their discretion to deny entry to anyone who could become a public charge (Ngai, 2004: 54–55). The new law also made the lack of a visa for inspection upon border crossing grounds for deportation, and the statute of limitations on deportation was eliminated (ibid.). Therefore, when Mexican migrants began to come into the US at unofficial crossings, they became 'unauthorised'. In 1965, national origins quotas were replaced with hemispheric quotas, including for the first time, caps on Western Hemisphere visas. Restrictions thus directly affected visa availability for Mexicans.

A fragmented policy space

In the US the federal government has exclusive authority over immigration policy, although the federal border enforcement agency increasingly coordinates efforts with state and local law enforcement. Subnational levels of government control many policy areas that directly impact immigrant integration, such as health, education and welfare, among others. Local governments experience immigrant flows and respond to them in one way or another, even if not formally engaged in immigration policy. In practice, then, immigration policy-making and implementation, broadly defined, occurs at all levels of government.

Federal immigration policy

The dominant element of US immigration policy is enforcement – in terms of dollars spent, policy activity and innovations. Most public statements from national elected officials and agency personnel emphasise various aspects of enforcement, including border control and enforcement inside the borders. Especially after the terrorist attacks of September 11, 2001, enforcement through detention and deportation has grown. This means that unauthorised immigrants, both actual and potential, are the central focus of federal policy, and the enforcement focus means that the outsider status of these immigrants is emphasised. As Meissner et al. put it, 'a philosophy known as "enforcement first" has become *de facto* the nation's singular response to illegal immigration, and changes to the immigration system have focused almost entirely on building enforcement programmes and improving their performance' (Meissner et al., 2013: 1). Their study found that, at $18 billion for fiscal year 2012, 'the US government spends more on its immigration enforcement agencies than on all its other principal criminal federal law enforcement agencies combined' (ibid.: 9).

Under presidents Bush and Obama, there has been increased use of two 1996 laws that facilitate detention and deportation. The Antiterrorism and Effective Death Penalty Act and the Illegal Immigration Reform and Immigrant Responsibility Act expedited procedures for exclusion and deportation, limited discretion in judicial review of deportation cases and limited the Attorney General's ability to grant asylum. Many violations were reclassified from civil to criminal, resulting in more 'criminal aliens' than had existed previously. The list of deportable crimes for legal noncitizens has grown. Secret and unlawfully obtained evidence can be used in deportation hearings (Smith, 2007). These departures from practices in the execution of criminal law in the US create a state of exception for immigrants, similar to that described in other chapters of this volume along the Mediterranean border in Europe.

In addition, the Obama administration has made use of a 1996 provision integrating state and local law enforcement into the immigrant enforcement apparatus through agreements drawn between federal and local agencies; as well as creating the Secure Communities programme, which required state and local police to send the fingerprints of arrested people to federal officials, who check for previous criminal records and prior deportation orders (Meissner et al., 2013: 113–117). The sum of immigration enforcement efforts under Obama has been a dramatic rise in detentions and deportations, with removals reaching a record in 2011 of 391,953 and detentions standing at 429,247 people in 2011 (ibid.: 11). As numbers of detained and deported immigrants have risen, many dangerous conditions and poor treatment in detention centres have also been exposed. The administration has been criticised both from internal reports, like the Department of Homeland Security's Inspector General, and human rights groups like American Civil Liberties Union (ACLU) and Amnesty International (Amnesty International, 2009; Office of Inspector General, 2011; see also Rodriguez, in this volume). A review by the National Immigration Forum of advocates' and government reports criticising detention summarised 47 reports produced between 2008 and 2011 (2011).

Rising criticism of the 'enforcement first' apparatus led to some 2011 shifts in policy that included directing enforcement administrators to focus on deporting those who had committed serious crimes and to consider length in country and family ties when making decisions to deport non-criminals. Reviews of backlogged cases that began in selected jurisdictions using these guidelines have closed many cases, stopping deportation proceedings. One year later, President Obama directed that removal proceedings be stopped against young people brought to the US as children and meeting certain eligibility criteria; this group was estimated to number about 1.7 million people (Meissner et al., 2013: 138–140).

These executive actions were President Obama's first that acknowledged aspects of the 'insider' status of undocumented immigrants, and he took these steps as the end of his first term and the presidential election in 2012 drew near. From the start of Obama's second term, his administration and a growing number of legislators began to formulate legislation that would offer more undocumented immigrants a path to legal status, and would enable more people to come to the US for high- and low-skilled jobs. The political and public discussions of immigration broadened beyond enforcement to include the role of immigrants throughout the American economy. The resulting Senate bill passed in June 2013 emphasised security and imposed penalties on undocumented immigrants even as it offered many of them a long path towards regularisation and citizenship (Preston, 2013). Yet opposition from conservative Republicans in the House of Representatives stalled legislative momentum for the remainder of the year.

State and local integration policy

In the US, the federal government has exclusive authority over immigration policy, although as noted above, it increasingly forms partnerships with local law enforcement. Federal agents also contract with state and local governments for detention facilities. Rodriguez (this volume) discusses the local impacts of such contracts. Yet the many policy domains in which the states have uncontested authority directly affect immigrant settlement and integration, and some states have been increasingly aware of these connections. These policy areas include voting and elections, public safety, public education, public health and labour, among others. Local governments also create and provide services in many of these spheres, control land use and regulate public space. Unlike in many European states and Canada, where formal integration policies exist, the US has no explicit policy focused on integration. Rather, one must survey the policies that affect the social process of immigrant integration to discover how policies shape the integration experience. This is why scholars have likened US integration policy to a 'loosely-stitched patchwork', with 50 states and thousands of local governments taking actions each day that affect immigrant settlement (Bloemraad and de Graauw, 2011).

Besides the dispersion of integration policy is the variety: without a centralising, coordinating role from the federal government, policies shaping integration vary across localities. Some places have policies that welcome immigrants while others are exclusionary. For example, states and localities have engaged in 'backdoor' immigration policy, such as requiring proof of legal status to access services or licences; adopting municipal codes that prohibit renting homes to, or hiring, undocumented immigrants; or anti-loitering ordinances that may be used to disrupt day labour hiring processes (Varsanyi, 2008; see Rodriguez, this volume). At the same time, other places have proactively addressed integration, issuing city identification cards, creating local offices for newcomers that coordinate services, or funding worker centres or language courses and more (Eaton, 2012; Ridgely,

2008). Together, the lack of explicit federal integration policy, the variety of local policies that shape integration, and the strongly punitive, enforcement-oriented thrust of national policy create a policy domain that is fragmented, diverse and that gives rise to conflicts between and within government scales.

Local immigrant advocacy: The case of Newark, New Jersey

Local immigrant organisations confront a fragmented policy field and a national policy discourse emphasising the problem of undocumented immigrants. This study considers how local organisations whose missions involve helping immigrants settle and forge lives in cities navigate this complex and even hostile policy domain. I draw on field research conducted in Newark, NJ, between 2008 and 2010, which focused on immigrant-serving organisations. I conducted 15 interviews with staff members and/or directors of immigrant organisations. I also consulted secondary sources and policy reports.

I find that the local organisational landscape is fragmented into various types of organisations and that different types of organisations interact with different levels of government and strategically frame the 'problem' of undocumented immigrants differently. Immigrant rights' organisations work most directly with the local consequences of national 'enforcement first' policies. Labour groups target the state and local policies that affect immigrant workers. Community development organisations focus on state and local policies affecting urban development and social welfare as they work to improve the quality of life for residents in particular neighbourhoods. Growing out of these missions and interactions with government, each group's staff members develop particular perspectives on the role that immigrants play in their city, and their needs. These understandings lead to distinctive frames used to pursue their goals.

New Jersey stands out as a top immigrant-receiving state. In raw numbers, New Jersey has the sixth largest immigrant population in the US, but in terms of population share, the state has the third largest percentage of immigrants after California and New York. Brookings Institute researchers call the NY-Northern NJ area a continuous immigrant gateway, with high levels of immigration over a long period of time (Hall et al., 2011). About 550,000 unauthorised immigrants were estimated to live in New Jersey in 2010 (Passel and Cohn, 2011). Newark is the state's largest city, with a population of about 275,000. At 26 per cent, its share of immigrants is higher than the state as a whole. Newark's immigrant groups come from Latin America, Europe and Africa. The top ten countries of origin are Brazil, Ecuador, Portugal, the Dominican Republic and El Salvador, followed by Ghana, Haiti, Jamaica, Nigeria and Mexico (US Census, 2010).

Newark is a quintessential American industrial city that thrived more or less through World War II and then entered a period of economic and population decline stemming from suburbanisation, economic restructuring and racial prejudice and discrimination, among other factors. The city is infamous for six days of riots in July 1967 sparked by the arrest and beating of a black cab driver by white police officers. State police and eventually the National Guard came to the city. Twenty-three people died during the riots, more than 700 were injured and 1500 people were arrested (Herman, n. d.). Vacant land dating from property destroyed during the riots continues to mark the city's landscape. Newark has struggled with high poverty rates, high crime rates and attendant social problems, along with economic disinvestment. Signs of revitalisation began to be noted in the 1990s and while slow and spotty, they have persisted, albeit slowed by the most recent economic downturn. Since 1970, Newark has been a majority-black city, and the city's first black mayor was elected in the early 1970s. The city experienced population decline for 40 years until around 2000, just at the time when immigration rates increased. Latinos now make up about a third of the city's population.

Both Newark and New Jersey as a whole have been relatively inactive in terms of explicit immigrant policy. The state has not adopted measures to make life easier for undocumented immigrants, such as allowing them to get driving licences or qualify for in-state tuition at state colleges and universities. However, the state also has not adopted explicitly restrictive measures. During Governor Jon Corzine's term from 2006 to 2009, he appointed a commission to study and to make recommendations about how the state could further immigrant integration. The commission produced a detailed report with recommendations spanning the policy areas of social services, labour and workforce, education, and state and local government. These recommendations were wide-ranging, addressing the needs of all immigrants in New Jersey, including those who are unauthorised and those with legal status. But they were not implemented because Corzine, a Democrat, did not get re-elected in 2009, and his successor, Republican Chris Christie, effectively stopped implementation.

In Newark, immigrant integration was not a signature policy of Mayor Cory Booker's two-term administration, from 2006 to 2013. Yet there is some activity primarily related to cultural recognition and to cooperation with federal immigration enforcement. Booker emphasised early in his first term that Newark has what is called a 'Sanctuary City' ordinance which states that city agencies will not ask about immigrants' legal status or share information about status with federal agencies. Also early in his term, he created the African Commission, a volunteer body aimed at raising awareness of African culture and African immigrants in Newark. About seven years later, in August 2013, the Newark Police Department became the first in New Jersey to decline to detain immigrants arrested for minor crimes for the purpose of turning them over to federal enforcement officers. The menu of proactive integration policies adopted by other cities do not exist in Newark; these include measures such as creating a city office for integration, featuring immigrants on the city's web site, enabling immigrants to obtain ID cards or business licences regardless of status, fostering the creation of a worker centre to manage the informal labour market in a way to limit worker exploitation, or ensuring language access at City Hall. New York City, just across the river, has a much more developed set of immigrant-friendly policies. Yet Newark's relative inactivity is more the norm for US cities than the exception.

Three immigrant-serving organisations in Newark

Across US cities, many non-governmental organisations serve and/or advocate for immigrants. Many of these organisations have explicit missions related to immigration and immigrants. Other community-based organisations with different missions come to serve immigrants as neighbourhoods change and immigrants come to constitute significant portions of their constituencies. The following analysis focuses on three local groups in Newark that serve immigrants. Two were formed explicitly to serve immigrants, while the third organisation serves a broader constituency. The aim is to show that organisations with different missions develop different narratives about unauthorised immigrants and different relationships with government agencies. These organisations – a legal services group, a labour group and a community development corporation – are common types of local NGOs serving immigrants in the US. While some studies of immigrant organisations focus only on those with official non-profit tax-exempt status and/or those whose work is singly focused on immigrants (e.g. de Graauw, 2008), this study looks more broadly to include local organisations that have adapted their work over time as immigrants come to make up part of their community.

My analysis of these groups is twofold – I seek to show that local organisations interact with different arrays of government agencies at different levels of the US system and that the narratives about immigrants – particularly unauthorised immigrants – vary according both to group mission and to the level of government with which groups interact. These narratives may have internal as well as external aims – they help organisations to mobilise constituencies, to address conflicts within the group or service area, and they also are meant to help organisations gain government support. The following profiles describe group activities, strategic frames and interactions with government. The cases are followed by a discussion of the general themes that the profiles raise.

Immigrants as rights-bearing individuals

Some organisations develop narratives about immigrants that emphasise their rights as human beings and as residents in the city, state or nation; often such organisations provide legal services for individual immigrants who have been detained by federal authorities and are subject to deportation. In Newark, the American Friends Service Committee (AFSC) offers an example. AFSC uses this narrative as its staff lawyers represent detainees in immigration courts, and its organisers work with families of detainees in efforts to lobby for national policy change. The group interacts most often with the national government, including the court system and the immigration enforcement system. It also aims to build support among national legislators for policy change. That being said, building local and state allies (including state government agencies) and mobilising local residents of the Newark metro area, is part of the work of lobbying for national change.

The AFSC's downtown Newark office is a local branch of a national social-justice organisation with offices in 37 cities and Washington, DC, as well as international sites in 13 countries and a United Nations office. The national group, founded by Quakers in 1917, and rooted in the Quaker religious tradition, has a broad social justice mission. Its offices work on many policy issues including poverty, youth, criminal justice systems, nuclear weapons, humanitarian crises and conflict resolution; one of the group's goals is 'humanely reforming immigration policy' (AFSC, n. d.). The Newark office focuses primarily on immigrant rights. AFSC's national web site describes its programme areas as united by 'the unfaltering belief in the essential worth of every human being, non-violence as the way to resolve conflict, and the power of love to overcome oppression, discrimination, and violence.' The organisation's funding comes from foundations, a national fund for legal services derived from taxes on legal fees, and state funds for specific programmes. Newark's office grew from a three-person staff in the mid-1990s to a 12–13 person-staff by 2001. The group's activities include provision of legal services, community organising and policy advocacy.

Activities: Legal services, community organising and advocacy

Staff attorneys help immigrants to gain legal status if they qualify for the few routes available through specific laws – for example, as refugees under laws about political asylum or because they are victims of domestic violence. If immigrants have family members or young children in the US, staff may be able to represent them and help them to gain status. AFSC staff also visit a local federal detention centre where they inform detainees about their rights and help them to find attorneys. They also meet with families of detainees, helping them cope with meeting basic needs in the absence of a caregiver or earner. Most recently the AFSC added a staff attorney to focus on unaccompanied immigrant youth, after recognising this growing population through work with the New Jersey's Division of Youth and Family Services. Indeed, state grant programmes fund much of the work for specialised immigrant populations.

In the early 2000s, the AFSC added community organising more strongly into its organisational mission and strategies, partly linking this programme with its legal work. Thus, one project works with families of immigrants being held in detention centres and families of immigrants who have been deported, teaching them to tell their stories to the public or government officials, and thereby to participate in immigrant rights advocacy. To help attract interest and attendance at community organising meetings, the AFSC will publicise the presence of staff attorneys who can answer questions about immigration law. Thus legal clients become participants in advocacy. Programmes aim to train people to become leaders in the immigrant rights cause. Staff members teach immigrants and other community members about US immigration history and policy, about the Universal Declaration of Human Rights, or about how the US legislative system works. They also learn how to facilitate a meeting, how to contact a Member of Congress, how to talk to the media and how to publicise a meeting.

Beyond this programme, the AFSC's advocacy work consists of organising or participating in cross organisational campaigns to spur changes to immigration law, whether targeted at the state or federal level. For example, one recent effort, New Jersey Phone Justice, focused on expensive telephone rates at a county jail in Newark where immigrants are detained. The AFSC publicises reports about the federal immigration system and its effects on individuals, organises rallies and speaks out on injustices of current immigration enforcement practices. The director and other staff regularly participate in local educational forums and rallies related to immigration policy. Several years ago, the AFSC helped to create a coalition of organisations, including many religious congregations, that gather to discuss immigrant detention and several times a year hold interfaith services, vigils at state detention centres and rallies protesting immigrant detention.

Framing of undocumented immigrants

The AFSC's general framing of undocumented immigrants is captured by the slogan 'No Human Being is Illegal', which features prominently on the organisation's web site, and appears on AFSC posters and literature at rallies and events. It contrasts with the common depiction of unauthorised immigrants as lawbreakers and illegitimate residents of the US. AFSC staff and volunteers depict immigrants as holders of rights whose mistreatment by federal authorities is unjust and causes suffering to family members and to communities disrupted by federal enforcement. For example, AFSC's web site features videos of immigrants telling the stories of their interactions with federal enforcement agents (AFSC, 2012). In one video, a 24-year-old woman who lived with her aunt and uncle in New Jersey tells of an early-morning raid when immigration officers and local police searched for her aunt and uncle, holding 20-year-old photographs of them when they came to the US. The family operated a local butcher shop and had raised five children. Her uncle was detained for seven months before being granted a stay of deportation for a year, while her aunt was required to wear an ankle monitor at home since she was nursing a newborn baby. 'It felt like he just disappeared, like he fell off the face of the planet', she said of her uncle's experience in a detention facility. 'I don't think anyone should go through that.' This narration of immigrant experiences serves to mobilise immigrants and others behind AFSC's work for national immigration policy reform, it challenges the dominant narrative used by opponents of immigration reform and it justifies the work for which AFSC seeks funding.

Immigrants as workers

A second type of narrative about immigrants focuses on their contributions to the workforce. Organisations using this narrative describe immigrants as integral parts of the local workforce who should be treated lawfully, regardless of their immigration status. Such organisations often work to reduce the exploitation of informal labourers and, more generally, to advance the well-being of immigrants in the workplace. In Newark, a group called New Labor takes on this task. It interacts most often with state and local government agencies whose purview includes worker protection and licensing, as well as with local elected officials. For some of New Labor's work, this frame was sufficient, but when the group sought to change a local licensing ordinance, members crafted a second narrative, which depicted immigrants as members of the city's political community.

New Labor is an organisation of immigrant workers, mostly Latino, and many undocumented, based in central New Jersey, but working in locations around the state, including Newark. Founded in 2000, the grassroots membership organisation works primarily with low-wage service-sector workers, such as those who are placed through temp agencies or hired informally as day labourers. New Labor's work in Newark has included organising day labourers and organising flower and ice-cream vendors to fight for improved work conditions, the ability to secure vending licences and against exploitation. The group also has scheduled buses to take its members to Washington, DC, to participate in rallies for national immigration policy reform. Laws and policies governing the workplace are primarily under state and local jurisdiction, so New Labor engages these levels of government most often in their work. Their campaigns against wage theft and other forms of exploitation are crafted with awareness of state law, which covers all people working in the state regardless of immigration status.

Activities: Direct actions, services and lobbying for policy change
New Labor staff and members canvass workers to learn about issues and develop programmes or campaigns to address them. Examples are direct

action campaigns against wage theft, provision of English and computer classes, and health and safety training programmes. The group receives funding from membership dues, foundations and a grant from the federal agency of Occupational Health and Safety. There is no office in Newark, so group meetings take place in a local church whose pastors actively support immigrant causes.

One major undertaking by New Labor in Newark was to organise flower and ice-cream vendors to lobby City Hall for policy change relative to business licences and treatment by local police officers. Although Newark is technically a 'Sanctuary City' where city employees are ordered not to inquire about legal status when providing local services, the licensing policy for street vendors in practice required legal status. Without licences, vendors were subject to fines and their carts could be impounded. In general, vendors (even those who had licences) reported bad relations with police officers, who ordered them away from certain corners, sometimes threw their flowers on the ground and spoke to them with insults.

The *Union de Vendedores* came to be part of New Labor when a community-based organisation closed in Newark and the community organiser who had helped the vendors began working for New Labor. The community organiser had met some of the vendors and learned that they were having trouble with city licensing laws. Because of a change in enforcement of licensing ordinances, vendors needed to obtain a background check as part of their application for a licence. But undocumented immigrants could not obtain this without drawing attention to their lack of status. The community organiser helped the vendors to create a local association and they began to lobby City Hall, meeting with mayoral staff. They tried to meet with police officers but several times after scheduling meetings, officers could not make it. The group also faced some internal conflicts among vendors. After about a year of meetings and lobbying, the *Union de Vendedores* secured a meeting with Newark's mayor, Cory Booker. About 40 people wearing orange New Labor t-shirts met in a hotel conference room where speakers described to the mayor and his staff members the problems they were having obtaining licences. The mayor told them that he would help them, the people in attendance smiled and cheered and afterward posed for photographs with the mayor. A temporary fix was secured that summer with the mayor's help, but as vending season approached the following year, no permanent policy change had occurred and the vendors were again at risk of being ticketed or having their carts impounded.

Framing of undocumented immigrants

As a labour organisation, New Labor generally emphasises the identity of undocumented immigrants as workers. Staff and members describe immigrants as seeking to support their families no differently from other

US workers and as entitled to treatment similar to other workers and with the same protections. While members employed the 'immigrants as workers' narrative in Newark, they also developed another narrative that cast immigrants as members of Newark's political community. Leaders of the flower and ice-cream vendors union recognised that local elected officials viewed them as a non-voting constituency, hurting their chances of securing support. They started to describe themselves as integrated into the fabric of the city's political life. They talked about their own children and family members who were US citizens, as well as their friends. These connections, they argued, put them in a position to communicate political information and to influence the political views of voters. They argued that they deserved government responsiveness because they worked and had family and friends right in Newark. Many were parents to US-citizen children. Union members also described themselves as resources for disseminating political information. They noted that although they were not able to vote, they spent their work days out in the streets among Newark's voters and often discussed politics and exchanged information with their customers. They sometimes even distributed flyers about local community programmes to their customers; they pointed out that they could help local officials publicise important city programmes. Recognising their political vulnerability in the absence of the right to vote, they aimed to establish themselves as legitimate constituents of the mayor and council members, deserving of government responsiveness to their needs.

Immigrants as community members

A third type of narrative about immigrants is similar to the one that union members created when they lobbied City Hall. It focuses on immigrants' place in city neighbourhoods, living alongside other city residents and like them, having legitimate claims and needs that stem from this residence. Neighbourhood-based organisations use this frame, often as part of the process of negotiating conflicts between groups within the neighbourhood they serve, as well as when seeking to mobilise community members around shared problems. In Newark, the Ironbound Community Corporation (ICC) is one such group. It runs a range of programmes and implements many state and local policies within the boundaries of the city's Ironbound neighbourhood. The ICC draws funding from local and state government (and private funders) to implement programmes related to social welfare, education, health and neighbourhood development.

The Ironbound Community Corporation is a community development corporation serving the Ironbound neighbourhood of Newark, located on the city's east side just beyond Penn Station. Its name derives from the railroad tracks that surround the area. About two-thirds of the 50,000 Ironbound residents are immigrants. Historically, the neighbourhood was home to Irish and Italian immigrants, then Eastern European immigrants, then Portuguese, and more recently Central and South American immigrants, many from Brazil. The ICC opened its doors in 1969, when residents organised to create a preschool and later built on their organising success to work on improving the neighbourhood in other ways. They fought to have environmental contamination cleaned up and to improve the poor neighbourhood facilities such as parks and schools. Today, the ICC is a multifaceted organisation providing services, creating community plans and engaging in community organising. Immigrants – legal and without status – along with other neighbourhood residents, come to local ICC offices and can become involved in community events, as well as getting the opportunity to learn about local services, city and state programmes, including housing, health, food stamps and welfare programmes and become involved in advocacy efforts.

Activities: Service provision, community building and advocacy
Many of the services that the ICC provides are funded by the state of New Jersey to help low-income families and senior citizens, many of whom are immigrants. These include implementing state social-welfare services focused on building self-sufficiency, registering families for social welfare programmes, providing meals to homebound seniors, implementing state weatherisation and energy efficiency programmes, and operating parenting classes and support groups. The group coordinates with the state's medical school to bring a medical van to the neighbourhood once a month. There are vocational training programmes and early childhood education programmes, as well as English-language classes and American citizenship classes.

The group also engages in community-building and community-development activities. Thus, organisers seek to bring together the different groups who share the neighbourhood, but do not always interact. For example, recent efforts in the East Ironbound ICC office have worked to create ties between the African-Americans who live in the neighbourhood's social housing complex, and the Central American immigrants who live in private housing in the area. Two programmes, both grant-funded, celebrated diversity and addressed misconceptions. The office's director used a state humanities grant to develop East Ironbound Cooks, a programme featuring the teachings and practice of the neighbourhood's cooks. Staff and volunteers asked neighbourhood residents to identify great home cooks, who were then interviewed and videotaped. The cooks – from the American South, Ecuador, Peru, Puerto Rico and Portugal – spoke about their dishes and cooking style at the local library. Participants could then sample the food. A display of artwork by neighbourhood youth was linked to the programme. A second programme was a series of workshops facilitated by the Black Alliance for Just Immigration, from Oakland, California. Two workshops were held, one with African-American residents and one with immigrant residents. A third workshop brought members of the two groups together for a discussion. The ICC also monitors and advocates for improvements to neighbourhood amenities, for attention to environmental contamination and public health problems, and for a voice in the redevelopment of former industrial sites.

In general, organisers engage residents in discussions as they canvass the neighbourhood to find out their key concerns. One reported that a common feeling among native-born residents is that immigrants 'are getting something they shouldn't'. In discussions with immigrants, she found immigrants believe that, as citizens, the native-born residents 'can get all kinds of stuff we can't get'. The organiser tries to educate both groups about the longstanding discrimination against African-Americans in the US, and the exclusion that undocumented immigrants face.

Framing of undocumented immigrants

As a neighbourhood-based organisation, ICC discourse understands and perceives immigrants, including the undocumented, as neighbourhood residents. Long-time organisers see immigrant presence as a fact of neighbourhood life stretching back decades. Recent flows and inter-group conflicts are only the latest iteration of an ongoing and practically inevitable process through which groups arrive, settle, and for some, move out. Older groups develop fears or resentments about newer groups. There is 'a tendency to blame people who are different from ourselves when things go bad' according to one ICC staff member. ICC staff members also see immigrants as contributing to the political weakness of the neighbourhood. They interpret their difficulties in getting attention from City Hall as stemming from low voter turnout that is linked to low levels of citizenship in the Ironbound neighbourhood. Because of immigrants, then, 'we are the least powerful community', one staff member said. Thus, although the ICC considers all residents, including non-citizen and undocumented immigrants, to be legitimate community members deserving of voice and responsiveness, staff also are aware that local officials have a different sense of who 'counts'.

The close-up view of neighbourhood residents that emerges from service provision and organising work means that the staff has a fine-grained understanding of the particular vulnerabilities of the undocumented. They see them as one part of their constituency with distinctive challenges; similarly other groups also have distinctive challenges. ICC staff members are aware of the difficulties the undocumented immigrants have in gaining access to higher education, to government-funded English classes and to the workforce. They know that undocumented immigrants are part of mixed-status families. They notice subtle changes in the immigrant population – knowing for example that more illiterate immigrants have arrived, or that newer immigrants speak indigenous languages rather than Spanish. Understanding cultural distinctions is part of the work of this community organisation that seeks to mobilise residents and build bridges between them. ICC staff thus understand that some immigrants are used to more collective life in their home country, and are thus 'ripe' for participating in community organisations.

Organisational type, undocumented immigrants and urban citizenship

These three case studies of NGOs serving immigrants in Newark, NJ, show the variety of work being done by and on behalf of immigrants at a local level, how the organisations position themselves vis-à-vis the government, and aim to achieve their goals through strategic framing of immigrants as deserving and positive members of the community. Each group developed a positive frame of unauthorised immigrants, but with a slightly different focus related to their organisational goals: as rights-bearing individuals, as workers and as community members. Consistent with Rygiel's ideas (this volume) about practising citizenship and Raissiguier's (this volume) analysis of how 'impossible subjects' turn into legitimate subjects, these organisations illustrate the variety of resistance to punitive and exclusionary national policy taking place at a local level, even in a city and state not particularly proactive on immigrant integration. Each group engages in what Rygiel refers to as 'making city spaces safe' for immigrants, especially unauthorised immigrants; many of the members, staff and volunteers working in the various NGO programmes are immigrants themselves; some of them are unauthorised. They exercise local citizenship as a route to improve their own lives but also to improve the quality of life in their communities, and paradoxically for some they do this work as simultaneously they are formally excluded from citizenship.

Each of these organisations contends with the effects of national immigration policy, interacts with government at different levels and serves and includes undocumented immigrants; each in its own way challenges internal borders that shape the lives of the undocumented in cities. Depending on their mission and their organisational type, they do so differently. The AFSC, an immigrant rights and legal-services organisation, navigates within the federal enforcement apparatus, where undocumented immigrants are intensely perceived as outsiders. New Labor, a labour organisation, seeks changes from state and local governments as it aims to improve work conditions for immigrant labourers, mostly undocumented. The ICC, a community-based organisation, interacts with state and local government service and development agencies in order to serve neighbourhood residents, including the undocumented immigrants who live in the Ironbound.

Each group in its own way seeks to empower its members. The AFSC represents the needs and claims of undocumented immigrants and their families in immigration court proceedings, and teaches them to become leaders and to claim their legitimacy as community members and human beings. New Labor organises immigrant workers to understand their rights in the workplace and supports their efforts to exercise and to protect these rights. The group also teaches workers to develop strategies aimed at making claims on government, particularly at the local level. The ICC advances an understanding of immigrants as part of a diverse neighbourhood, whose residents together should have voice in determining its fate, and ensuring it receives the attention it deserves from City Hall. It fosters cross-group dialogue and understanding.

Each group also contends with the political vulnerability of undocumented immigrants, with the AFSC focusing on the national policy and political scene, while New Labor and the ICC experience inattention at the city level. The AFSC and New Labor most directly confront exclusionary policies, interacting with the immigration legal system and city policies; the ICC understands political inattention as stemming from the low citizenship rates, and thus voting rates, of its majority-immigrant neighbourhood. This latter group most directly seeks to foster relationships across categories of residents by building on common ground and the fact of shared neighbourhood residence. With its geographic rather than group-based focus, the ICC shows the capacity for building mixed-group movements, or bridges across population groups. The other two organisations are less structurally inclined to build cross-group solidarity. Interestingly, neighbourhood borders to some extent help to overcome internal national borders experienced by the undocumented.

Each of these groups interacts with different levels of government and aspects of the immigration and integration policy sphere. In doing so, they mirror the sphere's fragmentation – it takes different kinds of groups to navigate different parts of the policy space. These NGOs confront the formal borders inside the national space by serving undocumented immigrants and trying to improve their lives in the US. At the same time, they bring to light the informal deconstruction of these borders that emerge as undocumented immigrants share neighbourhoods with other US residents, and make claims on government alongside the claims of other groups. At the time of writing, public opinion polls showed that strong majorities of the American public believed that there should be a path to citizenship for undocumented immigrants (Sullivan and Clement, 2013). The work of NGOs in American cities perhaps contributes to this level of support, chipping away bit by bit at the foundations of the borders inside the nation.

8
Conditions as Internal Borders: The Case of 'Security of Residence' for Third-Country Nationals in Austria

İlker Ataç

The recent literature on the rights of third-country nationals and their subsequent acquisition of residence rights and citizenship status highlights the fulfilment of integration requirements, such as language proficiency and citizenship tests (Joppke, 2007; Mourão Permoser, 2012). This has instigated scholarly and public debates on whether integration policies are in fact becoming a tool of an exclusionary immigration policy or whether they can be understood as an instance of symbolic politics, with the primary aim of sending a restrictive message to (potential) migrants. Such requirements exist likewise in Austria. I argue, however, that classification of aliens and the fulfilment of income requirements are powerful state technologies to assign rights and secure residence status to third-country nationals. Historically, the tendency has clearly been towards the expansion of residence rights for third-country nationals. The respective European Union directives were important milestones in harmonising the requirements and scope of rights. Focusing on the relevance of these new mechanisms – classification and income requirements – I attempt to contribute to comparative studies on the rights of third-country nationals by showing that the new requirements lead to new forms of inclusion and exclusion, and ultimately tend to reduce access to rights for many migrants.

Greater economic and social rights for third-country nationals have been discussed in the literature under the concept of denizenship. The extension of migrant rights was prominently coined by Soysal as an outcome of emerging post-national societies (Soysal, 1994). This approach has been challenged by authors such as Lydia Morris (2002), who focuses on how states construct forms of civic stratification in which specific migrant categories have different rights of entry and residence, and different access to rights in general. The literature on 'migration management' shows that current migration policies are characterised by a focus on security, but that a country's economic rationale also plays a significant role in creating an opening for some migrants in terms of entry, work and residence, and closure for others (Kofman, 2005). The introduction of integration requirements has been discussed as a new form of stratification (Joppke, 2007).

In this chapter I discuss the access of third-country nationals to certain rights in current migration policies. I concentrate in particular on how migrants acquire a secure residence status and identify policy changes and the shift in policies during the different phases of immigration policy in Austria. Austria is a fitting example with which to illustrate my argument. The EU15 average for long-term residence according to the Migrant Integration Policy Index (MIPEX) is 60 points, with Austria scoring an average of 58 points. In terms of subcategories, Austria is above the EU15 average with respect to scope of the rights associated with this status and eligibility of the same; it is below the EU15 average for migrants regarding the security of the residence status and the conditions for its acquisition. This makes Austria an interesting case for analysis, since it scores an average on the general scale but underscores in areas such as security of residence status and the conditions for acquisition of the same.

I will discuss the mechanisms and technologies at play when politics referring to third-country nationals intersect with immigration policies. I examine the circumstances under which an expansion or contraction of rights has occurred. What role do conditions and requirements play in achieving a safer status for immigrants? Similar to Kim Rygiel's statement in this volume, I argue that new politics of citizenship are characterised by simultaneous openings and closures (see also Ataç and Rosenberger, 2013).

Migration policies and the stratification of rights

Migration policies are about determining which groups should have the right to enter and stay in a country and under what conditions. For this purpose different categories of individuals are drawn up with respect to eligibility for rights. Policy decisions classify migrants as legal permanent residents, temporary non-immigrants, humanitarian migrants or undocumented migrants. They also determine the rights each migrant category enjoys (Cornelius and Rosenblum, 2005: 112). The chief rights dimensions discussed in the literature encompass economic, social and political rights and security of residence. Among the various factors that shape the outcome of migration policies are government decisions, economic interest groups, the judiciary, human rights norms, experts, civil society organisations and migrant self-organisations.

I discuss the issue with reference to the conceptual framework of the stratification of rights. The stratification literature documents a widening differentiation in entitlements between denizens, long-term residents and temporary permit holders. Temporary status is accompanied by limited access to economic and social rights. Labour migrants with temporary work and residence permits in particular are unable to establish an unbroken period of residence that would enable them to settle down and acquire denizenship rights. In addition, conditions based on testing and monitoring language skills and high-income requirements leads to increased residence uncertainty for specific migrant groups.

In her comparison of migrant rights in Germany, Italy and Britain, Morris works with the concept of civic stratification, which focuses on differentiated entitlement, access and delivery in the practice of rights. The concept of civic stratification describes 'a system of inequality based on the relationship between different categories of individuals and the state, and the rights thereby granted or denied' (Morris, 2003: 79). Formal inclusions and exclusions remain at the centre of her approach, which operates with respect to eligibility for rights. Governance through rights thus leads to a differentiated system of rights, which may vary nationally (Morris, 2003).

Access to rights from this perspective functions as a form of governance, whereby the elaboration of rights for categories of third-country nationals provides the opportunity and the means for surveillance and control. These tensions play out differently in the individual forms of migration (labour, family and asylum). Kofman (2005) argues that migration policy works through the classification, selection and stratification of migrants with access to a bundle of rights. Migration policy seeks to filter and distinguish between welcome and unwelcome strangers – a point elaborated in the previous chapter by Mara Sidney. Kofman and Sidney stress that migration policy is directed towards the selection of those who will be most advantageous to the economy, fit into a pre-existing national culture and not disrupt any supposed social and community cohesion.

Secure residence status were originally established in Western European countries to accommodate 'guest' worker migrants. Protection against deportation and access to social rights are the core of secure residence status. With the exception of most political rights, basic economic and social citizenship rights have been extended over time to resident non-citizens. A number of political rights, such as the right to vote in local council elections and some local governments, exist in some countries for resident third-country nationals. Hammar (1990) used the concept of denizens to describe the expansion of rights for migrants.

Access to social rights remains at the heart of debates on security of residence. The granting of social rights and access to social security systems is discussed against the background of whether citizens and non-citizens should have the same rights. Social rights are described as membership of the welfare state but not of the political community. With regard to social rights, the post-national thesis has argued that they arrived in Europe earlier than civil and political rights and more completely, thereby reversing Marshallian citizenship logic (Soysal, 1994). Yasemin Soysal developed the idea that national citizenship is losing ground to a more universal membership model entitled 'post-national membership'. She emphasised the formation of migrant rights as the outcome of an emergent post-national society in which migrants can draw on transnational rights located outside the nation-state (Soysal, 1994). From a European perspective there are two sources for the expansion of rights beyond national states: international conventions that secure the rights of aliens and the European Union (EU), which establishes mechanisms for free movement and supranational policies in the field of migration policy-making.

However, with respect to the social rights of third-country nationals the limits of denizenship status are evident, in particular the scope of rights that migrants can acquire. Joppke distinguishes between contributory and non-contributory benefits (Joppke, 2010). Since benefits such as unemployment benefits, pensions and healthcare are insurance based, labour participation and territory rather than citizenship constitute the basis for access to these social rights. Reciprocal insurance is the leading principle at work here (Söhn, 2011). The extension of social rights to non-citizens has occurred mostly in the case of contribution-based benefits (Joppke, 2007). In terms of gaining access to non-contributory, tax-based benefits such as housing, social assistance and family benefits, however, there are obvious differences between citizens and third-country nationals. Full benefit entitlement presupposes secure residence status. Repeated or long-term entitlement to these services by third-country nationals can endanger their residence status or at least hinder the consolidation of their residence security (Mohr, 2005). Joppke (2007) mentions that non-contributory benefits are the core of social citizenship. He underlines that access to these benefits is restricted by immigration laws that render the immigration authority the 'watchdog of the welfare state' (Baldwin, 1997, cited in Joppke, 2010: 90), which, in turn, may proscribe the termination of residence for non-citizens.

Over the last ten years many European states introduced integration requirements that coupled security of residence and family reunification with fulfilment of integration conditions, such as passing a language test. Joppke (2007) argued that integration policy in the form of integration conditions is used as a migration policy instrument, since states have the power to control the entry of 'unwanted family members' of third-country nationals. This tendency has been discussed as a shift from a rights-based understanding of integration to a form of 'repressive liberalism', whereby immigrant duties are emphasised over immigrant rights. Guild et al. criticise that integration conditions potentially exclude low-income and poorly educated immigrants in terms of access to rights (Guild et al., 2009). The current goals of integration policy are seen as an attempt to reduce the number of immigrants who stay in the territory and to restrict immigrant access to permanent residence rights and citizenship rather than to encourage integration and language learning.

Unlike political rights, which are deeply rooted in the national sphere, security of residence and the rights attached to this status are the outcome of steps taken by various actors at the national, international and supranational level. Rights stratify, discipline and divide but they also present a site of social struggle and frequently concretise contested visions of society (Morris, 2012: 42–43). A series of contradictions and tensions have become evident in the governing of migration in European countries (Kofman, 2002). A clash of principles arose between universal principles and economic interests and the preservation of national identities. International judges and European Union directives have played a major role in the context of expanding residence security. Government strategies at national level have swung in both directions: for expansion and for contraction of these rights.

I will analyse the development of policies referring to security of residence for third-country nationals in Austria and focus on the following questions: (1) What categories of third-country nationals have access to secure residence status? (2) What are the preconditions for secure residence status? (3) What rights are attached to this position? For further analysis, I make a distinction between three historical epochs in Austrian migration history from the end of the 1950s to the current phase. The overarching question is whether it comes to a contraction or expansion of these rights and whether this leads to a new form of citizenship regime.

The first three decades of migration in Austria: Reproducing precarious status through law

In the context of the economic boom in the late 1950s and early 1960s, labour shortages became a major issue in Austria and several other Western European countries. Employer representatives demanded liberalisation of the labour market in order to fill the gap, while the trade unions rejected the employment of foreign workers. In 1961, the social partners finally agreed on the employment of foreign workers. Agreements were signed between Austria and Turkey and Yugoslavia in 1964 and 1966, respectively (Mayer, 2009: 132). Originally designed as temporary, rotating migration, the system developed into a mixed form of circular and permanent migration (Kraler, 2011). Migrant workers arrived in Austria mostly through their own networks. In 1967, only one out of eight labour migrants was recruited through official channels (Parnreiter, 1994). Numerous migrants entered the country as tourists and later found work and were granted residence permits. Karakayali describes similar legalisation practices for Germany (Karakayali, 2008). An autonomous system of migration soon emerged, in which markets and migrant networks became decisive factors, while the impact of government regulation in the recruitment process remained limited.

In this first phase of labour immigration, which lasted until the end of the 1980s, immigrant workers had limited social and political rights, notably with regard to residence security and free choice of employer. This led to a dramatic reduction of immigrant workers in times of economic crisis. In the wake of the 'oil crisis' in 1973, the number of immigrants working in Austria between 1974 and 1976 declined in net by about 55,000 (Bauböck, 1996: 14). As in other European countries, measures designed to reduce the number of foreign employees led to settlement and increased family unification (Castles, 2004).

In response to the economic crisis, a new piece of legislation came into effect in 1975, strengthening the influence of social partners on the regulation of labour migration. The key component of the law stipulated that immigrant workers were to be employed only when the labour market permitted. This saw the introduction of an annual labour market quota, which has been the leading instrument for regulation. According to this new regulation, immigrant workers can receive a certificate of exemption (*Befreiungsschein*) restricted to two years, rendering them independent of their employer after eight years of continuous employment.

Basically, the new law held on the already failed guest worker regime with limited rights and rotation principle. Although there were clear signs of permanent immigration to Austria, the government persevered with policies that reproduced the temporary character of migration instead of facilitating migrant integration (Bauböck, 1996).

Labour migration worked in the context of an open border regime until the end of the 1980s (Parnreiter, 1998). The migrants who entered Austria on a tourist visa came for the most part from Turkey and Yugoslavia. Once they had found a job, legal work and residence permits were issued (see Gächter, 2000). Up until the reform of 1990, long-term work permits were, as a rule, reserved for those who could prove they had been legally employed in Austria for the previous eight years without significant interruption (Davy and Gächter, 1993: 270). Since the majority of migrants worked as unskilled or semi-skilled labourers, their jobs were subject to seasonal fluctuation, whereas the right to residence was dependent on permanent employment. In practice, migrants received a residence permit as long as they could prove they had an income and accommodation. At the same time, however, deportations were common. For the most part, decisions were taken autonomously by bureaucrats on a case basis (interview, Norbert Bichl, *Beratungszentrum für Migranten und Migrantinnen* (Counselling Centre for Migrants), 14 October 2011). The result was an ethnic segmentation of the domestic labour market and continuing dependency of migrant workers on their employers.

The impetus for a reform of the security of residence for labour migrants did not come from politics but from the judiciary in 1987. The Constitutional Court removed two paragraphs of the Aliens' Police Act (*Fremdenpolizeigesetz*) of 1954 with the argument that the ban on residence was at odds with Article 8 of the European Convention on Human Rights concerning respect for private and family life. For the first time since 1954, the law was amended in 1986. The first amendment by the government failed at the Constitutional Court. The second amendment in 1987 was the first major change to security of residence and confirmed that human rights are valid for labour migrants living in Austria (interview, Norbert Bichl, *Beratungszentrum für Migranten und Migrantinnen*, 14 October 2011). In the case of the residence ban, the new law was to give priority to the private and family life of immigrants over public interest (Bauböck and Perchinig, 2006). Another important change triggered by the government took place in 1988. An amendment to the Employment of Foreign Workers Act gave second-generation migrants access to a work permit *(Befreiungsschein)* and unrestricted access to the labour market, a step towards equality and recognition of the permanence of the migrants' presence in Austria (Mayer, 2009: 49; Kraler, 2011).

Towards the consolidation of rights: The period between 1992 and 2005

The new residence act implemented in 1992 was the first law to govern long-term residence. It introduced a strict regulation with a clear distinction between visas for tourists and those for people wanting to immigrate (Mayer, 2009: 52). The aim was to terminate the immigration regime via tourist employment that persisted until the end of the 1980s and to introduce a paradigm of control. The focus shifted from labour market regulation to border management. The new act stipulated the maximum number of residence permits to be issued annually (Mayer, 2009: 52).

The 1992 Residence Act affected settled migrants and their relatives in particular. Migrants were obliged to make an application to renew their papers four weeks prior to expiry of their permit. Since many migrants overlooked this date, they had to file their application from abroad under new restrictive conditions and with the result of losing their economic and settlement rights (interview, Norbert Bichl, *Beratungszentrum für Migranten und Migrantinnen*, 14 October 2011). Moreover, the children of third-country nationals born in Austria were included in the maximum number of permits, with the effect that new-born children found themselves in an 'irregular position' and received a deportation order due to an irregular stay (Perchinig, 2009). A residence permit did not automatically entitle the holder to an employment permit. Such was the case for family members. Loss of a job and hence of an employment permit could also lead to loss of the residence permit (Mayer, 2009: 52).

Çinar et al. found that the rights granted to labour migrants regarding security of residence and free movement of employment were clearly weak in Austria compared to other Western European countries (Çinar et al., 1995). Up until the reform of 1997, long-term residence did not lead to increased security of residence for immigrants. At the time 'a permanent residence permit could be withdrawn on any grounds sufficient for refusal of a visa, such as insufficient income, inadequate housing, acts against public security, peace and order, including traffic offences' (Groenendijk et al., 1998: 37). Even receipt of social benefits could lead to the loss of long-term residence status (Çinar et al., 1995: 37).

During this period, not only was access to security of residence restricted, but the scope of accessible rights was limited. Third-country nationals were excluded from emergency support *(Notstandshilfe)*. Only when a Turkish citizen who had been denied emergency support brought his case to trial at the beginning of the 1990s, it came to an amendment of the law. The Constitutional Court in Austria was in favour of a restriction. It argued that the availability of emergency assistance ad infinitum would invalidate the category of 'guest workers', who were expected to eventually return to their country of origin. With this decision the court ignored the reality of labour immigration for workers who had been settled for almost 30 years. When the European Court of Human Rights (ECtHR) ruled in favour of the applicant *(Gaygusuz v. Austria)* in 1997, the government finally amended the Unemployment Insurance Act, providing equal access to emergency assistance and removing the requirement of Austrian nationality as a prerequisite. The government linked eligibility for emergency assistance to the beneficiary's availability to the labour market and to residence criteria (Liegl et al., 2008). The decision of the ECtHR undermined the primacy of Austrian citizens in social policy (Cholewinski, 2004).

The leading step towards consolidation of the rights of third-country nationals took place with the 1997 Aliens Act, which came into effect on 1 January 1998. This provided for a comprehensive reform of the legislation on the residence of third-country nationals. The new legislation was adopted after strong criticism of the implementation of the previous Act of 1992. In this context, NGOs, migrant organisations and human rights organisations had criticised its exclusionary effects and campaigned for secure residence status notably for second- and third-generation migrants (Groenendijk et al., 1998). It was also decisive that the Constitutional Court addressed several issues contained in the 1992 Act. The Court held that the right to private and family life as stated in Article 8 of the Convention for the Protection of Human Rights and Fundamental Freedoms (ECHR) should prevail and that residence permits should not be withdrawn on the grounds of inadequate housing or insufficient income (Groenendijk et al., 1998).

Several provisions in the legislation of 1997 provided for a comprehensive reform of the legislation on the residence status of long-term aliens and reinforced their residence security. It introduced the principle of secure residence status under the slogan 'integration before new immigration' as a pathway to denizenship. The key innovation here was the principle of graded consolidation of security of residence for third-country nationals after five, eight and ten years (Groenendijk et al., 1998). According to this regulation, third-country nationals had the right to a permanent residence permit *(unbefristete Niederlassungsbewilligung)* after five years of uninterrupted residence provided they were in possession of adequate and regular income. They could no longer be expelled on the grounds of insufficient financial means or dependence on public assistance. Expulsion could take place after eight years of residence if an immigrant was convicted of a criminal offence and a continued stay in Austria was seen as a threat to public order and security. Immigrants could only be expelled after ten years of residence if they were given a prison sentence of at least one year for a specified serious crime (Groenendijk et al., 1998; Cholewinski, 2004).

While migrant rights have been improved, new restrictions were also imposed (Kraler, 2011). Legislation provided greater security of residence status for long-term migrants, but distinguished two types of residence permits: one for temporary residence *(Aufenthaltserlaubnis)* and the other for settlement *(Niederlassungsbewilligung)* (Groenendijk et al., 1998). The success of a residence permit application depends on whether the annual quota of new permits has been reached. Immigrants who fulfil the requirements may be granted security of residence. If third-country nationals are categorised as temporary residents, however, they cannot be given security of residence since their visas are issued for one year only and certain conditions must be fulfilled annually for an extension. Seasonal and rotational workers, as well as a number of other categories, were excluded from permanent residency. This form of classification or stratified rights is still a major component of denizenship policy. Furthermore, as a concession to the trade unions, proposals to harmonise immigration legislation and the Employment of Foreign Workers Act – linking a long-term residence permit to employment access – were not pursued (Kraler, 2011). Although steps were taken throughout the 1990s to consolidate immigrant rights, on the whole, policies continued to reproduce the fiction of migrants as a temporary presence and to legally exclude third-country nationals from several social and other rights, including access to the labour market and political rights (Kraler, 2011: 44).

Expansion of rights and introduction of new criteria: The phase from 2005 onwards

Important milestones for the consolidation of the rights of third-country nationals were introduced in 2005. The government undertook a complete revision of the legislation on aliens, which came into force in January 2006. It was based on the implementation of three European directives that extended the rights of immigrants.[1] The directive on long-term residents in particular granted increased security of residence to third-country nationals with a permanent status. Holders of the EU long-term resident status gained access to specific social rights. They were entitled to equal treatment with nationals in terms of access to the labour market, education, social and tax benefits, and to goods and services including housing (Strik and Böcker, 2011). In addition to formal rights, permanent resident status entitles the holder to take out a mortgage, which in most countries is not given by the banks to migrants with temporary residence permits (ibid.). In addition, the law introduced in 2005 finally correlated residence rights with employment rights (Kraler, 2011).

The new regulation enhanced the status of third-country nationals compared to the regulations in existence since 1997. Holders of a permanent resident permit do not lose their residence rights as a result of dependence on public assistance or of public order offences. The permanent residence permit could only be forfeited on the grounds of, for example, fraud, a long absence from the country, a long prison sentence or if the immigrant in question constituted a real and sufficiently serious threat to public policy or public security (Strik and Böcker, 2011).

While these changes improved the legal position of a number of immigrants, at the same time they constituted setbacks in the form of newly introduced restrictive changes. Absolute residence security for children born in Austria was revoked in 2006 and reinstated in 2011 with the change in government. During the 2006 implementation of the law, classifications for residency were also altered, removing entitlement for permanent residency to temporary residency for some professions – artists, religious preachers and researchers. The year 2006 can thus be seen as a milestone in the consolidation of rights referring to the security of residence for third-country nationals. Although the scope of rights has increased and access to them standardised, we need to take note of the tendencies that led to a contraction of these rights, in particular with regard to the access criteria for these rights, such as integration requirements and income. I will now therefore turn to the changing definitions of both the criteria and their impact.

Integration requirements

Many European governments define sets of integration requirements to be fulfilled by third-country nationals seeking permanent residence. The idea behind making permanent residence conditional on the passing of an examination is that migrants must show evidence of their integration as a precondition for their entitlement to secure status. Behind the European Commission's proposals for the directives on long-term residents (2003/109/EC) and on family reunion (2003/86/EC) is a reversal of the concept that secure status facilitates the integration process (Strik and Böcker, 2011). As a result of pressure from certain member states, such as Austria, Germany and the Netherlands, however, integration has been introduced as a requirement to the policy process. Consequently, the directive allows member states to demand the compliance of third-country nationals with integration conditions in accordance with the national law on long-term resident status.[2]

Third-country nationals admitted for non-temporary purposes have been required to sign an 'integration contract' since 2002. This obliges migrants to attend language courses and pass a final exam. The level of language to be met by migrants has been raised several times. With the reform of 2002, migrants were obliged to attend 100 hours (A1 level) of language courses. The 2005 reform raised the bar to 300 hours and the level of German proficiency from A1 to A2. In the amendment of February 2011, the language level increased again. Currently, third-country nationals must achieve B1 level German, which calls for an average of 600 hours of German language courses. With no exception, all applicants must pass this test to gain residence security.

The law reform in 2011 brought two further regulations. Migrants admitted for non-temporary stay must achieve A2 level German within two years of arrival as part of the integration requirements. The sanction for non-compliance is deportation. In this category, highly skilled labour migrants and their family members are exempt (Strik and Böcker, 2011). Integration requirements also focus on family members of third-country nationals already living in Austria, most of them relatives of first-generation migrants and their descendants. Another regulation was the set of pre-entry conditions introduced for family members. Applicants in the family reunification category are now required to take a language test before they travel to Austria. Pre-entry language requirements specifically target family relatives and call for A1 level German language proficiency. This prerequisite for obtaining a residence permit makes family reunification difficult.

The initial 2002 version of the integration agreement is discussed in the literature largely as a symbolic measure or symbolic politics, and as having only a limited influence on actual immigration policies (see Kraler, 2011; Mourão Permoser, 2012). The key explanatory factor here is an electoral shift towards the populist anti-immigrant Freedom Party (FPÖ), which became part of the coalition government. Thus the government has been under pressure to adopt discourses and positions that highlight the call for limited access to permanent residence (Strik and Böcker, 2011). In 2002, Peter Westenthaler, the parliamentary leader of the FPÖ, described the contract as a device for selection and the aim of the regulation as a message to immigrants and the wider public that 'abuse of the social system will no longer be possible' (Mourão Permoser, 2012: 184; Kraler, 2011). Hence the Freedom Party (FPÖ) heralded the introduction of the integration contract as a major political success and a paradigm shift towards a more restrictive immigration policy.

There is also evidence that the symbolic meaning of the regulation has little impact on everyday life. In the first year of the implementation of the regulation in 2002, for example, 90 per cent of migrants were exempted from taking the mandatory courses and were not obliged to sign the integration agreement (Mourão Permoser, 2012). However, the tendency to raise the required level of language proficiency and its potential impact has not yet been explored. The first cohorts of third-country nationals that complied with the language requirements had not yet fulfilled the five-year residence requirement at the time of research.

Although it is still too early to see the effects of changing integration requirements on permanent residence, some results can be observed: social workers and experts I interviewed stated that the required level of language proficiency (A2 in the first two years and B1 in five years) might be too high for immigrants with little formal education. If passing the A2 level exam in two years is difficult, reaching B1 level in five years could be an insurmountable difficulty (interview, Veli Çayci, *Beratungszentrum für Migranten und Migrantinnen*, 10 October 2011; interview, Johannes Peyrl, *Arbeiterkammer Wien*, 13 October 2011). The study by Strik and Böcker refers to statements of Austrian teachers, who pointed out that illiterate migrants cannot attain level A2 within the 75-hour literacy training period and 300 hours of language training provided in Austria (Strik and Böcker, 2011).

Third-country nationals who fail or refuse to comply with integration requirements are not eligible for secure residence status and the attendant rights. Consequently they are awarded a residence permit for one year only, which can be extended annually (Strik and Böcker, 2011). The overwhelming majority of the target group includes newly arrived immigrants who have been admitted for the purposes of family reunification. Here it is particularly difficult for older people who perform exhausting physical labour to obtain a permanent residence permit. In other words, these migrants will remain in a state of temporary inclusion and 'deportability' (De Genova, 2002). Apart from uncertainty and the ineligibility for certain social benefits, this leads to additional expense for the applicants, since the annual extension of a temporary residence permit amounts to €110.

Income requirements

Whether a government foresees possession of a defined amount of economic resources as a requirement for permanent residence or citizenship varies from one European state to another. Historically, income criteria have always been important. Up until the 1990s, third-country nationals were obliged to confirm regular income and a work contract prior to issue of a residence visa. Standardised rules were not in place, however, leaving the ultimate decision to the discretion of the bureaucrats concerned. Since 2005, the income requirements for third-country nationals have risen dramatically and now almost doubled. To access residence security, third-country nationals must have a regular fixed income enabling them to meet their current livelihood needs without resorting to welfare aid from local authorities.

Up until 2005, social assistance rates *(Sozialhilfesätze)* were used as a yardstick. The regulation of 2005 stipulated that the monthly income must coincide with the standard rates of the General Social Insurance Act (ASVG) *(Ausgleichzulagenrichtsätze)*. The calculation of adequate means for monthly subsistence for 2012 is €814.82 for single people, €1221.68 for married couples and €125.72 for each additional child. Credit payments and housing rent are included in the calculation of financial requirements, a burden that weighs heavily on low-income migrants. According to the standard rates in the General Social Insurance Act, only €260.35 (for 2012) is included as rent. If the rent is higher (assume €500), a married couple with two children must show evidence of an income amounting to €1712.77 (interview, Veli Çayci, *Beratungszentrum für Migranten und Migrantinnen*, 10 October 2011; Schumacher and Peyrl, 2012). Similar criteria apply when it comes to citizenship.

In the interviews, experts and stakeholders in the field stressed that besides the integration agreement, financial requirements are essential to a successful application for a long-term residency permit (interview, Veli Çayci, *Beratungszentrum für Migranten und Migrantinnen*, 10 October 2011; interview, Johannes Peyrl, *Arbeiterkammer Wien*, 13 October 2011). Some respondents saw the income requirements as a greater obstacle than the integration requirements. Stern points out that a full-time worker who earns the minimum wage according to the collective agreement in 2009 will not earn enough to fulfil the income requirement (Stern, 2012). Immigrants with low levels of education would have difficulty in fulfilling both requirements at the same time (Strik and Böcker, 2011). Furthermore, social workers emphasised that migrant workers in less qualified sectors frequently change their jobs, making it next to impossible to prove they had a regular fixed income (interview, Veli Çayci, *Beratungszentrum für Migranten und Migrantinnen*, 10 October 2011).

Conclusion

The case of the security of residence in Austria shows us that the policy phases and acting laws are an expression of conflicting political forces in Austrian politics, such as migrant organisations, judges, governing and far-right political parties, and EU and international law standards. Access to citizen rights lies at the centre of these social struggles, with several actors operating at the national, international and supranational level. Historically, there has been an expansion of rights for third-country nationals. Notably, the scope of rights and the circle of groups eligible for these rights have been enlarged and the criteria for access to this status standardised. While the literature highlights these levelling trends, I see the need to cast doubt. Studying the mechanisms and technologies at the intersection of citizenship and immigration policies in the case of Austria reveals a stratification of access to rights, in particular to secure residence status, for third-country nationals.

The technology of classification plays a major role when it comes to decisions about who is to be granted security of residence. The distinction between a residence permit and a settlement permit has remained characteristic for Austrian migration policy since the 1990s. For many migrants, the switch from temporary residence to permanent settlement is almost impossible in these cases, and 'undesirable' from an official migration policy perspective. Seasonal workers and other categories with temporary permits are excluded from permanent residency altogether.

The year 2005 was a turning point, since EU directives led to an expansion of rights. On the other hand, the introduction of formal demands and requirements under the integration agreement led to growing insecurity of residence status. As I have shown, for example, the level of language immigrants are required to meet was repeatedly increased in subsequent immigration reforms. Apart from the integration agreement, the fulfilment of financial requirements is also vital to the receipt of permanent residency. Furthermore, the technology associated with classification and additional conditionalities to secure the residence status, has gained significance in recent years. These factors have often been overlooked in the literature, which focuses primarily on 'cultural' integration requirements for the upgrading of a more secure residence status. While much of the literature sees cultural borders as new borders, I see language skills, economic conditions and the government technology of classification as equally important forms of drawing boundaries in terms of who has access to security of residence and its attendant rights.

Notes

1. The Directive on the Status of Long-Term Resident Nationals of Third Countries (2003/109/EC), the Directive on the Status of Third-Country Nationals, the Family Reunification Directive (2003/86/EC) and on the freedom of movement of EU citizens and their family members (2004/38/EC).
2. Similarly, Article 7(2) of the Family Reunification Directive allows member states to demand the compliance of third-country nationals with integration measures. This article is applicable to both admission and the granting of an autonomous residence permit (Strik and Böcker, 2011).

Part III
Introduction: Politics of Citizenship as Border Politics

Sabine Ruß-Sattar and Helen Schwenken

In large parts of migration and citizenship studies as well as in political theory, a notion of citizenship as a legal status that primarily focuses on the progressively inclusive effects and the allocation of membership rights also for immigrants (see Soysal, 1994 as the most often-cited author) has been predominant. However, recent contributions in citizenship studies turn around this implicitly normative notion and link it to the study of migration policies and border regimes – strands of research that have oftentimes been disconnected. They argue that citizenship policies also have their flip side and create inequality and can be used as a means to govern populations. Also, identity constructions and citizenship policies take place, as Mikuszies shows in her chapter, in the context of bordering policies, which assign emigration countries a specific geo-political position in the region. Hence, highlighting the politics of citizenship (Rygiel, 2010: 12), which can turn either way, can be an analytical angle to evaluate changes in citizenship regulations and related border policies.

The first chapter in Part III by Kim Rygiel therefore serves analytically as a bridge between border and citizenship studies by considering border controls as a citizenship technology in a Foucauldian sense. In a similar vein, the contributions of Helen Schwenken and Catherine Raissiguier stress the agentive focus on claiming citizenship by undocumented migrants. Critical migrations studies have approached the subject, but, up to now, tended either to over-estimate or under-estimate the no border activism: Thus, in the perspective of Agamben's 'logic of exception' (Agamben, 1995; cf. Rigby and Schlembach, 2013), migrants in camps are considered as immobilised and excluded subjects, while, to the contrary, authors who cling to the 'autonomy of migration' thesis, highlight the activism of undocumented migrants as social movement politics beyond citizenship. Therefore, Helen Schwenken's study critically tests these theoretical assumptions on the basis of the *Sansgatte* case. As Catherine Raissiguier demonstrates in her study of the French *sans papiers* movement, the citizenship concept is open to innovation and can be changed by migrants' agency. Actually, the *sans-papiers* do enact what Bosniak (2006) has proposed as a logical possibility: the citizenship of (undocumented) aliens. By their mobilisation the *sans-papiers* in France succeeded in rendering visible the various mechanisms that have placed them and keep them in zones of *infra-droit*. As Catherine Raissiguier points out, one of the most innovative moves made by the *sans-papiers* lies in their organising around an identity of lack, which enabled them to focus on the structural forces that shape their every-day lives and to ally with other groups that share this constructed lack. Beyond any doubt, this has been a brilliant move in the context of French political culture. However, one has to be aware of the fact that the political meaning of citizenship and the framing and political opportunity structures for migrants' agency vary among polities and their individual citizenship regimes.

The study of citizenship therefore is in need of comparative empirical research. In particular, there is a void within migration research with regard to citizenship regimes and citizenship policies of the countries of origin. Two chapters within this part therefore engage with countries of origin and their politics of citizenship entailing a re-nationalisation and multinationalisation of citizenship. In the following, the case studies on Morocco and Turkey explore more closely the construction of the citizenry of emigrants by different analytical perspectives. In contrast to Mikuszies' study of the official discourse on Moroccan diaspora, Jörg Nowak adopts the analytical tool of critical state theory to evaluate cross-border political activities. Thus, in his study on the activities of the Turkish right wing party MHP in Germany, he rejects the liberal dichotomy between political and economic spheres or the distinction *bourgeois vs. citoyen* and diagnoses migrant politics beyond borders as class politics backed by the state apparatuses of the country of origin as well as the host country. In this perspective, the crossing of borders – although the 'guest worker' programmes through which many of them migrated have been state-negotiated – implies for the migrant the risk to be subjugated to a doubled domination.

Totally opposed to this view is the concept of *citizenship à la carte* (Fitzgerald, 2009: 176) that has recently been proposed, suggesting a menu of rights to be chosen from by territorially absent citizens who also gain agency from their transnational orientation. But has migration really inverted the power relationship between sending state and emigrants in favour of the latter (Waldinger, 2013)? As Mikuszies' study clearly shows, overseas membership has certainly shifted from a control to a rhetorical courting of the diaspora, but 'lingering nationality' (Stasiulis, 2008: 142–143) still privileges 'patriotic duty' over freedom of rights. Interestingly, Esther Mikuszies finds a polyphonic assembly of argumentative patterns of the Moroccan king and government to refer to Moroccans living abroad, by which the diversity of Moroccans living abroad should be captured. However, it is important to note one exception: Similar to Sidney's finding in the second part of the volume, the status of undocumented migrants is highly sensitive and contested.

In the case of Morocco, the king and the state portray them as 'the bad' or 'unwanted' type of emigrant. Morocco even penalised irregular emigration. Only the legally abroad residing Moroccan is considered a legitimate citizen. Here, Morocco's geopolitical position could be an explanation, because Morocco attempts to maintain good political and cultural relations with the main countries of residence for Moroccans in Europe. Hence, Morocco uses its citizenship policies to support European border and immigration control claims. Furthermore, in this regard, its citizenship policy could be dubbed a non-manifest element of the *migration diplomacy* that increasingly becomes part of the new *high politics* in international relations as has been argued for the case of Turkey–EU relations by İçduygu and Üstübici in the first part of this volume.

9
Border Control Politics as Technologies of Citizenship in Europe and North America[1]

Kim Rygiel

In October 2009, 76 Tamils fleeing decades of civil war in Sri Lanka arrived off the coast of Vancouver Island, British Columbia, Canada, on the *Ocean Lady*. A year later, in August 2010, another boat carrying some 492 Tamil asylum seekers again arrived off the coast of British Columbia on the *MV Sun Sea*. Fearing that some might belong to the Liberation Tigers of Tamil Eelam (LTTE), listed as a terrorist organisation in Canada since 2006, these 'boat arrivals' galvanised the Canadian government to 'get tough' on irregular and uncontrolled migration. Despite heated opposition, in June 2011 the government of Canada quickly introduced 'anti-smuggling' legislation, the *Preventing Human Smugglers from Abusing Canada's Immigration System Act*, which was later rolled into an omnibus bill *Protecting Canada's Immigration System Act* that passed into law in June 2012. The anti-smuggling portion of this new legislation enables the government to create two classes of refugees by designating all those who arrive by boat en masse (including minors of 16 years and older) as 'irregular arrivals' and to detain irregular arrivals for up to a year as they wait for their refugee application to be processed. It also enables the government of Canada to deny those refugees designated as 'irregular arrivals' the right to apply for permanent residence for up to five years. During this time, this group of refugees may be prevented from travelling outside Canada or from sponsoring family members, all of which is contrary to both the Canadian *Charter of Rights and Freedoms* and international law.[2] This is but one example of the more punitive approach that the Canadian government has taken towards asylum seekers and irregular migrants in recent years. Canada, however, is not alone. The shift in Canadian policies is part of a larger trend across North America (see Rodriguez, in this volume), Australia (see Weber & Pickering, in this volume) and Europe of securitising mobility and migration in the post-9/11 period.

In Europe, governments are increasingly pursuing policies of 'push-back' and 'expulsion' that involve the externalisation of the detention of irregular migrants and asylum seekers to the borders of Europe. In order to deter asylum seekers from making multiple asylum claims, the Dublin Regulation of 2003 ('Dublin II') was implemented, requiring that asylum seekers be processed in the first country they pass though (European Commission, 2003). Countries on the external borders of the EU or the 'Schengen area', such as Greece, Italy, Malta (see Klepp, in this volume) and Spain, are now responsible for a disproportionate share of asylum seekers. This policy of 'push back' extends further to the increasing reliance of third, non-EU countries, such as Morocco, Turkey and Libya, to become Europe's border police, and to detain and accept irregular migrants and asylum seekers expelled and returned from countries in Europe (see Klepp, in this volume). Re-admission agreements and 'mobility partnerships' between EU countries or the EU and third countries are an important part of this process and one of the preferred methods of facilitating what is referred to more officially as the 'external dimension' of EU migration and asylum policy. In these agreements, countries often agree to accept returned irregular migrants and asylum seekers, often in exchange for money and development assistance (Europa, 2005; European Commission, 2013; Cassarino, 2010; see Mikuszies, in this volume).

In a period of supposedly heightened globalisation and free movement across borders, how are we to make sense of governments' growing reliance on more restrictive border controls to regulate the borders of European and North American countries? Just as physical mobility has become an ever more important resource and pathway towards upward economic and social mobility, governments are increasingly investing in border controls and security technologies with the aim of regulating and securitising mobility. As part of this, governments in the wealthier Global North are using discourses, technologies, practices and policies of citizenship as a means of governing mobile populations. Within this context, citizenship becomes, in the Foucauldian sense, a technology of government to regulate the very rights, access and ability to be and become mobile precisely at a time when, within an increasingly global and neoliberal economy, mobility has become one of the principle means by which individuals and groups are able to alter their conditions of life (fleeing war and violence, economic hardship or environmental devastation). In the current neoliberal era, moving often becomes the only survival strategy available to individuals and families, who often choose to invest in helping one relative re-locate to a wealthier country in Europe or North America in the hopes that this individual can then help support those back at home.

Yet, to look at how citizenship is used to regulate mobility across borders – citizenship as border control – reveals only part of the picture. For, as is revealed by the literature on the concept of the autonomy of migration, border controls often follow the agency of migrants and the pathways by which they choose to move. From this perspective, mobility is an important resource employed by migrants (e.g. Alioua, 2006; Rodriguez, 1996; Mezzadra and Neilsen, 2003, 2008; Mitropoulos and Neilson, 2006; Papadopoulos et al., 2008; Transit Migration, 2006). Restrictive border controls thus become important sites through which differentiated and stratified rights to movement are produced, negotiated and re-imagined (see Ataç, in this volume). On the one hand, from a perspective of *citizenship as government*, border controls place restrictions on migrants' mobility and generate new forms of inequality and exclusion. However, even as border controls restrict and exclude, they also generate social responses such as the growing activism of politicised groups of non-citizen migrants and those working in solidarity for migrants' rights. The remainder of this chapter sets out to outline the concept of *citizenship as government* to show how this approach bridges citizenship, border and migration studies.

Citizenship as government

'Citizenship' is often used as a term to refer, in a more narrow sense, to the institution of modern liberal citizenship as a legal status and membership in a political community, most commonly that of the nation-state. The liberal regime of citizenship is often associated with the history of the development of equal rights between all members of the nation-state, such as is articulated in the French *Declaration of the Rights of Man and Citizen* (1789) and the American *Declaration of Independence* (1776) as well as T.H. Marshall's (1950) well-known argument that liberal citizenship evolved through the extension of rights from civil rights in the eighteenth century to political rights in the nineteenth century and social welfare rights in the twentieth century. Modern liberal citizenship, however, is also tied as much to a history of exclusion as it is to one of inclusion. Historically, citizenship has also been a part and parcel of the more violent aspects of nation-building and state-making processes involving the exclusion and elimination of various groups of people from the polity. Citizenship is viewed, here, from the perspective of the dominant group against which others, non-citizens, are excluded from citizenship status, whether for reasons of nationality, ethnicity, religion, class, gender or sexuality (Isin, 2002: 275). However, what both of these readings of liberal citizenship miss, as Engin Isin (2002: X) observes, is the fact that '[c]itizenship and otherness are then really not two different conditions, but two aspects of the ontological that makes politics possible.' It would be a mistake, in other words, to equate and thereby reduce citizenship to either simply a progressive institution based on liberal rights or an exclusionary one, as both are integral parts of citizenship. Citizenship is constituted as an institution, status, or identity by those *excluded* from it – who have fought for or challenged the parameters of citizenship – as much as by the dominant classes and groups in society. It is for this reason that I use the term citizenship *as government* to place the idea of this politics of citizenship at the centre.

Following Foucault (1994), I use the term citizenship as government to refer to citizenship in a broader sense as the management or the 'conduct of conducts' of individuals and populations (Rygiel, 2010). Citizenship as government involves the practices, discourses, technologies and forms of power involved in governing individuals and populations, but which are also productive of ways of being political and of citizen and non-citizen political subjectivities (ibid.: 29). Within this context, border controls (e.g. travel policies using risk management and biometric technologies along with policies of detention and deportation) not only restrict the mobility and access to rights and resources of certain individuals and groups of people – for, as Foucault (1980: 139) observes, power is not simply constraining or limiting (power as that 'which says no') but power it also produces new responses, relations and subjectivities. Thus, while border controls often restrict movement, they also generate new forms of politics, ways of being political and political subjectivities. With the recent investment in risk management technologies across North America and Europe, for example, border controls are also productive of new ways of thinking about subjects, for example, as high and low risk travellers. As technologies of citizenship, border controls help to constitute notions of who can and cannot be a citizen and which non-citizens are constituted as less risky and permitted to circulate more freely within the spaces of citizenship (tourists or business travellers, for example) and which others, in contrast, are constituted as risky and even illegal, with their mobility restricted if not barred altogether from entry into the state (such as is the case with many irregular migrants and asylum seekers).

The emphasis of a *politics* of citizenship thus highlights the idea that citizenship is, at its core, a dialogical relationship between groups of people holding a gradation of statuses and rights, who engage with each other in ways that continually expand the boundaries of inclusion or conversely restrict it (Rygiel, 2010:38). As Engin Isin (2002, 2009; Isin and Nielsen, 2008) argues, citizenship has historically always been constituted as much by the non-citizen or 'others' to citizenship as it has by those who hold dominant positions in society whom we call 'the citizen' or 'active citizen' in the liberal sense of the term (as opposed to what Isin (2009) refers to as the 'activist citizen').[3] Women, for example, who historically were excluded from even being counted as political subjects, have pushed for the right to be recognised as legal persons and a series of related rights to vote, to work and to control their own bodies. From this perspective, the ontological condition of *being political* is a dialogical one integral to the concept of citizenship. As Isin (2002: X) explains, it is the moment when individuals constitute themselves as a group, 'simultaneously with and against others as an agent capable of judgment about what is just and unjust', in order to call into question the dominant workings of power and claim rights as political subjects.

This approach allows us to think about citizenship not only as dialogical but also as *performative* and *embodied* (Rygiel, 2010: 40–43). Citizenship is *performative* in that it involves not just legal status and membership, but also practices through which people engage in making claims to rights and, in the process, enact or constitute themselves as political subjects, that is as 'citizen subjects'. This means that one can engage and participate in the practice of citizenship, paradoxically, even if one lacks official legal citizenship status (see Raissiguier, in this volume). Such an approach to citizenship opens up space in which to talk about irregular migrant citizenship as that paradoxical moment when those without legal status can, by engaging in political tactics, practices and sociality, engage in either claiming rights that they do not have or materialising rights through practices. Here, the notion of 'acts of citizenship' (Nyers, 2003, 2008; Isin and Nielsen, 2008) explains how subjects (including non-citizens) enact themselves as political subjects by engaging in action and making claims to rights that they may not have, or have in theory but not in practice (as Isin argues, 'acts produce actors that do not exist before acts'). As Peter Nyers (2003: 1078) explains:

> The practices that enact political equality... are not necessarily coextensive with the legal status of citizenship. Acts of citizenship are as likely to be enacted by abject subjects as by citizen subjects. For Rancière, the point is that politics is 'a specific kind of connection' that 'comes about solely through interruption'. This involves those moments when abject subjects (in Rancière's terms, those who have 'no part' in the social order) articulate a grievance as an equal speaking being. For Rancière, this is a radical political moment. It qualifies as a quintessential political moment, what Isin identifies as the 'moment when the naturalness of the dominant virtues is called into question and their arbitrariness revealed'. Such moments enable the excluded – the abject – 'to constitute themselves as political agents under new terms, taking different positions in the social space than those in which they were previously positioned'.

The question that also arises here is whether such moments also include possibilities that may elude or even challenge notions of political subjectivity identified with citizenship. As Nyers and Rygiel (2012: 10) ask, 'Do we impose a category of citizenship subjectivity on peoples whose actions may not necessarily be framed this way? And, if so, do we eclipse other ways of being political?' We need to consider whether the terms of citizenship, even in its most radical potential, necessitate an embrace of the individual or population by government and if so, whether there might not also be ways of being political for which the terms of reference of citizenship might be at odds if the desire is to evade or remain invisible to the embrace of governmental authorities for example. While this is important to consider, citizenship nevertheless has historically been equated with political agency. Thinking about non-citizen migrant agency through the lens of citizenship can therefore be strategically useful if it opens up possibilities for disrupting the relationship and terms through which we currently think and practice our relationships within community and those positioned ontologically and physically on 'the other side'.

Finally, in addition to this performative aspect integral to the idea of 'acts of citizenship', citizenship is also always *embodied*, a point powerfully made by feminist scholarship (Hyndman, 2004; Biemann, 1999). As feminist scholars note, universal citizenship has 'historically taken on the characteristics of the perspectives and experiences of the white, male bourgeoisie. All experiences that have then differed – like women's experiences, which have historically been identified with sentiment and the realm of the body – are said to belong to the private rather than public realm and, therefore, as not properly belonging to the domain of citizenship (Young, 1989: 253)' (Rygiel, 2010: 38). Despite claims to universality, in other words, 'citizenship has historically been defined on the basis of a certain group of men's experiences and, as a result, has been restrictive of women's full and equal participation as citizens (Young, 1989; Yuval-Davis, 1999)' (Rygiel, ibid.).

Like citizenship, borders and mobility are also experienced differently by and through different bodies that are gendered, raced, classed and sexed in different ways. Those deemed to be risky or undesirable are often subject to much more restrictive controls and surveillance than those identified as desirable and less risky, a determination that has to do with a range of criteria including race and ethnicity, religion, class, gender and sex. In fact, the border often materialises through and on the body. As Shahram Khosravi (2010: 97) so powerfully explains in his chapter 'We Borders', 'My status as a Swedish citizen disappeared at the racialized border because of my face.... Borders have become invisible borders, situated everywhere and nowhere. Hence, undesirable people are not expelled by the border; they are forced to be the border.'

Viewed this way, citizenship is fundamentally about relations of governing and the constitution of political subjects. Citizenship evokes the language of social relations in connection to politics and subjectivity. This opens up space in which to strategically employ the language of citizenship to describe, on the one hand, the deployment of citizenship as discourse, policy and technologies of governing that utilise border controls as an essential means of regulating mobility while, on the other hand, also drawing attention to the contested nature of these processes involving struggles to negotiate and resist these controls. The benefit of such an approach is that it moves us away from the very strong border thinking that is so integral to, but which also limits, our thinking about citizenship as always being defined by the binary between non-citizen and citizen, and assuming these to be already ontologically settled identities. A politics of citizenship draws awareness, instead, to the idea that identities and subjectivities are produced through social and political relationships (they are not pre-societal, pre-political and settled) and thus, the nature of these relationships matter. They can potentially create different forms of what I would like to call a transgressive citizenship politics, which is an alternative way of thinking and doing citizenship based on acts of transgression of borders and boundaries motivated by concerns of social justice and solidarity. According to the Oxford Dictionary (1998, online edition), transgressive means 'to contravene or go beyond the limits set by a commandment, law etc.' or 'to infringe or go beyond the bounds of (a moral principle or other established standard of behaviour)'. Transgressive citizenship politics invokes the idea of a form of politics dependent on acts of crossing that disrupt a norm, rule or law. It involves forms of politics that are unconventional (crossing normative boundaries) but also transformative (in the sense that crossing disrupts the border). This would include political action that is transnational in nature, meaning acts that cross national and territorial borders, but also action that disrupts and displaces borders of belonging (the ontological, legal and political divide between the citizen and non-citizen) as definitive grounds upon which to legitimise claims and access to rights and resources.

Transgressive citizenship politics also speaks to the methodological challenges for those of us who wish to produce critical migration scholarship. One of the key methodological challenges is to give space to the voices, perspectives, knowledge and skills of people on the move (see also Schwenken, in this volume). But doing so demands that we find ways to simultaneously identify the very real constraints and injustices placed on certain non-citizens (irregular migrants, asylum seekers and refugees in particular) while simultaneously disrupting this citizen/non-citizen binary and the privileging of the citizen that accompanies it. Non-citizens are frequently portrayed as those simply lacking the qualities of citizens (power, status, rights, agency, voice) (Nyers, 2006a, 2006b). We need therefore to find ways of speaking about the restrictions of rights and mobility placed on non-citizens but doing so in ways that present non-citizens as power-full, that is as embodied with the capacity to act, despite being in unequal positions of power and lacking rights and status. For it is only when we recognise such agency that we can then move to having a conversation where we agree that all people should have rights to movement as political subjects, rights that then enable or prohibit access to a whole series of other rights such as employment, housing and social services (Anderson et al., 2012; McDonald, 2012; see Sidney, in this volume).

The tendency in much border and migration literature is to examine the security aspects, punitive consequences and violent effects of border controls on migrants. While this is certainly important, doing so without simultaneously paying attention to the agency of migrants who are involved in negotiating these border controls reduces migrants to the status of victims. All too frequently, discussion around migration (especially in academic and policy circles) tends to characterise the figure of the non-citizen 'irregular migrant', 'asylum seeker' or 'refugee' as either an 'illegal' body or criminal, a characterisation which is then used to create legitimacy for and justify a whole series of punitive responses. Alternatively, the non-citizen migrant/refugee tends to be characterised as a 'victim' in need of charity, a response that also is problematic because it denies agency and political subjectivity to the person (see also Johnson, 2011). It justifies assistance as charity but at the expense of the idea that persons are deserving of assistance simply because they are human beings and political subjects with a 'right to have rights' (Arendt, 1968: 297). Both positions erase the agency of groups of people on the move (such as irregular migrants, asylum seekers and refugees). As I have argued elsewhere (Rygiel, 2011b), such approaches can become complicit with the end goal of border controls that aim to strip people of rights, status and resources but also (as in the case of detention and deportation) to deny presence and voice and relationship to society and, as a result, to prevent this group of people – 'non-citizens' – from being seen by others – 'citizens' – as human beings with stories to tell. It is, in other words, an attempt to break any relations of solidarity, empathy and understanding from developing. A critical perspective on citizenship, such as evoked with a notion of citizenship as government hopes to draw attention to the way citizenship is used to create an exclusionary politics around the border and yet can also simultaneously be strategically invoked by those lacking citizenship status to make claims to political subjectivity and rights that they should have by virtue of personhood but do not have because they lack legal citizenship status.

Towards a transgressive politics of citizenship

As noted above, research on border controls tends to focus on the border and border controls as solely that which excludes and controls the movement of people, including migrants, across the border. While there is a need to continually bring the violence of the border to light and act against it, we need also to bring to light the politics of resistance that it also inspires. By violence, I am referring to a range of outcomes related to the negative consequences that borders have on people's lives. These include making legal movement difficult and thus forcing people into more precarious and irregular ('illegal') means of movement; restricting access to rights and resources and thereby preventing a larger global redistribution of the world's resources; and subjecting people to direct physical harm if they cross borders in unsanctioned ways, which can include forced detention, beatings, torture and death. Yet, even in the face of such violence, these very same borders can also, paradoxically, provide openings or act as bridges or what Nevzat Soguk (2007: 288) calls 'borderizations'. Soguk argues that borders should be defined not simply as walls of separation but as 'practices of relationality that become possible in moments of tensions, conflicts, and contradictions as well as unexpected convergences of intentionalities' that open up space for and can be 'productive of a transformative form of politics'. A few illustrative examples can be helpful here to elaborate on this in more concrete terms, the first of which is based on my own research in summer 2012 at the Turkey–Greece land border.

The Turkey–Greece land border has become in recent years a key entry point into Europe and a growing site of increased border control and violence at the border. Since 2010, the detection of illegal migrants and refusals of entry have dramatically increased at this land border. In its 2011 risk analysis report, Frontex (2011: 14) recorded a 45 per cent increase between 2009 and 2010 at the Greek land and sea borders with Turkey, and estimated that some 130,000 migrants cross into Greece by sea or along the Turkish border every year, with the Greek police arresting some 7000 migrants at the border in the month of September 2011 alone (Nielsen, 2012a). In an attempt to halt irregular migration, a new security fence was built along some 10 km of a 12.5 km stretch of land border between Greece and Turkey next to where the Evros/Meriç river runs equipped with watch towers and 23 thermal vision cameras (Nielsen, 2012b). Those migrants who attempt to cross are often subject to unofficial and illegal 'black deportations', which amount to a politics of pushing migrants back across the Evros/Meriç river to border points such as Edirne on the Turkish side of the border and off the Greek islands of Samos and Lesvos. This unofficial policy of pushing back migrants takes informal means whereby Greek border authorities may avoid processing asylum seekers and irregular migrants, preferring to return them instead across the border back to Turkey, often by precarious means, such as in rubber boats with holes poked into their sides (Pro Asyl, 2007). In the case of those pushed back to Turkey from Greece, asylum seekers may be picked up by Turkish police and placed in detention at the Edirne detention centre, once euphemistically referred to as a *misafirhane* or guest house and now a deportation centre. Recently rebuilt, the Edirne detention centre now shows whitish-pink walls and modern new facilities that include separate eating and sleeping quarters for men and women and a play area for children. Nevertheless, lest the new look should fool anyone, it is still very much a detention centre, where people are enclosed behind bars, their hands and faces peeking out from any available space between the bars placed over the windows in the hopes of catching a glimpse of the daylight on the other side. On the Greek side, migrants entering Greece from Asia or North and Eastern Africa are also held in detention, with plans now under way for the building of some 30 new detention centres, or 'closed hospitality centers' on unused military sites (Paphitsas, 2012). Greece has also begun renovations of existing detention centres after a powerful report by Pro Asyl et al. (2012)

documented the deplorable conditions of the detention centres in the Evros region. Alongside this violence of detention, deportations and the fence, there is also the horrific violence of death at the border as illustrated by the unmarked graves of a cemetery for illegal migrants who have died trying to cross the border. In a visit to the Turkish–Greek village of Sidiro, some 60 km away from the border and into the hills, the villagers there explained how they had buried eight migrants alone over the past week with a total of some 400 people now buried there (personal conversations, August 2012).

However, making visible this violence at the border and the restrictions placed on migrants' mobility is only part of the story. What a politics of citizenship adds here is to make visible the way the border has also become a bridge in 'practices of relationality' (Soguk, 2007: 288). What has emerged is a particular case of *transgressive citizenship politics*. This involves German and Greek activists working together as part of a transnational migrant solidarity network that brought them to discover the grave two years earlier and to work in solidarity with the families of the lost migrants to come to the village to reclaim their bodies. 'Welcome to Europe' is an NGO that campaigns on behalf of migrants and refugees in Greece and describes itself as 'a grassroots movement that embraces migration and wants to create a Europe of hospitality' (Welcome to Europe, n.d.). Its website posts extensive country-specific information directed at migrants to provide them with knowledge and advice about how to cross borders and make applications for asylum. This work is transgressive, because not only is the network a transnational one, but it also facilitates the ability of non-citizen irregular migrants, asylum seekers and refugees to cross country borders into Europe. By doing so, the network actively subverts the logics and intentions of governments to control their sovereign territorial borders through increased securitisation of the border aimed at preventing migrants from crossing borders and accessing European state territories. As the network explains, 'We welcome all travellers on their difficult trip and wish all of them a good journey – because freedom of movement is everybody's right!' (ibid.). The idea of the right to unfettered mobility expressed in this sentiment is itself transgressive, in that it challenges current normative frameworks around mobility within the international state system premised on the regulation of movement in and between states. For the last two years, members have been driving back and forth across Greece in a van they call the 'Infomobile', collecting information about undocumented migrants, asylum seekers and refugees, and helping trace relatives who have drowned or disappeared trying to cross the country's borders (conversation with Infomobile member, 26 July 2012). In this example of a transnational migrant solidarity network, the network is motivated by a transgression of the border – that is, by not just a crossing but also disruption of the borders, territorial and national borders, but also those ideological borders foundational to the European Union's notions of EU citizenship and belonging based on dividing people into citizen/non-citizen and legal/illegal subjectivities.

But the network's activities also transgress the border in other ways. By working with migrants and the families of lost migrants, these activist networks seek to reconstitute a politics of belonging in Europe that transgresses borders of citizen and non-citizen belonging. Motivated by social justice concerns and the right to dignity in life and in death, the network assists migrants in need and speaks out against the border, even holding memorials to honour those who have died crossing the border (Infomobile and Welcome to Europe, 2011: 10). Here, the network's actions are transgressive in the sense that they provide a space in which migrants and their families are key political actors working in solidarity with EU citizens. Migrants who have crossed into the EU can post any information about the border conditions they have experienced on the website in order to help others who might wish to cross while the families of migrants have become involved through the process of searching for lost relatives. The families make demands for rights to know about what happened to their missing relatives, and to identify and reclaim the bodies of their relatives, all of which makes much more visible the violence at the border.

In addition to this example of transnational activism, transgressive citizenship politics around the border can be seen in sites removed from the actual external border to city centres, for example, in Istanbul in the example of the Solidarity Kitchen (*Mutfak Kolektifi*) organised by the Migrant Solidarity Network (MSN). This project and the transgressive citizenship politics it illustrates bears a resemblance to the types of transgressive citizenship politics found in Sanctuary City movements (see Sidney, in this volume) and 'Don't Ask Don't Tell' campaigns undertaken in cities across North America, and the campaign undertaken by the Toronto chapter of 'No One Is Illegal' in particular. These two examples further illustrate how citizens, together with non-citizen migrants, engage in forms of citizenship politics that aim to disrupt citizenship/non-citizenship statuses and legalities and to challenge the presence of border politics not just at the external border, as the former example shows, but also within city spaces. In these examples, political action makes visible the way in which the external border is diffused throughout internal spaces of the state, such as within the everyday lives of migrants living in the city with the effect of restricting their abilities to access rights and resources.

The Solidarity Kitchen is located in Tarlabaşı, one of the poorer neighbourhoods of Istanbul, which is home to a number of migrants passing through Turkey on their way to the EU. It is also home to Kurdish residents, many of whom are also migrants who have relocated from the southeast and other parts of Turkey to Istanbul. The kitchen is described appropriately in the following promotional flyer: 'There is a kitchen in Tarlabaşı. It is not like any other kitchen. It has neither cooks nor customers. Here, everybody is a cook and all the food is shared. It belongs to the neighbourhood and everyone is welcome,' (Amargi Istanbul, n.d.). The Solidarity Kitchen provides an open space in which residents of the area can mingle with Turkish and non-Turkish activists, a number of whom are also migrants, with some passing through Istanbul on their way through to Europe and others having decided to stay and who are now living, working or studying in the city. On the day I visited the kitchen, I met people from Nigeria, the Democratic Republic of Congo, France, Switzerland, Turkey, Azerbaijan, the UK and the US. The kitchen provides a space in which different people come together through collaborative food production and have the opportunity to get to know each other as people. Every Saturday people come to the kitchen to prepare and cook food, provided by donations from local food suppliers and eco-farmers who support the kitchen in this way. After a full day of cooking, which includes a great deal of storytelling, laughing and listening to music, everyone has the chance to eat together. The remaining food is offered during the week on certain nights open to residents of the area. The Solidarity Kitchen also serves as an informal classroom for Turkish and English language instruction. The language classes are offered not only by Turkish residents but also by the non-citizen migrants, who are equal participants in all the activities of the kitchen project. As one of the organisers, Begüm Özden Fırat, explained, the idea of the project was motivated by the desire to find a way to bring people together not through charity but rather in a way where both migrants and Turkish people could be together (conversation 21 July 2012). Sharing food seemed a good way to do this. The kitchen is open to everyone to come in and work together to prepare the food and serves the neighbourhood, but it is also a space to create 'encounters' where Turkish and Kurdish residents in the area have the opportunity to get to know migrants coming from outside of Turkey from countries such as Nigeria and Ethiopia (ibid.).

This example illustrates transgressive citizenship politics in that it is organised around the idea of working together regardless of legal status and non-citizen/citizen identities. The activities are designed to disrupt such borders by bringing people together across a variety of different statuses and identities to engage with one another through acts of sharing in the cooking and eating of food together. The kitchen serves the community and acts as a drop-in social and educational place for Turkish and non-Turkish residents alike. The project is transgressive in that it disrupts traditional ways of thinking about citizenship politics, in which citizens, or those with legal status, are deemed to be the political actors in contrast to non-citizens, often portrayed to be either illegal or victims, and thus addressed through either punitive measures or charity. The Solidarity Kitchen challenges both types of responses. It develops forms of assistance in which non-citizen migrants are also the principle political actors of change working in collaboration with

Turkish citizens to make claims to basic rights such as food and a right to belong in the city.

The transgressive politics enacted through the Solidarity Kitchen also resembles the politics employed in the Sanctuary City and 'Don't Ask Don't Tell' campaigns promoted by North American migrant solidarity networks, such as by the Toronto chapter of 'No One Is Illegal'. Explaining the logic behind the politics of these campaigns, Jean McDonald (2012: 129), a member of 'No One Is Illegal' and a key figure in organising 'Don't Ask Don't Tell' campaigns writes: 'Policies at local, municipal levels that create accessible social rights and community services for all residents, regardless of immigration status, pose a challenge to state-defined "migrant illegality"... By making services accessible for people with precarious status... these governmentalized, internal borders can be circumvented, and migrant illegality can be "unmade"'. The idea behind such movements is to have cities pass resolutions that can challenge federal immigration laws at the municipal level to become in some ways 'sanctuary cities' for those without legal status. As McDonald (2012: 131) further explains:

> Over fifty cities have passed legislation that forbids the use of municipal funds, resources and workers for the enforcement of federal immigration laws. Others, such as Los Angeles, Chicago, Portland, Seattle, New York City and Minneapolis to name a few, have taken more proactive roles, whereby specific legislation bars city workers from inquiring into and/or disseminating immigration information regarding persons using city services (ibid. [National Immigration Law Center, 27 February 2004]). Resolutions passed in Baltimore, Austin, Cambridge, and several other cities affirm that no city service will be denied on the basis of formal citizenship status (ibid.). These changes in municipal policy were not simply 'granted' by municipalities; rather, these transformations were hard-won by (im)migrants, refugees and their allies through research, networking, advocacy and political action.

These politics are transgressive because they disrupt the normative politics of the border, where the identity of non-citizen and illegal status is imposed on a person, a status and identity that is then used to restrict access to social services within the city. Yet, they are also transgressive in that the campaign action is undertaken by non-citizen migrants working together in solidarity with citizens to make claims for rights to daily living needs on the grounds of being political subjects and residents of the city, regardless of legal citizenship status. In Toronto, the 'Don't Ask Don't Tell' campaign began in 2004 and works to promote the idea of access to public services for all members of the city regardless of citizenship status. The idea is to get municipalities to pass resolutions that prohibit city workers from asking about a person's status or revealing it to other officials, with the hope of ensuring that all city residents, legal or not, can access essential services without fear of arrest and/or deportation. In Toronto, the campaign established a policy, for example, with the Toronto District School Board to commit to working towards making this a safe zone for students regardless of status. It also worked to prevent school officials from collecting or passing on information to immigration officials about students' status. By engaging in political action to claim rights to the city, non-citizen migrants enact themselves as if citizens, that is as political subjects, making claims to rights. As McDonald observes (2012: 131):

> Municipal policies that affirm access to city services, regardless of formal legal status and without fear of information sharing with federal immigration enforcement enable a double reconfiguration. First, the potential of cities as spaces that enable substantive citizenship is re-affirmed. Second, active citizenship itself is reconfigured. The social space of migrant illegality, while certainly not abolished, is re-made through the establishment of (porous) city boundaries. Municipal policies affirming the right to public services for all members of the metropolis pose an important challenge to state definitions of migrant illegality.

These campaigns show parallels with the Solidarity Kitchen in Istanbul in that the goal of both is to make city spaces safe for non-citizen migrants to live, spaces in which they, too, can access basic needs such as food, community and, in the case of Toronto, access to public services such as the right for children, regardless of status, to receive an education. The campaigns embody a transgressive politics in that they reveal a practice of including both non-citizens and citizens working together as political actors and, through this, seeking to challenge the meaning of who is a citizen of the city (see for other cases Sidney, in this volume).

Conclusion

In this chapter I have sought to outline an approach to citizenship as government that links citizenship studies to border and migration studies. Citizenship as government refers to the ways in which discourses, practices and technologies of border controls are employed by governments to govern mobile populations. However, as Foucault points out, power is never simply constraining but is also always productive. In the process of regulating mobility, border controls are also constitutive of new mobile subjects and ways of enacting oneself as political through mobility. Such a perspective, I have argued, demands attention to the politics of citizenship. Rather than assuming that citizen and non-citizen identities are already defined, such subjectivities are always being made and re-made in relation to one another at and through the border. As I have briefly alluded to here, this can involve, for example, the constitution of mobile persons through categories of riskiness, as has also been shown in the case of Australia by Weber and Pickering and Sack in this volume. Yet, if we take seriously the insights of the autonomy of migration perspective that highlight the agency of migrants, border controls are always contested and borders can therefore also be constitutive of other mobile subjects such as what I refer here to as *transgressive citizen subjects*. The violence at and of the border is a moment that can also bring people together to act in solidarity and resistance across the territorial borders and citizen/non-citizen divide. What the empirical examples of transgressive citizenship politics illustrate are new ways of engaging with the border. The violence at/of the border emboldens new forms of migrant solidarity networks and transgressive citizenship politics that work transnationally across the border as well as within the state, in cities for example. The aim of such new border politics is to disrupt external border controls that restrict peoples' movements across borders as well as the ontological borders of citizens and non-citizens. In so doing, these new types of transgressive citizenship politics engage in a fundamental questioning of who can and cannot be a citizen and the association of status with basic rights to a decent quality of life.

Notes

1. This chapter is based on my talk at the International Symposium of the Network 'Critical Migration and Border Regime Research' (kritnet), Kassel, 13–15 July 2012. It builds on work published in *Globalizing Citizenship* (2010) and *Citizenship, Migrant Activism and the Politics of Movement* (2012), co-edited by Peter Nyers. Research on the Turkey-Greece border is made possible through funding from the Social Science and Humanities Research Council of Canada.
2. As James Hathaway (2005: 160) notes, refugees are entitled according to international law and the 1951 *Refugee Convention* (United Nations 1951) to a 'basic first order of rights', which includes at a minimum a prohibition against returning a refugee to a place where they risk being persecuted (i.e. Article 33 on *non-refoulement*). However, an expanded set of rights applies when refugees are simply 'physically present' in a state's territory regardless of how they arrive. These include 'rights to receive identity papers, to freedom from penalization for illegal entry, and to be subject to only necessary and justifiable constraints on freedom of movement' (Hathaway, 2005: 171). For example, Article 31 of the *Refugee Convention* stipulates that countries 'shall not impose penalties, on account of their illegal entry or presence' and 'shall not apply to the movements of such refugees restrictions other than those which are necessary'.
3. In contrast to the modern liberal notion of the citizen or 'active' citizen, who practices citizenship by voting, military service and paying taxes, Isin (2009: 380) suggests we think of the 'activist' citizen as one who, independent of legal status, enacts his or herself as a political subject through acts that present a 'sense of making a break, a rupture, a difference'.

10
Troubling Borders: *Sans-papiers* in France

Catherine Raissiguier

Border-making technologies are no longer simply at work at the geographical edges of the nation and governed only by state border regimes; they are now at play in myriad locations and implemented by a variety of state and non-state actors. In this essay, I draw from my recent work on the *sans-papiers* in France to illustrate some of the ways in which borders are being established through material and discursive practices that not only mark and bound the national territory, but also help sort which subjects – that is, *who* – belongs within (Raissiguier, 2010). Such practices draw from existing race-based, class-based and gender-based metaphors to construct certain subjects, who then have no choice but to reside on the borders of the Republic. While these subjects have affected the reality of many immigrants (documented and undocumented alike) and their French children – one only need to think of the treatment of young French men of North African origin in France today – this essay focuses primarily on the *sans-papiers*, who provide an excellent point of entry for the analysis presented herewith.

Sans-papiers are undocumented migrants and refugees often under threat of deportation. Organised through local collectives and broad activist networks, since the mid-90s they have been advocating the legalisation of their immigration status. The *sans-papiers* argue that it is the French state itself and its increasingly restrictive immigration policies that created them. By insisting they are not *clandestins* – a French word connoting both the illegal and the hidden – but simply without papers (and hence without rights), they point out and trouble the various mechanisms that locate them in social spaces where they lack the most basic of civil rights. In doing so, they help us see some of the contradictions that lie at the core of the French Republic. For example, the very presence of *sans-papiers* on French territory, their refusal to go away, and their bold politics call into question the notion of a French republican exceptionalism based on abstract rights and universal equality.

France – when it comes to its immigration politics – has long managed to hold onto and deploy both inside and outside its borders the idea of a *French exceptionalism*, while at the same time aligning itself with a broad EU trend of immigration control and border closure for third-country nationals.[1] In fact, it can be argued that the French exceptionalism narrative stands as one of the most successful, enduring and contradictory aspects of French political culture.[2] Here, I suggest that the 'exceptional' nature of the French political tradition resides rather in its ability to propagate a strong discourse of universal inclusion and equality along with its unique resistance to acknowledging past and present exclusionary and discriminatory discourses and practices. The former discourse has fuelled productive forms of resistance and contestation such as those produced by the *sans-papiers*. The latter has, on the other hand, certainly limited the potential for these immigrants to be liberated.

In his comparative study of France and Britain, Adrian Favell writes that French ruling élites, through the sheer reiteration of the 'French exceptionalism' narrative, participate in the 'reaffirmation of a particular national myth' (Favell, 2001: 43). Favell sees the myth of French republican citizenship as a public theory 'at pains to mask the recentness and artificiality of its construction and the incompleteness of the questions it focuses on' (Favell, 2001: 43). Belying the dominant 'French exceptionalism' narrative, Favell points to the growing influence of supranational forces (and the related declining role of national intellectual élites) on immigration policies in France. Interestingly, in the preface to the second edition of *Philosophies of Integration,* Favell also acknowledges the unique role played by the *sans-papiers* movement in challenging the republican myth of citizenship and, in the process, generating a growing awareness of the 'racially-inflected' position of 'black African migrants' in France: 'The outcome of the grassroots *sans-papiers* movement also revealed a new edge to French immigration politics, introducing critical arguments about human rights and "personhood" in a French debate normally dominated by nationally-bounded normative considerations,' (Favell, 2011: xvi–xvii).

The material and discursive positioning of undocumented immigrants

By disrupting business as usual and inserting 'critical arguments' within immigration discussions in France, the *sans-papiers* movement invites us to rethink French understandings of citizenship, national belonging and equality. In this essay, more specifically, I discuss some of the ways in which undocumented immigrants are positioned and maintained materially and discursively at the borders of the French Republic and, in turn, engage in political practices that upset these material and discursive borders.

In *Politics and the Other Scene*, Étienne Balibar argues that, today, borders are not only lines that divide and define territories; they are also mechanisms that produce identities. 'Every discussion of borders' Balibar writes, 'relates, precisely, to the establishment of definite identities, national or otherwise' (Balibar, 2002: 76). According to Balibar, the production of a collective 'us,' which is supposed to coincide with a delimited territory and – in the case of France – with a shared political culture, requires the parallel production of a collective 'them.' The racialisation of entire migrant communities – composed primarily of black and Muslim immigrants and their children – can be seen as a key element of this work of (national) identity production. Women, I argue, are central figures in this production. Thus, processes of racialisation and their gendered underpinnings must be seen as core elements of 'doing borders' in contemporary France.

Within the context of postmodernity, late capitalism and globalisation, Balibar continues, borders are now everywhere. They are ubiquitous: '*Some borders are no longer situated at the borders at all*, in the geographico-politico-administrative sense of the term. They are in fact elsewhere, wherever selective controls are to be found, such as for example, health and security checks' (Balibar, 2002: 84; cf. Rodriguez, in this volume, on housing control; Weber and Pickering, in this volume, on access to public services; Ataç, in this volume, on bureaucratic boundary drawing). Under these new conditions, Balibar argues, borders have thickened into zones or 'grids' where some people reside indefinitely. In that sense, borders are no longer external and clearly discernible objects. Rather, these 'inner' borders are often invisible and yet shape the daily reality of those who reside there. As a consequence, 'borders are becoming the object of protest and contestation as well as of an unremitting reinforcement' (Balibar, 2002: 92). Here, a focus on the *sans-papiers* is especially productive, as it affords unique insights into these borderzones, where some are made to reside in the most precarious of living conditions, as well as on the ways in which 'inner' borders are contested by those who reside there.

Bringing to bear current debates on borders (and border control) through Balibar's theoretical lenses on my recent analysis of the *sans-papiers*, this essay is organised around three related themes. In the next section, I provide a theoretical frame for conceptualising the *sans-papiers* as 'impossible subjects' of the French Republic. Then, I briefly illustrate some of the mechanisms that produce 'impossible identities' as well as some of the 'impossible' social locations – the inner borders invoked by Balibar – they are made to occupy. Finally, I look at some of the ways in which *sans-papiers* have been upsetting the borders of the Republic. Throughout, I pay particular attention to the gendered dimension of un/doing borders in the context of the *sans-papiers* movement.

Borders, citizenship and impossible subjectivities

Borders and citizenship are linked and are key elements of the modern nation-state; together, they stand as a precondition for popular representation (democracy) within a bounded national territory. However, both are also profoundly anti-democratic. Indeed, according to Balibar, the borders stand as

> the point where, even in the most democratic of states, the status of citizen returns to the condition of a 'subject,' where political participation gives way to the rule of police. They are the absolutely nondemocratic, or 'discretionary,' condition of democratic institutions. And it is as such that they are most often, accepted, sanctified and internalized.
>
> (Balibar, 2004: 109)

Similarly, as Linda Bosniak has convincingly argued in *The Citizen and the Alien*, for liberal democratic societies, citizenship is always dual and contradictory. On the one hand, and within a particular nation-state, citizenship functions as the basic framework for inclusion and democratic belonging (universal citizenship). On the other hand, citizenship presupposes the existence of a limited and bounded national community based on the exclusion of non-members (bounded citizenship). Bosniak highlights how, in many conventional accounts, these two meanings get conflated. This confusion not only reduces the usefulness of the concept but also obscures the very production of stratified 'others' embedded in the institution of citizenship. Pointing to the 'romanticism' inherent in hegemonic understandings of universal citizenship, Bosniak poses a crucial question: 'who' is it 'that rightfully constitutes the subjects of the citizenship that we champion?' (Bosniak, 2006: 1).

Societies committed to egalitarian democratic principles often attempt to solve this tension by promoting a politics of immigration control and regulation (a hardening of the exterior border) while asserting and protecting the rights of immigrants residing within the national territory (a softening of the interior). This compromise has certainly been the hallmark of the French politics of immigration since the 1970s. Political and legal theoretical models that build on this inside/outside dichotomy and rely on the insularity of the nation-state are flawed, Bosniak contends. They ignore the increasingly porous quality of borders and cannot address the ways in which rules of citizenship (which include the terms of residency and entry at the border as well as rights afforded to aliens on the inside), shape and construct one another.

Notwithstanding the political and analytical usefulness of Bosniak's study and her acknowledgment that 'identity' is indeed one of the core elements of citizenship, *The Citizen and the Alien* falls into a broad body of scholarship that treats citizenship primarily as a legal/political concept. By focusing on technologies of power that construct 'impossible subject' positions within the Republic as well as the resistance strategies that those who inhabit these positions are forced to deploy, in this essay I treat both borders and citizenship as mechanisms of subject formation. In addition to Étienne Balibar's notion of borders as producers of identities, I draw from the work of Aihwa Ong, who conceptualises citizenship as subject-making and calls for analyses that focus on 'the everyday processes whereby people, especially immigrants, are made into subjects of a particular nation-state' (Ong, 1996: 737).

For instance, increasingly restrictive immigration policies in France have turned large numbers of immigrants, among them many women, into '*clandestins.*' By intensifying police scrutiny and symbolically constructing certain immigrants as criminals and outsiders, recent immigration laws have, in fact, intensified the forms of civil and economic *précarité*, or 'precariousness', that many of them experience.[3] Against the backdrop of global economic transformations, the construction of Europe and increased national anxieties, it can be said that hegemonic discursive and material practices construct certain immigrants as 'impossible subjects' of the Republic.

I borrow the term '*impossible*' from a small group of scholars who use the concept of 'impossibility' to analyse related but different mechanisms of belonging and exclusion. In France, discursive constructions of foreigners as 'impossible citizens' date back to the beginnings of the French Republic. Sophie Wahnich, in her work on hospitality and national belonging in the context of the French Revolution, documents how the foreigner takes shape (*prend forme*) through a series of discourses and practices that posit him or her as a potential traitor to the budding nation-state between 1789 and 1794 (Wahnich, 1997). Wahnich documents, among other things, the emergence of a new administrative apparatus that singles out foreigners and, in the process, creates different types of subjects within the Republic:

> The dyad foreigner/national is constructed during the revolution on these bases, the nation can only be one and indivisible.... In a revolution where the stranger remains a paradox of announced universality, the territorialisation of identities is the avowal of an accepted closure of the revolutionary project.
>
> (Wahnich, 1997: 81)[4]

In the ongoing tension between dreams of hospitality and needs for security of the first years of the Republic, Wahnich argues that the stated formal rights of foreigners are sharply weakened by their increased surveillance (Wahnich, 1997: 123).

Mae N. Ngai (2004) charts a history of immigration restriction in the US that began after World War I, to uncover the dual and related production of illegal aliens as impossible subjects of the US as a modern nation. Restriction, Ngai argues,

> invariably generated illegal immigration and introduced that problem into the internal spaces of the nation. Immigration restriction produced the illegal alien as a new legal and political subject, whose inclusion within the nation was simultaneously a social reality and a legal impossibility – a subject barred from citizenship and without rights.... The illegal alien is thus an 'impossible subject,' a person who cannot be and a problem that cannot be solved.
>
> (Ngai, 2004: 4–5)

By focusing on South Asian queer politics in the US, Gayatri Gopinah (2005) analyses and challenges the various processes that elide the possibility of certain subjectivities within dominant nationalist and diasporic discourses. 'Given the illegibility and unrepresentability of a non-heteronormative female subject within patriarchal and heterosexual configurations of both nation and diaspora' Gopinah argues, 'the project of locating a "queer South Asian diasporic subject" – and a queer female subject in particular – may begin to challenge the dominance of such configurations. Revealing the mechanisms by which a queer female diasporic positionality is rendered impossible strikes at the very foundation of these ideological structures' (Gopinah, 2005: 16).

I use this concept of impossibility to illustrate the complex mechanisms that establish impossible subject positions within the French nation. These mechanisms include discursive practices that turn certain immigrants into inconceivable members of the national body as well as material/legal practices that locate them in spaces of impossibility. In addition, I point out the unnerving and 'unruly' forms of political interventions that these mechanisms elicit. Here, I draw on the work of Monisha Das Gupta on South Asian politics in the US to evoke the ways in which immigrants are involved in political practices that question nation-based understandings of civil membership and invent new ways to stake their claims and stage their battles (2006). In particular, like Das Gupta, I am interested in exploring the various ways in which certain immigrants 'fight against multiple techniques of subordination through claims that do not rely on citizenship' (2006: 2). Within a 'complex of rights' that draws on local, national and transnational laws, these immigrants creatively engage the political system that has created the social impasses in which they find themselves (Das Gupta, 2006: 16).[5]

The construction of *sans-papiers* as impossible subjects of the French Republic involves complex, intertwined and often contradictory processes.

They include political, academic and media discourses that render the *sans-papiers* and their claims unintelligible within the Republic; legal, social and political mechanisms that construe certain migrants and their communities as outside the reach of democratic inclusion; and administrative practices that exacerbate the precariousness and vulnerable nature of the living conditions *sans-papiers* are trying to escape. All are deeply gendered operations that place some immigrant women at the centre of border production in contemporary France.[6] In this essay, I will only briefly illustrate a couple of these processes and highlight how rules of entry and residency and rights afforded to immigrants within the national space shape and construct one another. In addition, my analysis sheds light on the ways in which social realities within France (such as the lack of affordable and decent housing for instance) impacts the social spaces where the *sans-papiers* are obliged to reside.

The *Sans-papières* on dwelling in/on the borders

In 2002, six years into the struggle initiated by some 300 undocumented immigrants in 1996, I collected interviews of men and women involved in the *sans-papiers* movement. This section of the paper is based on these interviews, as well as interviews collected by the French feminist activist network RAJFIRE – *Réseau pour l'Autonomie Juridique des Femmes Réfugiées/Immigrées* in 1998 (RAJFIRE, 2000).[7] Both sets of interviews illustrate some of the ways in which borders, despite their inherently porous quality, have both 'hardened' and 'thickened,' in the process producing more precarious and vulnerable living conditions for undocumented migrants in general and for women in particular.

Indeed, the interviews confirm the fact that, for most of these women, immigrating to France and especially staying there legally has become semi-impossible. This is partly due to the fact that visas have become much harder to obtain, and that family reunification laws have tightened considerably (Raissiguier, 2007). Maîmouna, for instance, points out the virtual impossibility for women like her to obtain anything but a short-stay visa:

> They [the people reviewing her regularisation application] told me that I did not have a long-stay visa [and on this basis denied my change of status]. But from Africa, when you go to France, that's not possible, if you're not a civil servant, if you're not rich. A poor woman like me cannot obtain a long-stay visa: that's not possible.
>
> (RAJFIRE, 2000)

The interviews also highlight how undocumented women have had to negotiate increasingly complex and arbitrary immigration regulations and controls. They document the arbitrariness of the decision-making mechanisms that render *sans-papiers* and *sans-papières*[8] much more vulnerable to all sorts of discriminatory and exploitative practices. Of particular interest here is the evaluation of familial ties that affect the ways in which applications are reviewed and decisions are made. Some women indicate that their single and childless status has worked against them, as in the case of Nathalie (RAJFIRE, 2000): 'Because I am single, I don't have children. I am not entitled to papers.' It is important to note here that despite the unevenness with which these matters are decided, women are often penalised not simply because they do not have familial ties in France, but because they still have familial connections 'back home.' Whether these connections are meaningful to the women themselves is, of course, of no importance to the French administration. Despite a 13-year stay in France, Khadidja, who has not been able to obtain a change of status, recounts in another RAJFIRE interview, 'in the negative decision I was sent [it says that] I am single. I don't have any dependents [in France] and my familial links are back home' (RAJFIRE, 2000).

Finally, they shed light on some of the gendered underpinnings of past and present French immigration policies, their implementation, and their impact on certain migrant communities. The women I interviewed had a variety of reasons for wanting to leave their countries. Some wanted to study abroad, others wanted to live full and independent lives, yet others wanted to be closer to family or access better healthcare, and many wanted to escape increasingly difficult living conditions. Despite great differences in these women's immigration trajectories, most of my interviews – like those conducted by the RAJFIRE activists – underscore the near impossibility of obtaining long-term visas and entering France through legal family reunification procedures. As a whole, they confirm the idea that the restrictive turn in immigration policies in France has greatly contributed to the '*clandestinisation*' and '*precarisation*' of certain immigrant women (Wihtol de Wenden and DeLey, 1986). Such processes of *clandestinisation* and *precarisation*, it has been argued, produce internal 'borderzones' where *sans-papiers* and *sans-papières* are forced to reside. Sami Naïr (1997) and Danièle Lochack (1985), for instance, have written about the creation of zones of *infra-droit* (substandard right) for immigrants in which policing, arbitrary administrative decisions and exclusionary practices have replaced the strict application of egalitarian principles and universal human rights often touted as the hallmark of French republicanism.

Most of the women I interviewed slipped into a 'clandestine' status only after they had exhausted other means of legal entry and stay. Lamria's story illustrates this gradual and inevitable process of *clandestinisation* well. Indeed, after several unsuccessful tries, Lamria – like most of the women I interviewed – decided to enter the country using a short-term (tourist) visa. Like most of them, she became undocumented after she overstayed her visa:

> In fact I arrived [in France] at the end of 1998 with a one-month tourist visa. I had tried to obtain a family reunification from there [Algeria], but

> I could not. I could not obtain the visa. In 1993, I came and stayed three months in France (I had taken a leave of absence back home) and since I saw how difficult it was... I wanted to register with the university.... I went back with an acceptance letter.
>
> I filed my request with the French consulate in Algeria. But I gave up – in respect to studying and starting something here. In 1993, I filed a request and I did not get an answer. In 1998, I filed again for a long-term visa and the consulate sent me a one-month tourist visa. I told myself, I will take this opportunity to stay.... My sister put me up (my sisters are married, have children and have the French nationality). In 1999, I married a Franco-Algerian with the French nationality, but with Algerian roots like me.

In spite of the fact that her family does reside legally in France and that some of her siblings are French nationals, Lamria clearly falls outside the limits of family reunification policy, because only children born in France to parents born in Algeria before 1962 are French at birth though the principle of double *jus soli*. Discouraged by her many rejections, Lamria entered the country legally but with the intention to overstay. This step-by-step movement away from legal stay (and more rarely entry) is common among the women I interviewed. Before accepting a future of living without papers, most try as hard as they can to work within the tight limits of French immigration law. It is only when all legal paths are exhausted that these women embrace more risky strategies.

Louisa is another example of what we might call the 'administrative production of illegality.' In her interview, she recounts her failure, as a child, to avail herself of the legal process of family reunification. While waiting to have her sister, who lives in France, become her legal guardian, Louisa entered the country on a tourist visa. Her brother, who is younger, stayed behind but intended to follow when the paperwork was done. In her interview, Louisa recalls the various mechanisms that, in the end, fail both of them in different ways.

> My parents are old, so we filed a request to have my sister become my and my little brother's guardian. At that time my little brother was 15 and I was 17. So I came with a tourist (short-term) visa, because it's impossible to obtain a long-term visa there.
>
> We started the paperwork in 1994. Then we received a notice to come to court. But later, in 1995, we were told that my sister could not become my legal guardian because [by then] I had turned 18. The request was granted for my little brother who had stayed in the Comoros, but we were not able to have him come because he was not granted a visa. So for me, who was

here, the request was denied. For my brother, who was there, the request was granted; but he could not come!

For both of them, a family reunification procedure would have to have been initiated by their sister and approved before they could come to France. The level of planning, the technical difficulties in obtaining the required documentation and the slowness of administrative decisions, as well as the arbitrariness of the decision-making process, all work towards the *clandestinisation* of the women I interviewed. Indeed, the combination of more restrictive immigration policies (family reunification included) and the generalisation of visa requirements, as well as the quasi-impossibility of obtaining long-term visas, have left many of them with the sole option of overstaying a tourist visa or entering the country illegally. Malika's experience illustrates the latter:

> That's right, she [my sister] sent me the papers I needed to show that she would put me up, she sent me everything, but it's Morocco; they did not grant me a visa because I was without a salary and I did not have a bank account; neither I nor my father. I did not have anyone [there] – my whole family is here.... What I wanted was a visa, even for two weeks only. But they did not grant me one and then, I decided to come in anyway, then I came in like that without a visa, illegally.

In Malika's case, it is the very structure of living and working in the Global South that makes it impossible for her to make a strong case for her visa request. Indeed, neither she nor her father could demonstrate steady employment (pay stubs) or sufficient income (a bank account) requested by the administration in charge of processing visas. Not being able to come through legal means, even for a short time, made Malika consider crossing the borders with someone else's papers. Of all the women I interviewed, however, she is the only one who has entered the country without a visa: 'I came through with the papers of someone who looked like me.'

Interestingly, some of the interviews illustrate also how past (gendered) immigration policies and practices in France affect present ones. In Lisa's case, for instance, a strategy from the 1960s of placing African male workers in special housing projects (*foyers de célibataires*) to limit family immigration would come to haunt her in the 1990s, when she and her husband tried to reunite.[9] Indeed, when Lisa's husband filed a request to bring his wife under the legal provision of family reunification, it was rejected because his housing arrangement is not adequate under the law. As Lisa explains,

> Before I came to France I had been married already, since 1996. I stayed in Algeria to wait for family reunification but it was not done because my

husband was living in a housing project for single men; and that [was] not possible.

Many immigrant men still live in these *foyers*, which offer an alternative to the prohibitive rents in the French housing market. Lisa's husband would have had to rent a large enough apartment months ahead of starting the application procedure in order to document adequate housing for his family reunification request. Needless to say, this is not likely to happen for many immigrants who have a hard time securing low-income housing in large French urban centres. It is interesting to note here – as an illustration of the localisation of border regimes – that the second Pasqua immigration law (1993) placed the assessment of 'adequate housing' for family reunification requests into the hands of city mayors.

Undocumented women experience greater levels of vulnerability within their own families and, in particular within their marital (and domestic) relationships. Aïcha, who was successfully leading a *sans-papiers* collective in Paris when I interviewed her, talked at great length about this aspect of the impact of current immigration laws on women. According to her, women who find themselves undocumented are more vulnerable and experience specific forms of exploitation and *precarisation* due to the fact that they are women – especially women with children:

> Undocumented women are more fragile. They sometimes find themselves in dramatic situations; sometimes someone proposes to marry them and later they find themselves on the street. There is also [the problem] of sexual exploitation.

Aïcha gave me two examples of these forms of gendered effects of French immigration law. In the first case, a young undocumented woman from Madagascar had married a compatriot with French citizenship; they had a child together. However, after her husband abandoned them, she found herself without papers. In addition, her husband's brother had tried to take advantage of the situation and was 'protecting' her. 'Without papers, she was especially vulnerable,' recounts Aïcha, 'She was afraid that Child Protective Services would take her child away from her.' Aïcha also recalled the situation of a woman who had three children and was also abandoned by her husband. Her husband had simply left her in France and moved to Austria. No longer attached to her husband's legal status, she became undocumented. Protective Services took her children away, but she was able get them back after her *régularisation*. Needless to say, undocumented women also have great difficulties in gaining access to basic services such as education, healthcare and legal representation in case of workplace conflicts.

Overall, the interviews illustrate some of the gendered mechanisms that create internal borders within the Republic and the precarious living conditions of those who are forced to reside in these borderzones. Despite living, working and having families in France for many years, *sans-papières* are placed outside societal norms through seemingly arbitrary processes. It must be noted here that, in addition to the legal/material processes discussed above, a variety of discursive practices construct non-European immigrant women as either invisible, unintelligible or victims of culture and tradition (Raissiguier, 2010). While not discussed in this essay, these discourses are part and parcel of the production of internal borders in France. Indeed, the deployment of gendered meanings in processes of racialisation of immigration and immigrant communities has contributed to the symbolic creation and reproduction of the collective 'Us/Them' mentioned at the beginning of this essay (see also Sidney, in this volume, on frames creating in- and outsiders). In turn, border-dwellers develop, out of necessity, impossible politics that at once highlight and challenge borders and border-making practices.

Troubling borders

Ever since their dramatic eruption on the French scene, in 1996, the *sans-papiers* have fought over political representation and the meanings attached to their presence in France. Among other things, *sans-papiers* have rendered visible their impossible social location and the various processes that have positioned them in extended borderzones within national boundaries through contentious political interventions ranging from occupation of public buildings and hunger strikes. In many ways the *sans-papiers*, then, enact and demand what Bosniak (2006: 15 and Chapter 4) proposes as a bold and logical – even if paradoxical – possibility: the citizenship of (undocumented) aliens. By 'coming out in broad daylight,' they render visible the various mechanisms that have placed them and keep them in zones of *infra-droit*. What the *sans-papiers* and their political interventions bring to light is that these processes also produce particular identities. At the most basic level, they help demonstrate that the *sans-papiers* are people who have been forced into a position of 'lacking' something they need to access human dignity and participate in the polity.

However, one of the most innovative moves made by the *sans-papiers* lies in their organising around an identity of this 'lacking,' which has enabled them to focus on the structural forces that shape their everyday lives and to collaborate politically with other groups that share this constructed lack. Within the confines of French political culture, indeed, this is a brilliant move. Focusing on a shared social location – the borderzone – makes it possible for the *sans-papiers* to make claims based on a principled rejection of the structural and systemic production of stratified 'others'. By avoiding the language of 'difference,' and focusing instead on the universal dignity of the person, they render these claims audible within the French Republic and open up the possibility for coalition politics both within France as well as beyond its borders. The *sans-papiers* do not make their claims on the basis of their belonging to a national community or on status citizenship, but rather on the rights that 'being here' affords them.[10] They thus draw on a variety of legal discourses that offer them different rights at the local, national and supranational levels. By de-linking citizenship from national belonging, the *sans-papiers* align themselves with current discussions that challenge the hegemony of the national-citizen coupling within liberal democratic societies (see also Rygiel, in this volume; Jacobson, 2008; Sassen, 1997; Soysal, 1994). Finally, by focusing on the concrete ways in which discursive and material practices undermine the basic rights to which they are entitled, the *sans-papiers* help disrupt the notions of abstract universalism that dominate French political parlance.

Taking *sans-papières*' narratives seriously and focusing on the gender underpinnings of the local and global forces that locate them in spaces of impossibility – or what have been called here borderzones – illustrates how the intersection of multiple social forces shapes French politics of immigration and immigrant women's everyday lives. The interviews included in this essay shed light on the ways in which past and present economic and political forces as well as gender stratification, for instance, have contributed to the *clandestinisation* and *precarisation* in the everyday lives of actual immigrant women in the context of the restrictive turn in immigration policies in France. Immigrant women are often trapped within traditions and the domestic sphere. This is one of the key mechanisms through which women are located within the borderzones in which they are forced to reside. *Sans-papières* critically engage French laws and administrative practices that continue to place them in zones of *infra-droit*. In particular, they demand that they be granted rights as individuals and not as members of families. Like other immigrant women before them, *sans-papières* understand and lobby for women's legal autonomy and the individuation of immigration rights.

Conclusion

In the process of trying to improve their lives and testing out a variety of strategies, most *sans-papières* develop a keen critique of the symbolic and structural forces that shape their everyday realities. They do see that collective efforts are often fruitful, even if not revolutionary and somewhat limited. Through their everyday practices, they reinvent old notions of citizenship and, in the process, invite us to redraw the borders of the Republic and redefine the terms of national belonging in France:

> Of course I am going to continue (to fight within the collective for undocumented gays). I have a lot of hope; we received quite a few positive

responses lately. For couples it is getting better, for single individuals, I don't know.

(Fatima)

No, there is no reason I should hide; I've been living in France for 13 and a half years, I totally have the right [to stay].... I have been living in France for 13 years and it entitles me to certain rights.

(Khadidja)

French republicanism is often described as a unique system that has generously opened the door to political refugees, established equal rights for individual immigrants settled within the national territory, and conceptualised nationality in terms of political membership rather than ethnic descent. The French republican model of immigration is said to have successfully integrated several waves of immigrants into the national community and socialised them into the French republican culture.[11] Feminist scholars, however, have forcefully argued that based on the doctrine of abstract individualism and on the strict division between a public (male) sphere and a private (female) sphere, the hegemonic rhetoric of 'the Republic' and 'universal citizenship' is in fact based on the exclusion of women (Gaspard et al., 1992; Viennot, 1996; Scott, 1996). Gender discrimination, they argue, is constitutive of the republican tradition. Scholars of colonialism, immigration and race relations have also demonstrated that the republican tradition is filled with contradictions that have shaped France's relationship with foreigners and colonial subjects and delineated the contours of its politics of immigration. These scholars highlight the presence of processes of exclusion and racialisation within the republican model of immigration and integration (Weil, 1991; Brubaker, 1992; Noiriel, 1994; Hargreaves, 1995; Wieviorka, 1997).

My analysis of undocumented immigrants in France suggests that it is the intersection of racial and gendered forms of exclusion that produces stratified 'others' and confines them in social spaces where they only have access to substandard rights. By analysing and linking borders and citizenship as mechanisms of subject formation (see also Rygiel, in this volume, on transgressive citizenship and related identities and practices), I highlight how – within the Republic – impossible subjects are produced and how, in turn, these subjects challenge the mechanisms that have constructed them. As they draw on the foundational discourse of the Republic at the same time and they point out its limits, the *sans-papiers* actively insert themselves within the French national and political community and, in the process, help us imagine how to transform the very terms of its belonging.

Notes

1. Third-country nationals are would-be immigrants who do not belong to other EU countries.

2. Scholarly writing in France, has contributed to this hegemonic narrative. Comparative studies help shed light on the enduring role of national intellectual traditions in shaping explanatory models and policy decisions. See, in particular, Favell (2001) and Lavenex (2005). Lavenex, for instance, looks at the discursive frames of reference that guide immigration research in France and Germany. She argues that, ironically and in contradistinction to commonly held views, ethnocultural concerns are more common in French discussions of 'assimilation' and 'integration.'
3. The concept of *précarité* has been used mostly in Europe to describe a social condition that lacks predictability or security and endangers a person's wellbeing. The term has been used to describe new labour conditions under globalisation and their attendant social precariousness.
4. Throughout, translations from French to English are mine unless indicated otherwise.
5. For a discussion of the ways in which *sans-papiers* in France have used EU structures to make their claims, see Castles and Davidson (2000).
6. These processes are explored at length in Raissiguier (2010).
7. These interviews were conducted in the Paris region by the *Réseau pour l'Autonomie Juridique des Femmes Réfugiées/Immigrées*; RAJFIRE (Network for the Legal Autonomy of Immigrant and Refugee Women) between July and December 1998. The RAJFIRE interviews were aired on feminist radio show *Femmes Libres* (Free Women) and published in *Brochure No. 2* (RAJFIRE, 2000). The interviews are on file with RAJFIRE and some of them are accessible online at www.rajfire.free.fr. As such, they stand as unique archival documentation of the early stages of the *sans-papiers* movement and of the women involved within. For a full discussion of these interviews, see Raissiguier (2010: 43–53).
8. *Sans-papières* is the female form of *sans-papiers* and is used by the women themselves.
9. In the 1960s, economic forces superseded France's plans to use immigration to stave off its population decline. Employers actively recruited workers in Southern Europe and the Maghreb. A minister publicly stated that illegal immigration should be considered as a solution to the country's need for labour. Indeed, the 1960s were laissez-faire years as far as immigration is concerned. See Bernard (1998: 80–81).
10. For a similar argument calling for citizenship on the grounds of residency (in the specific case of voting rights for foreign residents), see Bouamama (2000).
11. Texts that promote these ideas in France and elsewhere are too numerous to list here. For prominent ones, see Noiriel (1994); Weil (1991); and Brubaker (1992). Adrian Favell (2001) offers an interesting critique of the French republican hegemony.

11
From Sangatte to 'The Jungle': Europe's Contested Borderlands

Helen Schwenken

In September 2009, after riot police destroyed 'The Jungle' – a settlement of provisional tents of undocumented migrants in the forests around the French harbour city of Calais – in a cloak-and-dagger operation, some dozen Afghani men assembled in the morning. They were holding banners such as 'The jungle is our house. Plz. don't destroy it. If you do so, where is the place to go?' (Calais Migrant Solidarity, 2009; BBC News, 22 September 2009).[1] The destruction of the informal settlements as well as the protests by the migrants mark a decade of contestation and political mobilisation in those borderlands. The dynamic can be summarised as follows: refugees and migrants come to the Channel tunnel in order to reach the UK; police and private security from transportation firms try to stop them; at the local level, the population is split between those supporting the undocumented migrants out of political or humanistic motivations and those fighting 'illegal migration'; and politicians and parties try to capitalise on the conflicts. The Channel tunnel, Calais and the village Sangatte, where the Red Cross set up a shelter for the migrants, have become a synonymous with this conflict.

As this case shows, conflicts on immigration take shape as conflicts in borderlands. I define borderlands as the zones around borders in which border, surveillance and migration regimes are important elements of governance. One important characteristic of the Franco-British borderland is that it not only separates two countries by a sea border, but that France belongs to the Schengen area of the European Union (EU), while the UK has decided to opt out. Therefore, persons need to have valid border crossing papers. Borderlands are highly contested geographic spaces. Thus I suggest looking at them also as geographies or terrains of resistance (Pile and Keith, 1997; Routledge, 1993). In these borderlands, interactions and negotiations between governments, undocumented migrants and anti- as well as pro-migrant forces take place. Issues at stake include entry, exit, citizenship and identity.

In the decade under investigation – 1999–2009 – two principal mobilisation cycles can be identified. My hypothesis is that in both cycles the relation to and the usage of space has played a decisive role for the dynamics and outcomes. By doing so, I spell out what has been only implicitly assumed by existing analyses of the case (Millner, 2011; Rigby and Schlembach, 2013; Rygiel, 2011a, 2012). In the first protest cycle (1999–2002), migrants took advantage of divided government elites in the UK and France and the obvious discrepancy of the declared official policies and their outcome, the failure of control. The migrants managed to establish a practice and discourse of the 'autonomy of migration' which ran counter to existing migration control policies. A second frame in their protests was 'refugee protection'. This frame gained in relevance in parallel to the increase of police violence against the refugees and migrants. Comparing these two frames, I explain how the less universal one, the autonomy of migration frame, used to have more success than the human rights master frame. In the light of social movement studies in which universal master frames are considered the most powerful, this result may surprise. I argue that the specific geographic location of these protests in the borderlands between France and the UK turned this general wisdom in social movement research around. In this case, space made a significant difference. For the second protest cycle (2008–2009), immigration authorities applied more powerful spatial strategies and in combination with a modified refugee protection frame – the one of identifying 'real refugees' in mixed migration flows – finally resulted in the demolishing of 'The Jungle'.

In the chapter I first briefly review some of the literature regarding the mobilisations in the region of Calais, followed by the theoretical concept of geographies and terrains of resistance. The next portion of the text outlines the case study and the methodology. In the subsequent parts, the case is analysed according to the main research questions and the hypothesis.

At the epistemic margin: Mobilisations in borderlands

The conflict in the borderlands around Calais and the Red Cross centre in Sangatte has – until 2009 – rarely been analysed by academic scholars: Smain Laacher carried out an important baseline study surveying the social structure of the migrants in the Red Cross shelter (Laacher, 2002). He was able to document that migrant flows went up and down along the lines of the world's conflicts. Thus, the migrants present in the region were relatively homogeneous in terms of their ethnicity, class and gender – mainly (young) middle-class men who were selected by their families in Afghanistan or Iraq to move out of the war zones to then support their relatives from abroad. Marc Thomson carried out a discourse analysis of the British policies and the media representation of undocumented migrants, finding a widely negative representation of the migrants (Thomson, 2003). Kartik Varada Raj refers to Sangatte, but is in fact not interested in the specific dynamics, and instead takes it up as a symbol to discuss the function of European borders from a Marxist-feminist perspective. She claims that migrants 'become' borders (Varada Raj, 2006). Architects and critical cartographers have dissected the architecture and the organisation of daily life in Sangatte. They show how these are embedded in and are part of the security-driven border regime and the borderland (An Architektur, 2003). Publications in local and national media were mostly interested in the political struggles between France and Britain and in the specific incidents in the borderland such as police raids, destruction of border fences and reactions of local population and truck drivers. What was often overlooked is that the migrants organised themselves and tried to articulate and fight for their demands. They were an important factor in the actual political struggles. In the media they mostly appeared as an anonymous mass moving in the dark.

Much of the research in migration as well as in social movement studies is characterised by immobility – which is astonishing given that migration as such is in flow. There have been relatively few studies on the mobilisations of undocumented migrants in the moment of border-crossing or in transit. Many studies look at undocumented migrants already living in the receiving states and facing hardship due to their irregular status. Exceptions to the tendency of immobility are those studies in anthropology on the making of borderlands (e.g. Alvarez, 1995) and by some activist and artistic scholars (e.g. Transit Migration, 2007). They stress that borderlands are always in the making and contested, and that (undocumented) migrants thus must be considered a constitutive force. However, most of these studies on Calais do not provide a longer-term analysis of the dynamics; instead they provide a snapshot of a 'no border camp' in Calais in June 2009 (Rigby and Schlembach, 2013; Millner, 2011; Rygiel, 2011a). This snapshot perspective tends to overestimate the significance of the no-border activism as '[a] new politics? A politics beyond citizenship?' (Rigby and Schlembach, 2013: 169) or a 'solidarity ethos' (Millner, 2011). These diagnoses might be the result of a 'hyper-theoretisation' of the protest and of activist and migrant collaboration, which compared to other settings, has been extremely precarious and not based on a continuous basis. Kim Rygiel (2011a) offers an implicit explanation of this epistemic trend by reading the Calais case through two competing theoretical perspectives popular among critical migration and border regime scholars, which, however, both tend to simplify the complex situation: Referring to Agamben's notions of camps and a 'logic of exception' (cf. Rigby and Schlembach, 2013, on Calais), migrants in camps are considered as being immobilised and excluded; on the other hand, analyses through the 'logic of (autonomous) migration' consider the migrants as political agents involved in claiming rights and the makeshift camps as a resource for doing so.

With the following case study on mobilisations of undocumented migrants in borderlands, I attempt to bring forward the field of political mobilisations on migration issues. I show that borderlands are a rewarding location for study which offers insights differing from those analyses stuck in 'immobility'. My longer-term perspective enables us to see significant changes that take place throughout the decade of mobilisations. These changes can be best understood if the specific space and territorial strategies are taken into account.

Theorising contestations in borderlands: Geographies of resistance

My theoretical framework originates from two distinct scholarly traditions: From social movement research I make use of the methodological and conceptual approach of *political opportunity structure* and *framing*. In order to theorise the significance of the borderland as a specific space of contestation, I borrow the concept of *terrains and geographies of resistance* from political geography. A key idea is that 'geography makes possible or impossible certain forms of resistance' and 'resistance makes other spaces – or geographies – possible or impossible' (Pile, 1997: 2). In the case of the borderland and the contestation on immigration, this double movement allows consideration of even powerless actors such as undocumented migrants as significant. Their activities are shaped by the socio-political conditions in the borderlands and they themselves contribute in reifying the specific borderlands. This way of thinking moves the sole focus of attention away from institutions such as border patrols and border surveillance mechanisms. It also reminds us that borders are not pre-given, but always contested and under construction (cf. Anderson and O'Dowd, 1999).

Unauthorised border crossings and the mobilisation of migrants and their opponents make borderlands geographies or terrains of resistence. This concept has been developed prominently by the political geographer Paul Routledge: 'A terrain of resistance refers to a site of contestation and the multiplicity of [dialectic] relations between hegemonic and counter-hegemonic powers and discourses, between forces and relations of domination, subjection, exploitation and resistance' (Routledge, 1996: 516). Not every space is a terrain of resistance, though in general space is a necessary condition for political mobilisations. In the case of the borderlands around Calais, I argue that the undocumented migrants were only able to individually and collectively act relatively successfully during the first protest cycle, because the conflict took place in a specific spatial context: a borderland. They transformed this space into a terrain of resistance. For such a transformation, mobilisation processes and communication were needed and the practices of the migrants clearly are counter-hegemonic practices. In geographies of resistance, behaviour which follows the rationale of consensus is *not* positively sanctioned; instead, actors behave in a confrontational way. For other cases like lobbying policies, it is the other way around: only actors following the written and unwritten rules of lobbying are able to use the spatial and discursive opportunity structure. It can be concluded that the undocumented migrants in the French borderlands were only able to organise themselves because the space 'borderland' is a terrain of resistance and because the mobilisations became a conflict over the space itself and its significance. Thus, following the classical work of Henri Lefebvre, 'it is only *in* space that such conflicts come effectively into play, and in doing so they become contradictions *of* space' (Lefebvre, 1991 [1974]: 365).

The case study: The borderlands around Calais

As in other borderlands, it is not an uncommon situation that hundreds of migrants constantly stroll around. The transit population around Calais is composed of persons coming from the hot spots of civil and international war: in the mid- and late 1990s they came from Kosovo, then Chechnya, followed in the new millennium by people from the Kurdish parts of Iraq and from Afghanistan; in 2009 the border region had increasingly become a destination for Eritrean and Somali refugees. The large majority were male and rather well-educated (cf. Laacher, 2002). They have then tried to cross the Channel to the UK, which can take from days to months. In the high-peak phase between 2000 and 2003, about 80,000 persons, mostly from Iraq and Afghanistan, managed to cross the Channel in a clandestine way, either on ships, trucks or freight trains (ibid.). Some migrants get discouraged and return 'voluntarily' as promoted by the International Organization for Migration (IOM), which has an office in Calais; other migrants get arrested and deported; some migrants die while attempting to cross; and only an evanescent small minority decides to apply for asylum in France. The reasons for the small number of asylum applications lies in the logic of EU asylum procedures, according to which most asylum applicants would be returned to countries such as Italy or Greece, where they stepped on EU soil for the first time; besides that, the likelihood of being granted asylum in France is very small.

In order to deal with the challenges of the large and permanently changing transit population, in September 1999 the French Red Cross established a camp for irregular migrants in Sangatte. Sangatte is a small village within walking distance of the Channel tunnel. The Red Cross provided food and shelter, partly paid for by the French state; local charity organisations took care of the children and provided medical and legal assistance.

The large number of irregular border crossings and the existence of the Red Cross shelter led to diplomatic disputes between France and Britain at the turn of the millennium. The British government blamed the French government for tolerating and actively promoting the migrants' passage;

British politicians alleged that France aimed to get rid of the unwanted migrants. During the 2002 preliminary and run-off elections for the French presidency, the issue was one of the most important and controversial campaigning issues in France. The centre-conservative party RPR (*Rassemblement pour la République*) mobilised against the Red Cross centre. After they won the elections in 2002, everything changed quickly: It became a top-priority issue for the newly elected centre-right French Minister of Home Affairs, Nicolas Sarkozy, and Britain and France agreed on the closure of the centre. The centre was closed down at the beginning of December 2002, despite a series of mass protests by the migrants and anti-racism organisations.

However, the closure of the centre did not stop migrants from crossing the border. They occupied warehouses and other buildings in Calais, and set up camps in the outskirts of Calais. These camps were called 'The Jungle' by the media and the police, as well as by the migrants themselves. The squats and the jungle camps were arranged and governed according to national and ethno-religious groups. The Pashtun Afghans even set up infrastructure, like a grocery store and a mosque. In spring 2009, the situation again escalated (cf. Calais Migrant Solidarity, 2009). The French Minister of Immigration, Integration and National Identity, Éric Besson, and the Mayor of Calais, Natacha Bouchard, stated that they intended to make Calais and the borderlands 'migrant free'. The chasing of migrants and refugees by riot control police, the CRS, increased; police frequently destroyed their overnight refuges, sprayed tear gas, confiscated and destroyed sleeping bags and regularly arrested migrants. Charity organisations complained that police even arrested migrants at the places where they provided food, first aid and showers. In September 2009, national and local authorities announced the definitive closure of 'The Jungle'. On 22 September, the shelters were destroyed and 278 Pashtun Afghans, among half of them minors, were arrested and brought to a detention centre in Coquelles or to the south of France (adults) and a holding centre in Vitry-sur-Orne in Moselle (minors) (*La Voix du Nord*, 22 September 2009; BBC News, 22 September 2009). More than 1,000 persons were thought to have already left before the demolition (ibid.). 'The Jungle' was burned down and other potential places for setting up new temporary housing were fenced off and heavily controlled. After the closure of 'The Jungle', protests against the procedure were voiced by a broad range of local and national pro-migrant, human rights and charity organisations (La Belle Etoile et al., 2009). A group of Afghan refugees started a week-long hunger strike on 30 September. On 22 October a joint British–French deportation charter flight brought Afghan refugees to Kabul, one of them from the Calais 'Jungle'. It had been the first deportation flight to Afghanistan since 2005, which drew a lot of criticism from French civil society (Radio France, 2009) and among members of the European Parliament, who called upon

France to suspend the application of the Dublin II regulation (Hautala et al., 2009). In the following, I will shed some light on these political mobilisations. The conflict will appear in a different light than in most media, as the range of actors and their capabilities is much wider than usually assumed.

Methodology: Event analysis and frame analysis

The analysis was carried out with the help of protest event analysis and frame analysis. As the conflicts in the borderlands around Calais have not yet been researched systematically, no chronicle existed on which the analysis could build. I thus reconstructed the events from primary sources: local and national media articles in France and Britain, leaflets, speeches, emails, photographs, web blogs and other sources. The central unit of the sources which were taken into consideration was 'political mobilisation'. For the first conflict and protest cycle (1999–2002) I analysed 336 newspaper articles, from one local paper (*La Voix du Nord*) and one major national French paper (*Le Monde*); all articles during the course of the conflict were analysed. Articles from a number of other papers, including British newspapers, were included when important events took place.

A reconstruction of events which is based only on media coverage tends to over-represent spectacular or violent events, focus on speakers of a movement, complex issues are simplified and events are isolated. Thus I included other kinds of sources: more than 100 grey documents and publications of social movement organisations, over 150 documents by the government, parliament and parties of France and the UK, and another 30 documents by other European actors. In total the case study 'Sangatte' for the first protest cycle is based upon 600 documents. For the second protest cycle (2008–2009), about 100 documents from the same type of sources as during the first protest cycle were taken into account.

For the analysis, events were identified (more than 400 in total), information from the sources was summarised, coded and stored in a database, and the documents were archived. The analysis of frames allows us to identify the actors' competing argumentative pattern – their 'set of beliefs and meanings that inspire and legitimate the activities and campaigns of a social movement organization' (Benford and Snow, 2000: 614). These frames can be located within political opportunity structures. Hence there are frames which are closer to hegemonic argumentative structures and others which remain at the discursive margins. For actors to mobilise successfully, social movement scholars have detected certain patterns; for example, different elements of a frame need to fit together well and not contradict each other. As I will show, this has not been the case in the borderlands around Calais.

Framing unauthorised border crossings as legitimate actions in the first protest cycle

Analysing the empirical material of the first protest cycle (1999–2002), the 'Sangatte phase', two main frames by the undocumented migrants and refugees in Sangatte can be identified: I call the first one *autonomy of migration* and the second one *refugee protection frame*.

The first framing: 'Autonomy of migration'

The name of this frame is borrowed from a discussion which has mainly developed and been discussed among French intellectuals and antiracism activists since the 1990s (Moulier Boutang, 1993; Karakayali and Tsianos, 2005; Rygiel, in this volume). A starting point of the concept is the existing reality of undocumented migration, and it diagnoses the failure of migration control, while highlighting the agency of the migrants. We can identify the frame of autonomy of migration mainly in the actions performed by the undocumented migrants in Sangatte. The frame is seldom articulated discursively or discussed in a strategic way. On various occasions, a few hundred migrants penetrated the fenced territory of the Channel tunnel and entered the tunnel itself.[2] These mass invasions can be regarded as political actions for two reasons. The migrants are not so naïve as to hope to reach the other side of the tunnel without being caught. The second indicator are the chosen dates such as Christmas Day 2001, when public attention was quite high for the situation of despairing refugees (*La Voix du Nord*, 27 December 2001; *Le Monde*, 27 December 2001). On another occasion they invaded the tunnel when the French border control police was reorganised due to the change of government in spring 2002 (BBC, 17 May 2002). Each time that large numbers of migrants entered the tunnel, the media coverage was quite impressive.

At a demonstration in October 2001, the undocumented migrants demanded that the borders be opened within and into the EU (Réfugiés Afghans du camp, 2001; Réfugiés Afghans and Herin, 2001). This was one of the few occasions the frame 'autonomy of migration' was verbally expressed. Another example happened during the hot phase of the closure of Sangatte. When no further migrants were accepted to Sangatte, the migrants and their French supporters occupied a gym and a church (*Le Monde*, 10 November 2002). The migrants, most of them Iraqi Kurds, demanded a transit permit with a one-month validity period (*Le Monde*, 12 November 2002) in order to have enough time and the possibility to reach Great Britain without getting into trouble with the border police all the time.

These examples show the relevance of the 'autonomy of migration' frame for the political activities of undocumented migrants in Sangatte. Indeed, the refugees and migrants possessed authority (Pile, 1997: 15): they force others – politicians, the media and the border police – to play their game, although not only according to their rules, but also to the rules of the state. This usage of the specific space is constitutive not only of dominating forces, but also of resisting ones.

The second framing: 'Refugee protection'

The 'refugee protection' frame refers to the responsibility of nation-states and societies to provide safe havens for persecuted persons. It includes the right of asylum and other protective measures with regard to the Geneva Refugee Convention of 1951. This basis is shared by broader parts of political and civil society. The 'refugee protection' frame is mainly articulated in Sangatte by the undocumented migrants discursively via petitions and declarations, and on banners and in slogans at demonstrations. On 2 August 2001, the migrants demanded the mediation of the United Nations (UN) in their case (*Libération*, 3 August 2001; *La Voix du Nord*, 3 August 2001). Two weeks later, they wrote a letter to the United Nations High Commissioner for Refugees (UNHCR) in which they expressed their causes to flee, among them war, persecution and poverty (*Le Monde*, 23 August 2001), and they demanded fair asylum procedures. In a declaration by the Afghan refugees after 11 September 2001, they condemned the terrorist attacks and explained their experiences in Afghanistan during the Taliban regime as their main reason to leave the country (*Immigrés Afghans*, 2001; *Le Monde*, 20 September 2001; *La Voix du Nord*, 19 September 2001). These examples could be extended to every demonstration or to every petition delegations of undocumented migrants from Sangatte passed on to politicians or official representatives.

Confrontation wins over negotiation in borderlands

Both major frames during the first protest cycle refer directly or indirectly to international norms. The 'autonomy of migration' frame alludes to a right for everybody to choose his or her place to live and a right of free movement. The 'refugee protection' frame argues within the existing norm of granting asylum to persecuted persons. Although both frames are somehow rights-based, the legitimacy is very different: The 'autonomy of migration' frame can rarely build on cultural resonance and has a low degree of legitimacy because of the widely-shared nation-states' right to decide who is allowed to enter the territory and who is not. Therefore this frame is not suitable to mobilise broad support; it has a low degree of openness and elasticity. The frame is bounded to persons without papers or antiracism activists. However, the frame consistency and credibility of the 'autonomy of migration' frame is high, because the principles of the frame and the actions fit well together. The 'refugee protection' frame is a typical master frame due to its inclusiveness, openness, elasticity and its high cultural resonance. Master frames are not necessarily bounded to a single social movement. As a result, human rights organisations, NGOs, churches, welfare organisations and parts of the public can in principle refer to the frame and join in activities. Despite these potentials of a master frame, the case of Sangatte is characterised by large frame inconsistencies. Contradictions between the discursive parts of the framing and the actions can be analysed during the first protest cycle. The undocumented migrants demanded fair asylum procedures, whereas only very few migrants applied for asylum in France. Their actions follow the logic of the frame labelled 'autonomy of migration'. Furthermore, the main protagonists of the undocumented migrants were considered to lack credibility because they had been involved into the shadow migration regime.

The conflict ended in December 2002 with a positive result for most of the undocumented migrants, as they were allowed to legally enter the UK. They were even granted a work visa for two years; the other migrants were allowed to stay in France. How can this result be interpreted? If viewed from the perspective of the frame 'autonomy of migration', it means the realisation of the interests of the migrants to reach Great Britain through uncontrollable movements. The migrants used the specific terrain of the borderland for their subversive tactics; they defeated attempts by the state to control space. From the government's perspective, the closure of Sangatte is interpreted in a completely different way. It has nothing to do with the political mobilisations and border crossing tactics of the migrants or the various actors from the civil society, but only with a mediation of interests between two governments. From this perspective, space is not considered an issue which has affected the results of the conflict; the legitimate terrain is a governmental and parliamentarian one. These different views about the closure of Sangatte show that success, and the interpretation of it, is always relative and contested.

The second protest cycle: From the 'Jungle' to its demolition

After the Red Cross centre had been torn down, new refugees and migrants came into the region. They occupied empty houses and set up informal settlements in the forests around Calais. The intensity of the political mobilisations by the migrants decreased during this 'Jungle phase'. Nonetheless, local and national NGOs and charity organisations took care of the migrants' most basic needs and critically commented on the policies and police practices in the region. Antiracism activists from France, Belgium and the UK protested on various occasions against the situation in the borderland. In June 2009, for example, they organised a no-border camp in Calais, where hundreds of antiracism activists assembled for a week and organised political manifestations and pro-migrant activities; some of them included migrants, although their participation was hindered by local authorities and police, who threatened the migrants with deportation (Noborder, 2009a, 2009b; Rygiel, 2011a; Millner, 2011; Rigby and Schlembach, 2013).

The state intensifies territorial strategies in the second protest cycle

During the second protest cycle under investigation (2008 to October 2009), local and national state authorities intensified the repression against the migrants and refugees in the borderlands around Calais. This resulted in the demolition and burning of the tents and shelters in 'The Jungle' around Calais and squatters' housing in Calais at the end of September 2009. In comparison to the first protest cycle, the state authorities undertook more efforts to narrow down the space of manoeuvre for the migrants. One important precondition for the 'success' of the state this time was the dismantling of the institution 'Sangatte' in 2002. This resulted in an informalisation of migrants' housing and migrant services by charity organisations. The Red Cross centre in Sangatte functioned as a hub and safe haven for the migrants; there they were also able to gather and plan political activities and decide upon joint statements. After the September 2009 demolition of the informal jungle settlements of the refugees and migrants, the police immediately fenced potential alternatives, such as roofed open spaces, bridges and alternative campsites (Calais Migrant Solidarity, 2009). In this cat-and-mouse game, the migrants were confronted with an antagonist with much more power and resources. While the migrants for a long time relied on their ethnic networks, their border crossing tactics and their numbers, the police presence got stronger and stronger, and civil society supporters were systematically frustrated by the police or tamed – as some activists critically noted – by local authorities who introduced the instrument of round tables (Calais Migrant Solidarity, 2009).

'Law of the Jungle' in the borderland

In the Calais conflict, an interesting discursive figure is the one of the jungle. This term is full of associations, alluded to by the different protagonists in the borderland (see also Rigby and Schlembach, 2013: 163). The migrants protested against the demolition, claiming 'The Jungle' home and creating banners stating, for example, 'Destroying our homes will not make us disappear' (Calais Migrant Solidarity, 2009). They have developed a positive relationship to 'The Jungle' – it enables them to hide, find shelter and be in the companion of other migrants. France's Minister of Immigration, Integration and National Identity at that time, Éric Besson, scandalised the 'law of the Jungle' which threatened to make the borderlands an unruly space: 'On the territory of this nation, the law of the Jungle cannot endure' (BBC News, 22 September 2009). By emphasising that in France the rule of law is standard, he implicitly draws a line to states such as Italy or Greece which struggle in dealing with their migrant and refugee population. Some local NGOs denounce the fact that the police repression makes the migrants more vulnerable to traffickers and smugglers, hence the 'law of the mafias' (La Belle Etoile et al., 2009) rules in the borderlands; this was an argument shared by the French Minister of Minister of Immigration, Integration and National Identity, stating that the camps were 'a base for people traffickers' (BBC News, 22 September 2009). The signatory organisations of the civil society declaration 'Destroying the Jungle: a false solution' also redefined what police and the Calais mayor have called the 'law of the jungle' (La Belle Etoile et al., 2009). In their understanding, the European asylum system has failed and has led to an unlawful space where the 'law of the jungle' rules.

As shown, the term 'jungle' is interpreted in very different ways by the protagonists. Aside from the migrants, the other protagonists have criticised the borderland as a space in which the rule of law is not working adequately – either the laws to protect refugees or the ones to protect the border. In their attempt to enforce laws in the borderland, these different actors meet in the aim of recognising so-called well-founded refugees. The conflict in the borderland around Calais has taken place during a time in which the discussion on the challenges of 'mixed migration flows' is prevalent. I consider it a powerful sub-frame of the 'refugee protection' frame. It also represents a governmental technology to weaken the position of the refugees and migrants actually present in the borderlands.

'Mixed migration flows' as a technology of splitting mobile populations

During the 'Sangatte phase' of the conflict, the migrants and refugees used the frame of 'asylum and refugee protection', but it did not have much credibility in the way they did it. This has changed in the late 'Jungle phase' in light of Europe-wide discussions and controversies on the European asylum system. Even the European Commissioner for Justice and Home Affairs at that time, Jacques Barrot, commented on the Calais conflict. He said that

> A relevant number of the undocumented migrants from the 'jungle' are authentic asylum seekers who do not claim asylum due to their fear of being sent back to the country through which they entered the European Union.... They arrived in Greece and they are afraid of being sent back to this country where their demands have virtually no chance of being heard.
> (*La Voix du Nord*, 18 September 2009, own translation)

Despite the widely accepted critique on the European asylum policies, the British Immigration Minister at the time, Phil Woolas, insisted that the majority of the 278 people arrested in Calais must be illegal migrants, because otherwise they would have had claimed asylum in France or the first country of the EU they had arrived in (The Guardian, 22 September 2009). The point the European Commissioner for Justice and Home Affairs raised was a seriously discussed issue among the member states of the EU at that time (Euronews, 21 September 2009). It has been widely considered a problem that the asylum procedures in states such as Italy and Greece are deficient and that other states in the centre of Europe, such as Germany, receive fewer and fewer asylum seekers, while the exterior states have to deal with an increase. Another problematic dimension of the joint EU asylum policies that was identified was the different rates of recognition and treatment of asylum seekers in the 27 member states. Greece, for example, accepted less than 1 per cent of its asylum claims in 2008; Iraqi and Afghans had a 0 per cent success rate (The Guardian, 22 September 2009; Calais Migrant Solidarity, 2009). In the case of Calais, these problems of the European asylum policies can be seen like under a burning glass (France Terre d'Asile et al., 2009). One issue is the mixed composition of the flows, which means that undocumented migrants, refugees and asylum seekers are all coming together and in an irregular way (IOM, 2008: 2), as the lines are blurry anyway. However, only very few asylum seekers and refugees actually claim their rights, as mentioned before. The population of 'The Jungle' and the informal settlements during the second protest cycle under investigation is characterised not only by Afghan people and Iraqi Kurds, but also by Ethiopians and Somalis; these are migrant populations which are a typical example of these mixed migration flows, 'hoping to escape poverty, persecution and the never-ending violence raging in Mogadishu and South Central Somalia' (UNHCR, 2008: 1). Many of these 'refugee-migrants' had already been living in shanties next to the port while they waited to cross the Gulf of Aden towards Yemen (UNHCR, 2008: 2–4). Therefore it might not be a completely unknown way of living-in-transit when they come to Calais and its informal settlements at the Channel tunnel.

One technique to identify 'real' refugees in mixed migration flows is screening and profiling (UNHCR, 2007b: 3, 10). In this process, it is decided in a multi-step procedure whether newly arrived persons belong (a) to the group of potential asylum seekers, (b) to the group of persons which cannot be granted asylum, but which cannot be returned either, or (c) to the group which is not eligible for protection and thus subject to voluntary or forced return. This screening contributes, intended or not, to the re-emergence of the discursive figures of the 'bogus asylum seeker' and the 'economic migrant', as opposed to the 'real' refugee in need of protection. As studies on discourse and racism have shown, these constructions, often media-driven, have not been innocent in the emergence of racism against migrants and refugees in everyday knowledge (Jäger, 1996). Further, it promotes a victimising view of the refugees, often making invisible their own political mobilisations and articulations.

In the conflict in the Calais borderlands, another dimension is relevant when talking about mixed migration flows. Among the international organisations there is a division of labour – and competition – about which organisation deals with what category of migrants/refugees. The UNHCR and the International Organization for Migration are the key antagonists in this regard. In the conceptual approaches on mixed migration flows, this division is bridged and collaboration among 'key partners' such as governments and international organisations is an important issue (UNHCR, 2007b: 6). The history of the conflict in the Calais borderlands has witnessed some of these tensions as both organisations used to be present. The IOM was heavily criticised by the Sangatte migrants themselves, who felt that the advertisement for voluntary return options (for example to Afghanistan) was indeed no option at all, and also applied unethical means (one of the criticised documents: IOM, 2001). The UNHCR returned to Calais in 2009, a decision which has been applauded by many local protagonists. In the case of Calais, the UNHCR spokesperson Andrej Mahecic criticised the situation, noting that '[c]losing the so-called jungle camp does however not address the phenomenon of mixed and irregular migration, nor does it solve the problems of the people concerned, amongst whom there may be many with protection needs' (UNHCR, 2009a). In the case of Calais, the actual number of those claiming asylum has been very low. Until the demolition of the informal settlements, only 170 persons showed interest in claiming asylum and 50 in the end did so (BBC News, 22 September 2009). Nonetheless, the migrants themselves displayed banners after the camps were destroyed claiming 'We want asylum in Europe where we can get our human rights,' (Calais Migrant Solidarity, 2009). Given the situation of the European asylum policies as described before, and given the previous mobilisations in the first protest cycle, the migrants act within the same real-life and framing dilemmas: claiming rights which are not recognisable and refusing to claim asylum with the knowledge that their claims are either turned down due to procedural reasons (Dublin II regulations) or are rejected as not well-founded.

Conclusion

As shown, political protest against European migration policies and the EU border regime emerge in borderlands, for example in places like Calais where the border between the Schengen area and a non-Schengen country is located and postcolonial and family ties make the UK a desired destination for many refugee-migrants. As a result, the view of social movement scholars who only locate European protest in the field of migration policy in Brussels and at the nation-state level has to be corrected. Looking at the periphery of the EU offers important insights into the political struggles in 'hot spots' such as Calais, the Spanish exclaves of Ceuta and Melilla, the Greece–Turkey border (see Rygiel, in this volume), the Greek Mediterranean islands, Malta (see Klepp, in this volume) or the Italian Lampedusa. Despite the relatively closed political opportunity structures and the almost non-existing political participation possibilities for (undocumented) migrants, migrants have developed a considerable level of agency and political mobilisations, customised for the borderland space. This goes beyond simple uprisings, as strategic suggestions like the framing of the activities are considered. However, it should not be forgotten that these political mobilisations are very precarious and not comparable to a more stable social movement. Therefore I would not speak of a social movement as such, but of political articulation and mobilisation processes. Even prior to these political articulations, transnational communities existed, particularly among Kurdish and Afghan migrants in the Sangatte Centre and later in the informal settlements. What can be clearly stated is that the refugee-migrants in Sangatte could not refer to a European vocabulary of inclusion, as they were not welcomed. The analysis of the framing strategies, however, showed that the migrants did refer to the universal norm of 'refugee protection'. As the frame of 'autonomy of migration' shows, they acted on the basis of their knowledge of their numbers in the region; the mass invasions of the Channel tunnel were only performable with hundreds of undocumented migrants.

The situation in the French northern borderlands has dramatically changed over time: While in the 'Sangatte phase' (1999–2002) the state provided shelter for the undocumented refugees and migrants, they later had to self-sustain and self-organise during the early jungle phase (2002 to autumn 2008). Although police frequently arrested migrants, they were de facto tolerated by the police and the public. This changed dramatically during the late 'jungle phase' after autumn 2008 and the demolition of 'The Jungle' in September 2009. In that period, migrants were systematically chased and humiliated by riot control police. Recalling Pile's statement that 'geography makes possible or impossible certain forms of resistance' and 'resistance makes other spaces – or geographies – possible or impossible' (Pile, 1997: 2), the dynamics in the Calais borderland can be explained very well. The space for clandestine border crossings has become narrow; the space for political mobilisations has discursively been narrowed by the frame of mixed migration flows and the question of which of the migrants could be considered legitimate refugees. The extreme forms of dispersal among the migrants resulted in worse conditions for mobilisation and communication among the migrants as compared to the 'Sangatte phase' during which the migrants held plenary sessions on how to react to changing political environments. For the 'Sangatte phase', I characterised the borderlands around Calais as an enabling environment for the migrants; the migrants adapted to the confrontational logic within this space. During the 'Jungle phase' the political mobilisations decreased, and the migrants were organising their precarious lives and journeys. In the late 'Jungle phase' the situation escalated and the state made use of its power. The spatial conditions no longer allowed the migrants to act as before. Nonetheless, the situation in and around Calais has not changed significantly since. Despite worse conditions, refugees and migrants continue coming to Calais. They continue to set up new precarious settlements such as the Africa House Squat (Calais Migrant Solidarity, 2010) and new 'Jungles', such as the ones by Hazara Afghans (Quillet, 2010), or by Syrian or Eritrean refugees. They have been confronted with ever more strict surveillance mechanisms and regular arrests (Calais Migrant Solidarity, 2013). Calais Mayor Natacha Bouchart even called upon the local population via Facebook to denounce any new migrant settlements and has hoped that the Minister of the Interior installs a priority security zone, which would bring even more police into the region (*France 3*, 3 November 2013). However, the migrants continue their attempts to cross the border and if the conditions allow, some engage themselves culturally and politically, such as Syrian refugees sending an 'Open letter to Europe', asking for a safe haven (Syrians blocked in Calais, 2013).

Notes

1. As the research is based on media analysis, the media articles are not referenced.
2. Empirical evidence can be found, for example, in Home Office, 2001; *Le Monde*, 4 September 2001, 1 November 2001, 27 December 2001, 22 January 2002; *La Voix du Nord*, 27 December 2001; BBC, 17 May 2002.

12
Labour Migration, Postcolonial Nationalism and Class Politics beyond Borders: The Case of the Turkish Party MHP in Germany

Jörg Nowak

Literature on the politics of sending countries has burgeoned in the last decade (Østergaard-Nielsen, 2003a; Brand, 2006; Rodriguez, 2010), contributing to a focus beyond the politics of receiving countries (Soysal, 1994). It has been often discussed separately from the literature on borders and borderlands, although borders are not just constituted by what is conceived generally as the narrow field of border policies, but also by citizenship policies and the political and economic management of labour migration. Another approach, the one for autonomy of migration, proposed to debate borders in a more encompassing way (Moulier Boutang, 2007; Bojadzijev, 2008). It draws its case studies predominantly from the guest worker struggles of the 1970s, but also claims to be methodologically able to explain contemporary developments of borders.

This case study on the activities of the Turkish MHP (*Milliyetçi Hareket Partisi,* Nationalist Movement Party, MHP) in Germany from the 1970s to the present day adds up to several salient studies on migrant associations in Germany that have appeared in the last few years (Sökefeld, 2008; Yurdakul, 2009; Schiffauer, 2010; Sezgin, 2010), but did not include the MHP. It shows which shortcomings go along with the autonomy of migration approach that tends to ignore conservative formations of migrant associations and, therefore, is unable to grapple with the political significance of these associations. On the other hand, the existing research on migrant associations tends to ignore the integration of migrant associations into larger economic and political strategies and objectives: I chose the example of the MHP in order to show how this integration is established in different ways across various political conjunctures and how it is closely connected to the polities of sending countries. I embed the activities of the MHP in the larger context of political and economic government strategies and highlight 'class politics beyond borders' as transnational strategies to control immigrant workers.

Countering Thomas Faist's claim that liberal immigration policies furthered the emergence of migrant associations (Faist, 2000), I maintain that the exclusionary immigration policies of the 1970s in Germany and their production of a divided citizenship has an even stronger effect to enhance the importance of these associations for migrants in Germany (Bosniak, 2006). The isolation of migrants in Germany from social and political institutions of the receiving country, enforced by legal restrictions on their activities, made it attractive for them to join migrant associations which were often controlled, directly or indirectly, by Turkish political parties. Borders are created not just between states, but also, in the case of labour migration, inside of states, so that they remain effective. Borders are crucial devices in order to maintain wage differences between migrant workers and indigenous workers and cannot be conceived of independently of class politics without ignoring one of their basic political foundations.

By combining research on sending countries with the topic of migrant associations, I attempt to explore an aspect that has not yet been treated extensively: joint political action by the state apparatus and political parties in both sending and receiving countries, the aim of which was to repress the migrant workforce and gain political control of the migrant population. For this purpose, I contextualise both strands of research with relational state theory, which interprets activities and strategies of state apparatuses and political parties as the condensation of strategies and interests of class-based actors (Poulantzas, 1978).

The Turkish far-right MHP and its front organisations constituted the largest single Turkish immigrant organisation in Germany from 1973 to 1983, peaking in 1979 with a membership of 26,000. In 1984, MHP membership was outnumbered by the Islamist *Milli Görüs* and later, in 1993, by organisations linked to the Kurdish Workers Party (PKK), and by new organisations such as *Diyanet İşleri Türk İslam Birliği* (DITIB), *Türkischer Bund* (TBB) and the Alevi organisation, *Almanya Alevi Birlikleri Federasyonu* (AABF). Since the late 1980s, MHP membership in Germany has remained reasonably stable with between 7000 and 8000 members.

The MHP was and still is linked in various ways to the German and Turkish state apparatuses, although the nature and intensity of these connections has altered considerably over time. The racist shutdown of access to German political organisations paved the way for organisation in religious, social and political groups – in the case of Turkish emigrants – tied to Turkey's social and political landscape (Ögelman, 2003). I contend that the growing influence of the MHP in Germany was embedded in a control strategy for a potentially disruptive migrant workforce following the outbreak of several wildcat strikes by migrant workers in 1973. Thus, from the perspective of the autonomy of migration approach, which highlights the social and political activities of migrants (Moulier Boutang, 2007; Bojadzijev, 2011; see Rygiel, in this volume), the case of the MHP stands out as an example of the many attempts to gain control of this autonomy with joint action by institutions in two separate states.

State theory, migration and divided citizenship

Relational State Theory sees the state as an area of contention, where actors with conflicting interests compete in the context of highly unequal power relations. State institutions are therefore not neutral, and specific interests and strategies are inscribed in their mechanisms. The internationalisation of states and of labour migration did not emerge with the recent wave of globalisation but is, on the contrary, a long-standing phenomenon.

Relational state theory and the internationalisation of the state

Much of state theory sees society and the state as separate given entities (Skocpol, 1985; Evans et al., 1985). Taking this as a starting point, the question is to what extent can the state control society. Strong states distinguish themselves from weak states: strong states exert tax authority, establish territorial sovereignty and integrate capitalists into economic strategies proposed by the respective governments – a state image underpinned by the liberal and realist schools.

The relational state theory of Marxist Nicos Poulantzas takes a different angle and asks alternative questions. According to Poulantzas, the emergence of the bourgeois national state coincided with the rise of the bourgeoisie as a class. Having failed to achieve political unity in the economic sphere, however, the latter sought to establish a political sphere that would serve to attain a comparative albeit fragile unity of the bourgeoisie. While in the nineteenth century, members of the European bourgeois class extended their influence in political parties, the twentieth century saw more and more people from other classes in the governing role, albeit under the sway of the bourgeoisie as the hegemonic class. For a greater understanding, Poulantzas distinguished between *governing* and *hegemonic group* or *faction* (1973). That the state as an institution is a condensation of class power relations is his primary theoretical insight. Insofar as the bourgeoisie is in a position to establish its own rule, state institutions work as a filter to transform the interests of that class into general rules for the whole of society (1978). The concept of the relational nature of the state combines an understanding of Althusser's account of the structural conditions of statehood (1971), Gramsci's approach of the state as a battlefield where different factions compete for power and hegemony (2011), and Foucault's insights into the fragmented nature of power relations (1978). There are two consequences. First, different state apparatuses are bases for different class factions and, second, the working class likewise maintains a base within the state apparatus. The balance of power, however, only permits the dominance of the working class in less significant areas of the state.

Far from being subject to a unified bourgeois interest, many state institutions act independently and pursue the fragmented interests of various class factions. The government as the central agency of the state, however, is dominated by the hegemonic faction, which seeks to control state institutions and, should events grow out of control, to shackle their independence. This faction of the bourgeoisie and its allies form a so-called 'power bloc' – not necessarily identical with the government – and effectively dominate the state. A possible scenario would be a leftist party in government and a power bloc that holds sway in state institutions that are in a position to influence the government agenda (see Poulantzas, 1973).

Internationalisation of the state and labour migration to Germany

Poulantzas analysed the internationalisation of the state in the context of US interests in West European states (1975). Although the Greek government, for example, was formally independent, the power of the US ruling bloc made itself felt in Greece's ruling bloc politics, internalised via numerous channels of influence. The internationalisation of states, however, had begun long before this: colonial expansion internationalised state functions by exercising power in the colonies, with the aim of extracting raw materials through slave or other forms of forced labour. The German state colonised quite late, between 1884 and 1919, and faced a series of uprisings as a result of its treatment and exploitation of the indigenous people (Pogge von Strandmann, 2009). Another facet of internationalisation of the state was the expansion of German companies that dominated certain sectors of the world market, such as AEG, the company that split the global electronics market in a joint venture with General Electric (Lenin, 2010 [1916]).

A third method of internationalising states occurred in the form of labour migration. In the late nineteenth century Polish immigrants worked in the agrarian sector of Prussia. The second wave of industrialisation following World War I saw an influx of Polish workers to the Ruhr area. A proper guest worker system was first established during the German fascist regime. While millions of workers from Eastern Europe worked in a system of forced labour, fascist Germany launched a guest worker programme with Italy in 1937, in the course of which 350,000 Italians migrated to Germany. After the downfall of Mussolini in 1943, Italian workers were likewise integrated into the system of forced labour. The term 'guest worker' was established during fascist rule. It was predominantly used to describe workers who had not been forced to work in Germany but had migrated voluntarily (Herbert, 1999).

The second guest worker system began in 1955 and was again based on a contract with the Italian government. Contracts with other countries followed suit. In 1961, the German government signed a labour migration contract with Turkey. This second programme was the result of a compromise with the trade unions, since German employers – hampered by the labour shortage of the day – expected wages to continue rising. The growing incorporation of women into the labour market met with the opposition of the two political parties that supported the German breadwinner model, and of the trade unions, concerned that this vast increase of women in the workforce would undermine the existing wage system (Türkmen, 2010). There was consensus with the unions that foreign workers should be paid according to the German system of collective bargaining. Since most of the immigrant workforce was employed in low qualification jobs, however, wage differences between German and migrant workers remained substantial (Bojadzijev, 2008: 151).

The West German guest worker system entailed labour recruitment in other countries by state institutions in a concerted effort with trade unions and employer organisations. Cooperation with the governments in question went a long way to easing the labour bottleneck for West German capitalists, while the said governments anticipated a more relaxed domestic situation once some of the economically superfluous population had emigrated and would ultimately support their families at home with remittances. The guest worker system in West Germany licensed the ruling blocs of both receiving and sending countries[1] to exert class domination. This system of cooperation, however, was far from balanced; its strong economic position allowed the West German state to dictate the conditions. This cooperation between several states in a hierarchical relationship reveals the role of the border as a device for government by difference. The hierarchy of states on the world market is reproduced as a hierarchy of groups of workers.

Transnationalisation, divided citizenship and autonomy of migration: Turkish workers in Germany

The existence of migrant populations creates transnational political spaces. Migrants remain connected to the political context of their countries of origin, but also interact with the politics of countries of destination. 'This can result in anything from the formation of solidarity groups with persecuted movements to the defence of the homeland political regime,' (Østergaard-Nielsen, 2003b: 1).

It has been acknowledged in the literature that sending countries endeavour for a number of reasons to maintain links with their emigrant citizens (Mikuszies, in this volume). Migrant remittances to families at home are crucial to the national economies of sending countries, whose governments mobilise 'their' migrants for their own political aims. In addition, the qualifications that migrants acquire in the countries of destination could be of advantage to their home countries should the migrants eventually return

(Østergaard-Nielsen, 2003b). Migrant participation in political organisations in receiving countries is the first step towards citizenship in the cosmopolitical sense of the word, as citizens active in the community and/or the broader public sphere (Basch et al., 1994; Smith and Guarnizo, 1998). In the case of Germany, assigning migrants a legal status different to Germans has led to a phenomenon Linda Bosniak has termed divided citizenship (2006). It is her concept of 'divided citizenship' (Bosniak, 2006: 3) that I would like to explore here. Bosniak highlights the 'second-class citizenship' of most migrants: 'the individuals involved here enjoy many substantive citizenship rights even in the absence of formal citizenship status; and yet the scope of rights they enjoy is simultaneously constrained by virtue of citizenships' other substantive commitments, including a commitment to national exclusivity and closure.' (100).

The fact that sending states endeavour to control migrants abroad and are active in shaping their social and political identification has been highlighted by a number of scholars (Mahler, 2000; Smith, 2003; Brand, 2006). I take a closer look at what has been called political transnationalism in the literature, 'the various means by which nationals abroad participate in politics [...] back home' (Brand, 2006: 11). The crucial point is that 'politics back home' and 'politics abroad' often intersect (see Sezgin, 2010).

Turkish workers gradually began to take part in social and political life in Germany, albeit under certain conditions: they were not in possession of an unlimited residence permit, their families frequently remained in Turkey, and to all intents and purposes they were excluded from German political and social organisations (with the notable exception of small radical left-wing organisations; see Betriebszelle Ford, 1973), all of which propelled them into the arms of their own organisations. Extending the approach of Robyn Rodriguez, who shows how the Philippine state acts as a broker for citizens who go abroad as migrant workers (2010), this paper underlines the degree to which the Turkish state exported violent political control to Germany in the form of the nationalist MHP, on the one hand, and how much this was welcomed and fostered by German officials in state institutions.

Ludger Pries's theory of transnationalisation sees a dialectic between renationalisation and the emergence of transnational social spaces (2008: 16, 19): both processes evolve at the same time. In other words, the basis of and framework for the emergence of transnational social spaces is national identification, regardless of how broken or ambivalent it may be. Turkish immigrant associations belong to what Pries defines as diaspora transnationalisation (Pries, 2008: 156). They share a common reference point in the mother country. This diaspora link, however, is also determined by relations between the Turkish and German states and their respective internal political divisions along party lines, which are rendered visible by the presence of certain political parties in certain state institutions.

Transnational political spaces came into being when contracts for the migration of Turkish workers to Germany were put into practice. I will give prominence to an aspect hitherto underappreciated in the literature on migration. NATO, the Western form of political internationalisation to counter communist international organisations such as COMECON and the Warsaw Pact, also created transnational political spaces. The Gladio network, comprised of military units, intelligence services and fascist networks, was part of NATO's bulwark against communist forces (Ganser, 2005). Turkey and Germany shared information and training in police, intelligence and government institutions. This arrangement not only involved state apparatus personnel: fascist militias in countries such as Italy, Turkey and Germany were also in the process of entering these transnational political spaces, and the MHP was an important node to connect Turkish politics with the Gladio network. Links established through NATO gave state institutions an opportunity to control migrant workers. In the 1950s, for example, the German government made a request to the Italian government to investigate the case of 27,800 Italian workers in Germany for possible links to communist organisations (Schönwalder, 2001: 229). The ties between the MHP and German state institutions in the 1970s have been well documented. They have failed, however, to find their way into the current literature on transnational social spaces. Østergaard-Nielsen, for example, omitted the MHP entirely in her section on the close cooperation between migrant organisations and the German authorities (2003b: 78–81). Following Ögelman's claim that German exclusionary politics engendered the persistence of homeland politics among the Turks in Germany (Ögelman, 2003), I maintain that this development is a specific form of governing Turkish migrants and that its background is one of class politics.

Scholars emphasising the 'autonomy of migration' see migration itself as a social and political process that evades the strategies of state and corporate actors (Moulier Boutang, 2007: 170). I contend that such an autonomy exists but is limited by the efforts of states and other actors. One method of curbing this autonomy is a 'divided citizenship' regime that segregates the population along different entitlements to citizenship rights and political participation.

The claim to an 'autonomy of migration' draws attention to aspects of self-determination in migrant activities and establishes a close link between processes of capitalist exploitation and those of migration, upholding entitlement to the primacy of human mobility over the mobility of capital (Moulier Boutang, 2007: 169–170). Scholars working with this approach, however, did not spell it out sufficiently (see Mezzadra's self-criticism, 2010a). The claim to an 'autonomy of migration' operates with a post-structuralist misinterpretation of Mario Tronti's thesis that working-class resistance both precedes and causes capitalist restructuring (1966). The misinterpretation contains two aspects: first of all, Tronti's assumption cannot be transposed lightly from the field of class struggle to that of migration, due to the entirely different dynamics of these fields. Second, Michael Hardt and Antonio Negri's concept of the ontological primacy of resistance (Hardt and Negri, 2000) is intrinsic to the claim of an autonomy of migration. Operating with the notion of ontological primacy frustrates any attempt to grasp real social conflicts where no such primacy is given.

From the perspective of relational state theory, it is more productive to conceptualise the ways in which conflicts between migrant movements and strategies of state control and capitalist accumulation are managed. The notion of looking at processes of migration from the perspective of migrant struggles implies the involvement of conflict – inherent in conflict is its unpredictable outcome, which is ultimately determined by *relations* of forces that are subject to change. Institutions such as 'divided citizenship' are the result of social and political conflict, and are highly effective devices when it comes to freezing the autonomy of migrant struggles (Bosniak, 2006: 124).

The postcolonial nationalism of the MHP

Of the many political groups in Germany with connections to the Turkish government, I will focus on the nationalist right-wing MHP, since it has loomed large in the political activities of Turkish migrants in Germany for almost three decades. The MHP was founded in the late 1960s as a party deeply entrenched in Kemalist republican ideology (Bora, 2001; Taş, 2012). Kemalism defines itself as an anti-imperialist force for the defence of Turkey's national independence against European powers. Although Turkey was never colonised, Kemalist ideology bears a strong resemblance to the nationalism that emerged in former colonised countries such as Algeria, Morocco and Egypt, to name but a few in the same region. The backbone of the war fought by Atatürk against Britain and Greece between 1919 and 1923 was in fact a nationalist movement. As one characteristic of the 'dialectics of decolonisation' (Cooper, 1997), postcolonial nationalism became a means of class domination in decolonised/independent countries. Frederick Cooper outlines how the workers' struggle in support of the process of decolonisation in West Africa was effectively controlled and, subsequent to national independence, integrated into these former colonised states. Trade unions and workers' parties were obliged to submit to the national unity projects of the parties in power. Although circumstances in Turkey are quite different and the Turkish state was founded in 1921, this scheme can be applied to the Turkish case. The MHP was founded at a time when a left-wing party, the Soviet-oriented Workers Party (*Türkiye Işçi Partisi*), entered parliament for the first time in Turkish history with 15 delegates (in 1965, and again with two delegates in 1969), representing 3 per cent of the vote. The party was banned in 1971 when it acknowledged the demands of the Kurdish movement as legitimate. The massive wave of violent demonstrations and kidnappings by leftist groups in 1969 and 1970 was soon echoed and outnumbered by assassinations and killings on the part of the MHP. The MHP addressed conservative sections of the urban and rural working and middle classes. In this light, it can be seen as a typical example of postcolonial nationalism, a key device for control of the workforce during the first wave of industrialisation in Turkey (Bora, 2001; Taş, 2012).

Political developments in Turkey since the 1970s

In my research I focus on the period from 1970 up until today. The 1970s was a fragile period in Turkish political life. After successful industrialisation based on a strategy of import substitution, the Turkish economy faced a downturn in the 1970s that reached an all-time low in the second half of the decade. The military coup in 1971 was a response to the strike wave during the initial months of that year and focused on the repression of left-wing parties and trade unions. Martial law was introduced in April 1971, a status that was upheld for two years. From 1975 onwards, governments began to include the MHP and Erbakan's Islamist *Millî Selamet Partisi* (MSP) within their ranks. Both parties were backed by paramilitary units that carried out attacks against leftist activists and their organisations. The clashes between right-wing paramilitaries and left-wing organisations came close to civil war and were brought to an end by the military coup in 1980. After the coup, the aspiring Anatolian and Islamic bourgeoisie was gradually incorporated into the Kemalist Turkish-Islamic synthesis represented by Prime Minister Turgut Özal. Özal adopted a neoliberal export-oriented strategy that strengthened the textile industry and other world market production sectors in the Anatolian regions. The post-coup period from 1983 to 2002 was dominated by the conservative parties *Anavatan Partisi* (ANAP) and *Doğru Yol Partisi* (DYP), which represented the bourgeoisie of Istanbul and the upcoming Anatolian bourgeoisie. During this period, the Islamist *Refah Partisi* (Welfare Party) garnered more and more of the votes. The old confrontation between right- and left-wing militias petered out with the incarceration of activists on both sides. Leftist organisations were combatted with repression, while the organisational structures of the MHP remained more or less intact. A new area of conflict, however, was soon to emerge. In 1984, violent clashes broke out between the Turkish army and Kurdish rebels. Following the capture of the Kurdish rebel leader, Abdullah Öcalan, in 1999, hostilities ground to a halt for several years. Since the 1990s, Islamist political forces confronted the Kemalist elite more successfully. The Anatolian bourgeoisie, made up of textile company owners, now gave strong support to the theocratic *Refah Partisi* as an alternative means of political influence. The first government participation of Islamists from 1996–1997 was terminated by non-violent military intervention. The Islamist camp split into two fractions, the moderate, which has been in government since 2002 under the name AKP, and the radical, represented by the *Saadet Partisi*.

The MHP in Turkey

Founded in 1969, the MHP, in coalition with centre politician Demirel's *Adalet Partisi* (AP) and the Islamist MSP, was part of the Turkish government for the first time from 1975 to 1978. Pursuing a strong nationalist ideology, it drew its base from the lower middle class and from rural and industrial workers. The party leader, Alparslan Türkes, was among the 32 military officers who staged the 1960 coup in Turkey. In the national elections in 1973 it gained 3 per cent of the votes, in 1977 this rose to 6 per cent. The MHP was also present in the government that ruled from November 1979 to September 1980 prior to the coup. Although not widely supported in the elections, the MHP had considerable influence. Its paramilitary units, often collaborating with those of the Islamist MSP (representing 12 per cent of the votes in 1973 and 9 per cent in 1977), set about killing hundreds of Alevis, left-wing students and unionists around this time, and did so with government support. Daniele Ganser reports in his studies on Gladio that Abdullah Çatlı, a leading figure in the Turkish branch of Gladio, coordinated the MHP militia assaults on left-wing citizens (2005: 239).

MHP party leader Türkes was deputy prime minister from May 1975 to June 1977, and again from July 1977 to January 1978. The massacre of 105 Alevis by members of the MHP in Kahramanmaras in December 1978 prompted the introduction of martial law, while the military coup in 1980 was due in part to the conservative prime minister's refusal to abandon his government coalition with the MHP. The military had favoured a grand coalition of the two centre parties, Demirel's AP and the social democratic *Cumhuriyet Halk Partisi* (CHP) led by Bülent Ecevit. In the aftermath of the coup, the MHP was finally banned. In 1983 it reformed under a different name but in 1992 returned to the name MHP. In the course of the struggle against Kurdish rebels, Turkish armed forces cooperated extensively with paramilitary groups recruited by the MHP. Hence the MHP once again became an influential organisation (Bora and Can, 2004), gaining 8.8 per cent of the vote in 1995. Subsequent government coalitions with the MHP occurred from 1999 to 2002. The MHP reached a historical peak with 18 per cent of the votes in 1999. This was followed by 14 per cent in 2007. With 13 per cent in the 2011 national elections, the party stabilised its votes at a comparatively high level.

Activities of the MHP and the Turk Federation in Germany

Turkish migrant associations began to emerge in the early 1970s, gaining momentum in the mid-1970s – at a time when Turkish migrants in Germany outnumbered other national groups of immigrants. By 1977, Turks had become the leading national group with 515,000 workers, followed by those from Yugoslavia (376,000) and Italy (266,000) (Minister des Inneren, 1977).

This trend impacted on the significance of Turkish immigrant associations in Germany. The largest migrant associations in 1973 were VGD e.V., which was linked to the Greek Junta and had 5000 members, and the Italian Communist Party with 3500 members. Membership of several Turkish New Left groups reached a total of 2400, while the MHP boasted 2000 members (Minister des Inneren, 1973). This was soon to change. In 1975, MHP leader Türkes spoke as deputy prime minister of Turkey to 2000 party delegates in Germany (Özcan, 1989: 181). In the same year, membership of the party rose to 5800 members and peaked in 1979 with 26,000 members. FIDEF was the only Turkish migrant association in Germany with a similar number of members at that time. It was dominated by the Moscow-oriented Turkish Communist Party and had a membership of 5400 in 1977, and 18,000 in 1979 and 1980. By 1987, following a sharp decline, no more than 5000 members belonged to FIDEF.

1974 saw an increase in violent actions by MHP activists in Germany. The victims were Turkish leftists and trade unionists. The German trade union umbrella organisation, DGB, called for a ban on MHP structures (Özcan, 1989; Aslan and Bozay, 2000). In 1976, the MHP was forced to close down its German office when the Turkish government banned the activities of Turkish parties outside of Turkey. The old MHP structures in Germany were renamed 'associations of idealists' and later the 'Turk Federation'. The German conservative party CDU (Christian Democrats) had supported the emerging organisational structures of the MHP in the 1970s. According to several sources, the German foreign intelligence service, BND, took an active role in the foundation of the MHP in Germany (Aslan and Bozay, 2000; Argun, 2003: 141; Bozay, 2005: 206).

In 1978, when the influence of the MHP in Germany was at its peak, the leader of the MHP, Alparslan Türkes, met the leader of the Bavarian conservative party CSU, Franz Josef Strauß, and German employers (Roth and Taylan, 1981: 139; Bozay, 2005: 183). In the aftermath of this meeting, the CSU and its foundation provided strong financial support for the old MHP structures. At the time the Turk Federation had 170 local branches in Germany. The teachers, preachers and consulate officials who had been sent to Germany by the Turkish government were a key factor in swelling the ranks of the MHP between 1975 and 1980. When the party lost government power in 1978 and its members were increasingly charged with acts of political violence in Turkey, many of them sought asylum in Germany (Özcan, 1989: 191).

In the aftermath of the coup in 1980, the MHP was banned in Turkey. While the influence of the Turk Federation in Germany decreased rapidly as a result (Özcan, 1989: 191; Bozay, 2005: 183), Islamist groups experienced the opposite. Another reason for the demise of the MHP was the party's link to the professional killer and MHP member who had endeavoured to kill Pope John Paul II in 1981. The attempted assassination of the Pope and the MHP link to organised drug trafficking captured public attention in the early

1980s. Musa Serdar Celebi, head of the German Turk Federation from 1979 to 1982, was under arrest for several years in Italy as result of his participation in the event (Bozay, 2005: 183). Other reasons for the decline in membership numbers were the return of MHP activists to Turkey in the mid-1980s, an Islamist split-off from the MHP in 1987, and during the 1980s, the growth of Milli Görüs, which seemed a more attractive option and a 'young' political force within the conservative realm of Turkish politics.

In the early 1990s, the MHP began to retrieve some of its influence in Turkey: the escalation of the war against the Kurdish movement saw a strong presence of MHP members in paramilitary units, the military forces and the state apparatus. In the MHP-led Turk Federation numerous activists were simultaneously members of MIT, the Turkish intelligence service. Turk Federation activists clearly owed their relatively mild treatment by German officials to the close ties between the MIT and institutions such as the German police, intelligence agencies and conservative political parties (Argun, 2003: 149; Arslan, 2009: 147–148).

Massive mobilisation by the MHP during the 1990s failed to lead to a significant increase in membership of the Turk Federation in Germany. Islamist split-offs in the late 1980s and early 1990s led to a drop in membership numbers and ultimately stagnation. Current membership is estimated at around 7000 (Deutscher Bundestag, 2011). The Islamist split-off ATIB has a membership of around 8000 to 10,000 (Becker, 2006).

The development of the MHP in Turkey in the 1990s did not run parallel to that of the Turk Federation in Germany: the upswing of the MHP in Turkey since the 1990s was reflected in the surge of votes in the federal elections, with 19 per cent in 1999, 8 per cent in 2002, 14 per cent in 2007 and 13 per cent in 2011 (compared to 3 per cent in 1973 and 6 per cent in 1977). In Germany, on the other hand, both membership and influence ground to a standstill. The Turk Federation in Germany never recovered from two Islamic split-offs, ATIB and ATB. It nonetheless continues to play a major role in terms of financial and human resources of the mother party, MHP. Members of the German Turk Federation are repeatedly transferred to Turkey as politicians or to paramilitary units. Since the 2000s, however, there has been a lull in activities in Germany. While the MHP rose to the status of an established party in Turkey in the 2000s, its German counterpart found itself almost isolated from political life.

The immigrant wildcat strikes of 1973: Autonomy of migration or class politics beyond borders?

I will present a more detailed account of the wildcat strikes that occurred in 1973, and in particular of the strike at the Ford plant in Cologne, since this strike wave is a key reference point for German scholars working on the 'autonomy of migration' (Karakayalı, 2005; Bojadzijev, 2008: 148–196). The

Ford strike can furthermore be seen as a turning point in migrant political participation in Germany that is still relevant today. The strikes have been interpreted as proof of the existence of autonomous movements of migrant workers in Germany. The Ford strike in 1973 was the most significant labour dispute in post-war Germany that was led by migrant workers – at least in terms of numbers. The factory was occupied for four days by 17,000 workers, most of whom were Turkish (Hildebrandt and Olle, 1975). Preceded by similar strike waves across West Germany in 1969 and 1971, the Ford wildcat strike and its ultimate defeat in 1973 was decisive for the strike movement. It would take another 14 years for a comparable working-class movement to resurface in Germany (the dispute over the closure of a steel plant in Duisburg escalated in 1987/1988 throughout the entire Ruhr area). I contend that the collapse of the Ford strike in Cologne not only put an end to large-scale migrant labour unrest in Germany, but also to the mass strike movements of the German working class as a whole for many years to come.[2] Consequently, the class politics beyond borders deployed by the German and Turkish state apparatuses, German trade unions and German employers succeeded in the long run in containing the eruption of disputes in the early 1970s. The MHP was a device for the control of an unruly immigrant workforce.

The historical overview shows that the development of the German branch of the MHP was influenced by events in Turkish governments: the heyday of the MHP and its influence in Germany dates back to its participation in the government of Turkey in the second half of the 1970s. The political ties of German national and regional governments that, at least in part, supported the MHP in the 1970s are another essential variable. Despite the use of massive political violence, the organisations linked to the MHP were neither banned nor investigated by German officials. This contrasts with the treatment of left-wing Turkish and Kurdish associations in Germany (Østergaard-Nielsen, 2003b: 73–74). The close ties between the MHP and German and Turkish intelligence services are another aspect of its development (Solmaz, 1999). In addition, the support of German conservative parties for the MHP was not simply a matter of foreign policy, but a means of controlling the immigrant population. After the wildcat strikes and police clashes involving Turkish and Italian workers, which took place – with one exception – in automobile plants reached a climax in 1973 with strikes in Osnabrück, Mannheim, Aachen, Lippstadt, Neuss and Cologne (Bojadzijev, 2008: 156ff.), German employers and their political associates were happy to see an alternative political force at work in the process of organising immigrants.

The strike at the Ford automobile plant in Cologne was a response to the dismissal of 300 Turkish workers who had returned late from their holidays in Turkey. The wide range of strike demands included better wages for the migrant workers. 17,000 predominantly Turkish and Italian workers from a total of 33,000 workers struck and gained control of the factory for four days (Hildebrandt and Olle, 1975; Bojadzijev, 2008: 158). The strike was denounced by the official trade union of the metal workers, *IG Metall*, the elected Turkish strike leader and a number of other organisers were arrested, and the strike leader was deported to Turkey. When the strike ended, 100 Turkish workers were fired and another 600 had their contracts cancelled. A book on the strike written by several participants reports that three Turkish newspapers were distributed at the factory gate: *Milliyet*, *Hürriyet* and *Tercüman*. *Tercüman*, an MHP publication, is quoted as having been the most popular paper among Turkish workers (Betriebszelle Ford, 1973: 134–135). It condemned the strike as a 'Jewish and communist' intervention. The authors of the book state that conservative immigrant workers with religious and fascist worldviews likewise took part in the strike and elected representatives to the strike committee (222).

The strike at the Ford plant reveals crucial contradictions between the sympathisers of the German MHP branch and its leaders, since the rank and file of these workers sympathising with MHP joined the big strike at Ford, while the MHP newspaper went on to denounce the strike activities. The autonomy of the strike movement was confirmed by the participation of Turkish workers with conservative and fascist worldviews in the protest against the collective situation of migrant workers. The aim of the violence exercised by MHP activists during the 1970s against left-wing Turkish workers in Germany was to intimidate and harass them, and to separate the different groups of Turkish workers united along political lines in the strike wave of 1973. While the division between German and Turkish workers was marked by racism and by separate levels of integration and of status in terms of rights and citizenship, segregating groups of Turkish workers demanded something else: group violence among groups of workers, one of which was supported by the repressive apparatuses of two states, proved to be a successful tool in curtailing the autonomy of the strike movement.

Large-scale migrant labour unrest in Germany ceased in 1973. In the years that followed, the political mobilisation of migrants moved to other sites of conflict such as housing and education, albeit on a micro-scale (Bojadzijev, 2008: 197–227). United action with the majority of German workers and the trade unions failed in 1973. Neither did it occur at a later date. That autonomous labour struggles were kept at bay was evident from the defeat at the Ford plant in Cologne, which heralded the end of a cycle of strike movements. Without the support of German workers and their trade unions, migrant labour struggles were too weak to withstand the power of German employers.

Two factors were responsible for this defeat: on the one hand, the divided citizenship that set Turkish and German workers apart (Bojadzijev, 2008: 172) and, on the other hand, the surge in MHP membership since 1975, which exceeded that of leftist Turkish organisations in Germany. From this perspective, the spread of working class struggles was hampered by the 'autonomy of migration'. The dynamic and organisation of the wildcat strikes was confined to demands pertaining to migrant workers and other groups of low-skilled workers, and was not able to include other groups of workers in the course of the protest events. The trade unions and their integration into 'selective corporatism' (Esser et al., 1980) was yet another factor that impacted on the potential unity of the workforce, dividing it into mutually exclusive groups.

The specifics and management of the divided citizenship regime in Germany led and still lead in the twenty-first century to the separate organisation of Turkish migrants in migrant associations. Since the latter are mostly satellite institutions of Turkish political parties, political divisions in Turkey affect Turkish immigrants in Germany. In the 1990s, conflicts between members of the MHP and Kurdish associations linked to the PKK (Kurdistan Workers Party) dominated the scene. The violent clashes that erupted in June 2013 in Turkey over the politics of Prime Minister Erdogan produced a deep split in tenant organisations in Berlin, half of which sided with Erdogan, while the other half rejected his policies.

The ties of Turkish migrant associations in Germany to political life in Turkey continue to have a dual effect today: (1) Turkish immigrants in Germany tend to organise themselves separately from other citizens when it comes to political participation outside the workplace. (2) Their common concerns as immigrants in Germany (their expulsion from former social housing facilities, for example) are replaced or dislocated by conflicts among groups of immigrants anchored in political life in Turkey.

In terms of theoretical approaches to labour migration and class politics, the examples show that political parties, employers, citizenship regimes and state bodies designed strategies to manage the 'autonomy of migration': the Turkish migrant networks that emerged spontaneously in the mid-1970s and assumed organisational forms were limited, and the extension of Turkish political parties to German territory resulted in political control of a section of the immigrant population through class politics beyond borders. In 2013, the workforce at the Ford plant in Cologne is made up of 4400 workers, about 2000 of whom are members of a social organisation connected to *Milli Görüs*, the Islamist organisation associated with the conservative AKP and *Saadet Partisi* in Turkey.

Conclusion: Class politics beyond borders and divided citizenship

The results of research on the MHP in Germany correspond at least in one aspect to the findings of other scholars: migrant associations cannot be strictly categorised as oriented towards either sending or receiving countries (Sezgin, 2010: 202–203). They also restate the thesis that migrant associations combine the claims of their members with expectations of the state or country of destination and its institutional environment (Sezgin, 2008; Pries, 2010), thus refuting the earlier claim that migrant self-organisation necessarily implies a retreat from social life in the country of destination (Esser, 1996; Diehl, 2002).

In Germany, ongoing political exclusion of the Turkish population – ranging from lack of recognition as part of the population to exclusion from elections and citizenship – furthered migrant involvement in political groups identified with Turkish politics. Another variable is the relationship between different state apparatuses, in this case those of Turkey and Germany. The stable relationship between German conservative parties and Turkish governments ensures the absence of political pressure on groups associated with the Turkish government or state apparatus. MHP structures were investigated in Germany for a short period only, when the attempted assassination of the Pope pressured the German police into action.

To sum up, the racist exclusion of immigrants who were treated as 'guest workers' paved the way for the influence of the MHP in Germany. This was precisely the logic that prompted several German state institutions to support the MHP as the political representatives of immigrants in the 1970s, instead of facilitating immigrant access to German political associations and parties (with the notable exception of German trade unions). The representation of a section of Turkish immigrants by the MHP, which is linked to the Turkish government and several Turkish state institutions, converged in the 1970s with the logic of German immigration policies that saw Turkish immigrants as 'guests' who would soon return to their home country.

What conclusions, if any, can be drawn from these aspects for theories on the state and on parties as political organisations? A first conclusion is that political parties can be important nodes for connecting different state apparatuses beyond borders: in the case analysed, the influence of the MHP in Germany during the 1970s, German conservative parties utilised organisational and personal resources to link specific fractions of the Turkish state apparatus with the German intelligence services. Nicos Poulantzas claimed that the state as the sum of its apparatuses assumes the role of a party in the power bloc (1975). Political parties represent specific interest groups or lose this function. From the perspective of the German state, the CDU took the responsibility of organising a degree of political control over the unruly immigrant workforce, exploiting connections to a Turkish party that had both a working-class constituency and strong ties to repressive apparatuses of the Turkish state and a partly state-independent militia.

At this point, Michael Jäger's reformulation of Poulantzas's conceptualisation of parties comes into play. Parties are responsible for the coherence of state apparatuses, since they deploy ideologies that transcend them (Jäger, 2010: 244). Party rivalry is a crucial aspect of democratic states and party ideologies play a decisive role in power bloc unification. In the context of

Turkey, the function of the MHP and its ideology was to amalgamate certain elements of these repressive apparatuses. It was exported to Germany as a combination of street gang activity, drug trafficking and the opportunity for qualified activists to acquire official posts in Germany or Turkey. Striking here is the party involvement in unifying and strengthening power blocs in two countries simultaneously. The link to the German party, CDU/CSU, was vital to how the MHP functioned in the 1970s in Germany. This example verifies Jäger's claim that class struggle precedes the party system and the power bloc, but that the party system precedes the power bloc: political parties are the means by which power bloc unity is achieved.

The case of the MHP and Turkish labour migration shows that the autonomy of migrant struggles peaked during the 1973 strikes, but also reveals that the countermeasures taken by the German and Turkish states enabled German employers and German trade union leaders to manage this autonomy and prevent further upheaval. A key management tool was the exclusionary immigration policy of the German state combined with the racist exclusion of migrants from public life. This politics of divided citizenship brought forth a new border in Germany. Furthermore, the diverse political worldviews of Turkish workers were enforced with state-backed violence, thereby creating different group loyalties and preventing unity in the face of the bosses.

The case study and its theoretical framework in this text have helped to explain that the internationalisation of states is not a new phenomenon. The guest worker regime in Germany, that is, labour migration organised by the German state and German employers, was accompanied by the emergence of new transnational political spaces. These spaces were open to the influence of political currents: the development of Turkish migrant associations in Germany was highly volatile between 1970 and 1990 with fluctuating membership, but has remained more or less stable over the last 20 years. Transnational political spaces, however, are a highly contested terrain; this is where the power and resources of both the German and Turkish state apparatuses come into play. While it is evident that migration processes are accompanied by specific forms of social and political organisation of immigrants and corresponding forms of struggle, scholarship on the autonomy of migration tends to ignore the political activities of migrants in Germany that do not fit into their framework. Examples are mobilisation by the MHP or the successful build-up of Islamist organisations such as the *Süleymanci* in the 1970s or *Milli Görus* and DITIB in the 1980s (Wunn, 2007).

A full account of migrant activities calls first for acknowledgement that migrants themselves might well have restrained their autonomy, given that they were joining organisations linked to the state institutions of receiving and/or sending states. This would also work as an antidote to what Sandro Mezzadra has termed in his self-criticism the romanticisation of migration inherent in the idea of an autonomy of migration (2010).

Second, migrant struggles are specific conflicts and should be seen in terms of the overall context. Institutions such as citizenship regimes and the political strategies of state apparatuses are frequently in a position to contain autonomous immigrant activities. In this regard, the primacy of resistance over domination persists as a myth.

Third, fetishising the autonomy of migration as a value in itself can obstruct a broader vision. Focusing on the activities of migrants as migrants tends to reproduce their status as racialised 'others' and loses sight of the additional dimensions of their political activities. As an implicit or explicit activist strategy, reference to the common situation of migrants can be a resource for mobilisation (the Ford strike in 1973), but it can also curtail mobilisation if strike movements remain largely isolated from the bulk of non-migrant workers (the defeat of the Ford strike).

Notes

1. West Germany signed contracts with Italy, Greece, Spain, Turkey, Morocco, Portugal, Tunisia and Yugoslavia between 1955 and 1968.
2. Other scholars share the same view. Scholars of industrial relations see the events and outcome of the strikes in 1973 as the basis for 'selective corporatism' in Germany, which excludes the lower working-class strata from social security and collective agreements (Esser et al., 1980; Birke, 2007: 339). Manuela Bojadzijev, too, emphasises that the year 1973 saw decisive ruptures in the situation of migrants in Germany (2008: 229).

13
Emigration Policies and Citizenship Rhetoric: Morocco and Its Emigrants in Europe

Esther Mikuszies

Scholars have classified modes of governing the diaspora via policies that range from encouragement to return, banishing and simultaneously monitoring emigrants through export of the security apparatus, to official promotion of national identity abroad (Collyer, 2013; Ragazzi, 2009; Levitt and de la Dehesa, 2003; Østergaard-Nielsen, 2003a). More and more countries embrace territorially absent citizens symbolically as part of the 'imagined community' (Anderson, 1991) of a global nation that offers membership, services and rights beyond territorial borders. Analogous to immigration policies, the global trend towards diaspora cultivation can be characterised as a means of replacing territorial fences with those that construct and control emigrant identities (Ragazzi, 2009).

This chapter analyses how the Moroccan political elite involved in homeland policies under the rule of King Mohammed VI used transnational policy and discursive strategies towards their emigrant population in Europe between 2000 and 2010. Morocco has a long tradition of labour migration to Europe. Since the state began to stimulate emigration in the 1960s, over 4.5 million Moroccan nationals – approximately 12 per cent of the population – have been officially registered abroad, 85 per cent of them in Europe (Cherti et al., 2013). The country's strategic shift in the 1990s from close surveillance to diaspora policies of courting and promoting Moroccan identity abroad has been thoroughly explored (de Haas, 2007; Brand, 2006; Belguendouz, 2006). Only decades after Moroccan development had charged emigrants with the generation of remittances to and investment in the homeland, they were rendered visible as a state category in a special ministry and a number of agencies. The comparatively late cultivation of the diaspora was part of a broader shift to co-opt former opponents to the makzhen, a branched but centralised network of the king's loyal followers, in preparation for the rule of Mohammed VI. The latter succeeded his father in 1999 as political and spiritual leader, as 'Commander of the Faithful' (*amir al-mu-'minin*) of Moroccan Muslims (Boukhars, 2011; Zisenwine, 2007).

Building on present perspectives on emigration policies, the Moroccan case invites further exploration of rhetorical patterns in the construction and promotion of emigrant subjectivities as good citizens. The Moroccan monarchy actually has established a conglomerate of institutions for emigrants. In consequence, the actors officially involved in the making of emigrant subjectivities are as heterogeneous as their corresponding rhetorics are. The analysis identifies the following rhetorical patterns on (emigrant) citizenship:

- *Diversity as a mode of governance*: the rhetoric of diversity and the uncoordinated reach-out to different categories of emigrants is coupled with the declaration of flexible, antagonistic and changing expectations and imperatives.
- *The emigrant as a multi-sited good citizen*: the transnational imperatives 'integrate yourself over there' and 'be a good Moroccan' assume unlimited freedom of action.
- *Islamic subjectivity as the call for an interventionist and disciplinary state*: the construction of 'the seducible faithful emigrant' abroad justifies control and religious instruction.

All three patterns exemplify power asymmetries on both shores of the Mediterranean and the specific features of the Moroccan case. Morocco's territorial integrity is permanently challenged in the complex border situation that includes the unresolved issues of Western Sahara, the closed border with Algeria, and claims to the coastal enclaves of Ceuta, Melilla and several islands. Setting the three taboos of territorial integrity, primacy of Islam and legitimacy of the king as discernible boundaries in the construction of nationhood is closely linked to the idea of the nation-state as the optimal form of existence, although the diaspora discourse crosses territorial borders and the notion of exclusive citizenship.

I will first of all provide the theoretical background to the construction and promotion of emigrant subjectivities. In the same way that studying immigration policies in isolation was perceived as one-sided, so too would ignoring the interactive dynamics of identity construction and fencing in the asymmetric Euro-Mediterranean power constellation be a biased approach. Second, I present a bird's eye view of transnational diaspora strategies in Morocco, and third, illustrate and discuss three dominant rhetorical patterns in the construction of emigrant subjectivities in the light of current literature on the diaspora, transnationalism and the international management of religion. My findings draw on the analysis of documents such as national emigration programmes, speeches of the king and other policy-makers, and expert interviews.[1] I conclude by discussing how members of the political elite in Morocco construct and promote different emigrant subjectivities, and by outlining future avenues of research.

The theoretical landscape: Constructing and fencing emigrant identities interactively

Contemporary research on diaspora strategies concentrates on the design of diaspora-state relations, shifts in national sovereignty and critiques of a neoliberal rationality in the government of emigrants (Levitt and de la Dehesa, 2003; Ragazzi, 2009; Kunz, 2012). Most authors agree on the global trend whereby states re-invent themselves to actively encourage emigration and reinforce lasting transnational involvement. The construction and promotion of diaspora identities has been theorised under the premise of different epistemological and ontological positions. Scholars following a Foucauldian tradition reject the opposition of the individual and the state, arguing that diaspora government works best through rather than against the subjectivities of emigrant citizens (Kunz, 2012; Ragazzi, 2009; Rodríguez, 2010). They claim that involvement of the diaspora is a more social method of government intervention, one that aims at legitimisation and consolidation of the neoliberal forms of government that have spread globally (Kunz, 2012).

Since emigration renders the cohesion between territorially present and absent citizens vulnerable, the state seeks to create a stable and coherent citizenry unified by a shared political allegiance, solidarity and symbolic identification with the state as an imagined community. Diaspora scholars highlight the constructed nature of diasporas, which are not given, and static entities but constituted by the symbolic politics of the home state (Barry, 2006). The following analysis underscores the premise that citizenship and relations between emigration and immigration states are hierarchical. Citizen rhetoric and emigration policies are interlinked, even interactive in the sense that both show attempts to cope with receiving state expectations while constructing the subjectivities of emigrant citizens. Although homeland policies are not necessarily coordinated with immigration countries, scholars have demonstrated two parallel dynamics: first, extending European migration policies beyond the external frontier of the European Union (EU) has involved state and non-state institutions in neighbouring countries in the making of irregular migration (Transit Migration, 2007). Second, government policies of European host states that offer citizenship to the wanted immigrant have pressured sending countries to respond to the needs of legalised emigrants (Brand, 2006).

Migrants' legal subjectivities are designed by sovereigns in at least two states, namely, in the state of residence and in the state of origin. Depending on the historical, situational and geographical context, scholars have described migrants as dually dehumanised, dually absent or dually present. Hannah Arendt (2011 [1951]) examined how states collectively denaturalised human beings in the interwar period and made them stateless refugees, who found it impossible to find a new home or government protection, and to act with conviction. By portraying migrants as *dually absent* (Sayad, 2004), French–Algerian sociologist Abdelmalek Sayad describes a spatial antagonism that refers to the immigrant excluded in the receiving society and the physically absent emigrant in the society of origin. According to Sayad, the emigrant is never completely included in the receiving society and never fully excluded or forgotten in the homeland society. Some voices in the current debate on Sayad's intellectual legacy pick up on the idea of a dual bond to argue that migrant citizens are now dually present.

Although many decolonised countries link emigrant citizenship to patriotic commitment rather than freedom of choice (Hansen and Stepputat, 2005), Fitzgerald's metaphor of a *citizenship à la carte* summons the notion of a possible increase in agency to be gained by territorially absent citizens. '[E]migrants can enjoy the substance of their homeland citizenship à la carte from a menu of rights and obligations, whereas residents must take the rights and obligations together at a relatively fixed price,' (Fitzgerald, 2009: 176). In a similar vein, Waldinger asserts that migration inverts the power relationship between sending state and emigrants in the sense that the once poor, ignored and at times persecuted migrants 'now possess resources that emigration countries dismiss at their peril' (Waldinger, 2013: 92).

Moroccan diaspora strategies in the Euro-Mediterranean constellation

The Moroccan monarchy developed its relations with emigrant citizens in Europe in a complex asymmetric constellation of states and populations in the Mediterranean. Although numerous Moroccans migrated to the Gulf States, Western scholars often neglect this constellation (Khachani, 2009). Gulf monarchies are the strongest investors in Morocco and allies of the Moroccan monarchy (Cembrero in: El País, 25 November 2011). Morocco has historical links with the European continent as a result of French and Spanish colonialism, and its economy depends heavily on Europe.

The Moroccan case has long been the textbook example of a diaspora policy that banishes part of the population abroad and at the same time controls it via an exported security apparatus (Ragazzi, 2009). Political exiles and migrant workers were not simply absent in both societies, as Sayad described, but dual suspects, at times even criminalised, following the official immigration stop in Europe in the 1970s. Moroccan state officials declared left-wing exiles particularly suspicious and were party to the Moroccan secret service kidnapping and executing of their opponent Ben Barka. In the long run, however, border-crossing mobility has also jarred global hierarchies of citizenship. Numerous migrant workers upgraded their position in Moroccan society through their mobility and suddenly had something to offer to their homeland. With poverty an unresolved problem in Morocco, emigration has been central to the country's development strategy since the 1970s. Some 5 million Moroccans still live on less than €1 per day (*El País*, 26 February 2012) and despite the wealth of the monarchy suffer social inequality, low alphabetisation and rural poverty. In 2010, Moroccan emigrants remitted approximately $6400m or almost 7 per cent of GDP (World Bank, 2011). Having gained experience with European versions of citizenship, emigrant citizens ultimately succeeded in convincing their king to appropriate the topic of migrant interests as his own.

In the context of a broad authoritarian restructuring in the 1990s, King Hassan II altered his strategic position towards the diaspora (de Haas, 2007; Brand, 2006; Belguendouz, 2006). A wide conglomerate of overlapping institutions and programmes directed at emigrants has been established by successive monarchs (Belguendouz, 2006), making the group officially involved in the making of emigrant subjectivities as heterogeneous as citizenship rhetoric. Global nation policies encouraged emigrants to stay abroad, to integrate into the resident society, but to cultivate diaspora relations. A series of institutions aimed at fostering economic, political and cultural ties between the diaspora and the homeland were established: the Hassan II Foundation for Moroccans living abroad, the Mohammed V Foundation for Solidarity, the Council of the Moroccan Community Abroad, the Moroccan Council of Ulemas for Europe and the Ministry of Moroccans Residing Abroad. Several projects abroad offer courses in Arabic and the national culture, partnership programmes with local and regional authorities worldwide, cultural events, and religious instruction for the preservation of the Moroccan community's Muslim identity. A number of schemes are directed at homeland tourists within the framework of *Opération Marhaba* (Arabic for operation welcome): a National Day of Moroccans Abroad, a Summer University, and transport and logistics assistance for annual holidays at home. The organisers spread the welcome message to encourage Moroccan travellers to spend money in their homeland on their return.

The political elite gradually began to see emigrant citizens as permanently absent, but to value them as unbroken members of the homeland political community. Mohammed VI (2005) courted emigrant citizens in a historical speech as the 'highest trump for the new Morocco'. He announced a 'new emigration policy', full political citizenship, including active and passive voting rights, and the creation of a council of the Moroccan Community Abroad. King Hassan II uniquely carried out external voting in five extraterritorial circumscriptions for the legislative period from 1984 to 1993. External voting was re-introduced in the 2011 constitution as a response to the Arab spring protests. At the same time, the monarch made efforts to yield to European demands for the successful integration of Moroccan residents into European societies. As members of the council of the Moroccan Community Abroad he chose those

> who enjoy a *good moral reputation in the host country*, and who are known for their commitment to the nation's sacred institutions, its immutable values and its unified multi-faceted identity, as well as from among those who make up the lifeblood of the nation and are known for their competence, experience, credibility and special input.
> (Royal Decree, 21 December 2007; emphasis added)

Six working groups were established to deal with political rights and citizenship, the rights of women and of new generations, culture, education and identity, administration and public policies, scientific competences and religious instruction. Whereas transnational initiatives such as *Daba 2012 pour tous*, the *Mouvement des Marocains démocrates résidants à l'étranger* and the *Forum Civil des Marocains d'Europe* demanded the immediate introduction of external voting, the council persevered in activities with a cultural bias. It financed and promoted publications, exhibitions, cultural events, research and expert meetings, all of which led to overlapping, intersecting and even contradictory rhetorical patterns in the construction of diaspora subjectivities, which I will explore in the following.

Constructing, promoting and fencing identities: Rhetorical patterns in Moroccan diaspora discourse

The following sub-sections explore and discuss three complex and dynamic patterns in the identity construction and fencing of emigrant citizens in Morocco.

- Uncoordinated parallel discourses on the diaspora reach out simultaneously with various expectations and imperatives to different categories of emigrants.
- The transnational imperative of 'integrate yourself over there' and 'be a good Moroccan' constructs emigrants as *multi-sited good citizens*.
- Religion can *call for an interventionist and disciplinary state* to control the 'easily seducible faithful'.

I argue that the involvement of numerous actors in homeland policies entails divergent, intersecting and sometimes contradictory rhetorical patterns that do not necessarily attempt to homogenise the imagined community of the Global Nation beyond the common, albeit no longer exclusive bond of Moroccanness (*'marocanité'*). The construction of heterogeneous Moroccan subjectivities creates flexible junctions that allow for the government of different categories of emigrants in different situations.

Diversity and the uncoordinated reaching out to different groups of emigrants

Legalised Moroccan migrants have gradually become dually present and recognised individuals both in the country of immigration and in the homeland, where sovereigns seek to govern them through the construction of different subjectivities. The political elite involved in homeland policies address emigrants predominantly as economic subjects and as part of a highly qualified entrepreneurial elite, but occasionally as needy migrant workers, as people more oriented to the host country or as faithful subjects of the king. By assigning contradictory and overlapping identities to emigrant citizens, the political elite can enforce varying imperatives and expectations: remittances, maintenance of family ties in Morocco, integration into the receiving country, departure from Morocco through lawful channels only, and loyalty and religious obedience to the king, whose role is constitutionally defined as Commander of the Faithful.

Policy-makers in Morocco have for a long time clearly charged 'the Moroccans of the World' with contributing to the country's welfare with remittances and investments. At the same time, a spokesman for the Council of the Moroccan Community Abroad characterises the homeland as proud, virtuous, caring and fully committed to emigrant citizens, 'leaving doors and windows permanently open for emigrants... respecting their autonomy and independence' (first international forum of Moroccan migrant organisations active in the local development of Morocco, 10 August 2009). The recognition and caring of the heroic emigrant citizen represents a form of earned citizenship. The political elite appreciates migrants' knowledge, *savoir-faire* and economic contribution to development to the extent that 'they deserve that we are interested in them' (interview Ministry for Moroccans Residing Abroad, 26 May 2010). Migrant rights activist and scholar Belguendouz, on the other hand, has long criticised that Moroccan residents abroad are reduced to 'passive milk cows' (2004: 8), but excluded and forgotten as political beings. The Emigration Ministry's Five-Year Plan from 2008 to 2012 honours remittances and investment as a 'crucial commitment to the stability and economic, social, human and political development of the whole country' (Ministère Chargé des Marocains Résidant à l'Étranger et des Affaires de la Migration, 2008). The authors of the Plan mildly concede, however, that 'Moroccans from elsewhere wish to be more than a simple "bank identity"' (ibid.).

The political elite began to express awareness and solidarity when Moroccans in Europe became highly concerned about the unemployment that resulted from the global economic and financial crisis. The Minister for Moroccan Residents Abroad mentioned 'help and priority in future emigration policies for those people who are in emergency for the state of economy' (Ministère Chargé des Marocains Résidant à l'Étranger, 2012).

Although emigrant citizens are courted as economic subjects, they are constructed differently when it comes to political subjectivity. According to a survey of the Council of the Moroccan Community Abroad, only 20 per cent of the sample wished to participate in political life in Morocco, whereas 54 per cent saw political participation in the resident country as important (CCME and BVA, 2010: 57). Given that emigrant workers are less informed and less interested in political participation in the homeland, a spokesman for the council suggested introducing a complex three-level procedure prior to launching external voting. Moroccan intellectuals should first of all be mobilised to debate the topic and only then, second, should the debate be open to the general public. Third, a democratic debate on the situation of emigrants should be conducted without contesting the integration requests of the destination country (interview CCME, 1 June 2010). In this context, the monarchy's mantra that Morocco primarily needs economic growth and is not yet ready for democracy (Boukhars, 2011) loses its credibility in the emigrant community, which now has something to offer the homeland.

In addition to the economically worthy emigrant citizen and the unqualified, needy emigrant worker who needs to be protected and looked after, homeland actors have reproduced the legal Moroccan resident abroad as the wanted emigrant. Illegal migrants, on the other hand, are objects of the Mediterranean security partnership and not mentioned in discursive diaspora strategies. Many sending states reproduce the illegal emigrant as an 'impossible subject' – Raissiguier's definition – as a 'subject barred from citizenship and without rights...a person who cannot be and a problem that cannot be solved' (Ngai, 2004 quoted in: Raissiguier, 2010: 3). In the area of irregular migration, Moroccan legislation makes strong concessions to European demands. The Moroccan migration act, passed in 2003, fines those who leave Moroccan territory illegally between €250 and €900 or sends them to prison for a period of one to six months. Policy evaluation studies meanwhile call for depenalisation of irregular emigration to enable the voluntary return of illegal migrants (Cherti et al., 2013).

This sub-section illustrated how the political elite involved in homeland policies construct and value different subjectivities of the diaspora. While emigrants are highly desirable as remittance senders and investors, their subjectivity is rendered impossible in the case of illegal border-crossing.

Transnational imperatives: 'integrate yourself over there' and 'be a good Moroccan citizen'

Although most migrants remain involved in at least some cross-border activity, the proportion of transmigrants who take part in activities of higher intensity is relatively small and dependent on the sphere of participation (Waldinger, 2013). Rhetoric that reaches out to emigrants with the expectation of living the best possible transnational lifestyle coupled with specific patriotic commitments is, nevertheless, not a Moroccan particularity per se (Østergaard-Nielsen, 2003b).

The political elite involved in homeland policies addresses emigrants as 'Moroccan Residents Abroad' or 'Moroccan Communities Abroad'. They appeal to Moroccan nationhood and more hesitantly to the integration expectations of resident countries. Rhetorical patterns oscillate between the subtle imperatives of 'integrate yourself over there' and the request to be a good citizen of the homeland. Both patterns assume the unlimited agency of emigrants and confront them with the expectation of being a good citizen all over the world.

By positioning them transnationally in terms of sameness and otherness, the political elite promotes the members of the diaspora as potentially good *transmigrants*. Preservation of the identity of origin is considered a potential resource for both resistance to and integration into European societies. Hence Moroccan policy programmes seek to protect and strengthen Moroccan identity and not merely turn out economically productive citizens. According to a spokesman of the Hassan II Foundation, Moroccan nationality is a source of identity that can be transformed into rationalised economic behaviour, thus creating a win-win situation for all involved: the emigrants themselves and the countries of residence and of origin. The aim of the Foundation is to equip emigrants with the prerequisites for integration and economic prosperity in host countries by providing them with courses in culture and the Arabic language. 'It has always been better to have two stools or choices than sitting somewhere between two stools,' (interview Hassan II Foundation, 30 May 2010). Knowledge of one's roots, however, is also perceived as an instrument of resistance to and emancipation from European pressure to integrate, while benefiting from multiple belongings. Awareness of one's roots would compensate for the inferiority complex said to have evolved as a consequence of mobility (ibid.).

Another argumentation strand reverses the notion of sameness and otherness, claiming that Moroccan residents abroad are first of all citizens of their country of residence and only then Moroccan citizens. Policy-makers in the Council of the Moroccan Community Abroad refer to the resident country's territorial integrity, anticipate possible loyalty conflicts and use the otherness of emigrants as an argument. 'It is important that Moroccan state decisions do not hinder good integration and a good rooting of those who have become dual nationals, who are no longer exclusively Moroccans,' (interview Emigration Council, 1 June 2010). Arguing that the mentality and the customs of Moroccan residents abroad differed from those of their non-mobile fellow citizens on Moroccan territory, this strand positions the emigrant as the partially 'other' in the homeland rather than in the receiving society. Simultaneously, the argument of the territorial integrity of European states is exploited to negate the responsibility of the Moroccan state towards their emigrant citizens. 'When a Moroccan worker in Europe has a legal problem and contacts the political community in Morocco, he is on the wrong path. Morocco is not entitled to examine the policies of others,' (interview Emigration Ministry, 26 May 2010).

The transnational imperative to be a good, multi-local citizen is not a Moroccan particularity. Morocco, however, is an exemplary case of citizenship in the Arab world, where kinship and religion link the ruler and the ruled (Parolin, 2009). The principle of perpetual allegiance forbids Moroccan nationals to renounce their citizenship, which they inherit *jus sanguinis* (Nationality Code, 1958). Although multi-local bonds are constantly encouraged and Moroccan national identity is no longer exclusive, the diaspora discourse shares the idea that the optimal condition for political existence is still the nation-state.

The role of Islam: Constructing and promoting religious subjectivities

Whether via the creation of the secular subject in Europe (Mavelli, 2013) or the construction of the seducible faithful in Morocco, states on both shores of the Mediterranean call for a more 'interventionist' and disciplinary state, one that is expected to control the faithful emigrant. With few exceptions (Laurence, 2012; Brand, 2006), little attempt has been made to investigate the role of Islam in emigration policies and citizenship rhetoric. Adherents of a psychoanalytic tradition generally treat religion as a plaster on the wound of battered identity or an instrument to govern (de)colonialised populations (Benslama, 2011). Some scholars do not take religion seriously, reducing it to ideology or banishing it to the pre-scientific sphere or pre-modern era.

The Moroccan case demonstrates that the national version of Islam is one of several dimensions in the official construction of a diaspora identity. It exemplifies Muslim states in which nationality is neither exclusively secular nor exclusively religious, but 'involves concepts of citizenship, concepts of ethnicity and concepts of religion in an ambiguous connection to each other' (Lapidus, 2001: 47). Tradition and religious forms of legitimacy coexist with constitutional sources of legitimacy imported from Western countries (Badie, 1987). Following decolonisation, the monarchy constructed a Muslim community of the king's subjects and regained its central political position by launching a myth about the martyr sultan (Frégosi and Zeghal, 2005).

The purpose of promoting a Moroccan Islam abroad is to respond to European expectations, to discredit groups that question the king's religious and political authority, and to multiply influence and competitiveness in relation to other Islamic influences in Europe. The monarchy began to discipline religious scholars and to use spiritual instruction to undermine Islamic groupings that have questioned the king's role as Commander of the Faithful since the 1970s, such as *Al Adlwa al Ihssane* (Bouasria, 2012). In Europe, the struggle for hegemony at the *Grande Mosquée de Paris* is evidence of the tense relationship between Algeria and Morocco. Morocco countered the Algerian takeover of the *Grande Mosquée de Paris* in 1982 with support for the French Muslim federation, embarking on a campaign of 'Islamic awakening' in Moroccan and European universities (Laurence, 2012). The monarchy has considerable experience of sending preachers and religious guides to Europe during the month of Ramadan and of providing spiritual support and instruction abroad. Central agencies are the Hassan II Foundation, the Ministry of Habous and Islamic Affairs and the Council of Ulemas for Europe established in 2008. The management of religion across borders is legitimised in accordance with European expectations. 'If we failed to offer religious instruction, certain countries would complain that we did not have our migrants under control,' (interview Hassan II Foundation, 30 May 2010).

The Casablanca attacks in 2003 shattered the image marketed to international donors of a kingdom immune to terrorism. The attacks accelerated enactment of the immigration act that penalises irregular border-crossing and pushed for the securitisation of Islam on Moroccan territory (Bouasria, 2012). Policy-makers involved in the management of Islam abroad are concerned about the rise of 'green fear' in the aftermath of 9/11, which led to the dominant perception of Moroccans as Muslims rather than Arabs. A spokesman for the Hassan II Foundation explained the need for spiritual instruction of the religious emigrant metaphorically: 'If someone practises the Islamic religion, I prefer them to take the right direction. This is comparable with the right to water. There are many types of water: poisoned water, water with microbes and controlled water. Shouldn't we give controlled water to the thirsty?' (interview Hassan II Foundation, 30 May 2010).

The faithful abroad are constructed as seducible ignorant subjects unable to emancipate themselves autonomously on the spiritual level and therefore in need of instruction. This argument is reminiscent of the popular dichotomy prevalent in colonial literature and anthropology between a popular but retrograde Islam in the countryside and a formal, progressive Islam of Arabs and the Ulema elite in the cities (El Ayadi et al., 2006: 20). At the same time, scholars in the Ministry of Habous and Islamic Affairs, for example, push the search for philosophical and historical traces of universalistic values in Islam and parallels to Christianity with regard to peacefulness, solidarity and justice. The golden age of Al-Andalus is remembered as an important historic reference for reciprocal enrichment between Jewish and Muslim intellectuals in Andalusia (interview Ministry of Habous and Islamic Affairs, 2 June 2010; Bensadoun, 2007). Whereas policy-makers reach out to Moroccan emigrants in terms of rights and freedom, religion appears as the opportunity to strengthen a relationship of obedience between the king as Commander of the Faithful and his subjects.

Conclusion

While numerous scholars have examined citizenship policies and rhetoric in receiving societies, this article focuses on the reverse side: the complex and overlapping diaspora policies and discourses, taking the Moroccan case as an example. The country's complex border situation, its position in the Euro-Mediterranean constellation, the meaning of kinship and religion in citizenship and the convergence of the religious and political spheres are among the particularities of the Moroccan case that invite deeper analysis of identity construction and fencing across borders. Three contradictory and complementary rhetorical patterns stimulate reflection on current blind spots in homeland research and inspire further avenues of research.

First, the section on diversity and the construction of multiple diaspora identities has shown that the uncoordinated reaching out to elitist emigrants, needy emigrant workers, loyal and potential remittance senders and faithful emigrants, proceeds with multilayered expectations and imperatives. A more detailed empirical study on the production of the irregular migrant as an 'impossible subject' (Raissiguier, 2010) based on current research on the making of irregular migration in eastern neighbouring countries of the EU (Transit Migration, 2007) is called for, especially for the North African region and the post-Arab spring era. Research could furthermore focus on the few emigration states that have adopted alternative citizenship rhetoric, such as Ecuador with its 'we are all migrants' state philosophy.

Second, the section on the twofold imperatives of 'integrate yourself over there' and 'be a good Moroccan' illustrated that the idea of political monogamy has not only been challenged in the Western world. The political elite expect emigrants to be virtuous citizens in Europe and Morocco simultaneously. What this entails needs to be explored in the context of Arab citizenship, which links the access and loss of nationality to religious beliefs.

Third, the section on the role of religion in emigration policies and citizenship rhetoric made a plea to overcome the secular bias in homeland policy research by integrating religion, for instance, as one of several dimensions of identity construction in the diaspora. Complementary to the construction of the secular subject in Europe (Mavelli, 2013), the Moroccan case demonstrates that the creation and promotion of a specific Moroccan Islamic identity can similarly be mobilised to call for an 'interventionist' and disciplinary state. Constructing and fencing the emigrant as an 'easily seducible and ignorant faithful' justifies policies that control and instruct Moroccan nationals abroad. Future research should ask to what extent the global revival of Islam during the final decades of the twentieth century and the current collapse of states in the Arab world have challenged the idea of the nation-state as the optimal form of existence. The Moroccan constitution of 2011 recognises emigrants for the first time as legal persons with voting rights, but has only slightly altered the rhetoric towards emigrants. The constitutional text emphasises the monarchy's commitment to protect migrant rights and its wish to reinforce emigrant contributions to homeland development and strengthen the friendship and professional ties between the Moroccan government and the societies of resident countries.

Although the diaspora discourse extends beyond territorial borders, all three rhetorical patterns clearly sustain the idea that the nation-state remains the optimal form of existence.

Note

1. The analysis is based on the 21 interviews I conducted in Morocco in spring 2010 with several representatives of institutions that had a voice in designing diaspora policies: transnational migrant organisations, the Council of the Moroccan Community Abroad, the Ministry of Moroccans Residing Abroad, the Hassan II Foundation for Moroccans Residing Abroad, the Ministry of Habous and Islamic Affairs, academic activists and political parties. The analysis is confined to the French-speaking, hegemonic discourse.

14
Coda

Sabine Ruß-Sattar and Helen Schwenken

Border studies have addressed the phenomenon of borders primarily with reference to analytical categories of governance, state or globalisation (Donzelli, 2013) – taking the border as something that demarcates sovereign states. In this vein, it is commonly assumed that citizenship issues come across as a stratified access to all kinds of rights as soon as a person enters a state territory. This volume, in contrast, was conceptualised to explore the intertwined relations between borders and citizenship at a local, national and international level. The common argument of the authors rests on the premise that the mechanisms of bordering can only be fully grasped by revealing their relation to the ambivalent and shifting construction of citizenship. A glance at contemporary politics reveals the political character of this construction. The heated debate on immigration reform in the US during the second term of the Obama presidency, for example, is glaring evidence of the bargaining processes that link border and citizenship construction: by introducing a probationary status, the bill approved by the US Senate in June 2013 (US Senate, 2013) has paved the way for 11 million undocumented migrants in the US to acquire citizenship (O'Keefe, 2013). Senate approval was based on the compromise that the legalisation of irregular migrants would come into operation parallel to a 'border surge' involving a dramatic increase in the militarisation of the US–Mexico border. This is made possible – despite a tremendous budget deficit – by revenue accrued from regularising the status of undocumented migrants. Immigrants will therefore pay for citizenship inclusion with future immigrant exclusion. As this example shows, processes of constructing borders and citizenship are based on straightforward binary codes such as inside/outside, inclusion/exclusion or citizen/non-citizen. Our empirical findings, however, challenge these dichotomies and indicate that more contradictory and more complex mechanisms are at work here. This is evidenced by the third major category in our analytical concept (albeit not explicitly mentioned in the title of the volume): the migrant. We deliberately focus on the political agency and subjectivity of migrants and border crossers, refusing to reduce them to mobile objects of border security, labour exploitation or immigration control. Nevertheless, as Nowak and Mikuszies assert in this volume, economic aspects co-determine the politics of citizenship, both in the form of class politics (Nowak) and of emigration policy and remittances (Mikuszies).

Resuming the empirical observations presented in this volume, we identify three forms of politics that reflect the contested relation between border and citizenship: first, border(land)s as arenas of contested *juridical politics,* second, transgressive border politics as a generator of new forms of citizenship and, third, border politics as *domopolitics* with the attendant deterioration of (social) citizenship.

The border(land) as an arena of contested *juridical politics*

One of the key border functions – controlling a territory and a population – is now carried out with technologies that stretch way beyond territorial borderlines (Weber and Pickering; Sack, both in this volume). At first sight, this seems to suggest increased mobility constraints and a worsening of migrant circumstances. As Sack argues in the case of airports as inner border(land)s, however, the tension between deterrence and human rights associated with contemporary border phenomena is gaining momentum: on the inside, the presence of lawyers, associations and higher courts, all of them intent on enforcing the rule of law, can render the executive accountable and even change the rules in use by implementing international law. The migrant as a non-citizen is endowed with a new status and becomes a juridical cosmopolitan subject. On the outside, however, the migrant's juridical situation changes utterly. As Klepp illustrates in her case study of the Mediterranean border in this volume, unclear responsibilities can prevent the application of rules, frequently with fatal consequences for irregular boat migrants. Responsibilities are indeed imprecise, even deliberately so, when a state is engaged in joint operations, in operations in the territorial waters of another state or those on the high seas. Klepp's findings reveal the negotiable and political character of the drafting and implementation of law in the 'multi-sited arena of negotiation' (Benda-Beckmann et al., 2005: 9) of the Search and Rescue (SAR) system in the Mediterranean Sea. At sea, the humanitarian law of the sea is either ignored or modified to accommodate political considerations and the government manoeuvres of the coastal states that dominate the sea. At the same time, the politically explosive nature of sea migration questions the very legitimacy of legally binding SAR regulations.

As these and other cases in this volume demonstrate, legal regulations on migration, border control and migrant categories (Ataç, in this volume) are by no means set in stone. In line with critical legal theory, they confirm that migration policy struggles are also legal struggles, and that legal provisions are one important outcome of societal struggles (see also Buckel, 2013).

Transgressive border politics: The border as generator of a new form of citizenship

In the case of *transgressive border politics* (Rygiel, in this volume), border violence generates political solidarity between migrants and residents. This form of border politics is also found on the inside, where non-government organisations (NGOs) at a local level are tearing down internal barriers by actively promoting solidarity and the inclusion of undocumented migrants (Sidney, in this volume). Furthermore, the contesting of borders by undocumented migrants can be seen as an act of citizenship, notwithstanding the legal status of the actors (Raissiguier, in this volume). Rygiel and Raissiguier found some empirical evidence for the 'autonomy of migration' thesis advanced, among others, by Mezzadra (2010b), confirming political subjectivity beyond the legal citizenship status in migrant practices. In this sense, *transgressive border politics* constitute a new form of politics beyond citizenship, although the fate of the frequently cited Sangatte 'jungle' case does put some water in the wine, since it shows that the success of this kind of political experience has so far turned out to be temporary (Schwenken, in this volume).

New border politics as *domopolitics* and the deterioration of (social) citizenship

The other side of the coin is *domopolitics*, with ongoing border securitisation and the attendant impact on rights and citizenship. New policies of migration control use security measures and control technologies both inside and outside, as well as on the territorial borderline. As Rodriguez's case study on New Jersey in this volume demonstrates, the securitisation of borders is coupled with a bunch of measures and policies that lead to a deterioration in the living conditions of undocumented migrants in terms of work and accommodation. She points out that the internalisation or localisation of border enforcement in the US case generally takes place in suburban areas in the form of outright expulsion, prohibition of settlement (restrictions on work and accommodation) and intimidation of and violence against migrants on a daily basis. Interestingly, the agents of *domopolitics* are not only (local) government representatives but also so-called citizen organisations and ordinary citizens who discriminate against their 'illegal' neighbours. Rodriguez claims that American citizenship, particularly social citizenship, is at stake when benefits and entitlements are confined exclusively to those deemed to be genuine citizens. County prisons built in the midst of Latino and Muslim communities, for instance, are striking examples of policies of intimidation and deterrence at the local level. *Domopolitics* makes the marginalised feel uncomfortable. *Domopolitics* implies a reconfiguring of the relations between citizenship, state, and territory. At its heart is a fateful conjunction of home, land and security. It rationalizes a series of security measures in the name of a particular conception of home' (Walters, 2004: 241). The individual components of these politics may not be brand new, but the coalition of government and non-government actors, and the combined practices of control and discrimination in a multi-sited and multi-levelled field of action introduce new and unprecedented dynamics into border and citizenship politics.

Similar dynamics emerge in the case of the Australian border control policy, hitherto known for its harsh offshore practices of detention and deportation. It also has an 'onshore' strategy that closely resembles the internalisation of border control in the US and many European countries, insofar as it likewise restricts the social citizenship of non-citizens and undocumented migrants by denying access to work and public services. This ensemble of measures constitutes the 'structurally embedded border' (Weber and Pickering, in this volume) and stands for a new form of border governance that aims at shaping individual decision-making to promote 'voluntary' compliance with migration management goals at both onshore and offshore locations. 'Intent management' technologies and the structurally embedded border correspond to a neoliberal belief in rational choice and 'responsible' citizen and non-citizen subjectivities.

That the above forms of border and citizenship politics are at odds with each other is immediately evident – *domopolitics* counteract *transgressive border politics*. The upsurge in bordering technologies and their contestation leads to a growing differentiation and hierarchisation of migrant statuses: there is no demarcation line between citizen and non-citizen but rather between the numerous migrant categories (see Ataç, in this volume) ranging from the cosmopolitan juridical subject (Sack, in this volume) to the 'impossible subject' (Raissiguier, in this volume). As controversies on internal EU migration or 'poverty migration' demonstrate, stratification and classification – central features of new border and citizenship politics – gather momentum where wealthier member states tend to curtail the mobility of EU citizens from new member states such as Bulgaria or Romania by curbing their access to the benefits of social citizenship.

Research gaps

Our common reflection leads us to the conclusion that the following aspects are worth further investigation:

The 'structurally embedded border' concept: we consider this concept to be a particularly valid instrument to capture the current entanglement of border and citizenship politics and the internalisation of border control. We are well aware that the explicit notion of 'embeddedness' also opens up the research on borders to embrace the question of hegemonic societal ideologies.

'Migration diplomacy': the concept of migration diplomacy is used in different contexts and has yet to be defined precisely. It contains the idea that changing border and asylum policies can be regarded as an indirect form of foreign policy (Thiollet, 2011; İçduygu and Üstübu, in this volume). Some authors interpret legal struggles on migration and border control in the European Union as a constitutive element of a 'European state project' (Buckel, 2013: 14). The management of migration challenges the relationship between governments, forcing them to negotiate. (The perception of) domestic policies of integration can likewise impact on foreign relations (Ruß-Sattar, in this volume). It can be assumed that migration issues will gain even more ground in international relations in the future, calling for a more systematic study of the logics of negotiation. In contrast to this interpretation of the term, *migration diplomacy* can also be understood in the sense that migrants are political actors in international relations. In this context, the discussion on a renewed EU policy towards Mediterranean neighbour states after the so-called Arab Spring is instructive. Up to now, the EU offer of 'mobility partnerships' has been rejected by the Arab states as shifting the burden of border management onto their shoulders. As critics of EU policy point out, the proclaimed priority shift in EU policy on the promotion of development and democracy necessitates a change in its own immigration policy. The argument is as follows:

> The better migrants are integrated in their host society, the more efficient they are in contributing to their home society's development. In the same way, political participation granted to long-term migrants at local level in the host country may well bring 'democratic remittances' to the home country. The EU and its Member States should grant political participation for long-term migrants at the local level.
> (Fargues and Fandrich, 2012: 14)

These snapshots illustrate potential research topics on the different ways in which migration constitutes 'a stake' (see also Squire, 2011) in international relations.

The role of religion and culture in constructing borders and citizen identities: The role of religion and culture in the construction of borders and citizen identities is twofold. In Europe, bordering processes on the inside and outside are accompanied by a culturalist discourse on identity, which identifies Islam as the essential 'other' (İçduygu and Üstübu; Ruß-Sattar, in this volume). In the postcolonial constellation, we see a growing threat of neo-racism based on culturalist rather than biological arguments (Balibar and Wallerstein, 1991). Religion and culture, on the other hand, can intervene differently in the construction of citizenship and fundamentally challenge the Western institution of citizenship based on the secular subject (Mavelli, 2013). As Mikuszies argues in this volume, the Moroccan case demonstrates that the promotion of a specific Moroccan Islamic identity calls for an 'interventionist' and disciplining state. The extent to which the global revival of Islam during the final decades of the twentieth century and the current collapse of states in the Arab world have put a strain on the institution and the idea of the nation-state as the optimal form of existence is a topic for future research.

The role of emigration countries: non-Western conceptions of citizenship and bordering: Much of the scholarship on migration, borders and citizenship is characterised by an epistemological 'Western' standpoint, with an analytical and normative bias towards powerful social interest groups in Western immigration countries and their perspectives. Recent scholarship on the policies of emigration countries (such as on the Philippines, Rodriguez, 2010; on Mexico, Kunz, 2011 and Fitzgerald, 2009) has shown that governments and civil society in these countries are not merely dependent on labour demand and migration control policies at the 'receiving' end, but actively contribute to these policies, both on the inside and the outside. Dünnwald (2013) provides impressive insights into the sensitive issue of the involvement of a country of origin in return policies, an issue of great concern to human rights activists – the emigration policies of countries such as the Philippines and Mexico have largely been analysed. This is not the case, however, for the rest of the world. As Mikuszies argues in her chapter on Morocco's emigration policy, the production of irregular migrants as 'impossible subjects' (Raissiguier, 2010 and in this volume) calls for more detailed empirical research, particularly for the North African region and the post-Arab Spring era. Also worthy of further research are emigration states that have adopted alternative citizenship rhetoric, such as Ecuador with its 'we are all migrants' state philosophy. Here post-colonial scholarship could interact productively with migration and citizenship studies.

We are aware that our volume's contribution to research can only give cursory glimpses of the ongoing dynamics of a political field that is gradually shifting to the very core of politics. Our hope is that it will advance the discussion 'among all those who no longer believe the struggles of migration to be a sideshow of history' (Bojadžijev and Karakayalı, 2010).

References

Abadan-Unat, Nermin (ed.) (1976) *Turkish Workers in Europe 1960–1975*. Leiden: E.J. Brill.
Abadan-Unat, Nermin (2002) *Bitmeyen Göç: Konuk İşçilikten Ulus-Ötesi Yurttaşlığa* [Never Ending Migration: From Guest Workers to Transnational Citizens]. Istanbul: Bilgi Üniversitesi Yayınları.
Adler, Rachel H. (2006) '"But they Claimed to Be Police, Not La Migra": The Interaction of Residency Status, Class and Ethnicity in a (Post-Patriot Act) New Jersey Neighborhood'. *American Behavioral Scientist*, 50, 1, 48–69.
AFSC, American Friends Service Committee (n. d.) 'Our Work'. https://afsc.org/our-work, accessed 7 December 2013.
Agamben, Giorgio (1995) *Homo Sacer: Sovereign Power and Bare Life*. Stanford: Stanford University Press.
Agamben, Giorgio (2005) *State of Exception*. Chicago: University of Chicago Press.
Akgündüz, Ahmet (2008) *Labour Migration from Turkey to Western Europe, 1960–1974: A Multidisciplinary Analysis*. Aldershot: Ashgate Publishing.
Alaya, Ana M. (2006) 'Spanish McDonald's Ad Prompts Talk of a Boycott: Bergen Town's Mayor Calls Billboard "divisive"'. *The Star-Ledger* [NJ], 8 July.
Alioua, Mehdi (2006) 'Silence! People Are Dying on the Southern Borders of Europe'. In: Ursula Biemann (ed.) *The Maghreb Connection: Movements of Life across North Africa*. Barcelona: Actar, 85–105.
Althusser, Louis (1971) 'Ideology and Ideological State Apparatuses'. In: Louis Althusser (ed.) *Lenin and Philosophy and Other Essays*. New York, London: Monthly Review Press, 121–176.
Alvarez, Robert R. (1995) 'The Mexican-US Border: The Making of an Anthropology of Borderlands'. *Annual Review of Anthropology*, 24, 447–470.
Amargi Istanbul (2012) 'Solidarity Party for Migrant Kitchen'. http://amargigroupistanbul.wordpress.com/2012/07/31/solidarity-party-for-migrant-kitchen/, accessed 17 October 2013.
Amnesty International (2009) 'Jailed without Justice: Immigrant Detention in the USA'. http://www.amnestyusa.org/research/reports/usa-jailed-without-justice?page=show, accessed 7 December 2013.
An Architektur (2003) 'Grenzgeografie Sangatte'. *An Architektur*, 03. http://www.anarchitektur.com/aa03_sangatte/aa03_sangatte.pdf, accessed 25 March 2010.
Anderson, Benedict (1991) *Imagined Communities: Reflections on the Origin and Spread of Nationalism*. London and New York: Verso.
Anderson, Bridget, Nandita Sharma and Cynthia Wright (2012) 'We Are All Foreigners: No Borders as a Practical Political Project'. In: Peter Nyers and Kim Rygiel (eds.) *Citizenship, Migrant Activism and the Politics of Movement*. London: Routledge, 73–91.
Anderson, James and Liam O'Dowd (1999) 'Borders, Border Regions and Territoriality: Contradictory Meanings, Changing Significance'. *Regional Studies*, 33, 7, 593–604.
Andreas, Peter (2009) *Border Games: Policing the U.S.–Mexico Divide*. Ithaca: Cornell University Press.
Andrijasevic, Rutvica (2010) *Migration, Agency and Citizenship in Sex Trafficking*. Houndmills, Basingstoke: Palgrave.

Arendt, Hannah (1968) 'The Decline of the Nation-State and the End of the Rights of Men'. In: *The Origins of Totalitarianism*. San Diego, New York and London: Harcourt, 266–302.

Arendt, Hannah (2011 [1951]) *Elemente und Ursprünge totaler Herrschaft. Antisemitismus, Imperialismus, totale Herrschaft*. 14th ed. München: Piper.

Argun, Betigül Ercan (2003) *Turkey in Germany. The Transnational Sphere of Deutschkei*. New York, London: Routledge.

Armour, Stephanie (2009) 'More Families Move in Together during Housing Crisis'. *USA Today*, 3 February.

Arslan, Emre (2009) *Der Mythos der Nation im transnationalen Raum. Türkische Graue Wölfe in Deutschland*. Wiesbaden: VS Verlag für Sozialwissenschaften.

Arvanitopolous, Constantine (2009) *Turkey's Accession to the European Union: An Unusual Candidacy*. Berlin, Heidelberg: Springer Verlag.

Aslan, Fikret and Kemal Bozay (2000) *Graue Wölfe heulen wieder. Türkische Faschisten und ihre Vernetzung in der BRD*. 2nd ed. Münster: Unrast Verlag.

Ataç, Ilker and Sieglinde Rosenberger (2013) 'Inklusion/Exklusion als relationales Konzept der Migrationsforschung'. In: Ilker Ataç and Sieglinde Rosenberger (eds.) *Politik der Inklusion und Exklusion*. Göttingen: Vienna University Press V&R unipress, 35–52.

Avci, Gamze and Kemal Kirisşci (2006) 'Turkey's Immigration and Emigration Dilemmas at the Gate of the EU'. *Migración y Desarrollo*, 2, 123–173.

Badie, Bertrand (1987) ' "État" et "Légitimité" en Monde Musulman: Crise de l'Universalité et Crise des Concepts'. *Annuaire de l'Afrique du Nord*, 26, 19–30.

Bağış, Egemen (2012) 'Visa Restrictions are Shutting Turkey out of the EU'. *The Guardian*, 14 July. http://www.theguardian.com/commentisfree/2012/jul/14/visa-restrictions-turkey-eu, accessed 23 September 2013.

Baldwin, Peter (1997) 'State and Citizenship in the Age of the Globalization'. In: Peter Koslowski and Andreas Follesdal (eds.) *Restructuring the Welfare State*. Berlin: Springer, 95–118.

Balibar, Étienne (2002) *Politics and the Other Scene*. New York: Verso.

Balibar, Étienne (2004) *We, the People of Europe? Reflections on Transnational Citizenship*. Princeton and Oxford: Princeton University Press.

Balibar, Etienne and Immanuel Wallerstein (1991) *Race, Nation, Class: Ambiguous Identities*. London: Verso.

Barlow, Andrew L. (2003) *Between Fear and Hope: Globalization and Race in the United States*. Lanham, MD: Rowman & Littlefield.

Barry, Kim (2006) 'Home and Away: The Construction of Citizenship in an Emigration Context'. *New York University Law Review*, 81, 11, 11–59.

Basch, Linda, Nina Glick Schiller and Cristina Szanton Blanc (1994) *Nations Unbound: Transnational Projects, Postcolonial Predicaments, and Deterritorialized Nation-States*. Langhorne, PA: Gordon and Breach.

Bauböck, Rainer (1996) 'Nach Rasse und Sprache verschieden. Migrationspolitik in Österreich von der Monarchie bis heute'. *Political Science Series No. 31*. http://www.ihs.ac.at/publications/pol/pw_31.pdf, accessed 7 December 2013.

Bauböck, Rainer and Bernhard Perchinig (2006) 'Migrations- und Integrationspolitik'. In: Herbert Dachs, Peter Gerlich, Herbert Gottweis, Helmut Kramer, Volkmar Lauber, Wolfgang C. Müller and Emmerich Tálos (eds.) *Politik in Österreich: Das Handbuch*. Vienna: Manz, 726–742.

Bauman, Zygmunt (2002) *Society under Siege*. Cambridge: Polity Press.

Becker, Hildegard (2006) 'Der organisierte Islam in Deutschland und einige ideologische Hintergründe'. In: Bundesamt für Migration und Flüchtlinge (ed.) *Integration und Islam*. Nürnberg: German Federal Department of Migration and Refugees (Bundesministerium für Migration und Flüchtlinge, BAMF), 62–85.

Behar, Cem (2006) 'Demographic Developments and "Complementarities": Ageing, Labor and Migration'. *Turkish Studies*, 7, 1, 17–31.

Belguendouz, Abdelkrim (2004) *'M.R.E.' Quelle marocanite?* Salé: Imprimerie Beni Snassen.

Belguendouz, Abdelkrim (2006) 'Le traitement institutionnel de la relation entre les Marocains résidant à l'étranger et le Maroc'. http://cadmus.eui.eu/handle/1814/6265, accessed 31 January 2012.

Benda-Beckmann, Franz von and Keebet von Benda-Beckmann (2007) 'Transnationalisation of Law, Globalisation and Legal Pluralism: A Legal Anthropological Perspective'. In: Christoph Antons and Volkmar Gessner (eds.) *Globalisation and Resistance: Law Reform in Asia since the Crisis*. Oxford and Portland: Hart Publishing, 53–80.

Benda-Beckmann, Franz von, Keebet von Benda-Beckmann and Anne Griffiths (2005) 'Mobile People, Mobile Law: An Introduction'. In: Franz von Benda-Beckmann, Keebet von Benda-Beckmann and Anne Griffiths (eds.) *Mobile People, Mobile Law: Expanding Legal Relations in a Contracting World*. Aldershot and Burlington: Aldershot, 1–25.

Benford, Robert D. and David A. Snow (2000) 'Framing Processes and Social Movements: An Overview and Assessment'. *Annual Review of Sociology*, 26, 611–639.

Bensadoun, Mickael (2007) 'The (Re)fashioning of Moroccan National Identity'. In: Bruce Maddy-Weitzman and Daniel Zisenwine (eds.) *The Maghreb in the New Century: Identity, Religion, and Politics*. Gainesville: University Press of Florida, 13–35.

Benslama, Fethi (2011) *Soudain la révolution! De la Tunisie au monde arabe: la signification d'un soulèvement*. Paris: Denoël.

Benz, Martina and Helen Schwenken (2005) 'Jenseits von Autonomie und Kontrolle: Migration als eigensinnige Praxis'. *PROKLA. Zeitschrift für kritische Sozialwissenschaft*, 35, 3, 363–377.

Berger, Joseph (2008) 'A Place Where Indians, Now New Jerseyans, Thrive'. *The New York Times*, 27 April. www.nytimes.com/2008/04/27/nyregion/nyregionspecial2/27indianj.html?pagewanted=all, accessed 14 May 2013.

Bernard, Philippe (1998) *L'Immigration: Les Enjeux de l'Intégration*. Paris: Editions Le Monde.

Bernstein, Nina (2006) '9/11 Detainees in New Jersey Say They Were Abused with Dogs'. *The New York Times*, 3 April.

Bernstein, Nina (2007) 'In a New Jersey Town, an Immigration Fight Pits Brother against Brother'. *The New York Times*, 4 September. http://www.nytimes.com/2007/09/04/nyregion/04brothers.html?pagewanted=all, accessed 14 May 2013.

Bernstein, Nina (2009) 'Immigrant Detainee Dies, and a Life Is Buried, Too'. *The New York Times*, p. 2. Apr.www.nytimes.com/2009/04/03/nyregion/03detain.html?pagewanted=all&_r=0, accessed 15 May 2013.

Betriebszelle Ford der Gruppe Arbeiterkampf (eds.) (1973) *Streik bei Ford Köln*. Köln: Rosa-Luxemburg Verlag.

Biemann, Ursula (1999) *Performing the Border*. Film: Switzerland, Mexico, 42 minutes.

Birke, Peter (2007) *Wilde Streiks im Wirtschaftswunder. Arbeitskämpfe, Gewerkschaften und soziale Bewegungen in der Bundesrepublik und Dänemark*. Frankfurt/Main: Campus.

Bloemraad, Irene (2006) *Becoming a Citizen: Incorporating Immigrants and Refugees in the United States and Canada*. Berkeley: University of California Press.

Bloemraad, Irene and Els de Graauw (2011) *Immigrant Integration and Policy in the United States: A Loosely Stitched Patchwork*. Institute for Research on Labor and Employment, UC Berkeley, Working Paper Series.

Böcker, Anita G.M. (1995) 'Migration Networks: Turkish Migration to Western Europe'. In: Rob van der Erf and Liesbeth Heering (eds.) *Causes of International Migration*. Luxembourg: European Communities, 151–171.

Bojadzijev, Manuela (2008) *Die windige Internationale. Rassismus und Kämpfe der Migration*. Münster: Westfälisches Dampfboot.

Bojadzijev, Manuela (2011) 'Das "Spiel" der Autonomie der Migration'. *Zeitschrift für Kulturwissenschaften*, 6, 1, 139–145.

Bojadžijev, Manuela and Serhat Karakayalı (2010) 'Recuperating the Sideshows of Capitalism: The Autonomy of Migration Today'. In e-flux link: http://www.e-flux.com/journal/recuperating-the-sideshows-of-capitalism-the-autonomy-of-migration-today/, accessed 9 February 2014.

Bora, Tanıl (2001) 'Der nationale Reflex: Die fundamentalistische Disposition des Nationalen in der Türkei und der proto-faschistische Nationalismus der MHP'. *Sociologus*, 51, 1/2, 123–139.

Bora, Tanıl and Kemal Can (2004) *Devlet ve Kuzgun. 1990'lardan 2000'lere MHP*, İstanbul: İletişim.

Bosniak, Linda (2006) *The Citizen and the Alien: Dilemmas of Contemporary Membership*. Princeton and Oxford: Princeton University Press.

Boswell, Christina (2003) 'The "External Dimension" of EU Immigration and Asylum Policies'. *International Affairs*, 79, 3, 619–638.

Boswell, Christina and Andrew Geddes (2011) *Migration and Mobility in the European Union*. Basingstoke: Palgrave Macmillan.

Bouamama, Saïd (2000) *J'y Suis, j'y Vote! La Lutte pour les Droits Politiques aux Résidents Étrangers*. Paris: Éditions L'Esprit frappeur.

Bouasria, Abdelilah (2012) 'The Second Coming of Morocco's "Commander of the Faithful". Mohammed VI and Morocco's Religious Policy'. In: Bruce Maddy-Weitzman and Daniel Zisenwine (eds.) *Contemporary Morocco: State, Politics and Society under Mohammmed VI*. London and New York. Routledge, 37–56.

Boukhars, Anouar (2011) *Politics in Morocco: Executive Monarchy and Enlightened Authoritarianism*. London: Routledge.

Bozay, Kemal (2005) *'Ich bin stolz, Türke zu sein!' Ethnisierung gesellschaftlicher Konflikte im Zeichen der Globalisierung*. Schwalbach/Ts.: Wochenschau Verlag.

Brand, Laurie A. (2006) *Citizens Abroad. Emigration and the State in the Middle East and North Africa*. Cambridge: Cambridge University Press.

Brewer, Kelly and Deniz Yükseker (2006) A Survey on African Migrants and Asylum Seekers in Istanbul. Istanbul: Mirekoç.

Brubaker, Roger (1992) *Citizenship and Nationhood in France and Germany*. Cambridge, MA: Harvard University Press.

Brunstein, Joshua (2008) 'Immigration Stirs Up Bound Brook, Again'. *The New York Times*, 8 August. http://www.nytimes.com/2008/08/10/nyregion/nyregionspecial2/10boundnj.html, accessed 14 May 2013.

Bruter, Michael (2005) *Citizens of Europe? The Emergence of a Mass European Identity*. New York: Palgrave.

Buckel, Sonja (2013) *'Welcome to Europe'. Die Grenzen des europäischen Migrationsrechts. Juridische Auseinandersetzungen um das 'Staatsprojekt Europa'*. Bielefeld: Transcript.

Bulmer, Simon J. and Claudio M. Radaelli (2004) *The Europeanization of National Policy*. Queens' Papers on Europeanization, 1/2004. Queens University Belfast.

Bundesamt für Migration und Flüchtlinge (2012) *Das Bundesamt in Zahlen 2011.* Nürnberg: German Federal Department of Migration and Refugees (Bundesministerium für Migration und Flüchtlinge, BAMF).
Bundesverfassungsgericht [German Constitutional Court] (1996) *2 BvR 1516/93*, 14 May, Karlsruhe.
Bundesverfassungsgericht [German Constitutional Court] (2011) *1 BvR 699/06*, 22 February, Karlsruhe.
Buzan, Barry, Ole Waever and Jaap de Wilde (1998) *Security – a New Framework for Analysis.* Boulder: Rienner.
Calais Migrant Solidarity (2009) 'Come to Calais to Protest against the Destruction of Camps and Squats of Migrants! International Solidarity Actions in Front of all French Embassies in Europe!'. http://www.statewatch.org/news/2009/sep/france-calais-migrants.pdf, accessed 10 November 2013.
Calais Migrant Solidarity (2010) 'Latest Information from Activists and Migrants on the Ground in Calais'. http://calaismigrantsolidarity.wordpress.com/, accessed 25 March 2010.
Calais Migrant Solidarity (2013) 'Fight for Basic Rights. Don't Let Them Take Away Our Shelter'. 8 November. http://calaismigrantsolidarity.wordpress.com/, accessed 10 November 2013.
Cardwell, Paul James (2009) *EU External Relations and Systems of Governance.* London and New York: Routledge.
Carling, Jørgen and María Hernández-Carretero (2011) 'Protecting Europe and Protecting Migrants? Strategies for Managing Unauthorised Migration from Africa'. *The British Journal of Politics and International Relations*, 13, 42–58.
Carmody, Rebecca (2000) 'Sharks, Crocodiles and Snakes to Scare off Illegal Immigrants'. *The ABC World Today Archive*, 15 June. http://www.abc.net.au/worldtoday/stories/s140600.htm, accessed 6 November 2013.
Carnevale, Roberta, Stefan Ihrig and Christian Weiss (2005) *Europa am Bosporus erfinden? Die Diskussion um den Beitritt der Türkei zur Europäischen Union in den britischen, deutschen, französischen und italienischen Zeitungen. Eine Presseanalyse.* Frankfurt/Main: Peter Lang.
Cassarino, Jean-Pierre (2010) 'Readmission Policy in the European Union'. *Report for European Parliament.* http://www.europarl.europa.eu/committees/en/libe/studies download.html?languageDocument=EN&file=35488, accessed 9 February 2014.
Castles, Stephen (2004) 'Why Migration Policies Fail'. *Ethnic and Racial Studies*, 27, 2, 205–227.
Castles, Stephen and Alastair Davidson (2000) *Citizenship and Migration: Globalization and the Politics of Belonging.* London and New York: Routledge.
Castles, Stephen, Heather Booth and Tina Wallace (1984) *Here for Good, Western Europe's New Ethnic Minorities.* London: Pluto Press.
CCME (Conseil de la Communauté Marocaine à l'Étranger) and BVA (2009) 'Enquête auprès de la population marocaine résidant en Europ'. *Rabat.* http://www.ccme.org.ma/images/activites/fr/2009/07/CCME-BVA-Etude_Marocains_dEurope.pdf, accessed 30 May 2010.
CFCU, Central Finance and Contracts Unit, Prime Minister, Republic of Turkey (2012) *Technical Assistance for Impact Assessment Study of a Possible TR/EU Re-admission Agreement in Turkey.* Impact Assessment Report. B&S Europe and Ministry of Interior of the Turkish Republic: Ankara.
Cherti, Myriam, Brhmie Balaram and Miklos Szilard (2013) *Retour des Migrants Irréguliers au Maroc. Quelle Politique de Réintégration?* London: Public Policy Research Institute.

Cholewinski, Ryszard (2004) *The Legal Status of Migrants Admitted for Employment – A Comparative Study of Law and Practice in Selected European States*. Strasbourg: Council of Europe.

Çinar, Dilek, Christoph Hofingerand and Harald Waldrauch (1995) *Integrationsindex Zur rechtlichen Integration von AusländerInnen in ausgewählten europäischen Ländern*. Vienna: Institut für Höhere Studien. http://aei.pitt.edu/32445/1/1264672251_pw_25.pdf, accessed 7 December 2013.

Collyer, Michael (2013, ed.) *Emigration Nations. Policies and Ideologies of Emigrant Engagement*. New York: Palgrave Macmillan.

Comando Generale del Corpo delle Capitanerie di Porto (2007) *Relazione Attività Antimmigrazione Anno 2006*. Internal Paper of Guardia Costiera [given to the author].

Cooper, Frederick (1997) 'The Dialectics of Decolonization. Nationalism and Labor Movements in Postwar French Africa'. In: Frederick Cooper and Ann Laura Stoler (eds.) *Tensions of Empire. Colonial Cultures in a Bourgeois World*. Berkeley, Los Angeles and London: University of California Press, 406–434.

Cooper, Michael (2012) 'Census Officials, Citing Increasing Diversity, Say U.S. Will Be a "Plurality Nation"'. *The New York Times*, 12 December, p. A20.

Cornelius, Wayne A. and Marc R. Rosenblum (2005) 'Immigration and Politics'. *Annual Review of Political Science*, 8, 99–119.

Corzine, Jon S. and Anne Milgram (2007) 'Attorney General Law Enforcement Directive 2007–2003'. http://www.nj.gov/oag/newsreleases07/ag-le-directive-2007-3.pdf, accessed 17 October 2013.

Council of Europe (1991) 'Recommendation 1163 on the Arrival of Asylum-Seekers at European Airports'. http://assembly.coe.int/Main.asp?link=/Documents/AdoptedText/ta91/EREC1163.htm, accessed 9 February 2014.

Council of the European Union (2003) *Regulation 343/2003. Establishing the Criteria and Mechanisms for Determining the Member State Responsible for Examining an Asylum Application Lodged in One of the Member States by a Third-country National*. Brussels, 18 February.

Council of the European Union (2005) *Council Directive 2005/85/EC on Minimum Standards on Procedures in Member States for Granting and Withdrawing Refugee Status*. Brussels, 1 December.

Council of the European Union (2008) *2008/157/EC: Council Decision of 18 February 2008 on the Principles, Priorities and Conditions Contained in the Accession Partnership with the Republic of Turkey and Repealing Decision 2006/35/EC*, Brussels. http://eur-lex.europa.eu/legal-content/EN/ALL/?uri=CELEX:32008D0157, accessed 9 February 2014.

Council of the European Union (2009) *Note from: The Cyprus, Greek, Italian and Maltese Delegations to: Delegations, Subject: Combating Illegal Immigration in the Mediterranean (5689/09)*. Brussels, 23 January.

Coutin, Susan Bibler (2007) *Nations of Emigrants: Shifting Boundaries of Citizenship in El Salvador and the United States*. Ithaka: Cornell University Press.

Coyne, Kevin (2008) 'Turbans Make Targets, Some Sikhs Find'. *The New York Times*, 15 June. http://www.nytimes.com/2008/06/15/nyregion/nyregionspecial2/15colnj.html, accessed 14 May 2013.

Cuperus, René (2005) 'Not the Copenhagen Criteria, but the Berlin-Kreuzberg Criteria'. *Speech in Brussels*, 5 October. http://www.esiweb.org/pdf/turkeynetherlands/Cuperus%20Speech%20in%20Brussels%202005.pdf, accessed 10 December 2013.

Curr, Pamela (2012) 'A Warehouse for Human Beings'. *New Matilda*. http://newmatilda.com/2012/11/05/warehouse-human-beings, accessed 6 November 2013.

Cuttitta, Paolo (2008) 'The Case of the Italian Southern Sea Borders: Cooperation across the Mediterranean?' *Documentos CIDOB Migraciones*, 17, 46.
Das Gupta, Monisha (2006) *Unruly Immigrants: Rights, Activism, and Transnational South Asian Politics in the United States*. Durham, NC and London: Duke University Press.
Davy, Ulrike and August Gächter (1993) 'Zuwanderungsrecht und Zuwanderungspolitik in Österreich'. *Journal für Rechtspolitik*, 1, 2, 155–174 and 1, 3, 257–281.
De Genova, Nicholas P. (2002) 'Migrant "Illegality" and Deportability in Everyday Life'. *Annual Review of Anthropology*, 31, 419–447.
De Genova, Nicholas P. (2007) 'The Production of Culprits: From Deportability to Detainability in the Aftermath of "Homeland Security"'. *Citizenship Studies*, 11, 5, 421–448.
De Genova, Nicholas and Nathalie Peutz (eds.) (2010) *The Deportation Regime. Sovereignty, Space, and the Freedom of Movement*. Durham, NC and London: Duke University Press.
de Graauw, Els (2008) 'Nonprofit Organizations: Agents of Immigrant Political Incorporation in Urban America'. In: S. Karthick Ramakrishnan and Irene Bloemraad (eds.) *Civic Hopes and Political Realities: Immigrants, Community Organizations, and Political Engagement*. New York: Russell Sage Foundation Press, 323–350.
de Haas, Hein (2007) *Between Courting and Controlling: The Moroccan State and 'its' Emigrants*. Working Paper 54. Oxford: Centre on Migration, Policy and Society. http://www.imi.ox.ac.uk/about-us/pdfs/between-courting-and-controlling-the-moroccan-state-and-its-emigrants, accessed 31 January 2012.
de Haas, Hein (2011) 'Mediterranean Migration Futures: Patterns, Drivers and Scenarios'. *Global Environmental Change*, 21, 59–69.
Department of Homeland Security (2006) 'Treatment of Immigration Detainees Housed at Immigration and Customs Enforcement Facilities'. http://www.oig.dhs.gov/assets/Mgmt/OIG_07-01_Dec06.pdf, accessed 2 December 2013.
Department of Information of Malta (2010) 'Another Amnesty International Report Riddled with Inaccuracies, Misinformation and Glaring Omissions'. *Press Release No. 0985 (2010)*. http://www.doi.gov.mt/en/press_releases/2010/05/pr0985.asp, accessed 19 July 2010.
Deportation Class (2002) 'Archive of Press Releases'. http://www.noborder.org/archive/www.deportation-class.com/lh/index.html, accessed 4 January 2013.
Deutscher Bundestag (2000) *Antwort der Bundesregierung auf die Kleine Anfrage der Abgeordneten Ulla Jelpke, Rosel Neuhäuser und der Fraktion der PDS zum Flughafenverfahren und §18a Asylverfahrensgesetz*, Drucksache 14/2898, 14 March.
Deutscher Bundestag (2001) 'Antwort der Bundesregierung auf die Kleine Anfrage der Abgeordneten Ulla Jelpke und der Fraktion der PDS. Abschiebungen auf dem Luftweg im Jahr 2000'. Drucksache 14/5734, 30 March.
Deutscher Bundestag (2011) 'Antwort der Bundesregierung auf die kleine Anfrage der Abgeordnete Ulla Jelpke, Jens Petermann, Frank Tempel und der Fraktion DIE LINKE'. Drucksache 17/7624, 8 November. http://dip21.bundestag.de/dip21/btd/17/076/1707624.pdf, accessed 10 May 2013.
Deutscher Bundestag (2012) 'Antwort der Bundesregierung auf die Kleine Anfrage der Abgeordneten Ulla Jelpke, Jan Korte, Sevim Dagdelen, weiterer Abgeordneter und der Fraktion DIE LINKE'. Drucksache 17/8834, 2 March.
DIAC, Department of Immigration and Citizenship Australia (2012) 'Department of Immigration and Citizenship Annual Report 2011–12'. http://www.immi.gov.au/about/reports/annual/2011-12/pdf/, accessed 7 November 2013.

Diehl, Claudia (2002) *Die Partizipation von Migranten in Deutschland. Rückzug oder Mobilisierung?* Opladen: Leske und Budrich.

Donohue, Brian (2007) 'Raids Nab Twice as Many Illegal Immigrants'. *The Star-Ledger* [NJ], 5 December.

Donzelli, Stefanie (2013) *Border Studies, Theoretical Approaches, Themes of Inquiry, and Suggestions for Future Research*. Working Paper No. 571, The Hague: International Institute for Social Studies.

Duffy, Jamie (2009) 'New Jersey Pro-immigration Leaders Call for a Halt to 287(g) on the Steps of Town Hall'. *NJ.com*, 8 October.

Dünnwald, Stephan (2013) 'Voluntary Return: The Practical Failure of a Benevolent Concept'. In: Martin Geiger and Antoine Pécoud (eds.) *Disciplining the Transnational Mobility of People*. Basingstoke: Palgrave Macmillan, 228–250.

Eaton, Susan (2012) 'The Other Side of Immigration: Humane, Sensible, and Replicable Responses in a Changing Nation'. *Poverty and Race Research Action Council News*, 21, 2, 1–5.

Education Week (2008) 'ACLU Faults New Jersey Districts for Asking Immigration Status'. *Education Week*, 28, 3, 4.

El Ayadi, Mohammed, Hassan Rachik and Mohamed Tozy (2006) *L'islam au quotidien. Enquête sur les valeurs et les pratiques religieuses au Maroc*. Casablanca: Prologues.

Erzan, Refik and Kemal Kırışci (2006) 'Conclusion'. *Turkish Studies*, 7, 1, 1–11.

Erzan, Refik, Umut Kuzubaş and Nilüfer Yıldız (2006) 'Growth and Immigration Scenarios: Turkey-EU'. *Turkish Studies*, 7, 1, 33–44.

Esbenshade, Jill and Barbara Obzurt (2007–2008) 'Local Immigration Regulation: A Problematic Trend in Public Policy'. *Harvard Journal of Hispanic Policy*, 20, 33–47.

Esser, Hartmut (1996) 'Ethnische Kolonien: "Binnenintegration" oder gesellschaftliche Isolation?' In: J.H.P. Hoffmeyer-Zlotnik (ed.) *Segregation oder Integration: Die Situation der Arbeitsmigranten im Aufnahmeland*. Mannheim: Verlag Forschung, Raum und Gesellschaft, 106–117.

Esser, Josef, Wolfgang Fach and Georg Simonis (1980) 'Grenzprobleme des "Modells Deutschland"'. *Prokla*, 10, 3, 40–63.

Europa (2005) 'Readmissions Agreements. MEMO/05/351'. http://europa.eu/rapid/press-release_MEMO-05-351_en.doc, accessed 18 October 2013.

Europarlamento 24 (2013) 'Malmström: Eurosur will Help Better Manage Migrants Flow'. 4 October. http://www.europarlamento24.eu/malmstro-m-eurosur-will-help-better-manage-migrants-flow/0,1254,107_ART_4080,00.html, accessed 10 December 2013.

European Council (2003) 'Council Regulation (EC) No 343/2003 of 18 February 2003 Establishing the Criteria and Mechanisms for Determining the Member State Responsible for Examining an Asylum Application Lodged in One of the Member States by a Third-country National'. *Official Journal L 050, 25/02/2003*, 0001–0010. http://eur-lex.europa.eu/LexUriServ/LexUriServ.do?uri=CELEX:32003R0343:EN:HTML, accessed 18 October 2013.

European Commission (2004) 'Communication from the Commission to the Council and the European Parliament – Recommendation of the European Commission on Turkey's Progress Towards Accession'. http://eur-lex.europa.eu/smartapi/cgi/sga_doc?smartapi!celexplus!prod!CELEXnumdoc&lg=en&numdoc=504DC0656, accessed 31 July 2013.

European Commission (2007) *Report from the Commission to the European Parliament and the Council on the Evaluation of the Dublin System*. Brussels.

European Commission (2013) 'Specific Tools. Home Affairs'. http://ec.europa.eu/dgs/home-affairs/what-we-do/policies/international-affairs/global-approach-to-migration/specific-tools/index_en.htm, accessed 18 October 2013.

European Court of Justice (2011) '*C-411/10; C-493/10*'. Press Release 140/11, Luxembourg, 21 December. http://curia.europa.eu/jcms/upload/docs/application/pdf/2011-12/cp110140en.pdf, accessed 10 February 2014.

European Parliament (2006) 'European Parliament Resolution on the Situation with Refugee Camps in Malta'. Doc. No. P6_TA (2006) 0136.

European Parliament and the Council of the European Union (2008) 'Directive 2008/115/EC on Common Standards and Procedures in Member States for Returning Illegally Staying Third-country Nationals'. Brussels, 16 December 2008.

European Stability Institute (2006) *The German Turkey Debate under the Grand Coalition*. Berlin, Brussels, Istanbul.

European Union (2009) *Lisbon Treaty: Treaty on the Functioning of the European Union*. Brussels.

Europol (2009) 'Facilitated Illegal Immigration into the European Union'. http://meilleurdesmondes.be/blog/wp-content/uploads/2011/06/Europol-Illegal_Immigration_Fact_Sheet_20091.pdf, accessed 4 August 2013.

Eurostat (2013) 'Passenger Volume at European Airports'. http://epp.eurostat.ec.europa.eu/statistics_explained/index.php?title=File:Thousand_passengers_handled_in_top_airports_monthly_data_2011_and_2012s1.png&filetimestamp=20121018073816, accessed 4 January 2013.

Evans, Peter B., Dietrich Rueschemeyer and Theda Skocpol (1985) 'On the Road Toward a More Adequate Understanding of the State'. In: Peter B. Evans, Dietrich Rueschemeyer and Theda Skocpol (eds.) *Bringing the State Back In*. Cambridge: Cambridge University Press, 347–366.

FAFF – Forum Abschiebungsbeobachtung am Flughafen Frankfurt/Main (2009) *Jahresbericht 2008–2009*. Frankfurt/Main.

FAFF – Forum Abschiebungsbeobachtung am Flughafen Frankfurt/Main (2010) *Jahresbericht 2009–2010*. Frankfurt/Main.

Fahim, Kareem (2007a) 'Housing Crackdown Hits Indian Immigrants'. *The New York Times*, 6 August. http://www.nytimes.com/2007/08/06/nyregion/06crowd.html?pagewanted=all&_r=0, accessed 14 May 2013.

Fahim, Kareem (2007b) 'Should Immigration Be a Police Issue?'. *The New York Times*, 29 April.

Fahim, Kareen (2008) 'Immigration Referrals by Police Draw Scrutiny'. *The New York Times*, 23 March.

Faist, Thomas (2000) 'Grenzen überschreiten. Das Konzept Transstaatliche Räume und seine Anwendungen'. In T. Faist (ed.) *Transstaatliche Räume: Politik, Wirtschaft und Kultur in und zwischen Deutschland und der Türkei*. Bielefeld: Transcript, 9–56.

Fargues, Philippe and Christine Fandrich (2012) *Migration after the Arab Spring*. MPC Research Paper 2012/09, Robert-Schuman Center for Advanced Studies Florence. http://www.migrationpolicycentre.eu/docs/MPC%202012%20EN%2009.pdf, accessed 3 December 2013.

Favell, Adrian (2001) *Philosophies of Integration: Immigration and the Idea of Citizenship in France and Britain*. New York: Palgrave.

Fischer, Frank and John Forester (1993) *The Argumentative Turn in Policy Analysis and Planning*. Raleigh, NC: Duke University Press.

Fisher, William (2007) *Audit Finds Multiple Abuses in Immigration Jails*. New York: Inter Press Service News Agency.

Fitzgerald, David (2009) *A Nation of Emigrants: How Mexico Manages Its Migration*. Berkeley, Los Angeles: University of California Press.

Flughafen-Sozialdienst (1998) *Dokumentation. Evangelischer Regionalverband Frankfurt am Main*. Frankfurt/Main: Caritas-Verband Frankfurt e.V.

Fortress Europe (2013) 'I numeri del Canale di Sicilia anno per anno'. http://fortresseurope.blogspot.com/2006/01/i-numeri-del-canale-di-sicilia-anno.html, accessed 13 January 2013.

Fotakis, Constantinos (2004) 'EU Population Ageing: Challenge and Policy Responses in Turkish Family, Health and Planning Foundation, Population Challenges, International Migration, and Reproductive Health'. In: *Turkey and the European Union: Issues and Policy Implications*. Istanbul: TAP Publication, 203–217.

Foucault, Michel (1978) *The History of Sexuality. Volume 1: An Introduction*. London: Allen Lane.

Foucault, Michel (1980) *Power/Knowledge: Selected Interviews and Other Writings 1972–1977*. New York: Pantheon Books.

Foucault, Michel (1994) 'The Subject and Power'. In: Paul Rabinow and Nikolas Rose (eds.) *The Essential Foucault: Selections from Essential Works of Foucault 1954–1984*. New York and London: The New Press, 126–145.

Fourquet, Jérôme and Bénédicte Simon (2008) *L'adhésion à l'entreée de la Turquie dans l'Union Européenne*. Paris: IFOP.

France Terre d'Asile, British Refugee Council, European Council on Refugees and Exiles and Forum Réfugiés (2009) 'Calais is the Symptom of a Flawed European Asylum System'. Paris, 21 September.

Franz, Erhard (1994) *Population Policy in Turkey*. Hamburg: Deutsches Orient-Institut.

Frégosi, Franck and Malika Zeghal (2005) 'Religion et politique au Maghreb: les exemples tunisien et marocain'. http://www.ifri.org/files/PP_11_kmf_fregosi_zeghal.pdf, accessed 31 January 2012.

Frontex (2007) *Frontex General Report 2007*. Warsaw: Frontex.

Frontex (2008) *Frontex General Report 2008*. Warsaw: Frontex.

Frontex (2009) *Frontex General Report 2009*. Warsaw: Frontex.

Frontex (2010) *Beyond the Frontiers. Frontex: The First Five Years*. Warsaw: Frontex

Frontex (2011) *Frontex Annual Risk Analysis*. Warsaw: European Agency for the Management of Operational Cooperation at the External Borders of the Member States of the European Union. http://www.frontex.europa.eu/news/annual-risk-analysis-2011-uGgHEQ, accessed 18 October 2013.

Frontex (2013) *To the Rescue . . . .* http://frontex.europa.eu/feature-stories/to-the-rescue-ILWGXf, accessed 10 December 2013.

Fuller, Graham E. (2008) *The New Turkish Republic. Turkey as a Pivotal State in the Muslim World*. Washington, DC: United States Institute of Peace.

Gächter, August (2000) 'Austria: Protecting Indigenous Workers from Immigrants'. In: Rinus Penninx and Judith Roosblad (eds.) *Trade Unions, Immigration, and Immigrants in Europe, 1960–1993. A Comparative Study of the Attitudes and Actions of Trade Unions in Seven West European Countries*. New York, Oxford: Berghahn Books, 65–89.

Ganser, Daniele (2005) *NATO's Secret Armies: Operation Gladio and Terrorism in Western Europe: An Approach to NATO's Secret Stay-Behind Armies*. London: Cass.

Garland, David (1997) '"Governmentality" and the Problem of Crime: Foucault, Criminology, Sociology'. *Theoretical Criminology*, 1, 173–214.

Gaspard, Françoise, Claude Servan-Schreiber and Anne Le Gall (1992) *Au Pouvoir les Citoyennes: Liberté, Égalité, Parité*. Paris: Éditions du Seuil.

Geiger, Martin and Antoine Pécoud (eds.) (2010) *The Politics of International Migration Management*. Houndsmills, Basingstoke: Palgrave.
Geiger, Martin and Antoine Pécoud (eds.) (2012) *The New Politics of International Mobility. Migration Management and Its Discontents*. Special issue 'IMIS-Beiträge', 40. Osnabrück: IMIS.
Geiger, Martin and Antoine Pécoud (eds.) (2013) *Disciplining the Transnational Mobility of People*. Basingstoke: Palgrave Macmillan.
Giannakopolous, Angelos and Konstadinos Maras (eds.) (2005) *Die Türkei-Debatte in Europa. Ein Vergleich*. Wiesbaden: VS Verlag.
Gilbert, Liette (2009) 'Immigration as Local Politics: Re-Bordering Immigration and Multiculturalism through Deterrence and Incapacitation'. *International Journal of Urban and Regional Research*, 33, 1, 26–42.
Gitmez, Ali S. (1983) *Yurtdışına İşçi Göçü ve Geri Dönüşler* [Labour Migration to Abroad and Returns]. Istanbul: Alan Yayıncılık.
Glazer, Andrew (2004) 'Housing-code Raids Scaring Immigrants: Crackdown on N.J. Apartments'. *The Chicago Tribune*, 1 February. http://articles.chicagotribune.com/2004-02-01/business/0402010470_1_illegal-apartments-inspectors-attic, accessed 14 May 2013.
Goldring, Luin, Carolina Berinstein and Judith K. Bernard (2009) 'Institutionalizing Precarious Migratory Status in Canada'. *Citizenship Studies*, 13, 3, 239–265.
Gopinah, Gayatri (2005) *Impossible Desires: Queer Diasporas and South Asian Public Cultures*. Durham, NC and London: Duke University Press.
Government of Australia (2012) 'Australia by boat – no advantage!' Video. http://www.youtube.com/watch?v=5Kt-PEuDnfw (last accessed 24 February 2013).
Gramsci, Antonio (2011 [1929–1935]) *Prison Notebooks*. New York: Columbia University Press.
Grech, Herman and Kurt Sansone (2009) 'Shrinking Malta's Search and Rescue Area is "not an option". Italy Applying Pressure Directly and Indirectly'. *Times of Malta*, 26 April.
Griffin, Laura (2011) 'When Borders Fail: "Illegal", Invisible Labour Migration and Basotho Domestic Workers in South Africa'. In: Elspeth Guild and Sandra Mantu (eds.) *Constructing and Imagining Labour Migration. Perspectives of Control from Five Continents*. Farnham, Burlington: Ashgate, 15–38.
Groenendijk, Kees, Elspeth Guild and Halil Dogan (1998) *Security of Residence of Long-term Migrants, A Comparative Study of Law and Practice in European Countries*. Strasbourg: Council of Europe.
Große-Hüttmann, Martin (2005) Die öffentliche Debatte um einen EU-Beitritt der Türkei in Deutschland. In: Giannakopolous, Angelos and Konstadinos Maras (eds.) *Die Türkei-Debatte in Europa. Ein Vergleich*. Wiesbaden: VS, 34–45.
Guild, Elspeth and Sandra Mantu (eds.) (2011a) *Constructing and Imagining Labour Migration. Perspectives of Control from Five Continents*. Farnham: Ashgate.
Guild, Elspeth and Sandra Mantu (2011b) 'Introduction'. In: Elspeth Guild and Sandra Mantu (eds.) *Constructing and Imagining Labour Migration. Perspectives of Control from Five Continents*. Farnham, Burlington: Ashgate, 1–14.
Guild, Elspeth, Kees Groenendijk and Sergio Carrera (2009) 'Understanding the Contest of Community: Illiberal Practices in the EU?' In Elspeth Guild, Kees Groenendijk and Sergio Carrera (eds.) *Illiberal Liberal States: Immigration, Citizenship and Integration in the EU*. Farnham: Ashgate, 1–28.
Hall and Partners (2012) 'The Management of Enforced Removals from Australia: A Client Perspective'. *Report to DIAC by Hall & Partners Open Mind*. www.immi

.gov.au/media/publications/research/_pdf/management-of-enforced-removals-in-Australia.pdf, accessed 7 November 2013.

Hall, Matthew, Audrey Singer, Gordon F. De Jong and Deborah Roempke Graefe (2011) 'The Geography of Immigrant Skills: Educational Profiles of Metropolitan Areas'. Brookings Institution. www.brookings.edu/~/media/research/files/papers/2011/6/immigrants%20singer/06_immigrants_singer.pdf, accessed 7 December 2013.

Hamid-Turksoy, Nilyufer (2012) 'Turkey's Representation in the European Media: A Glimpse to France, Germany and Britain'. In Can Tan Bilgili and Nesrin Tan Akbulu (eds.) *Broken Grounds 1: Mass Communication and Cultural Transformation*. Sofia: Prof. Marin Drinov Publishing House, 135–152.

Hammar, Tomas (1990) *Democracy and the Nation State: Aliens, Denizens, and Citizens in a World of International Migration*. Aldershot: Avebury.

Hancıoğlu, Banu, Atilla Ergöçmen and Turgay Ünalan (2004) 'The Population of Turkey at the Turn of the XXI Century: Post Trends, Current Situation and Future Prospects'. In: Turkish Family, Health and Planning Foundation (eds.) *Population Challenges, International Migration, and Reproductive Health in Turkey and the European Union: Issues and Policy Implications*. Istanbul: TAP Publication, 43–50.

Hannam, Kevin, Mimi Scheller and John Urry (2006) 'Editorial: Mobilities, Immobilities and Moorings'. *Mobilities*, 1, 1, 1–22.

Hansen, Thomas Blom and Finn Stepputat (eds.) (2005) *Sovereign Bodies: Citizens, Migrants, and States in the Postcolonial World*. Princeton, NJ: Princeton University Press.

Hardt, Michael and Antonio Negri (2000) *Empire*. Cambridge, MA: Harvard University Press.

Hargreaves, Alec (1995) *Immigration, 'Race' and Ethnicity in Contemporary France*. London and New York: Routledge.

Hassan, Minhaj (2007a) 'Morristown Deputizing Plan Stirs up Outcry: Advocates Oppose Town Cops Serving as Immigration Agents'. *Daily Record* [Morristown, NJ], 27 March.

Hassan, Minhaj (2007b) 'Morristown Plan to Police Immigrants Sparks Town Hall Debate'. *Daily Record* [Morristown, NJ], 27 March.

Hassan, Minhaj (2008) 'Morris Detained 600 People for Immigration in 18 Months'. *Daily Record* [Morristown, NJ], 30 November.

Hathaway, James C. (2005) *The Rights of Refugees under International Law*. Cambridge: Cambridge University Press.

Hautala, Heidi (2009) 'MEPs Appeal to Prevent any Charter to Afghanistan'. http://www.heidihautala.fi/2009/10/meps-appeal-to-prevent-any-charter-to-afghanistan/, accessed 10 November 2013.

Herbert, Ulrich (1999) *Fremdarbeiter. Politik und Praxis des 'Ausländer-Einsatzes' in der Kriegswirtschaft des Dritten Reiches*. Bonn: Dietz Verlag.

Herman, Max (n. d.) 'Newark Riots, 1967'. http://www.67riots.rutgers.edu/introduction.html, accessed 7 December 2013.

Hertog, Leonhard den (2012) 'Two Boats in the Mediterranean Sea and Their Unfortunate Encounters with Europe's Policies towards People on the Move'. *CEPS Papers in Liberty and Security in Europe*, 48, July.

Hess, Sabine and Bernd Kasparek (eds.) (2010) *Grenzregime: Diskurse – Praktiken – Institutionen in Europa*. Berlin, Hamburg: Assoziation A.

Hildebrandt, Eckart and Werner Olle (1975) *Ihr Kampf ist unser Kampf: Ursachen, Verlauf und Perspektiven der Ausländerstreiks 1973 in der BRD*. Offenbach: Verlag 2000.

Home Office (2001) 'Measures Announced to Improve Immigration Control'. 19 September 2001, 214/01. http://www.ind.homeoffice.gov.uk/news.asp?NewsId= 86&SectionId=1, accessed 27 May 2002.
Hopf, Ted (2002) *Social Construction of International Relations: Identities and Foreign Policies*. Moscow, Ithaca: Cornell University Press.
Huber, Bertold (2004) 'Das asylrechtliche Flughafenverfahren'. In: Karl-Heinz Hohm, Achim Schunder, and Reiner Stahl (eds.) *Verwaltungsgericht im Wandel der Zeit. Fünfzig Jahre Verwaltungsgericht Franfurt am Main*. München: Beck, 145–159.
Hungarian Helsinki Committee (2008) Access to Protection at Airports in Europe. Report on the Monitoring Experiences at Airports in Amsterdam, Budapest, Madrid, Prague, Vienna, Warsaw. http://helsinki.hu/wp-content/uploads/books/en/Access_at_Airports.pdf, accessed 24 January 2014.
Huysmans, Jef (2000) 'The European Union and the Securitization of Migration'. *Journal of Common Market Studies*, 38, 5, 751–777.
Huysmans, Jef (2006) *The Politics of Insecurity. Fear, Migration and Asylum in the European Union*. London: Routledge.
Hyndman, Jennifer (2004) 'The (Geo) Politics of Mobility'. In: Lynn. A. Staeheli, Eleonore Kofman and Linda Peake (eds.) *Mapping Women, Making Politics: Feminist Perspectives on Political Geography*. New York, London: Routledge, 169–185.
İçduygu, Ahmet (2003) *Irregular Migration in Turkey*. Geneva: International Organization for Migration.
İçduygu, Ahmet (2006) *Türkiye-Avrupa Birliği İlişkileri Bağlamında Uluslararası Göç Tartışmalar Tartışmaları* [Debates on Issues of International Migration in the Context of Turkey-EU Relations]. Istanbul: TÜSİAD Yayınları.
İçduygu, Ahmet (2010a) 'The Politics of Demography and International Migration: Implications for the EU–Turkey Relationship'. *Journal of Balkan and Near Eastern Studies*, 12, 1, 59–71.
İçduygu, Ahmet (2010b) *International Migration and Turkey*, 2010 OECD SOPEMI Report, Istanbul.
İçduygu, Ahmet (2011) 'The Irregular Migration Corridor between the EU and Turkey: Is It Possible to Block It with a Readmission Agreement?', *EU–US Immigration Systems [2011/2014]*, Robert Schuman Center for Advanced Studies, European University Institute. http://cadmus.eui.eu/handle/1814/17844, accessed 4 August 2013.
İçduygu, Ahmet (2012) '50 Years after the Labour Recruitment Agreement with Germany: The Consequences of Emigration for Turkey'. *Perceptions*, XVII, 2, 11–36.
İçduygu, Ahmet and Ayşem Biriz Karaçay (2012) 'Demography and Migration in Transition: Reflections on EU–Turkey Relations'. In: Seçil Paçacı Elitok, and Thomas Straubhaar (eds.) *Turkey, Migration and the EU: Potentials, Challenges and Opportunities*. Hamburg: Hamburg University Press, 19–38.
İçduygu, Ahmet and Deniz Sert (2009) 'Country Profile Turkey', *Focus Migration, Country Profile No. 5*. http://www.focus-migration.de/uploads/tx_wilpubdb/CP_05_Turkey_2009.pdf, accessed 4 August 2013.
İçduygu, Ahmet and Deniz Sert (2012) 'Introduction'. In İçduygu Ahmet and Deniz Sert (eds.) *Borders Under Stress*. Istanbul: ISIS Press, 13–31.
İçduygu, Ahmet and Kemal Kirişci (2009) 'Introduction: Turkey's International Migration in Transition'. In: Ahmet İçduygu and Kemal Kirişci (eds.) *Land of Diverse Migrations*. Istanbul: İstanbul Bilgi University Press, 1–25.
İçduygu, Ahmet and Deniz Yükseker (2012) 'Rethinking Transit Migration in Turkey: Reality and Re-presentation in the Creation of a Migratory Phenomenon'. *Population, Space and Place*, 18, 4, 441–456.

İçduygu, Ahmet and Şule Toktaş (2002) 'How Do Smuggling and Trafficking Operate via Irregular Border Crossings in the Middle East? Evidence From Fieldwork in Turkey'. *International Migration*, 40, 6, 25–54.

ICE, Immigration and Customs Enforcement (2012) 'Fact Sheet: Delegation of Immigration Authority Section 287(g) Immigration and Nationality Act'. 31 December. http://www.ice.gov/news/library/factsheets/287g.htm, accessed 10 May 2013.

ICE, Immigration and Customs Enforcement (2013) 'Enforcement & Removal: Facility Locator'. http://www.ice.gov/detention-facilities/, accessed 26 November 2013.

Immigrés Afghans, Sangatte (2001) 'Les Afghans de Sangatte contre les terroristes et l'anéantissement de leur pays. Déclaration écrite parvenue à l'AFP'. 26 September. http://hns.samizdat.net/article.php3?id_article=369, accessed 25 March 2010.

IMO, International Maritime Organization (1974) 'International Convention on the Safety of Life at Sea (SOLAS Convention)'. http://www.imo.org/about/conventions/listofconventions/pages/international-convention-for-the-safety-of-life-at-sea-%28solas%29,-1974.aspx, accessed 24 February 2013.

IMO, International Maritime Organization (1979) 'International Convention on Maritime Search and Rescue (SAR Convention)'. http://treaties.un.org/doc/Publication/UNTS/Volume%201405/volume-1405-I-23489-English.pdf, accessed 24 February 2013.

Infomobile/Welcome to Europe (2011) 'Lost-at-Border'. http://www.scribd.com/doc/78567527/Lost-at-Border, accessed 17 October 2013.

IOM, International Organization for Migration (2001) *Dignity or Exploitation, the Choice Is in Your Hands*. Calais: IOM.

IOM, International Organization for Migration (2008) 'International Dialogue on Migration 2008: Challenges of Irregular Migration: Addressing Mixed Migration Flows'. *96th Session*. MC/INF/294. 7 November. http://www.iom.int/jahia/webdav/shared/shared/mainsite/about_iom/en/council/96/MC_INF_294.pdf, accessed 10 November 2013.

IRB, Immigration and Refugee Board of Canada (2013) *Sri Lanka: Treatment of Tamil Returnees to Sri Lanka, Including Failed Refugee Applicants; Information on Specific Asylum Cases, Including the Tamil Asylum-seeker Boat that Stopped in Togo, the Return of Sri Lankan Asylum Seekers from Australia in 2012, and any Cases of Voluntary Repatriation (August 2011–January 2013) [LKA104245.E]*, European Country of Origin Information Network. http://www.ecoi.net/local_link/240922/350350_en.html, accessed 2 February 2014.

Isin, Engin F. (2002) *Being Political: Genealogies of Citizenship*. Minneapolis, MN: University of Minnesota Press.

Isin, Engin F. (2008) 'Theorizing Acts of Citizenship'. In: Engin F. Isin and Greg Marc Nielsen (eds.) *Acts of Citizenship*. London: Zed Books, 15–43.

Isin, Engin F. (2009) 'Citizenship in Flux: The Figure of the Activist Citizen'. *Subjectivity*, 29, 367–388.

Isin, Engin F. and Greg M. Nielsen (eds.) (2008) *Acts of Citizenship*. London: Zed Books.

Jacobson, Robin Dale (2008) *The New Nativism: Proposition 187 and the Debate over Immigration*. Minneapolis: University of Minnesota.

Jäger, Michael (2010) 'Machtblock und Parteien bei Poulantzas'. In: Alex Demirovic, Stephan Adolphs and Serhat Karakayali (eds.) *Das Staatsverständnis von Nicos Poulantzas. Der Staat als gesellschaftliches Verhältnis*. Baden-Baden: Nomos, 241–257.

Jäger, Siegfried (ed.) (1996) *BrandSätze. Rassismus im Alltag*. 4th ed. Duisburg: DISS.

Johnson, Heather (2011) 'Click to Donate: Visual Images, Constructing Victims and Imagining the Female Refugee'. *Third World Quarterly*, 32, 6, 1015–1137.

Joppke, Christian (2007) 'Beyond National Models: Civic Integration Policies for Immigrants in Western Europe'. *West European Politics*, 30, 1, 1–22.
Joppke, Christian (2010) *Citizenship and Immigration*. Cambridge: Malden.
Kaina, Viktoria (2010) ' "Wir" und "die Anderen" – europäische Identitätsbildung als Konstruktion von Gemeinsamkeit und Differenz'. *Zeitschrift für Politik*, 57, 4, 413–433.
Kaiser, Bianca (2003) 'Lifeworlds of EU Immigrants in Turkey'. In Emrehan Zeybekoğlu and Bo Johansson (eds.) *Migration and Labour in Europe – Views from Turkey and Sweden*. Istanbul: MURCIR and NIWL, 269–289.
Kalinock, Sabine and Danica Göller (2007) *Jahresbericht der Abschiebungsbeobachtung am Flughafen Frankfurt am Main 2006/2007*. Frankfurt/Main: Bistum Limburg, Evangelischer Regionalverband Frankfurt/Main.
Kalinock, Sabine and Stella Schicke (2008) *Zweiter Jahresbericht der Abschiebungsbeobachtung am Flughafen Frankfurt am Main 2007/2008*. Frankfurt/Main: Bistum Limburg, Evangelischer Regionalverband Frankfurt/Main.
Kalm, Sara (2012) 'Global Migration Management, Order and Access to Mobility'. In: Martin Geiger and Antoine Pécoud (eds.) *The New Politics of International Mobility: Migration Management and Its Discontents*. IMIS-Beiträge, special issue. Osnabrück: IMIS, 49–73
Karakayali, Serhat (2005) 'Lotta Continua in Frankfurt, Türken-Terror in Köln. Migrantische Kämpfe in der Geschichte der Bundesrepublik'. In: Bernd Hüttner, Gottfried Oy and Norbert Schepers (eds.) *Vorwärts und viel vergessen*. Bremen: AG Spak, 121–134.
Karakayali, Serhat (2008) *Gespenster der Migration. Zur Genealogie illegaler Einwanderung in der Bundesrepublik Deutschland*. Bielefeld: Transcript Verlag.
Karakayali, Serhat and Vassilis Tsianos (2005) 'Mapping the Order of New Migration. Undokumentierte Arbeit und die Autonomie der Migration'. *Peripherie. Zeitschrift für Politik und Ökonomie in der Dritten Welt*, 97/98, 35–64.
Kaya, Ayhan and Ferhat Kentel (2005) *Euro-Turks: A Bridge or a Breach between Turkey and the European Union? A Comparison of German-Turks and French-Turks*. Brussels: Center for European Policy Studies.
Kaytaz, Esra (2006) *Turkey as a Country of Transit Migration: The Case of Christian Iranian Asylum Seekers*. Unpublished M.Phil. thesis. Oxford: University of Oxford.
Khachani, Mohamed (2009) 'La Migration Marocaine Dans Les Pays du Golfe'. *CARIM Notes d'analyse et de synthèse*, 34, Florence.
Khosravi, Shahram (2010) *'Illegal' Traveller: An Ethnography of Borders*. Basingstoke: Palgrave Macmillan.
Kirişci, Kemal (2002) *Justice and Home Affairs Issues in Turkish-EU Relations*. Istanbul: TESEV Publications.
Kirişci, Kemal (2007a) 'Turkey: A Country of Transition From Emigration to Immigration'. *Mediterranean Politics*, 12, 1, 91–97.
Kirişci, Kemal (2007b) 'Border Management and EU-Turkish Relations: Convergence or Deadlock'. *Carim RR 2007/03*. Robert Schuman Centre for Advanced Studies, San Domenica di Fiesole (FI): European University Institute.
Kirişci, Kemal (2008a) 'Informal "Circular Migration" into Turkey: The Bureaucratic and Political Context'. *Carim AS 2008/21*. Robert Schuman Centre for Advanced Studies, San Domenica di Fiesole (FI) European University Institute.
Kirişci, Kemal (2008b) 'Religion as an Argument'. In: Jan Gerhards (ed.) *Religion, Politics and Turkey's Accession to the EU*. Houndmills, Basingstoke and New York: Palgrave Macmillan, 19–39.

Kirişci, Kemal (2012) 'Turkey's New Draft Law on Asylum: What to Make of It?'. In: Seçil Paçacı Elitok and Thomas Straubhaar (eds.) *Turkey, Migration and the EU: Potentials, Challenges and Opportunities*. Hamburg: Hamburg University Press, 63–83.

Kirkham, John (2011) 'After 9/11, A New Era in The Business Of Detaining Immigrants'. *Huffington Post*, 9 September. http://www.huffingtonpost.com/2011/09/09/911-immigrant-detention-business-for-profit-prison_n_951639.html, accessed 2 December 2013.

Kivisto, Peter and Thomas Faist (2007) *Citizenship: Discourse, Theory and Transnational Prospects*. Oxford: Blackwell.

Klepp, Silja (2010) 'A Contested Asylum System: The European Union between Refugee Protection and Border Control in the Mediterranean Sea'. *European Journal of Migration and Law*, 12, 4, 1–21.

Klepp, Silja (2011) *Europa zwischen Grenzkontrolle und Flüchtlingsschutz. Eine Ethnographie der Seegrenze auf dem Mittelmeer*. Bielefeld: Transcript.

Kofman, Eleonore (2002) 'Contemporary European Migrations, Civic Stratification and Citizenship'. *Political Geography*, 21, 8, 1035–1054.

Kofman, Eleonore (2005) 'Citizenship, Migration and the Reassertion of National Identity'. *Citizenship Studies*, 9, 5, 453–467.

Kohler-Koch, Beate and Berthold Rittberger (2006) 'Review Article: The "Governance Turn" in EU Studies'. *JCMS: Journal of Common Market Studies*, 44, 1, 27–49.

Kraler, Albert (2011) 'The Case of Austria'. In: Giovanna Zincone, Rinus Penninx and Maren Borkert (eds.) *Migration Policymaking in Europe: The Dynamics of Actors and Contexts in Past and Present*. Amsterdam: Amsterdam University Press, 21–59.

Krieger, Hubert and Bertrand Maitre (2006) 'Migration Trends in an Enlarging European Union'. *Turkish Studies*, 7, 1, 45–66.

Küçük, Bülent (2008) *Die Türkei und das andere Europa. Phantasmen der Identität im Beitrittsdiskurs*. Bielefeld: Transcript.

Kunz, Rahel (2011) *The Political Economy of Global Remittances. Gender, Governmentality and Neoliberalism*. London and New York: Routledge.

Kunz, Rahel (2012) 'The Discovery of the Diaspora'. *International Political Sociology*, 6, 1, 103–107.

Kunz, Rahel, Sandra Lavenex and Marion Panizzon (2011) *Migration and Mobility Partnerships: Unveiling the Promise?*. London: Routledge.

Laacher, Smaïn (2002) *Après Sangatte...Nouvelles Immigrations, nouveaux enjeux*. Paris: La Dispute.

La Belle Etoile, French Coalition for the Right of Asylum, GISTI, Secours Catholique, C'sur, Salam, Migrants Fraternity Collective (Angres), Terres D'errances Norrent-Fontes, Terres D'errances Steenvoorde, Calais Migrant Solidarity, The Exiles of 10° (Paris), The Ligue de Droits de L'homme (Pas-de-Calais Regional Federation), Medecins du Monde, Cimade, the Greens, NPA Calais, Amnesty International (2009) 'Joint Declaration: Destroying the Jungles: A False Solution'. Calais, 21 September. http://calaismigrantsolidarity.wordpress.com/2009/09/22/joint-declaration, accessed 10 November 2013.

Lagro, Esra (2008) 'Why Is President Sarkozy Actually Against Turkish Accession to the EU? Facts and Challenges'. *Perceptions*, 8, 58–78.

Land Hessen (2005) *Hessische Erstaufnahmeeinrichtung für Flüchtlinge in Gießen – Außenstelle Flughafen*. Frankfurt/Main: HEAE.

Landman, Todd and Edzia Carvalho (2010) *Measuring Human Rights*. London and New York: Routledge.

Lapidus, Ira M. (2001) 'Between Universalism and Particularism: The Historical Base of Muslim Communal, National, and Global Identities'. *Global Networks*, 1, 1, 37–55.
Laurence, Jonathan (2012) *The Emancipation of Europes Muslims. The State's Role in Minority Integration*. Princeton: Princeton University Press.
Lavenex, Sandra (2005) 'National Frames in Migration Research: The Tacit Political Agenda'. In: Michael Bommes and Ewa T. Morawska (eds.) *International Migration Research: Constructions, Omissions, and the Promises of Interdisciplinarity*. Aldershot, UK: Ashgate, 243–264.
Lefebvre, Henri (1991 [1974]) *The Production of Space*. Oxford and Cambridge: Blackwell.
Leggewie, Claus (ed.) (2000) *Die Türkei und Europa*. Frankfurt/Main: Suhrkamp.
Leifeld, Philip and Sebastian Haunss (2012) 'Political Discourse Networks and the Conflict over Software Patents in Europe'. *European Journal of Political Research*, 51, 3, 382–409.
Leisering, Britta (2008) 'Menschenrechtsschutz in politisch bestimmten Räumen – zur Effektivität juristischer Kontrollmechanismen'. Working Paper 2008/03, Institut für Weltgesellschaft, Bielefeld: University of Bielefeld.
Lenin, Vladimir Iljitsch (2010 [1916]) *Imperialism, the Highest Stage of Capitalism*. London: Penguin Classics.
Levitt, Peggy and Rafael de La Dehesa (2003) 'Transnational Migration and the Redefinition of the State: Variations and Explanations'. *Ethnic and Racial Studies*, 26, 4, 587–611.
Lieberman, Samuel S. and Ali S. Gitmez (1979) 'Turkey'. In: Ronald E. Krane (ed.) *International Labor Migration in Europe*. New York: Praeger Publishers.
Liegl, Barbara, Kerstin Buchinger and Astrid Steinkellner (2008) 'Final Case Study Report Austria Draft April 2008'. Project report prepared for the JURISTRAS project funded by the European Commission, DG Research, Priority 7, Citizens and Governance in a Knowledge Based Society.
Lipsky, Michael (1980) *Street-Level Bureaucracy. Dilemmas of the Individual in Public Services*. New York: Russell Sage Foundation.
Liptak, Adam (2012) 'Court Splits Immigration Law Verdicts; Upholds Hotly Debated Centerpiece, 8–0'. *The New York Times*, 26 June, late ed., A1.
Llorente, Elizabeth (2008) 'Morris Rejects Jail Wing for Illegals'. *NorthJersey.com.*, 22 February. http://www.lcnj.org/287g/Morris%20rejects%20jail%20wing%20for%20illegals.pdf, accessed 26 November 2013.
Llorente, Elizabeth and Miguel Perez (2005) 'Policing Illegal Immigration: Dilemma Can Turn American Dream into Nightmare'. *The Record* [Bergen County, NJ], 26 June, A01.
Lochak, Danièle (1985) *Étrangers: de quel droit?* Paris: Presses Universitaires de France.
Mahler, Sarah J. (2000) 'Constructing International Relations: The Role of Transnational Migrants and Other Non-State Actors'. *Identities: Global Studies in Culture and Power*, 7, 2, 197–232.
Malta Today (2006) 'Exclusive: November Migrants' Shipwreck Tragedy. "Keep at distance" from Boat People, Rescuers Told'. 16 April.
Marshall, Thomas H. (1950) *Citizenship and Social Class*. Cambridge: Cambridge University Press.
Massey, Douglas (2007) 'Borderline Madness: America's Counterproductive Immigration Policy'. In: Carol Swain (ed.) *Debating Immigration*. New York: Cambridge University Press, 175–188.
Mavelli, Luca (2013) 'Between Normalisation and Exception: The Securitisation of Islam and the Construction of the Secular Subject'. *Millennium*, 41, 2, 159–181.

Mayer, Stephanie (2009) 'Migration and Labour Markets. Political Discourse in Austria'. In: Stephanie Mayer and Mikael Spång (eds.) *Debating Migration: Political Discourses on Labour Immigration in Historical Perspective*. Innsbruck: Studienverlag, 25–73.

McCairns, Gavin (2011) 'Serious and Organised Crime: Promoting Visa Integrity – DIACs Response to the Commission of Serious Migration Offences'. http://www.aic.gov.au/media_library/conferences/2010-isoc/presentations/mccairns.pdf, accessed 6 November 2013.

McDonald, Jean (2012) 'Building a Sanctuary City: Municipal Migrant Rights in the City of Toronto'. In: Peter Nyers and Kim Rygiel (eds.) *Citizenship, Migrant Activism and the Politics of Movement*. London: Routledge, 129–145.

McKeown, Adam M. (2008) *Melancholy Order. Asian Migration and the Globalization of Borders*. New York: Columbia University Press.

Meissner, Doris, Donald M. Kerwin, Muzaffar Chishti and Claire Bergerton (2013) *Immigration Enforcement in the United States: The Rise of a Formidable Machinery*. Washington, DC: Migration Policy Institute.

Menz, Georg (2009) 'The Neoliberalized State and Migration Control: The Rise of Private Actors in the Enforcement and Design of Migration Policy'. *Journal of Contemporary Central and Eastern Europe*, 17, 3, 315–332.

Merry, Sally Engle (1997) 'Legal Pluralism and Transnational Culture: The Kaho'okolokolonui Kanaka Maoli Tribunal, Hawai'i, 1993'. In: Richard A. Wilson (ed.) *Human Rights, Culture and Context: Anthropological Perspectives*. London: Routledge, 28–48.

Merry, Sally Engle (2005) 'Human Rights and Global Legal Pluralism: Reciprocity and Disjuncture'. In: Franz von Benda-Beckmann, Keebet von Benda-Beckmann and Anne Griffiths (eds.) *Mobile People, Mobile Law: Expanding Legal Relations in a Contracting World*. Aldershot and Burlington: Aldershot, 215–232.

Mezzadra, Sandro (2010a) 'Autonomie der Migration – Kritik und Ausblick. Eine Zwischenbilanz'. *Grundrisse*, 35, 22–30.

Mezzadra, Sandro (2010b) 'The Gaze of Autonomy. Capitalism, Migration and Social Struggles'. In: Vicki Squire (ed.) *Contesting the Securitization of Migration: Borderzones and Irregularity*. London: Routledge, 121–143.

Mezzadra, Sandro and Brett Neilson (2003) 'Né qui, né altrove. Migration, Detention, Desertion: A Dialogue'. In: *borderlands*, 2, 1. http://www.borderlandsejournal.adelaide.edu.au/vol2no1_2003/mezzadra_neilson.html, accessed 9 February 2014.

Mezzadra, Sandro and Brett Neilson (2008) 'Border as Method, or, the Multiplication of Labor'. *Transversal – eipcp Multilingual Webjournal* 2008, 3. http://eipcp.net/transversal/0608/mezzadraneilson/en, accessed 24 January 2014.

Miller, Peter and Nikolas Rose (2008) *Governing the Present: Administering Economic, Social and Personal Life*. Cambridge: Polity.

Millner, Naomi (2011) 'From "refugee" to "migrant" in Calais Solidarity Activism: Re-Staging Undocumented Migration for a Future Politics of Asylum'. *Political Geography*, 30, 320–328.

Minister des Inneren [Minister of Home Affairs, Germany] (1973) *Betrifft: Verfassungsschutz*, Bonn.

Minister des Inneren [Minister of Home Affairs, Germany] (1977) *Betrifft: Verfassungsschutz*, Bonn.

Minister for Immigration and Citizenship, Australia (2012) 'No Advantage Onshore for Boat Arrivals'. http://www.minister.immi.gov.au/media/cb/2012/cb191883.htm, accessed 24 February 2013.

Mitropoulos, Angela and Brett Neilson (2006) 'Exceptional Times, Non-governmental Spacings, and Impolitical Movements'. *Vacarme*, 34. http://www.vacarme.org/article484.html, accessed 9 February 2014.

Mohammed VI (2005) 'Royal Speech on the Occasion of the 30th Anniversary of the Green March'. 6 November 2005. https://www.maroc.ma/fr/discours-royaux/discours-de-sm-le-roi-%C3%A0-loccasion-du-30%C3%A8me-anniversaire-de-la-marche-verte, accessed 9 February 2014.

Mohr, Katrin (2005) 'Stratifizierte Rechte und soziale Exklusion von Migranten im Wohlfahrtsstaat', *Zeitschrift für Soziologie*, 34, 5, 383–398.

Moïsi, Dominique (2006) 'Examination as Witness, House of Lords European Union Committee: The Further Enlargement of the EU: Threat or Opportunity?' 53rd Report of Session 2005–2006, 161–168 www.publications.parliament.uk/pa/ld200506/ldselect/ldeucom/273/273.pdf, accessed 7 July 2011.

Monitor (2013) 'EU-Agentur Frontex gibt Menschenrechtsverletzungen an EU-Außengrenzen zu – Frontex-Chef Ilkka Laitinen hält Praxis für "nicht akzeptabel"'. *Press Report* 17 October. http://www.wdr.de/tv/monitor/presse/2013/meldung_131016.php5, accessed 10 December 2013.

Morris, Lydia (2002) *Managing Migration: Civic Stratification and Migrants' Rights*. London: Routledge.

Morris, Lydia (2003) 'Managing Contradiction: Civic Stratification and Migrants' Rights'. *International Migration Review*, 37, 1, 74–100.

Morris, Lydia (2012) 'Citizenship and Human Rights: Ideals and Actualities'. *The British Journal of Sociology*, 63, 39–46.

Moulier Boutang, Yann (1993) 'Interview mit Yann Moulier-Boutang, Paris'. *Materialien für einen neuen Antiimperialismus*, 5, 29–55.

Moulier Boutang, Yann (2007) 'Europa, Autonomie der Migration, Biopolitik'. In: Marianne Pieper, Thomas Atzert, Serhat Karakayali, and Vassilis Tsianos (eds.) *Empire und die biopolitische Wende*. Frankfurt, New York: Campus, 169–177.

Mourão Permoser, Julia (2012) 'Civic Integration as Symbolic Politics? Insights from Austria'. *European Journal of Migration and Law*, 14, 2, 173–198.

MSC, Maritime Security Committee (2004a) 'Maritime Security Committee (MSC) Resolution 153 (78) 2004'. *International Maritime Organization*. http://www.imo.org/OurWork/Facilitation/IllegalMigrants/Documents/MSC.167%2878%29.pdf, accessed 24 February 2013.

MSC, Maritime Security Committee (2004b) 'Maritime Security Committee (MSC) Resolution Guidelines on the Treatment of Persons Rescued at Sea 167 (78) 2004'. *International Maritime Organization*. http://www.imo.org/OurWork/Facilitation/IllegalMigrants/Documents/MSC.167%2878%29.pdf, accessed 24 February 2013.

Mykyta, Laryssa (2012) 'Economic Downturns and the Failure to Launch: The Living Arrangements of Young Adults in the U.S. 1995–2011'. *Working Paper*. Washington, DC: US Census Bureau.

Naïr, Sami (1997) *Contre les lois Pasqua*. Paris: Arléa.

National Immigration Forum, United States (2011) 'Summaries of Recent Reports on Immigrant Detention'. http://www.immigrationforum.org/images/uploads/2010/DetentionReportSummaries.pdf, accessed 7 December 2013.

National Immigration Law Center (2004) 'Annotated Chart of Laws, Resolutions and Immigration Laws'. www.nilc.org/immlawpolicy/LocalLaw/Local_Law_Enforcement_Chart_FINAL.pdf, accessed 27 February 2004.

NCSL, National Conference of State Legislators, United States (2013) '2012 Immigration-Related Laws and Resolutions in the States (1 January–31 December

2012)'. http://www.ncsl.org/issues-research/immig/2012-immigration-related-laws-jan-december-2012.aspx, accessed 17 May 2013.

Newman, Marie (2002) 'Five Children of Illegal Immigrants Return to School After the State Intervenes'. *The New York Times*, 24 September. http://www.nytimes.com/2002/09/24/nyregion/five-children-of-illegal-immigrants-return-to-school-after-the-state-intervenes.html, accessed 13 May 2013.

Newton, Lina (2005) 'It is Not a Question of Being Anti-Immigration: Categories of Deservedness in Immigration Policy Making'. In: Anne L. Schneider and Helen M. Ingram (eds.) *Deserving and Entitled: Social Constructions and Public Policy*. Albany: SUNY Press, 139–172.

Ngai, Mae M. (2004) *Impossible Subjects: Illegal Aliens and the Making of Modern America*. Princeton: Princeton University Press.

Nielsen, Nikolaj (2012a) 'Greece Opens First Migration Detention Centre'. *EU Observer*, 30 April. http://euobserver.com/social/116083, accessed 17 October 2013.

Nielsen, Nikolaj (2012b) 'Fortress Europe: A Greek Wall Close Up'. *EU Observer*, 21 December. http://euobserver.com/fortress-eu/118565, accessed 17 October 2013.

NJ.com (2009) Video: Morristown Mayor Cresitello's immigration Talk at Yale. 14 April. www.nj.com/morristown/index.ssf/2009/04/video_morristown_mayor_cresite.html, accessed 21 May 2013.

NJCFIC, New Jersey Citizens Forum for Immigration Control (2012) 'Stop the Invasion'. http://www.njcic.com/, accessed 21 May 2013.

Noborder (2009a) 'Calais No Border Camp'. 23–29 June. http://calaisnoborder.eu/org/sites/default/files/Camp%20Callout%20A4%20Dble%20Sided.pdf, accessed 25 October 2009.

Noborder (2009b) 'Nomade. Daily Newspaper of Calais No Border Camp. No. 1'. 24 June. http://calaisnoborder.eu.org/taxonomy/term/2, accessed 25 October 2009.

Noiriel, Gérard (1994) 'La Nationalité au Miroir des Mots'. In: Bernard Falga, Catherine Wihtol de Wenden, and Claus Leggewie (eds.) *De l'Immigration à l'Intégration en France et en Allemagne*. Paris: Cerf, 21–31.

NPR, National Public Radio (2007) 'One Third America: Asian and Hispanic Numbers Surge'. *National Public Radio*, 18 May. http://www.npr.org/templates/story/story.php?storyId=10254921, accessed 10 May 2013.

Nyers, Peter (2003) 'Abject Cosmopolitanism: The Politics of Protection in the Anti-Deportation Movement'. *Third World Quarterly*, 24, 6, 1069–1093.

Nyers, Peter (2006a) 'The Accidental Citizen: Acts of Sovereignty and (Un)Making Citizenship'. *Economy and Society*, 35, 1, 22–41.

Nyers, Peter (2006b) *Rethinking Refugees: Beyond States of Emergency*. New York, Routledge.

Nyers, Peter (2008) 'No one is Illegal: Between City and Nation'. In: Engin F. Isin, and Greg Marc Nielsen (eds.) *Acts of Citizenship*. London: Zed Books, 160–181.

Nyers, Peter and Kim Rygiel (2012) 'Introduction: Citizenship, Migrant Activism and the Politics of Movement'. In: Peter Nyers, and Kim Rygiel (eds.) *Citizenship, Migrant Activism and the Politics of Movement*. New York: Routledge, 1–19.

OECD (2010) *International Migration Outlook*. Paris: OECD.

Office of the Inspector General, Department of Homeland Security (2011) 'Management of Mental Health Cases in Immigrant Detention'. http://www.oig.dhs.gov/assets/Mgmt/OIG_11-62_Mar11.pdf, accessed 7 December 2013.

Ögelman, Nedim (2003) 'Documenting and Explaining the Persistence of Homeland Politics among Germany's Turks'. *International Migration Review*, 37, 1, 163–193.

O'Keefe (ed.) (2013) 'Senate Approves Comprehensive Immigration Bill'. *The Washington Post*, 27 June 2013. http://www.washingtonpost.com/politics/senate-poised-to-approve-massive-immigration-bill/2013/06/27/87168096-df32-11e2-b2d4-ea6d8f477a01_story.html, accessed 10 February 2014.

Öner, Selcen (2008) 'An Analysis of European Identity within the framework of the EU: The Case of Turkey's Membership'. In: Wolfgang Gieler and Christian Johannes Henrich (eds.) *Türkisches Europa – Europäische Türkei*. Bonn: Scientia Bonnensis, 163–182.

Ong, Aihwa (1996) 'Cultural Citizenship as Subject-Making: Immigrants Negotiate Racial and Cultural Boundaries in the United States'. *Current Anthropology*, 37, 5, 737–762.

Öniş, Ziya and Suhnaz Yilmaz (2009) 'Between Europeanization and Euro-Asianism: Foreign Policy Activism in Turkey During the AKP Era'. *Turkish Studies*, 10, 1, 7–24.

Onuf, Nicholas G. (1989) *World of Our Making: Rules and Rule in Social Theory and International Relations*. Columbia, SC: University of South Carolina Press.

Oppeln, Sabine von (2006) 'Die Debatte über den EU-Beitritt der Türkei im deutsch-französischen Vergleich'. In: Matthias Wächter (ed.) *Die Türkei auf dem Weg in die Europäische Union – Aspekte und Perspektiven*. Meeting of Isik University in Istanbul, Berlin: Berlin Akademie Verlag, 11–30.

Østergaard-Nielsen, Eva (2003a) *International Migration and Sending Countries: Perceptions, Policies and Transnational Relations*. Houndsmills: Palgrave Macmillan.

Østergaard-Nielsen, Eva (2003b) *Transnational Politics: Turks and Kurds in Germany*. London, New York: Routledge.

Oxford Dictionary (1998, Canadian edition). Toronto, Oxford, and New York: Oxford University Press. http://oxforddictionaries.com.

Özcan, Ertekin (1989) *Türkische Immigrantenorganisationen in der Bundesrepublik Deutschland*. Berlin: Hitit.

Palmer, Mick J. (2005) *Inquiry into the Circumstances of the Immigration Detention of Cornelia Rau*. Canberra: Department of Immigration and Multicultural and Indigenous Affairs.

Papadopoulos, Dimitris, Niamh Stephenson and Vassilis Tsianos (2008) *Escape Routes: Control and Subversion in the Twenty-First Century*. London: Pluto Press.

Paphitisas, Nicholas (2012) 'Greece Plans Detention Sites for Illegal Migrants'. *Boston Herald*, 26 March. http://www.boston.com/news/world/europe/articles/2012/03/26/greece_plans_detention_sites_for_illegal_migrants/, accessed 17 October 2013.

Parla, Ayşe (2007) 'Irregular Workers or Ethnic Kin? Post-1990s Labour Migration from Bulgaria to Turkey'. *International Migration*, 45, 3, 157–181.

Parla, Ayşe (2011) 'Undocumented Migrants and the Double Binds of Rights Claims'. *Differences*, 22, 1, 64–89.

Parnreiter, Christof (1994) *Migration und Arbeitsteilung: AusländerInnenbeschäftigung in der Weltwirtschaftskrise*. Vienna: Promedia.

Parnreiter, Christof (1998) 'Von Mauern mit Löchern: Grenzpolitik, Migration und Arbeitskraftregulierung'. *Diskus*, 98, 3. www.copyriot.com/diskus/3_98/3.htm, accessed 7 December 2013.

Parolin, Gianluca (2009) *Citizenship in the Arab World: Kin, Religion and Nation-State*. Amsterdam: Amsterdam University Press.

Passel, Jeffrey and D'Vera Cohn (2012) 'Unauthorized Immigrants: 11.1 Million in 2011'. *Pew Research Center, Pew Hispanic Center*. http://www.pewhispanic.org/2012/12/06/unauthorized-immigrants-11-1-million-in-2011/, accessed 7 December 2013.

Passell, Jeffrey and D'Vera Cohn (2011) *Unauthorized Immigrant Population: National and State Trends, 2010*. Washington, DC: Pew Research Center, Pew Hispanic Center.
Pearsall, Richard (2006) 'Latinos Praise Election Results in Riverside'. *Courier Post* [Camden, NJ], 15 November.
Perchinig, Bernhard (2009) 'Von der Fremdarbeit zur Integration? (Arbeits)migrations- und Integrationspolitik in der Zweiten Republik Österreich'. *Geschichte und Literatur*, 53, 3, 228–246.
Perez, Miguel (2005) 'Group Seeks N.J. Support to Halt Illegal Immigration; Bogota Rally Draws Protesters'. *The Record* [Bergen County, NJ], A4.
Però, Davide and John Solomos (2010) 'Introduction: Migrant Politics and Mobilization: Exclusion, Engagements, Incorporation'. *Ethnic and Racial Studies*, 33, 1, 1–18.
Pew Hispanic Center (2013) 'A Nation of Immigrants: A Portrait of the 40 Million, Including 11 Million Unauthorized'. Washington, DC: Pew Research Center.
Pew Research Center (2006) *Global Attitudes Project*. http://www.pewglobal.org/2006/07/18/islam-and-the-west-searching-for-common-ground/, accessed 12 August 2013.
Pew Research Center (2011) *Global Attitudes Project*. http://www.pewglobal.org/2011/07/21/chapter-1-the-rift-between-muslims and the west/, accessed 12 August 2013.
Pickering, Sharon and Leanne Weber (2014) 'New Deterrence Scripts in Australia's Rejuvenated Offshore Detention Regime for Asylum Seekers'. *Law and Social Inquiry*, early view: http://onlinelibrary.wiley.com/doi/10.1111/lsi.12088/abstract?campaign=wolearlyview, accessed 7 July 2014.
Pile, Steve (1997) 'Introduction. Opposition, Political Identities and Spaces of Resistance'. In: Steve Pile and Michael Keith (ed.) *Geographies of Resistance*. London: Routledge, 1–32.
Pile, Steve and Michael Keith (eds.) (1997) *Geographies of Resistance*. London: Routledge.
Pogge von Strandmann, Hartmut (2009) *Imperialismus vom Grünen Tisch. Deutsche Kolonialpolitik zwischen wirtschaftlicher Ausbeutung und 'zivilisatorischen' Bemühungen* Berlin: Christoph Links Verlag.
Polchi, Vladimiro (2009) 'Sbarchi, allarme del Viminale: "Nel 2009 sono raddoppiati" '. *La Repubblica*, 24 September.
Poulantzas, Nicos (1973) *Political Power and Social Classes*. London: New Left Books.
Poulantzas, Nicos (1975) *Classes in Contemporary Capitalism*. London: New Left Books.
Poulantzas, Nicos (1978) *State, Power, Socialism*. London: New Left Books.
Preston, Julia (2013) 'Beside a Path to Citizenship, a New Path on Immigration'. *The New York Times*, 16 April. http://www.nytimes.com/2013/04/17/us/senators-set-to-unveil-immigration-bill.html?pagewanted=all, accessed 7 December 2013.
Pries, Ludger (2008) *Die Transnationalisierung der sozialen Welt. Sozialräume jenseits von Nationalgesellschaften*. Frankfurt/Main: Suhrkamp.
Pries, Ludger (2010) '(Grenzüberschreitende) Migrantenorganisationen als Gegenstand der sozialwissenschaftlichen Forschung: Klassische Problemstellungen und neuere Forschungsbefunde'. In: Ludger Pries and Zeynep Sezgin (eds.) *Jenseits von 'Identität oder Integration'*. Wiesbaden: VS Verlag für Sozialwissenschaften, 15–60.
Pro Asyl (2007) *The Truth may Be Bitter but It Must Be Told: The Situation of Refugees in the Aegean and the Practices of the Greek Coast Guard*. Frankfurt: Pro Asyl, 1–27.
Pro Asyl (2008) *Flüchtlinge im Verschiebebahnhof EU. Die EU-Zuständigkeitsverordnung 'Dublin II'*. Frankfurt/Main: Förderverein Pro Asyl e.V.

Pro Asyl, Greek Council for Refugees, and Infomobile (2012) 'Walls of Shame. Accounts from the Inside: The Detention Centres of Evros'. *Pro-Asyl in Cooperation with the Greek Council for Refugees and Infomobile/Welcome to Europe*. http://www.proasyl.de/fileadmin/fm-dam/q_PUBLIKATIONEN/2012/Evros-Bericht_12_04_10_BHP.pdf, accessed 9 November 2013.

Pugh, Michael (2004) 'Drowning not Waving: Boat People and Humanitarianism at Sea'. *Journal of Refugee Studies*, 17, 1, 50–69.

Quillet, Matthieu (2010) *Chez les Afghans Hazaras à Calais*. Film, 3:12 min. http://www.dailymotion.com/video/xbs0im_chez-les-afghans-hazaras-a-calais-l_news, accessed 10 November 2013.

Ragazzi, Francesco (2009) 'Governing Diasporas'. *International Political Sociology*, 3, 4, 378–397.

Raissiguier, Catherine (2007) 'French Immigration Laws: The Sans-Papières' Perspectives'. In: Thomas Spijkerboer and Sarah Van Walsum (eds.) *Women and Immigration Law in Europe: New Variations of Feminist Themes*. London and New York: Routledge, 204–221.

Raissiguier, Catherine (2010) *Reinventing the Republic: Gender, Migration, and Citizenship in France*. Stanford: Stanford University Press.

RAJFIRE, Réseau pour l'Autonomie Juridique des Femmes Réfugiées/Immigrées (Network for the Legal Autonomy of Immigrant and Refugee Women) (2000) Brochure 2.

Refugee Protest March to Berlin (2012) 'Second Press Release', 13 September. http://www.refugeetentaction.net/index.php?option=com_content&view=article&id=76:zweite-pressemittei-lung-der-fussgruppe-des-protestmarsches-der-asylbewerber-innen-nach-ber-lin&catid=18&Itemid=150&lang=de, accessed 10 December 2013.

Réfugiés Afghans and Christophe Herin (2001) 'Calais: manifestation de "réfugiés" afghans du camp de Sangatte le mercredi 31 octobre 2001'. http://maison-des-sans.org/palabre.php3?id_article=17, accessed 12 January 2003.

Réfugiés Afghans du camp, Sangatte (2001) 'Manifestation', Calais, 31 October 2001. http://www.gisti.org/dossiers/sangatte/actions.html, accessed 10 November 2013.

Reiter, Bernd (2013) *The Dialectics of Citizenship: Exploring Priviledge, Exclusion and Racialization*. East Lansing, MI: Michigan State University Press.

Republic of Turkey (2005), *National Action Plan for the Adoption of the 'EU acquis' in the Field of Asylum and Migration*, March 2005. http://www.carim.org/public/legaltexts/LE2TUR003_EN.pdf, accessed 14 February 2014.

RFI, Radio France International (2009) 'Empörung über Abschiebung von afghanischen Flüchtlingen', 22 October. http://www.rfi.fr/actude/articles/118/article_1903.asp, accessed 10 November 2013.

Richardson, Roslyn (2010) 'Sending a Message? Refugees and Australia's Deterrence Campaign'. *Media International Australia*, 135, 7–18.

Ridgely, Jennifer (2008) 'Cities of Refuge: Immigration Enforcement, Police, and the Insurgent Genealogies of Citizenship in U.S. Sanctuary Cities'. *Urban Geography*, 29, 1, 53–77.

Rigby, Joe and Raphael Schlembach (2013) 'Impossible Protest: Noborders at Calais'. *Citizenship Studies*, 17, 2, 157–172.

Rittberger, Berthold and Arndt Wonka (2011) 'Introduction: Agency Governance in the European Union'. *Journal of European Public Policy*, 18, 6, 780–789.

Robertson, Campbell (2012) 'Alabama Gets Strict Immigration Law as Governor Relents'. *The New York Times*, 18 May. http://www.nytimes.com/2012/05/19/us/alabama-gets-strict-immigration-law-as-governor-relents.html?_r=1&, accessed 15 May 2013.

Rockland, Michael A. (2008) 'Those People'. *New Jersey Monthly*, 30 January. http://njmonthly.com/articles/lifestyle/people/those-people.html, accessed 10 May 2013.

Rodriguez, Néstor (1996) 'The Battle for the Border: Notes on Autonomous Migration, Transnational Communities, and the State'. *Social Justice*, 23, 3, 21–37.

Rodriguez, Robyn Magalit (2010) *Migrants for Export: How the Philippine State Brokers Labor to the World*. Minneapolis, MN: University of Minnesota Press.

Rose, Niklas (2000) 'Government and Control'. *British Journal of Criminology Special Issue on Criminology and Social Theory*, 40, 321–339.

Roth, Jürgen and Kamil Taylan (1981) *Die Türkei: Republik unter Wölfen*. Bornheim-Merten: Lamuv-Verlag.

Routledge, Paul (1993) *Terrains of Resistance: Nonviolent Social Movements and the Contestation of Place in India*. Westport, London: Praeger.

Routledge, Paul (1996) 'Critical Geopolitics and Terrains of Resistance'. *Political Geography*, 15, 6/7, 509–531.

Royal Decree (2007) *Dahir N° 1–07–208 Regarding the Setting up of the Council for the Moroccan Community Abroad*. 21 December 2007. http://www.ccme.org.ma/images/conseil/Dahir_CCME_ANGLAIS.pdf, accessed 9 February 2014.

Russakoff, Dale and Dan Eggen (2007) 'Six Charged in Plot to Attack Fort Dix'. *The Washington Post*, 9 May. http://www.washingtonpost.com/wp-dyn/content/article/2007/05/08/AR2007050800465.html, accessed 10 May 2013.

Ryan, Bernard and Valsamis Mitsilegas (eds.) (2010) *Extraterritorial Immigration Control: Legal Challenges*. Leiden: Brill.

Rygiel, Kim (2010) *Globalizing Citizenship*. Vancouver: University of British Columbia.

Rygiel, Kim (2011a) 'Bordering Solidarities: Migrant Activism and the Politics of Movement and Camps at Calais'. *Citizenship Studies*, 15, 1, 1–19.

Rygiel, Kim (2011b) 'Governing Borderzones of Mobility Through e-borders: The Politics of Embodied Mobility'. In: Vicki Squire (ed.) *The Contested Politics of Mobility: Borderzones and Irregularity*. London, New York: Routledge, 143–168.

Rygiel, Kim (2012) 'Politicizing Camps: Forging Transgressive Citizenships in and Through Transit'. *Citizenship Studies*, 16, 5/6, 807–825.

Sack, Detlef (2000) 'Step Across the Border, Stopp at Frankfurt's Frontier! Zum "Flughafenverfahren" in Frankfurt/Main'. *vorgänge 150*, 39, 2, 14–22.

SafeCom (n. d.) 'Keeping Perspective: Australia's Boat Arrivals'. http://www.safecom.org.au/pdfs/boat-arrivals-stats.pdf, accessed 9 November 2013.

Salamon, Lester M. (1995) *Partners in Public Service: Government-Nonprofit Relations in the Modern Welfare State*. Baltimore: Johns Hopkins University Press.

Santos, Fernanda (2006) 'Coming to Terms with the Men on the Corner'. *The New York Times*, 17 December. http://www.nytimes.com/2006/12/17/nyregion/nyregionspecial2/17Rday.html?pagewanted=all&_r=0, accessed 14 May 2013.

Sassen, Saskia (1997) 'Immigration Policy in a Global Economy'. *SAIS Review*, 17, 2, 1–19.

Sayad, Abdelmalek (2004) *The Suffering of the Immigrant*. Cambridge: Polity Press.

Schaefer, Sarah, Greg Austin and Kate Parker (2005) *Turks in Europe: Why Are We Afraid?* London: The Foreign Policy Centre.

Schiffauer, Werner (2010) *Nach dem Islamismus – Die Islamische Gemeinschaft Milli Görüs. Eine Ethnographie*. Berlin: Suhrkamp.

Schneider, Anne L. and Helen Ingram (1997) *Policy Design for Democracy*. Lawrence, KS: University Press of Kansas.

Schönwalder, Karen (2001) *Einwanderung und ethnische Pluralität: Politische Entscheidungen und öffentliche Debatten in Großbritannien und der Bundesrepublik von den 1950er bis zu den 1970er Jahren*. Essen: Klartext.

Schumacher, Sebastian and Johannes Peyrl (2012) *Fremdenrecht*. 4th ed. Wien: ÖGB Verlag.
Schwenken, Helen (2006) *Rechtlos, aber nicht ohne Stimme. Politische Mobilisierungen um irreguläre Migration in die Europäische Union*. Bielefeld: Transcript.
Schwiertz, Helge (forthcoming, 2014) ' "Für uns existiert kein Blatt im Gesetzbuch". Migrantische Kämpfe und der Einsatz der radikalen Demokratie'. In: Stefan Rother, Uwe Hunger and Roswitha Pioch (eds.) *Migration und Demokratie: Studien zu einem neuen Forschungsfeld*. Wiesbaden: Springer VS.
Scott, Joan Wallach (1996) *Only Paradoxes to Offer: French Feminists and the Rights of Man*. Cambridge: Harvard University Press.
Semple, Kirk (2011) 'U.S. Orders 72 Indonesians in New Jersey to Leave'. *The New York Times*, 7 December.
Sezgin, Zeynep (2008) 'Turkish Migrants' Organizations: Promoting Tolerance towards the Diversity of Turkish Migrants in Germany'. *International Journal of Sociology*, 38, 2, 80–97.
Sezgin, Zeynep (2010) 'Türkische Migrantenorganisationen in Deutschland – Zwischen Mitgliederinteressen und institutioneller Umwelt'. In Ludger Pries and Zeynep Sezgin (eds.) *Jenseits von 'Identität oder Integration'*. Wiesbaden: VS Verlag für Sozialwissenschaften, 201–232.
Skocpol, Theda (1985) 'Bringing the State Back In: Strategies of Analysis in Current Research'. In: Peter B. Evans, Dietrich Rueschemayer and Theda Skocpol (eds.) *Bringing the State Back In*. Cambridge: Cambridge University Press, 3–37.
Smith, Michael Peter and Luis Eduardo Guarnizo (eds.) (1998) *Transnationalism from Below*. New Brunswick, NJ: Transaction Publishers.
Smith, Robert C. (1997) 'Reflections on Migration, the State and the Construction, Durability and Newness of Transnational Life'. In: Ludger Pries (ed.) *Transnationale Migration. Soziale Welt*, Sonderband 12. Baden-Baden: Nomos, 197–217.
Smith, Robert C. (2003) 'Migrant Membership as an Instituted Process: Transnationalization, the State and the Extra-Territorial Conduct of Mexican Politics'. *International Migration Review*, 37, 2, 297–343.
Smith, Rogers (2007) 'Alien Rights, Citizen Rights, and the Politics of Restriction'. In: Carol M. Swain (ed.) *Debating Immigration*. Cambridge: Cambridge University Press, 114–126.
Smith, Steven Rathgeb and Michael Lipsky (1993) *Nonprofits for Hire: The Welfare State in the Age of Contracting*. Cambridge, MA: Harvard University Press.
Soguk, Nevzat (2007) 'Border's Capture: Insurrectional Politics, Border-Crossing Humans, and the New Political'. In: P.K. Rajaram and Carl Grundy-Warr (eds.) *Borderscapes: Hidden Geographies and Politics at Territory's Edge*. London and Minneapolis: University of Minnesota Press, 283–308.
Söhn, Janina (2011) *Rechtsstatus und Bildungschancen. Die staatliche Ungleichbehandlung von Migrantengruppen und ihre Konsequenzen*. Wiesbaden: VS.
Soja, Edward W. (1995) *Postmodern Geographies*. London: Verso.
Sökefeld, Martin (2008) *Struggling for Recognition: The Alevi Movement in Germany and in Transnational Space*. Oxford and New York: Berghahn.
Solmaz, Ali (1999) 'Deutschland als zentrales Operationsfeld des türkischen Geheimdienstes MIT'. *Trend*. http://www.trend.infopartisan.net/trd0200/t210200.html, accessed 31 December 2012.
Soysal, Yasemin Nuhoglu (1994) *The Limits of Citizenship: Migrants and Postnational Membership in Europe*. Chicago: University of Chicago Press.

Spiegel Online (2000) 'Lufthansa: "Deportation Class" sorgt für Tumulte'. 15 June 2000. http://www.spiegel.de/wirtschaft/lufthansa-deportation-class-sorgt-fuer-tumulte-a-80926.html, accessed 3 February 2014.

Spiegel Online (2001) Online-Demo: Flop-Flop, Hurra! 20 June 2001. http://www.spiegel.de/netzwelt/web/online-demo-flop-flop-hurra-a-140626.html, accessed 3 February.

Spoto, MaryAnn (2006) 'Town Settles Suit on Latino Laborers: Freehold Must Pay $278,000 in Fees and Respect Rights of Migrants'. *The Star-Ledger* [NJ], 15 November.

Squire, Vicki (ed.) (2011) *The Contested Politics of Mobility: Borderzones and Irregularity*. London, New York: Routledge.

Stasiulis, Daiva (2008) 'The Migration-Citizenship Nexus'. In: Engin F. Isin (ed.) *Recasting the Social in Citizenship*. Toronto: University of Toronto Press, 134–161.

Stelzenmüller, Constanze (2007) 'Turkey's EU Bid: The View from Germany'. In: Nathalie Tocci (ed.) *Conditionality, Impact and Prejudice in EU-Turkey Relations*. IAI-TEPAV Report, July. Rome: Istituto Affari Internazionali, 105–118.

Stern, Joachim (2012) 'Ius Pecuniae – Staatsbürgerschaft zwischen ausreichendem Lebensunterhalt, Mindestsicherung und Menschenwürde'. In: Julia Dahlvik, Heinz Fassmann and Wiebke Sievers (eds.) *Migration und Integration – wissenschaftliche Perspektiven aus Österreich. Jahrbuch 1/2011*. Göttingen: V&R unipress, 55–74.

Stone, Deborah (2002). *Policy Paradox: The Art of Political Decision Making*. New York: W.W. Norton.

Strik, Tineke and Anita Böcker (2011) 'Language and Knowledge Tests for Permanent Residence Rights. Integration Tests, Help or Hindrance?'. *European Journal of Migration and Law*, 13, 2, 157–184.

Sullivan, Sean and Clement Scott (2013) 'The Debate over a Path to Citizenship is Resolved among the Public, if not in Congress'. *The Washington Post*, 29 March. http://www.washingtonpost.com/blogs/the-fix/wp/2013/03/29/the-debate-over-a-path-to-citizenship-is-resolved-among-the-public-if-not-in-congress, accessed 7 December 2013.

Surdin, Ashley (2009) 'Crossover Appeal: Border Patrol Uses Music to Cross a Cultural Line'. *The Washington Post*, 15 March. http://www.washingtonpost.com/wp-dyn/content/article/2009/03/13/AR2009031304234.html, accessed 24 February 2013.

Swyngedow, Eric (1997) 'Neither Global nor Local: "Glocalization" and the Politics of Scale'. In Kevin R. Cox (ed.) *Spaces of Globalization: Reasserting the Power of the Local*. New York and London: The Guilford Press, 137–166.

Syrians blocked in Calais (2013) 'Open letter to Europe', 25 October. http://calaismigrantsolidarity.wordpress.com/page/2/, accessed 10 November 2013.

Taş, Savaş (2012) *Der ethnische Dominanzanspruch des türkischen Nationalismus. Eine diskursanalytische Studie zur Ideologie des türkischen Staates und der MHP*. Münster: Westfälisches Dampfboot.

Tekin, C. Beyza (2010) *Representation and Othering in Discourse. The Construction of Turkey in the EU Context*. Amsterdam: John Benjamins Publishing Company.

Teixere, Fiona (2006) *At the Gate of Fortress Europe: Irregular Immigration and Malta*. Rennes: Unpublished master thesis.

Thiollet, Helene (2011) 'Migration as Diplomacy: Labor Migrants, Refugees, and Arab Regional Politics in the Oil-Rich Countries'. *International Labor and Working-Class History*, 79, 1, 103–121.

Thomson, Mark (2003) 'Images of Sangatte: Political Representations of Asylum Seeking in France and the UK'. Sussex Migration Working Papers

No. 18. https://www.sussex.ac.uk/webteam/gateway/file.php?name=mwp18.pdf& site=252, accessed 10 November 2013.
Tolley, Erin and Robert Young (eds.) (2011) *Immigrant Settlement Policy in Canadian Municipalities*. Montreal and Kingston: McGill-Queens University Press.
Tondini, Matteo (2012) 'The Legality of Intercepting Boat People Under Search and Rescue and Border Control Operations'. *Journal of International Maritime Law*, 18, 59–74.
Transit Migration (2006) 'Topics: The Autonomy of Migration'. www.transitmigration.org/homethemen_e.html, accessed 17 October 2013.
Transit Migration (2007) *Turbulente Ränder. Neue Perspektiven auf Migration an den Grenzen Europas*. Bielefeld: Transcript.
Tronti, Mario (1966) *Operai e capitale*. Turin: Einaudi.
Türkmen, Ceren (2010) 'Rethinking Class Making'. In Günther Thien (ed.) *Klassen im Postfordismus*. Münster: Westfälisches Dampfboot, 202–234.
UK Border Agency (2009) 'Report of the Independent Monitoring Board on the Short Term Holding Facilities at the Heathrow Airport', February 2008–January 2009. http://www.imb.gov uk/annual-reports/09-annual-reports/Heathrow_2008 -2009.pdf?view=Binary, accessed 4 January 2013.
UNHCR, United Nations High Commissioner for Refugees (2007a) 'Advisory Opinion on the Extraterritorial Application of the Non-Refoulement Obligations under the 1951 Convention relating to the Status of Refugees and its 1967 Protocol'. http://www.unhcr.org/cgi-bin/texis/vtx/refworld/rwmain?docid-=45f17a1a4& page=search, accessed 14 January 2013.
UNHCR, United Nations High Commissioner for Refugees (2007b) 'Refugee Protection and Mixed Migration: A 10-Point Plan of Action'. http://www.unhcr.org/4742a30b4 .html, accessed 10 November 2013.
UNHCR, United Nations High Commissioner for Refugees (2008) 'Mixed Migration Flow: Pictures and Testimonies from Bossaso'. *UNHCR Somalia*. http://www.unhcr.org/487b44f92.html, accessed 10 November 2013.
UNHCR, United Nations High Commissioner for Refugees (2009a) 'France Dismantles a Migrant Camp at Calais'. *Briefing notes*, 22 September. http://www.unhcr.org/4ab8a65a9.html, accessed 10 November 2013.
UNHCR, United Nations High Commissioner for Refugees (2009b) 'UNHCR Deeply Concerned over Returns from Italy to Libya'. *Press Release*, 7 May. http://www.unhcr.org/4a02d4546.html, accessed 19 July 2010.
UNHCR, United Nations High Commissioner for Refugees (2012) 'Letter to Chris Bowen, Minister for Immigration and Citizenship Australia'. 9 October. http://unhcr.org.au/unhcr/images/121009%20response%20to%20minister%20on%20 png.pdf, accessed 21 November 2013.
UNHCR, United Nations High Commissioner for Refugees and IMO, International Maritime Organization (2006) 'Rescue at Sea, A Guide to Principles and Practice as Applied to Migrants and Refugees'. http://www.imo.org/OurWork/Facilitation/IllegalMigrants/Documents/Leaflet%20Rescue%20at%20sea.pdf, accessed 24 February 2013.
United Nations (1951) 'Convention Relating to the Status of Refugees'. 28 July. http://treaties.un.org/pages/ViewDetailsII.aspx?&src=UNTSONLINE&mtdsg_no= V~2&chapter=5&Temp=mtdsg2&lang=en, accessed 18 October 2013.
United Nations (1982) 'United Nations Convention on the Law of the Sea (UNCLOS Convention)'. http://www.un.org/Depts/los/convention_agreements/texts/unclos/closindx.htm, accessed 24 February 2013.

Uprooted People (2001) 'Newsletter Issue 14, February 2001'. http://www.wcc-coe.org/wcc/what/international/uprooted/uproot14.html, accessed 9 November 2013.

US Census Bureau (2010) 'Race and Hispanic Origin of the Foreign-Born Population in the United States: 2007'. www.census.gov/prod/2010pubs/acs-11.pdf, accessed 7 December 2013.

US Senate (2013) *Border Security, Economic Opportunity and Immigration Modernization Act* (Sponsor Sen. Schumer, Charles), Committee Report 113–040. http://thomas.loc.gov/cgi-bin/cpquery/R?cp113:FLD010:@1%28sr040, accessed 10 February 2014.

USAK (2009) 'Fourth USAK Foreign Policy Perception Survey 2009'. 16 August. http://www.turkishweekly.net/news/86952/4th-usak-turkish-foreign-policy-perception-survey-2009.htm, accessed 9 December 2010.

Varada Raj, Kartik (2006) 'Paradoxes on the Borders of Europe'. *International Feminist Journal of Politics*, 8, 4, 512–534.

Varsanyi, Monica W. (2008) 'Immigration Policing Through the Backdoor: City Ordinances, the "right to the city," and the Exclusion of Undocumented day Laborers'. *Urban Geography*, 29, 1, 29–52

Vasilache, Andreas (2008) 'Die Partikularisierung des Staates: Ein Problemaufriss'. *sozialer sinn*, 9, 121–140.

Viennot, Éliane (1996) 'Les femmes d'Etat de l'Ancien Régime'. In: Éliane Viennot (ed.) *La démocracie 'à la Française' ou les Femmes Indésirables*. Paris: Université Paris XII, 51–61.

Viviano, Francesco (2007) 'Tre giorni fra le onde le navi non ci aiutavano'. *La Repubblica*, 28 May.

Vobruba, Georg (2010) 'Die postnationale Grenzkonstellation'. *Zeitschrift für Politik*, 57, 4, 434–452.

Wahnich, Sophie (1997) *L'Impossible Citoyen: L'Étranger dans le Discours de la Révolution Française*. Paris: Albin Michel.

Waldinger, Roger D. (2013) 'Beyond Transnationalism: An Alternative Perspective On Immigrants' Homeland Connections'. In: Marc R. Rosenblum and Daniel J. Tichenor (eds.) *The Oxford Handbook Of The Politics Of International Migration*. Oxford: Oxford University Press, 74–102.

Walter, Jochen (2008) *Die Türkei – 'das Ding auf der Schwelle': (De)konstruktionen der Grenzen Europas*. Wiesbaden: VS Springer.

Walters, William (2004) 'Secure Borders, Safe Haven, Domopolitics'. *Citizenship Studies*, 8, 3, 237–260.

Weber, Bernd (2010) 'Europe's neighbourhood between Conditionality, Network Governance and Bargaining'. *CERI-Sciences Po Study*. http://www.ceri-sciencespo.com/themes/ue/articles/enp_weber.pdf, accessed 9 July 2013.

Weber, Leanne (2006) 'The Shifting Frontiers of Migration Control'. In: Sharon Pickering and Leanne Weber (eds.) *Borders, Mobility and Technologies of Control*. Amsterdam: Springer, 21–44.

Weber, Leanne (2013) *Policing Non-Citizens*. Abingdon: Routledge.

Webber, Frances (2011) 'How Voluntary are Voluntary Returns?'. *Race & Class*, 52, 98–107.

Weil, Patrick (1991) *La France et ses Étrangers: L'Aventure d'une Politique de l'Immigration de 1938 à nos Jours*. Paris: Gallimard.

Weinzierl, Ruth and Ursula Lisson (2007) 'Grenzschutz und Menschenrechte – Eine europarechtliche und seerechtliche Studie'. Berlin: German Institute for Human Rights.

Welcome to Europe (n. d.) 'Homepage'. http://www.w2u.net, accessed 7 November 2013.

Welge, Ines (2009) *Hastig, unfair, mangelhaft: Untersuchung zum Flughafenverfahren gem §18 AsylVfG*. Frankfurt/Main: Förderverein Pro Asyl e.V.
Wieviorka, Michel (1997) *Une Société Fragmentée? Le Multiculturalisme en Débat*. Paris: La Découverte.
Wihtol de Wenden, Catherine and Margo Corona DeLey (1986) 'French Immigration Policy Reform and the Female Migrant'. In: Rita Simon James and Caroline B. Brettell (eds.) *International Migration and the Female Experience*. Totowa, NJ: Rowman and Littlefield, 197–212.
Willis, Andrew (2010) 'Economic Realism Will Ease Anti-Turkish Feeling, Joschka Fischer Says'. *EU Observer*, 1 October. http://euobserver.com/news/30932, accessed 24 January 2014.
Wilpert, Czarina (1984) 'Returning and Remaining: Return among Turkish Migrants in Germany'. In: Daniel Kubat (ed.) *The Politics of Return: International Return Migration in Europe*. Rome: Centro Studi Emigrazione, 101–112.
Wilson, Dean and Leanne Weber (2008) 'Surveillance, Risk and Pre-emption on the Australian Border'. *Surveillance and Society*, 5, 2, 124–141.
Wimmel, Andreas (2006) *Transnationale Diskurse in Europa. Der Streit um den Türkei-Beitritt in Deutschland, Frankreich und Großbritannien*. Frankfurt/Main, New York: Campus.
Wong, Tom K. (2012) '287(g) and the Politics of Interior Immigration Control in the United States: Explaining Local Cooperation with Federal Immigration Authorities'. *Journal of Ethnic and Migration Studies*, 38, 5, 737–756.
World Bank (2011) *Migration and Remittances Factbook 2011*. Washington, DC: World Bank.
Wunn, Ina and Asiye Berge-Traore (2007) 'Die Union der Türkisch-Islamischen Kulturvereine in Europa e.V./ATIB und ihre Vorläufer'. In: Ina Wunn (ed.) *Muslimische Gruppierungen in Deutschland: Ein Handbuch*. Stuttgart: W. Kohlhammer, 65–70.
Yanow, Dvora (1996) *How Does a Policy Mean? Interpreting Policy and Organizational Actions*. Washington, DC: Georgetown University Press.
Young, Iris Marion (1989) 'Polity and Group Difference: A Critique of the Ideal of Universal Citizenship'. *Ethics*, 99, 250–274.
Yükseker, Deniz (2004) 'Trust and Gender in a Transnational Marketplace: The Public Culture of Laleli, Istanbul'. *Public Culture*, 16, 47–65.
Yurdakul, Gökçe (2009) *From Guest Workers into Muslims: The Transformation of Turkish Immigrant Associations in Germany*. Newcastle, UK: Cambridge Scholars Press.
Yuval-Davis, Nira (1999) 'The "Multi-Layered Citizen": Citizenship in the Age of "Glocalization"'. *International Feminist Journal of Politics*, 1, 1, 119–136.
Zaman (2007) 'Babacan: No "date" means Turks not Wanted in Europe'. In: *Today's Zaman*. 17 February. http://www.todayszaman.com/news-103155-babacan-no-date-means-turks-not-wanted-in-europe.html, accessed 23 September 2013.
Zaman (2013) 'EU Needs New Vision on Relations with Turkey, Turkish FM Urges'. In: *Today's Zaman*, 22 May. http://www.todayszaman.com/news-316666-eu-needs-new-vision-on-relations-with-turkey-turkish-fm-urges.html, accessed 23 September 2013.
Zedner, Lucia (2007) 'Pre-Crime and Post-Criminology?'. *Theoretical Criminology*, 11, 261–281.
Zentrum für Türkeistudien (2006) *Türkei Jahrbuch*. Essen: Klartext.
Zisenwine, Daniel (2007) 'From Hassan II to Muhammed VI: Plus Ca Change?' In: Bruce Maddy-Weitzman and Daniel Zisenwine (eds.) *The Maghrib in the New Century. Identity, Religion, and Politics*. Gainesville: University Press of Florida, 132–149.

Index

Abschiebungsbeobachtung (detention monitoring), 86
activism, activists, 5, 12, 51, 89, 97, 101, 137, 143–4, 150–2, 155–6, 162–3, 173, 178–81, 195–204, 211, 217, 223
  see also campaign; mobilization; movement; protest
advocacy, 11, 86, 111, 114–15, 119, 153
Afghanistan, Afghan, 47, 50, 57–8, 171–2, 175–6, 178–9, 183–6
AFM, Armed Forces Malta, 30–1, 33, 36–43
Africa, 32, 49–50, 57, 105–6, 111, 149, 162, 186, 194, 216, 223
AFSC, American Friends Service Committee, 114–16, 121–2
Agamben, Georgio, 5, 78, 137, 173
airport, 10, 74, 77–9, 80–9, 95
  detention at, 79, 86
  see also deportation
AKP, *Adalet ve Kalkınma Partisi*, 68, 195–6, 201
Algeria, Algerian, 83, 163–5, 194, 206, 208, 214
Amnesty International, 75, 83, 86, 109
Andalusia, *Al Andalus*, 215
Ankara Agreement, 51
anti-immigrant, 11, 72, 90–1, 100–1, 133
antiracism, 178–80
antiterrorism, 109
apprehension, apprehending, 50, 58, 90, 92, 96–7, 101–2
Arab spring, 209, 216, 222–3
Arendt, Hannah, 148, 208
  see also right to have rights
argumentative pattern, 11, 62–9, 87, 97, 138, 157, 177, 213, 222
  see also discourse
Arizona, 90, 95
Armenia(n), 67
associations (of migrants, political), 12, 57, 65, 88–9, 117, 155, 187–8, 192, 196–7, 199, 201–3, 219

asylum, asylum seekers, 1, 6, 9–10, 17, 20–5, 28, 32, 34–7, 44–58, 73–8, 80–1, 84, 86, 109, 114, 125, 141–2, 144, 147–50, 175, 179–80, 182–4, 197, 222
  see also refugees
Australia, 2, 8–9, 16–25, 27–9, 57, 73, 80, 91, 141, 155
Austria, Austrian, 4, 7, 11, 57, 63, 72, 123–4, 127–36, 166
autonomy of migration, 4, 137, 142, 155, 170, 172, 178–80, 185–8, 191, 193–4, 198, 200–4, 220

backdoor immigration, 110
backdoor immigration control, 6
  see also border control
Balibar, Étienne, 70, 156–60, 222
Balkan(s), 50, 65
Barka, Ben, 208
Belgium, 57, 180
beliefs, 44, 177, 221
  see also argumentative pattern; discourse
biometric technologies, 141
border
  borderisation, 71, 149
  borderland(s), 10–12, 61, 73–4, 77–89, 171–87
  borderline, 7, 61, 219–20
  border-making technologies, 3, 5–7, 9–11, 15, 17, 20, 71–2, 76–7, 141–2, 144, 154, 156, 182
  borderzone(s), 16, 158, 163, 167–8
  control, 3, 6–7, 9–11, 15–20, 23, 29–30, 34, 37, 52, 71, 81, 83–4, 88, 90, 108, 141–2, 149, 158, 178, 219–22
  external, 1, 3–4, 10, 16, 20, 25, 29–30, 46, 71–2, 104, 121–3, 153, 167
  externalisation, 5, 16–17, 142
  interiorisation, 5, 10, 90–4, 96, 102

253

border – *continued*
  internal, 1, 3–4, 6–8, 11, 20, 28–9, 53, 71, 104, 121–3, 153, 163, 167
  offshore, 5, 17
  onshore, 5
  postnational border constellation, 16, 61
  regime, 3, 5, 7, 9, 11, 15–16, 49, 51, 72, 128, 137, 155–6, 166, 173, 184
  structurally embedded, 3, 7–8, 17, 25, 72, 221
Bosporus, 70
bureaucracies, bureaucrats, 8, 11, 51, 58, 128, 134, 158

camp, 1, 23, 74, 86, 89, 137, 173–84, 195
campaign, 17, 20–2, 68, 86, 98–100, 115–17, 130, 150–4, 177, 215
  see also activism; mobilization; movement; NGO; protest
Canada, 104–6, 110, 141, 155
capitalism, capitalist, 12, 60, 158, 189, 191, 193–4
CCME, Council of the Moroccan Community Abroad, *Conseil de la Communauté Marocaine à l'Étranger*, 211–13, 217
CCTV, Closed Circuit Television, 77, 84
Ceuta, 184, 206
children, childhood, 40, 72, 86, 91, 99, 104–9, 114–19, 129, 132, 135, 149, 154–8, 163–6, 175
Christian, Christianity, 69–70
church, 83–4, 86, 88, 117, 178–9
citizenship, 1–12, 18, 22–3, 49, 54, 60, 64, 66, 69, 72, 91, 93–4, 99, 102, 104, 110, 119–27, 134–5, 137–9, 141–8, 150–5, 157–62, 164, 166–74, 176, 178, 180, 182, 184, 186–94, 196, 198, 200–12, 214–16, 218–23
  acts of, 1, 5, 85–6, 89, 92, 145–7, 152, 197, 220
  à la carte, 138, 208
  enact oneself as citizen/political subject, 145, 154, 167
  exclusive, 206
  as government, 143–4, 148, 154
  regime, 4, 127, 138, 143, 193, 201, 204
  social, 6, 91, 93, 125–6, 219–21

city level, 8, 65, 67, 87, 91–2, 96, 99, 105, 110, 112–13, 116–22, 151–5, 166, 171, 215
  policies, 122
  see also localization; municipality
clandestine, clandestinisation, 156, 160, 163, 165, 168, 175, 185
  see also irregular
coalition, 10, 74–5, 77, 79–81, 83, 88–9, 115, 133, 168, 196, 221
  see also activism; campaign; movement; mobilisation
coercive power, practices, 9, 17, 19–20, 29, 76
colonial(ism), colony, 12, 69, 169, 190, 194, 208, 214–15, 223
constructivist, social construction, 3, 6, 9, 17, 29, 44–5, 57, 62–3, 69, 74, 123, 137–8, 156–7, 160–2, 167, 169, 174, 183, 205–7, 210–11, 214, 216, 218, 222
contention, 21, 53, 80, 167, 189
  see also campaign; movements; mobilization; protest
crime
  crime control, 17
  criminalised, 54, 208
  criminal justice, enforcement, 18, 108–9, 114
  criminal offence, crime, criminality, 17, 78, 90, 92, 96, 107
  criminals, criminal networks, 15, 21, 92
  deportable crimes, 109, 112, 131
  immigrant criminality, 95–7, 107, 109, 131, 148, 169
  post-crime orientation/logic, 18
  pre-crime society, 18
critical geography, 77
culturalism, 10, 60, 66–70, 222
Cyprus, 61

death of migrants, 9, 15, 24, 32, 86, 148, 150
democracy, democratic, 2, 24, 159, 162, 202, 212, 222
  Christian democratic, 64, 81, 83, 88
  Social democratic, 64, 66, 81, 83, 196
denizen(ship), 123–6, 130–1

deportability, 134
  see also detention, detainees, detainment
deportation(s), 9–10, 17–18, 24, 28, 37, 74, 85–7, 90–4, 104–9, 114, 116, 125, 128–9, 133, 144, 148–50, 154, 156, 175–6, 180, 200, 221
  airport, 10, 74, 76–8, 80–9, 95, 176
  of convicted criminals, deportable crimes, 109, 112, 131
  see also removal
detention, detainees, detainment, 17, 20, 22, 25, 28–9, 36, 50, 76–9, 82–6, 91–8, 104–6, 141–4, 148–50, 176, 221
  duration, 25, 83
  for (minor) crimes, 109, 112, 131
  offshore, externalized, 17, 20–1, 25, 74, 142, 221
DIAC, Department of Immigration and Citizenship (Australia), 18–20, 24–8
diaspora, 3, 7, 138, 161, 192, 205–10, 212–14, 216–17
diplomacy, 9, 16, 44–6, 51, 53, 56–7, 61, 70, 139, 222
discourse, 6, 10–11, 15, 45, 66–7, 74–5, 77, 79–81, 83, 88–9, 96, 104, 106, 111, 120, 138, 146, 157, 169, 172, 183, 206, 210, 214, 217, 222
  diasporic, 161, 206, 210, 214, 216–17
  discourse coalition, 10, 74–5, 77, 79–81, 83, 88–9
  dominant, hegemonic, 11, 77, 106, 162, 174
  gendered, 167
  official, 45, 63, 74, 106, 138, 162
  opposing, counter-hegemonic, 67, 74, 88, 172, 174
  struggle of, 77, 79, 88
  see also argumentative pattern; belief
domopolitics, 7, 10–11, 72, 94, 102, 219–21
Dublin II, 34, 75, 86, 142, 177, 184

Ecuador(ian), 111, 119, 216, 223
emigration, emigrant, 2, 7–8, 12, 46–9, 55, 57, 137–9, 188, 191, 205–6, 219, 223
employer(s), 25, 41–2, 71, 91, 99, 127–8, 170, 191, 197, 199–201, 203

  organization, 191, 199–203
  sanction, 26, 91
employment, 1, 10, 26, 48, 53, 91, 93, 98–9, 127–9, 131–2, 147, 165
enforcement, 5, 7, 9, 17, 19–20, 24–5, 28, 32, 38, 90–102, 104, 106–12, 114–15, 117, 121, 153–4, 220
Erdoğan, Recep Tayyip, 65
Ethiopia, 152, 183
Europe
  borders of Europe, 6, 10–11, 16, 30, 44, 50, 60–70, 77, 139, 141–2, 171
  Eastern, 57–8, 118, 190
  EU acquis, 47, 54
  Europeanisation, 10, 44, 47, 56–7, 72
  European Area of Justice, Freedom and Security, 80
  European border agency Frontex, 15–16, 42, 53, 76, 149
  European Commission, 15, 46, 52, 58, 61, 75, 132, 142, 182
  European Court of Human Rights, 37, 78, 130
  European Court of Justice, 15, 75
  European identity, 52, 61, 63
  European Parliament, 34, 46, 58, 76, 89, 176
  European refugee protection system, 9, 30, 36, 182
  European state project, 222
  European Union (EU), 6–10, 16, 30–1, 34, 37, 41, 44–9, 51–70, 73–7, 80–1, 86, 88, 123, 126–7, 131, 135–6, 139, 142, 150–1, 157, 169–71, 175, 178, 182–4, 207, 216, 221–2
  Europol, 53
  Eurosur, European Border Surveillance System, 15
  Eurotunnel, 12
  Euro-Turkey relations, border, negotiations, 6, 45–8, 62–70
  Fortress Europe, 16, 61
  Welcome to Europe, 150–1
exception
  French Republican, 156–7
  logic of, 137, 173
  state of, 10, 74, 78, 80, 88, 109
expulsion, *see* deportation

externalisation, 5, 8–9, 16–17, 142
extraterritorial, 37, 71, 78, 209

family, 21, 25, 28, 48–9, 86, 94, 103, 109, 114–16, 118, 125–6, 128–30, 132–4, 136, 141, 162–6, 184, 211
  life, 129–30
  members, 49, 114–15, 118, 133, 136, 141
  reunification, 48, 126, 133–4, 136, 162–6
  ties, 109, 184, 211
federal, 1, 10, 12, 29, 48, 72, 81, 90–7, 100, 108–17, 121, 153–4, 198
female, *femme*, 161–2, 169–70
  see also women
feminist theories, 146, 162, 169–70, 173
FIR, Flight Information Region, 33
forced, 22, 27–8, 37, 56, 83, 101, 146, 148, 160, 163, 167–8, 183, 190, 197
  forced return, 183
Foucault, Michel, 5, 11, 71, 77, 137, 142, 144, 154, 189, 207
FPÖ, Freedom Party (Austria), 133
framing, 115, 117, 120–1, 138, 174, 178–80, 184–5
France, 4–5, 10–12, 57, 60–70, 78, 138, 152, 156–70, 171–86
free movement, 51–3, 58, 126, 129, 142, 179
Frontex, 15–16, 42, 53, 76, 149

gender, 5, 39, 84, 96, 143, 146, 156, 158, 162–3, 165–9, 172, 193
Geneva Refugee Convention, 35, 51, 78, 179
Germany, 1, 5, 10, 12, 45, 48, 58, 60–70, 77, 80–3, 89, 125, 127, 132, 138, 170, 183, 187–204
Gezi, 61
Ghana, 111
governance, 5, 17, 19, 29, 44, 104, 125, 171, 206, 218, 221
  good, 46, 56
governmentality, 5, 153
Greece, 54, 59, 75, 84, 142, 149–50, 155, 175, 181–4, 190, 194, 204
guest worker regime/system, 48, 55, 125, 128, 130, 138, 187, 190–1, 202–3

hegemony, hegemonic, 11, 52, 159–60, 168–70, 174, 177, 189–90, 214, 217, 222
heteronormative, 161
homeland, 93, 191, 193, 205, 207–13, 216
  homeland security, 91–5, 97, 102, 109
housing, 91, 93, 97–9, 119, 126, 130, 132, 135, 147, 158, 162, 165–6, 176, 181, 200–1
human rights, 10, 19, 23, 35–7, 45, 61, 65, 73–5, 77–81, 83–4, 86, 88–9, 109, 115, 128–30, 157, 163, 172, 176, 179, 184, 219, 223

ICE, United States Immigration and Customs Enforcement, 95–7, 102
identity, 6, 52, 60–1, 63, 66, 68, 117, 137–8, 143, 153, 155, 158–9, 167, 171, 176, 181, 205–6, 209–11, 213–14, 216, 222–3
  collective, 60–1
  construction, 137, 206, 210, 214, 216, 222
  European, 52, 61, 63
  national, 6, 63, 68, 158, 176, 181, 205, 213–14
IIRIRA, Illegal Immigration Reform and Immigrant Responsibility Act (United States), 92
illegal migration, migrants, illegality, *see* irregular
  illegal 'black' deportations, 149
  illegal practices, 9, 31, 41, 149
  'no one is illegal' network/group, 86, 115, 151, 153
imagined community, 3, 61, 73, 77, 205, 207, 210
immigration
  act, 107, 215
  authorities, 27, 126, 172
  control, 11, 19, 71–2, 100–1, 139, 157, 159, 219
  country, 47, 57, 65, 207
  enforcement, 7, 9, 28, 91–7, 102, 108–9, 112, 114–15, 154; *see also* apprehension
  law, 28, 115, 153, 160, 164, 166

officials, 20; *see also* bureaucrats
policy, 6, 48–9, 53–4, 92, 105, 108, 110, 114–16, 123–4, 133, 135, 156, 157, 160, 163, 165, 168, 188, 202–6, 222
reform, 92, 109, 136, 218
regime, *see* migration; regime
restriction, 92, 161–2
state, 2, 207
status, 26, 96, 98, 107, 116, 153, 156
stop, 208
system, 46–7, 56, 108, 115, 127, 141
see also migration
immobility, immobilised, 4, 137, 173–4
IMO, International Maritime Organization, 32–3, 35, 39–40
impossibility, 160–3, 165, 168
impossible subjects, 5, 121, 158–9, 160–1, 169, 216, 223
India, Indian, 98, 105
inequality, 7–8, 48, 125, 137, 143, 209
infra-droit, 138, 163, 167–8
see also rights
integration
agreement, 133, 135–6
conditions, 126, 133
difficulties, 45, 66
European, 44, 56, 60–1, 67
language, 11, 126
of migrants/immigrants/emigrants, 49, 52, 55, 63–4, 66–7, 70, 108, 111–13, 121, 128, 187
policy, 11, 110–11, 122–4, 126
process, 47, 132
requirements, 11, 123–6, 132–6
intellectual, 66, 157, 170, 178, 208, 212, 215
intent management, 6, 9, 17–24, 29, 85, 88, 221
interiorisation, 5, 10, 90–4, 96–7, 99, 102
internationalisation, 8, 12, 189–90, 193, 203
intersectional(ity), 135, 168–9
IOM, International Organization for Migration, 57, 175, 183–4
Iran, 47, 50, 54, 57, 63
Iraq(i), 50, 54, 57, 63, 172, 175, 178, 183
irregular migration, migrants, irregularity, 5–8, 10–12, 15, 24, 33–4, 38, 41, 45, 48–54, 58, 68, 72, 76–7, 86, 90–2, 94–102, 103–22, 124, 129, 137, 139, 141–2, 144–5, 147–50, 156–7, 162–3, 166–9, 171–85, 207, 212, 215–16, 218–21, 223
citizenship of irregular/undocumented migrants, 138
irregular emigration, 139, 212
Islam, Islamic, Islamist, 10, 60, 63, 65–8, 95, 188, 195–8, 201, 203, 206, 214–17, 222–3
Islamic awakening, 215
Islamophobic, 45
Istanbul, 151–2, 154, 195
Italy, 4, 15, 30–3, 36–9, 42, 63, 125, 142, 175, 181, 183, 190, 193, 196, 198, 204

juridical politics, 219
Jus sanguinis, 214
jus soli, 164

Kemalism, 194–5
kidnapping, 194, 208
Kurdish, Kurdistan, Kurd(s), 48, 54, 65, 151–2, 175, 178, 183, 185, 188, 194–6, 198–9, 201

labour, 12, 20, 46, 48–9, 51–3, 55–6, 91, 95, 99, 101, 106–8, 110–13, 116–17, 121, 125–34, 170, 183, 187–91, 199–201, 203, 205, 219, 223
demand, 107, 223
force, 56, 106
labour unrest/struggles, 199–200; *see also* trade unions
market, 46, 51–3, 56, 113, 127–30, 132, 191
migration, 12, 49, 125, 127–9, 133, 187–91, 201, 203, 205
organizations, *see* trade unions
recruitment, 48, 191
rights, 126–7
Lampedusa, 15, 184
language proficiency, language test, 11, 123, 126, 133–4
Latin America, Latina/Latino, 90–1, 93, 96, 98–101, 105–6, 111–12, 116, 220

law, 2, 9–10, 19, 25, 30–43, 50, 54, 57, 65, 67, 71, 73–6, 78, 80–1, 88–90, 95–7, 104, 108–10, 115–16, 127–30, 132–3, 135, 141, 147, 153, 155, 164–6, 181–2, 195–6, 219
  basic, 80–1, 153, 155, 168
  enforcement, 96–7, 104, 108–10
  humanitarian, 9, 30, 32–3, 36, 41, 219
  immigration, 28, 95, 115, 126, 153, 164, 166
  international, 9–10, 30, 33, 35, 73–8, 88–9, 135, 141, 160, 219
  maritime, 32, 38
  migration, 19, 57
  refugee, 35–7, 43
  rule of, 89, 147, 219
  of the sea, 9, 30, 32–3, 35–6, 38, 41, 219
  unlawful, 15, 17, 25–7, 29, 182
legalisation, 51, 75, 107, 127, 156, 207, 211, 218
Libya, 30–8, 42, 142
lobby, 65, 67, 72, 114, 116–18, 168, 175
  see also advocacy
localisation, 5, 10, 77, 90–4, 97, 99, 102, 110, 166, 220

Malta, 9, 30–43, 142, 184
manifestation, 17, 21, 180
  see also mobilisation; demonstration; movement
map, 45, 99
Marx(ist), 173, 189
media, 16, 19, 21, 39–40, 63–6, 94, 106, 115, 162, 172–3, 176–8, 183, 186
  analysis, 186
Mediterranean Sea, 4–5, 9, 15, 30–7, 41, 73, 219
Merkel, Angela, 62
method
  discourse analysis, *see* discourse
  ethnography, 30–43
  event analysis, 177
  frame analysis, 115, 117, 120–1, 138, 174, 178–80, 184–5
  interviews, 26, 31, 33–4, 37–8, 40, 43, 76, 111, 119, 128–9, 134–5, 162–8, 211–15, 217
  media analysis, 186
  methodological challenges, 147
  triangulation, 31
Mexico, Mexican(s), 8, 24–5, 90–1, 96, 98, 105–8, 111, 218, 223
MHP, *Milliyetçi Hareket Partisi*, 12, 138, 187–8, 192–203
Migration, migrants
  autonomy of, 4, 137, 142, 155, 168, 170, 172, 178–9, 180, 185, 187–8, 191, 193–4, 198, 201, 203–4, 220
  deaths, *see* death
  diplomacy, 9, 16, 44–6, 51, 53, 56–7, 61, 70, 139, 222
  family, 125, 144, 165
  governance, government, 3–4, 7, 16, 46, 56, 104–5, 127, 207; *see also* immigration, policy; policies
  Irregular, *see* illegality; irregularity
  managed, 12, 18–19, 23, 157, 172, 175, 194
  Migrant integration Policy Index (MIPEX), 124
  mixed flows, 172, 182–5
  organizations, *see* associations; movements; mobilization
  regime, 10, 44–5, 49, 50, 57, 129, 171, 180
  rights, 123, 125–6, 131, 211, 216
  system, *see* immigration system
  transit, 5, 16, 44–6, 48–51, 54, 58, 143, 173, 207, 216
  undocumented, *see* illegality; irregularity
  see also immigration
mobilization, 12, 19, 79, 98, 100, 113–21, 138, 171–85, 191, 198–206, 208–17, 223
  anti-immigrant, 11, 67, 72, 90–1, 100–1, 133, 171
  pro-immigrant, 11, 72, 105, 171, 176, 180
  see also movement; activism; protest
Mohammed VI, 205
Morocco, Moroccan, Moroccanness, *marocanité*, 8, 12, 138–9, 142, 165, 194, 204–17, 223
movement, 3–5, 11, 19, 30, 49–54, 58, 86, 89, 99, 107, 122–9, 136–7, 142–55, 157–70, 172–85, 187–204
  anti-racism, 86, 89

free, 51–3, 58, 126, 129, 142, 179
migrants/migration, 30, 49, 194
sans-papier(s), 157–8, 162, 170
social, 137, 172–4, 177, 179, 184–5
strike, 199, 200, 204
see also activism; mobilization; protest
municipal(ity), 10, 90, 93–5, 97–8, 100–2, 110, 153–4
Muslim, 49, 52, 62–3, 65–6, 68–70, 97, 101, 158, 206, 209, 214–15, 220
Muslimness, 68
see also Islam

narration, narrative, 3, 11, 60, 77, 105, 107, 113–14, 116, 118, 157, 168, 170
see also argumentative pattern; discourse
nation, 2–4, 6, 10–11, 16, 20, 25, 30–1, 34, 36, 41, 47–9, 56, 63, 66–9, 71, 92, 99, 103, 106, 113, 156, 160, 161, 168, 189, 191, 194, 196, 199, 205–7, 209, 210, 214, 218
nationalism, nationhood, 6, 8, 12, 45, 60, 161, 187, 192, 194–6, 206, 213
nationality, 24, 33, 39, 43, 78, 96, 130, 138, 143, 164, 169, 213–14, 216
post-national, 60
neighbour(hood), 8, 11, 70, 72, 93, 101–2, 104, 111, 113, 118–22, 151–2, 206, 213, 220, 222
neoliberal(ism), 9, 17, 19, 25, 29, 142, 195, 207, 221
New Jersey, 10, 91, 93–102, 105, 111–12, 114–16, 119, 220
New Public Radio, 95
NGO, Non-Governmental Organisation, 22, 74–5, 78–80, 83–4, 88–9, 91, 103–5, 113, 121–2, 130, 150, 179–81, 220
9/11, 10, 60, 64, 92, 94–5, 97, 101, 141, 215
non-refoulement, 35–7, 42–3, 74, 76, 78, 155
normalisation, 96, 100
of border control, 6, 9–10, 16–17, 19, 30, 71, 90, 221
North America, 11, 141–2, 144, 151

Obama, Barack, 109–10, 218
offshore, 5, 17, 20–1, 39, 74, 221

onshore, 5, 17, 29, 221
overstaying, overstayer, 25–6, 48, 50, 163–5
see also irregular

Pakistan, 50, 57
Paris, 67, 78, 80, 166, 170, 214
Peru, Peruvian, 96, 119
Philippine(s), 105, 192, 223
PKK, 188, 201
place of safety, 30, 33, 35–7
police, policing, 18–19, 25–6, 29, 38, 54, 73, 86, 90–2, 95–101, 109, 112, 115, 117, 128, 142, 149, 159–60, 163, 171–3, 176, 178, 180–2, 185–6, 193, 198–9, 202
local, 91, 95–101, 103–4, 109, 111, 115, 117–18
self-police, 26
policies, 2, 6 12, 17, 23, 29, 30 2, 44, 46, 48, 50–3, 56–8, 68, 75, 77–8, 87, 91–2, 94, 98, 103–4, 106–7, 110–13, 116, 118, 122–4, 126–8, 131, 133, 135, 137–9, 141–2, 144, 153–4, 156–7, 160, 163, 165, 168, 172, 175, 180, 182–4, 187–8, 201–2, 205–7, 209–17, 220, 222–3
asylum, 44, 48, 53, 142, 182–3, 222; *see also* asylum; European refugee protection system
citizenship, 2, 137–9
federal (policy), 92
immigration, 6, 53–4, 92, 105, 107–8, 110, 114–16, 122–4, 133, 135, 156–7, 160, 163, 165, 168, 188, 202–3, 205–6, 222
local, 103–4, 111, 118
local-federal cooperation, 95–6, 109
security, 92; *see also* border, control; enforcement
postcolonial, 12, 184, 187, 194–5, 222
see also colony
postnational border constellation, 16, 61
Poulantzas, Nicos, 189, 202
precarious(ness), precarisation, *précarité*, 6, 25, 127, 148–9, 153, 158, 160, 162–3, 166–8, 170, 173, 185
principle of *non-refoulement*, *see non-refoulement*
pro-immigrant, 11, 72, 105

protest, 1, 4–5, 12, 61, 83–4, 86, 115, 158, 171–4, 176–84, 200–1, 209
  protest cycle, 172, 174, 177–9
  protest event analysis, 177, 201
  see also activism; campaign; coalition; mobilization; movement

racialisation, 93, 146, 158, 167, 169, 204
racism, 33, 78, 86, 89, 100, 176, 178–9, 183, 200, 222
raid, 97, 115, 173
refugee, 1, 4–5, 9–10, 15, 18, 20–4, 30–3, 35–7, 43, 48–51, 54, 57–8, 73–6, 78–81, 83, 86, 88–9, 114, 141, 147–8, 150, 153, 155–6, 169–72, 175–6, 178–86, 208
  see also asylum
regime, 1, 3–5, 7–11, 15–16, 19, 22, 31–2, 36, 42, 44–5, 47, 49–52, 55, 57, 72, 92, 102, 127–9, 137–8, 143, 155–6, 166, 171, 173, 179–80, 184, 190–1, 193, 201, 203–4
  see also more specific; citizenship, regime; immigration/migration regime
regularisation, 20, 27, 106–7, 110, 162, 218
  see also legalisation
remittances, 191, 205, 209, 211–12, 216, 219, 222
removal, 20, 24, 26–8, 76, 79, 81, 83–4, 86, 109
  see also deportation
Republic, (neo)republican, *république*, 69, 156, 169
  Republican exceptionalism, 156–7, 161–2
  Republic model of integration, 66, 68, 169
resettle(ment), 22–3, 34, 51
residence status, 4, 7, 123–7, 130–1, 134, 136
resistance, 5, 10–11, 26–8, 74, 85–6, 89, 104, 121, 146, 148, 155, 157, 160, 171–2, 174–5, 179, 185, 193–4, 204, 213
  see also mobilization; movement; protest

return, 22–4, 27–8, 43, 48, 53, 58, 76, 78–9, 130, 149, 175, 183–4, 191, 198, 202, 205, 209, 212, 223
  compulsory, 28
  forced, 183
  voluntary, 17, 20, 23, 24, 27–8, 183–4, 212
rights, 1–2, 4–7, 10–11, 15, 19, 23, 30–1, 35–7, 44–5, 54, 60–5, 71–90, 96–9, 101–4, 107, 109, 111, 113–15, 121–38, 141–8, 151–63, 168–73, 176, 179, 183–4, 187, 192–3, 200, 205, 208–12, 215–20, 223
  citizenship, 4–7, 99, 123–7, 135, 138, 142–5, 147–8, 151, 157, 159, 161, 168, 170, 192–3, 200, 208–10, 212, 216, 218–20
  human, 1, 10, 19, 23, 35–7, 45, 61, 65, 73–5, 77–81, 83–4, 86–9, 109, 113–15, 128–30, 157, 163, 172, 176, 179, 184, 219, 223
  immigrant/migrant, 6, 11, 31, 54, 63, 97, 99, 101–2, 107, 111, 113–15, 121–4, 126, 130–4, 136, 137, 159, 161–3, 169, 211
  infra-droit, 138, 163, 167–8
  right to have rights, 1, 148
  social, 99, 123–7, 131, 153
Romania, 50, 221

Sangatte, 11, 171–3, 175, 177–82, 184–5, 220
  see also Eurotunnel; tunnel
sans papiers, sans papières, 11, 137–8, 156–8, 161–3, 166–70
  see also irregular; illegalised
SAR, Search and Rescue, 30, 32, 36–7, 73, 219
Sarkozy, Nicolas, 62, 68
Sayad, Abdelmalek, 208
Schengen area, 142, 171, 184
screening, 24, 37, 183
securitisation, 4, 7, 10, 15, 44, 77, 87–9, 92, 97, 141–2, 150, 215, 220
  of borders, 44, 150, 220
security, 6–7, 15–16, 18, 20, 25–6, 30–2, 37, 39, 42, 47, 50, 53–4, 58, 77, 80, 84, 86–7, 91–3, 94–5, 97, 99, 102–4, 109–10, 123–36, 142, 147, 149, 158,

160, 170–1, 173, 186, 204–5, 208, 212, 219, 220, 221
of residence, 11, 124, 127–36
see also homeland security
shipwreck(ed), 9, 16, 30, 35, 40
smugglers, smuggling, 15, 21–2, 50, 141, 181
solidarity, 57, 91, 104, 122, 143, 147–8, 150–5, 171, 173, 176, 181, 183–4, 186, 191, 207, 209, 211, 215, 220
Solidarity kitchen (Istanbul/Turkey), 151–4
Somali(a), 15, 57, 175, 183
SOS, 37, 40
sovereign(ity), 3, 5–6, 8–9, 12, 30, 71, 150, 189, 207, 211, 218
space, 11–12, 16, 74, 77, 80, 82–3, 86–8, 93, 108, 110, 121, 151, 154, 171–2, 174–5, 179–82, 185
social, 145, 154, 156, 162, 169
spatial strategies, 172
transnational social, politics, 12, 191–3, 203
state, 1–4, 6–12, 16–22, 25, 30, 32–5, 37–8, 40, 43–5, 50, 52, 56–8, 60–3, 65–6, 68–9, 71–80, 83–97, 99–100, 102–6, 108–16, 118–19, 121, 123, 125–6, 132–4, 136, 138–9, 143–4, 150–1, 153–6, 159–60, 173, 175, 179–85, 188–94, 198–208, 210–14, 216 23
apparatuses, 93, 138, 188–90, 199–200, 202–4
of exception, 10, 74, 78, 80, 88, 109
internationalisation of, 12, 189–90, 203
theory, 138, 188–9, 194
state of exception, 10, 74, 78, 80, 88, 109
stratification, 4–5, 7, 72, 123–5, 127, 131, 135, 143, 159, 167–9, 218, 221
strike, 176, 188, 195, 198–204
subject, 2–5, 8, 11, 24, 28–9, 31, 37, 45, 56, 58, 63, 76, 78–81, 85–7, 89–90, 106, 114, 117, 121, 128, 137, 144–9, 151, 153–6, 158–61, 169, 183, 190, 194, 206–7, 209–12, 214–16, 218–19, 221, 223
abject, 145
enact oneself as political subject, 145, 154, 167

formation, 2, 160, 169
impossible, 5, 121, 158–60, 169, 212, 221, 223
suburb(anisation), 7–8, 11, 94, 96, 102, 112, 220
Sudan, 57, 86
surveillance, 9, 15, 26, 38, 77, 84, 88, 92, 125, 146, 160, 171, 174, 186, 205
Sweden, Swedish, 57, 146
Syria(n), 54, 58, 63, 186

technologies
border, crime, migration control, 3, 5–7, 17, 71, 77, 88, 142, 154, 156, 219–21
of citizenship, 11, 137, 141, 144
governmental, 4, 7, 9, 11, 17, 25, 71, 76, 135, 144–6
IT, 19
risk-based, 19
terrorism, 92, 95–7, 101, 109, 215
see also anti-terrorism
tourism, 18, 50, 127–9, 144, 163–5, 209
trade unions, 117, 121, 131, 183, 191, 194–5, 197, 199–203
transit, 5, 10, 16, 21–3, 45–7, 49–54, 56–8, 74, 76–83, 85, 89, 143, 173, 175, 178, 183, 207, 216
transit zone, 10, 74, 76–83, 85, 89
transmigrants, 212–13
transnational, 7, 12, 31, 41, 49, 62, 77, 81, 126, 138, 147, 150–1, 155, 161, 185, 187, 191–3, 203–7, 210, 212–14, 217
tunnel, *see* Eurotunnel; Sangatte
Turkey, Turk(ish), 6, 8–10, 12–13, 44–59, 60–70, 84, 127–8, 130, 138–9, 142, 149–52, 155, 187–8, 191–204

UK Border Agency, 79–80
UK, United Kingdom, 5, 57, 63, 70, 79–80, 152, 171–2, 175, 177, 180, 184
UN, United Nations, 21, 31–2, 48, 79, 114, 155, 158, 179
United States Immigration and Customs Enforcement, ICE, 95–7, 102

UNHCR, 21–2, 24, 31, 35–9, 43, 48, 58, 79, 86, 179, 183–4
undocumented migration, *see* clandestine; illegality; irregular
US, United States, 7–8, 10–11, 20, 24, 60, 72, 90–102, 103–22, 152, 161, 190, 218, 220–1
Us/Them, 60, 167

victim, victimising, 84, 96, 114, 148, 152, 167, 183, 197

visa, 3, 9, 17–20, 23, 25–7, 47–8, 50, 54–5, 58, 108, 128–31, 134, 162–5, 180
(in)visibility, 16, 28, 74, 87
voting, 70, 110, 118, 122, 155, 170, 209–12, 216
   external, 210, 212

women, 33, 38, 40, 64, 144, 146, 149, 158, 160, 162–70, 191, 210
   see also gender; female, *femme*

Printed and bound by CPI Group (UK) Ltd, Croydon, CR0 4YY